SOCIAL
SKETCHES
OF AUSTRALIA

Humphrey McQueen started life in Brisbane, and
taught at a high school in Victoria. He also taught
twentieth-century Australian history at the Australian
National University. Since 1975 he has worked as a free-
lance historian from Canberra. From 1985 to 1988, he
was a member of the Bi-Centennial Committee to
Review Australian Studies in Tertiary Education. He
taught at Tokyo University in 1988 and 1989. His fourteen books include *A New Britannia* and *Australia's
Media Monopolies*. He serves on the editorial board of
Seeing Red, the quarterly magazine of the Socialist
Alliance.

SOCIAL SKETCHES OF AUSTRALIA

Humphrey McQueen

UQP

Third edition published 2004 by University of Queensland Press
Box 6042, St Lucia, Queensland 4067 Australia
First published 1978 by Penguin Books Australia

www.uqp.uq.edu.au

Typeset by University of Queensland Press
Printed in Australia by McPherson's Printing Group

Distributed in the USA and Canada by
International Specialized Book Services, Inc.,
5824 N.E. Hassalo Street, Portland, Oregon 97213–3640

Cataloguing in Publication Data
National Library of Australia

McQueen, Humphrey, 1942– .
    Social sketches of Australia.

    3rd ed.
    Bibliography.
    Includes index.

    1. Australia — History — 20th century. 2. Australia —
    Social life and customs — 20th century. I. Title.

994.04

ISBN 0 7022 3440 0

To John Hooker,
friend, comrade and publisher,
who commissioned the first edition as a 'rude,
radical and gutsy story of Australia for people
who hate history'

CONTENTS

THE WEBS WE WEAVE

These 'Social Sketches' offer a glimpse of what it has been like to live in Australia since 1888. Although this book is about Australia's past, it is not history in any meaningful sense. Rather, the pages sketch a few of the features through which Australians have coped with the dynamics and structures of a capitalist system, as it moved through industrialisation and ur-banisation. Personal accounts, anecdotes and jokes can evoke the temper of those times. By these means, it is hoped to woo people who avoid twentieth-century Australia because it seems no more than a procession of dull prime ministers, torn-up treaties and failed amendments to the constitution. And sheep. The richness of daily life points beyond such mat-ters to wholly different ways of seeing how we got to where we are. The book will succeed only if readers become impa-tient for works that analyse how and why these developments took place.

On the surface, this volume is arranged on chronological lines, with each chapter covering a decade or so, starting with 1889 to 1900. The material can be read from start to finish by any-one seeking a panorama. Several other approaches are possible.

One: Each chapter is built from seven recurrent themes — work, life in the cities, life in the country, health, Aborigines, White Australia, and our views of the world. These topics are marked in the text and the index. Thus, someone interested in

Aborigines could follow that theme from 1888 to 2001. The themes always appear in the same order within the chapters, although occasionally a topic will not appear.

Two: In addition to the seven themes set out in this way, several other major and minor issues run through the book. The index has been set up to make these implicit topics visible. For example, because women hold up half the sky they are too important to be consigned to a box of their own. By putting together aspects of all the chapters, a substantial account of women is available, as the index indicates. Food and transport are two minor aspects that can be traced in the same way.

Three: The brief chapters on single years, such as 1888 or 1970, offer opportunities to reflect and to sum up. They could be taken as a block, perhaps after the whole has been read.

Four: Some segments discuss particular events in detail, for example the Tuckiar case in Chapter Six.

The pattern invites readers to construct their own account by rearranging and supplementing the information on offer.

Humphrey McQueen
Canberra
2004

1888: ONE HUNDRED YEARS AFTER INVASION

Historians have a bad habit of breaking the past up into decades and centuries, which do not suit the ways in which a society develops. For instance, to start a survey of contemporary Australia in 1901 would be misleading because that date cuts across the specifics of the long twentieth century. The prime features of the recent past have been the emergence of monopolising forms of capitalism with mass marketing; the political reorganisation of the Federation; and the rise of a movement to defend the working people. These sketches, therefore, begin in 1888, which happens to coincide with the centenary of European invasion. Events of that year highlighted the jealousies between the colonies, disputes between workers and bosses, and anti-Asian attitudes.

The centenary in 1888 of the arrival of convicts was an unlikely occasion for national rejoicing. Indeed, it was the economic boom, which gold had sparked and British investors had fuelled, which called the public to worship. What was celebrated was not the hundredth anniversary but the achievements of the past forty years; not convict stains but the triumph of blotting them out with cash. Consequently, the *Official Record of the Centennial Exhibition* steered around the embarrassment by describing the convicts as 'pioneer colonists'; just as predictably, the *Bulletin's History of Botany Bay* stressed the iron chains, the lash and the gallows in order to

'expose the corrupt origins of despotism and the British connection' with the hope of ending them both.

Melbourne's leading role in the centenary celebrations confirmed that it was recent wealth and not early beginnings
which was being reviewed, though not scrutinised. A vast
Exhibition, Melbourne's seventh since 1854, lasted from 1
August 1888 to 9 March 1889. Two million people, over four
times the population of the city, passed through the gates.
Some were attracted by displays from European and American
governments, while some were drawn by local science in the
form of a model dairy which made cheese on Mondays and
Tuesdays and butter for the rest of the week. Others came to
amuse themselves in shooting galleries and the like, or to enjoy
the 3000 works of art and daily piano recitals. Visitors were
advised to bring plenty of change.

To counter the city's reputation as 'Marvellous Smel-
bourne', the organisers publicised the Exhibition's lavatory
arrangements: pans were removed with air-tight lids and
deodorised between six and eight each evening. The opening
of Foster's Brewery added to the enthusiasm at the International Temperance Convention. When the Exhibition finished,
most Victorians thought it had been worthwhile, though the
spending of a quarter of a million pounds was perhaps a little
too much. Even this doubt would not have arisen if Victoria's
Chief Justice Higinbotham had not made a point of resigning
as Chairman of the Planning Commission in protest.

Because of gold, Melbourne's population had bounded
ahead of Sydney's in the 1850s. By 1888 it was still 20 per cent
greater. Sydney might claim to be the cradle of the nation,
New South Wales might see itself as the 'Ma Colony', and
Henry Lawson might declare that 'New South Wales is Australia', yet there could be no doubting that Melbourne was the
city of the Southern Hemisphere. Sydney's celebrations were
held before Melbourne's, for which they were no more than a
warm-up. A brave face was attempted. Foundation stones

were lain. Despite Sir Henry Parkes's election slogan 'Now who will stand hat my right' and, hand build the Bridge with me?', the obvious outcome was the opening of the Domain as a public park. The Easter Show was spoilt by rain, disputes over prizes and rioting. It suffered further indignity with the minuteness of its loss — only £5000. How appropriate that Sydney began its festivities by handing relief supplies to the deserving poor.

In an article for the *Centennial Magazine*, the Rev. James Jeffries suggested that the successful mixing of the races and the solution to the 'social problem' could be 'Australia's mission and opportunity'. Before the year was half over, he had reason to doubt the early achievement of either. Violence took place during two industrial disputes, and the anti-Chinese movement gained new support.

When scab labourers turned up at Brooking Station, 80 kilometres south-west of Wagga Wagga, they were attacked by union shearers before the owner called the police. Eight unionists were sent to prison. At the same time, on the coalfields around Newcastle the miners presented the pit owners with a new set of claims. When these demands were turned down, a thirteen-week strike followed. Scab labour arrived, with the result that seven miners were arrested on charges of riot. The government sent an artillery unit of seventy-seven officers and men with a Nordenfelt machine-gun. At the miners' trials, the judge criticised the police for drawing their batons when they did not intend to use them. It was safer, he reminded the forces of law and order, to shoot directly into a crowd than to fire warning rounds over their heads.

These strikes and the violent reaction to them gave warning of the far greater clashes that would start two years later. A new element was about to be added, slowly, fitfully, reluctantly, to Australian society: a militant and organised working class. In the first issue of the *Centennial Magazine* for 1889, the Rev. Jefferies returned to the optimism of his earlier article.

He now feared that 'there would be many such strikes as that at Newcastle before we get to know the limits of justice and possibility'.

Moreover, if true justice were possible for non-whites in Australia, there were few signs of it. As part of the *Bulletin*'s contribution to the celebrations, the weekly announced that its issue for 14 April would be a special anti-Chinese affair showing why 'The Leper Must Change His Spots'. Heavily illustrated with horrible, comic and sex-crazed Chinamen, the *Bulletin* overflowed in essay, verse and fiction with its warnings of race war. That theme was explored in William Lane's novel *White or Yellow*, then being printed by the Brisbane newspaper the *Boomerang*. Fear of Asiatic invasion was to play a lively role in the achievement of Federation and in supporting what passed for Australian sentiment.

Uneven economic developments extended beyond the differences between Victoria and New South Wales. After years of decay, Tasmania and Western Australia were jolted into life by discoveries of silver, tin and gold. South Australia was in the rip of a depression which was soon to be felt through the eastern half of the continent. The battles between colonies and classes were later to be fought out in ways which make 1888, for all its difficulties and disputes, shine through as a high point of Australian unity.

1 1889–1901 'NEVER GLAD MORNING AGAIN'

Australians are drawn to the 1890s as a time of radicalism, nationalism, artistic creativity and industrial militancy. The Labor parties are founded, Federation is achieved, the *Bulletin* and the Heidelberg school of painting flourish, great clashes between capital and labour roll from the ports through the mining towns and on into the shearing camps. Here is the stuff of human drama. Yet this vision splendid is somewhat more than the truth. The Labor parties stayed small; the federal movement was less than democratic; the writers and painters were already off 'Home' to England; the strikes were defeated and the unions almost destroyed. What the 1890s meant to most people was hard times. Australia was gripped by economic depression and drought. The Australian dream was fading. The white community could no longer be certain that tomorrow meant a better day.

WORK

No matter what else people do, there are some actions which we must perform in order to live: we must make food, clothing and homes. Work, in all its forms, is therefore the starting point for understanding Australia. We must set out from

The miner cradling washdirt by the creek,
Or pulled through darkness dripping to the plat,

The navvy boring tunnels through the peak:
The farmer grubbing box-trees on the flat:
The hawker camping by the roadside spring:
The hodman on the giddy scaffolding ...

(Bernard O'Dowd, 'The Bush')

If men had not dug out coal, shorn sheep and driven trains, and if women had not taken in washing and dressmaking and kept assembly lines running, there would be no sport, no music, no wars, no parliament: nothing at all. In 1889 the man who would soon write the first draft of the Commonwealth Constitution, Samuel Griffith, argued that all new wealth was the product of labour. Moreover, 'the true view is that a man's labour is not something outside of himself, but is part of himself, and cannot properly be the subject of sale'. Yet almost everyone had to sell this part of herself or himself 'in order to procure the means of livelihood'. This injustice and inequality could be balanced, Griffith concluded, only 'by combination on the part of the laborers' in trade unions.

Constructing dams and railways required camps for a thousand or more men. Private employers were in charge of most of this work and they set up their headquarters near the site, close to running water and good timber. The men would follow. Once the labourers were employed, the contractor did not care how they fared, as long as they kept away from where the bosses lived. The navvies rarely had their wives with them. They lived in tents or shacks which they built for themselves. The authorities took almost no interest in sanitation. Camps became centres for diphtheria and typhoid, which spread to the surrounding countryside, and from there, in milk supplies, to the cities. Employers opposed suggestions that they should provide sanitary collection services for the camps, dismissing such suggestions as fetters on free enterprise.

In their small way, these camps were typical of the attitudes of the whole community towards public health. The assumption was that individuals had the responsibility to keep

themselves healthy. Governments should not interfere with
the liberty of citizens. Just how ridiculous this attitude was in
practice can be seen in the navvies' camps, where men had to
work ten hours a day for six days a week. No matter how
much they wanted better sanitation, they had neither the time
nor the energy to attend to it. What was everybody's business
became nobody's business because there was no profit in it for
the contractors. To them, even the death of a navvy was no
loss, because he had cost nothing to train and could be
replaced at no expense.

Far from making life easier for workers, technical progress
made work more dangerous when employers refused to install
safety devices, or to reduce hours of work on risky and tiring
jobs. For example, the introduction of underground drills into
Victoria's gold mines resulted in a sharp rise in chest complaints because of the fine dust that the new machines produced. Eaglehawk miners had a death rate from tuberculosis
six times greater than that of the general community. Mechanisation threatened jobs and rearranged the necessary skills.
Poorly paid junior and female labour could be taken on, especially in the clothing industry.

Workers who served the public had to put in very long hours.
Butchers and bakers slaved from 4 am till 10 pm. Barmen
served 15 to 17 hours a day, 6 days a week, with 2 hours more
on Sunday. Shop assistants worked from 7 am till 7 or 9 pm on
weekdays, and until just before midnight on Saturdays. Their
bosses were religiously opposed to working on Sundays. Public support rallied around the Early Closing Association,
which sometimes included shopkeepers feeling the strain of
the long hours. Owners of larger stores occasionally set a good
example by shutting at 6 pm during the week and at 1 pm on
Saturday. But almost all shop workers put in a 60-hour week.
Grocers' assistants and drapers faced a 12-hour day, 6 days a
week. Even after early closing laws were passed, employers

found lots of ways to get around them. The 1900 Queensland Act left barmen, butchers, waitresses, clerks and one-fifth of all shop assistants unprotected. On top of their health-destroying hours, hardly any workers were paid for overtime, for public or annual holidays, or for sick leave.

Barmaids had a particularly rough time. A Victorian Royal Commission in 1884 found them working from 14 to 18 hours a day for about 15 shillings a week. They were employed for their ability to attract customers, since the quality of colonial beer was at best uneven and generally pretty crook. One witness to the Commission claimed:

> As soon as a girl gets rather faded in one house she goes to a house of a lower grade, and down and down until no publican will have her; and next time you find her knocking about Lonsdale or Little Bourke Streets, and then she goes among the Chinamen, then to the hospital and then into the grave.

Waitresses were only slightly better placed and frequently worked 75 hours a week.

Laws controlling conditions in factories were either useless or did not exist before the mid-1890s. Victoria then brought its bits and pieces of controls together into one fairly progressive Act. The principal weakness of the law was its definition of a factory as a place where more than five people worked. This rule meant that the worst 'sweat shops', and all out-work, were not controlled. Although Queensland's 1900 Act defined a factory as any place where more than one person worked, an investigator found that over one-third of the women in dress-making and hat-making rooms earned no more than five shillings a week. They walked to and from work to save the fare. Sanitation in factories improved for a time as a result of panic after the 1900 bubonic plague. Rats were hunted down, rubbish removed and some of the worst buildings destroyed.

Even the most thorough Factory Act was useless unless there were enough inspectors willing to enforce it. Sometimes an inspector would give advance notice of a visit so that the employer could send home any under-age children or any workers beyond those allowed by the fresh-air regulations. Real improvement required a strong union movement, with representatives on every job reporting to full-time officials backed up by governments and the threat of a strike. Such a combination of forces would not exist for years to come.

LIFE IN THE CITIES

Everything in Australian cities started from scratch. Unlike European cities, ours had no canals, cathedrals or cobbled roads around which new services could be built. This lack put the building industry and public works at the crux of economic activity. The need to begin at the beginning also gave Australia an opportunity to have the most up-to-date equipment and to use the most modern methods. Adelaide, Canberra, Griffith and the centre of Melbourne show signs of what was possible. Most Australian towns bear the mark of private enterprise, that is, public neglect. Every city and large town had to provide certain basic services, whether well or badly. Towards the close of the nineteenth century, these needs included transport, water, sanitation and power.

The public transport system in Sydney was at once complicated and simplified by the harbour. A journey from the North Shore to any of the south-western suburbs required a ferry to Circular Quay, then a tram to the railway terminus at Redfern. The building of Central Station did not start until 1901.

In Melbourne, private companies had opened a few railway branch lines from Princes Bridge to Windsor and Hawthorn through Richmond. These were bought up by the government in 1878 to link with the Gippsland line through Caulfield to Oakleigh. Flinders Street and Spencer Street stations were joined to each other in the early 1890s. Camberwell and Lilydale had been connected to the city by the end of 1882. That construction brought claims of corruption against the ex-premier Sir John O'Shanassy. So that the line could pass through property that he owned, the engineers designed a track so steep that the carriages had to be taken up a few at a time. When they got to the top, they were still half a mile north of Camberwell village. A line had already been built from Spencer Street in a great sweeping arc through the western suburbs and then north-east to Whittlesea. At the opening of this extension, one speaker pointed out that in the bad old days it took an hour to travel to Melbourne, 'but with the advancing times and railway communication they could now do the journey in one hour and a half'. By the time that the 1890s depression knocked the bottom out of the land develop-ment schemes, the rail system had covered most areas of the city. The gap between Collingwood and the city was not plugged until 1901.

Privately owned horse-drawn buses were still popular, pos-sibly because they had a very easy attitude towards passengers. In Brisbane, drivers would wait for people as they shopped in the main street, or they would drag passengers out of shops. In an effort to make Sydney horse-drawn buses more comfort-able, damp straw was placed on the floor in winter to collect the mud from the dirt roads. When women started sitting on the tops of buses, 'decency boards' were added to stop men peering at their ankles. An English lady visitor to Melbourne wrote about the upsetting appearance and behaviour of her fellow bus travellers; after a few trips, she admitted that she had become hardened to them. In England, she had never even thought of using public transport. In Melbourne, she said, ser-vants cost so much, and were so rude, that she could not afford a driver and groomsman; she was forced to mix outside her class.

Very few streets were sealed. An early kind of tarred metal had been tried but came unstuck in summer. By the mid-1880s the streets of Sydney's inner area were paved with wooden blocks, which kept the dust down but were slippery for horses and twisted with the rain. A start was made to number sub-urban houses and erect street name-plates. As private and public transport became horseless, better roads and more signs were necessary.

Two developments in the later 1880s turned the bicycle from a dangerous device into a highly popular means of trans-port. These improvements were the low-wheeled 'safety bicy-cle' and blow-up tyres. Bicycles allowed skilled tradesmen and clerical workers to travel longer distances. In the bush, shearers could pedal hundreds of miles in a season on bikes that were very much cheaper to maintain than a horse. The bike helped prepare public attitudes for the motor car. They also boosted female freedom because they let young ladies move about without a coachman or chaperone. The bicycle required fashion changes which saw women wearing slacks, although these remained daring. Cyclists formed associations to press for separate pathways, two of which were built in Sydney in 1900. Long-distance races placed cycling on the front page of newspapers around the world. Not everyone was convinced of the value of the bicycle. The Mt Gambier author-ities made anyone riding after dark ring a bell all the time, as well as showing a red light in front.

Electricity speeded up the mechanisation of factories. The lighting made it easier for firms to operate outside daytime. Evening entertainments also expanded. Public transport and communication were revolutionised. No single invention has given rise to as many changes in the past hundred years. Its spread was quite uneven. It reached Penrith by the mid-1890s but did not get to Camberwell till 1911. Launceston enjoyed electric streetlights a few years earlier than Sydney. If a com-munity had been rich enough to install gas in the 1880s, it did not give up this investment in favour of electricity, especially not in the hard economic times of the 1890s.

Electricity seemed almost magical. Its home uses alarmed people who were not used to machines of any kind. The strangeness of electricity is well shown in the fate of a Sydney man who, in 1913, was struck by a falling tram wire and received a 3800-volt shock which turned him blue from head to foot. After eleven weeks in hospital, he regained his normal colour but retained an enormous charge of electricity which caused him considerable pain. He went to New Guinea because a British surgeon had told him that malaria might sweat the electricity out. Mosquitoes were repelled by his electric condition and he had to be injected with the virus.

Supplying endless quantities of fresh, pure water to every home is a problem faced by every city and town. Dams must be built and the water cleaned before being carried in pipes that will not spoil its taste. It was well into the twentieth century before many town dwellers felt that the public water was pure, 'soft', and regular enough to let them give up their galvanised iron tanks which caught rain water from the roofs. For the householder, another problem was how to heat water for washing and bathing. One popular solution was to make Monday 'wash day', and to have one night as bath night, often with more than one person using the same tub of water, together, or in turn.

Getting water into houses was almost as difficult as getting garbage and human waste out of them. Brisbane's inner-city dumped its waste into a creek bed a kilometre from the Post Office. To get rid of human waste, some earth privies used the two-pan system 'whereby the full pan was carted away with a sealed lid and was replaced with a disinfected empty pan'. Others had the single-pan system in which 'each pan was emptied into an open dray and was then replaced, uncleaned and undeodorised'. So as not to take up valuable floor space, the earth privies in several of Melbourne's taller buildings were in attics at the top. When they were on the roof it didn't matter too much if they stank a little. In outer suburban areas, cess-pools were dug, or families buried or dumped their own waste. In 1900, Townsville, with a population of 10 000, was described by a visiting government officer as having

> stenches in the main street worse than any I had encountered since Shanghai. Every vacant allotment was covered with rubbish, affording splendid cover for rats. There was no provision for the collection of kitchen refuse, and rat food was easily obtainable. On the town common I counted eighteen rotting horse carcases.

Market-gardens flourished on the shortcomings of the sanitary system.

Long working hours and the problems of storing food resulted in shops staying open late at night. Saturday evening was usually the busiest time of the week. Scattered throughout the suburbs were corner stores, usually owner-operated. Their presence meant that most household goods could be replaced without a long journey. The inner-city districts contained several large department stores employing hundreds of assistants and supplying a wide range of goods, from finery and food through to furniture and farm machinery. A hire-purchase system existed for a limited number of the well-to-do. Almost everyone could obtain some credit, though perhaps only with the corner store and only for five shillings worth of groceries. So many tradesmen came door-to-door that, for a long time, it was possible to do almost all one's shopping at home. Carts brought milk and bread, vegetables, fruit, meat, fish, clothes-props and soft drinks. Salesmen with patent medicines, cosmetics, biscuits and cooking preparations called with display cases and mail-order catalogues.

Land prices had soared in the boom of the 1880s. They fell to almost nothing in the depression of the 1890s. Sites in the centre of Northcote, Melbourne, had sold at £210 a metre in 1888. Twenty years later, they were going for a mere £24. The fall in land prices was not much help to the working man trying to build a home. During the 1890s he was as likely to be unemployed as to have spare savings.

A good type of working-man's dwelling was a long semi-detached or terraced house with a central hall running its full length. Three bedrooms and a bathroom led off the hall on one side; on the other were a parlour, then the living room, kitchen and laundry. The front parlour was rarely used, though it contained a piano, family portraits, an illustration of the British king or queen, any honours, certificates or awards, and a reproduction of one of the nineteenth century's favourite paintings.

For the better-off, two changes were improving the quality of private housing. Marseilles tiles were imported in the tens of millions before the Great European War; they provided a roof which was both cooling and waterproof. A local discovery, the cavity brick wall, offered similar comforts. Another architectural response to the climate did not catch on outside Queensland, where the heat from the iron roofs was partly overcome by the use of wide, latticed verandas and high stumps so the air could circulate.

Slums marked the inner parts of all the big cities. Towards the end of the 1880s, nearly 700 of the worst houses in Melbourne were declared unfit for humans to live in. While their clean-up was under way, brand new slums were being put up next door in Collingwood, where six terraces were built on a 29 metre (96 ft) frontage, with single brick walls between them. In Brisbane, the *Courier* complained that 'No city in the United Kingdom or in Europe would tolerate the wretched, cheap, inconvenient, jerry built, unsightly shanties which here line some of our principal streets'. That condemnation applied to all Australia's capitals.

LIFE IN THE COUNTRY

Work for a seventeen-year-old boy on a wheat farm could be

dull. His prospects were worse when the property was too small ever to make him rich and too dry even to turn a profit. For William Stagg of Tarcowie (SA) life was depressing, but never to the point of despair. His diary is rich with the detail of country life and work:

1885

January 12: *Finished reaping. I am glad too. I was sick of driving two horses, besides the platform of the machine is twisted. We cropped 132 acres this last year.*

January 19: *Carted wheat to Caltowie. Flies very bad this year. I've found out two cures for bung eyes and lips. First to rub instantly till smarts. Second to put carbonate of soda in the place where the fly bites on the lip or in the eyes.*

January 25: *Went Sunday School morning and afternoon. Bill Richardson said 116 verses against my 98. There is a race between us.*

January 31: *Took last load of wheat to Caltowie. In all, our wheat this year brought us £110/15/6.*

February 8: *Mother is not very well. Mrs Cubby came over. Father went on the road, cannot give that up yet because every little helps to make a living. The horses and cows went to water for the first time this year. I don't like going to the water. Grubbed 2 trees. Mother better.*

February 10: *Grubbed 2 trees and took the cattle to water. Had an easy day.*

March 13: *Carting dung. Father ploughing. Sowed some cabbages and cauliflower seed. Beauty had a heifer calf.*

April 14: *Ploughing. Father uses old worn shares now it is wet. The ground has never been ploughed properly and never will while he uses old shares. To save 1/- he loses 5/- I say.*

May 8: *Ploughing. The ground is frightful hard. I long to go to a foreign clime for I am disgusted with this one. I will therefore watch my opportunity to get to America as it is my favourite country.*

June 23: *We killed another pig, we are killing them as quick as possible for the feed is running short.*

June 29: *Father on the road. I have money to the amount of 5/3d on which I mean to lay the foundation of my future proceedings in money matters. I am determined to get on and I think I can with economy and perseverance.*

William Stagg came no closer to the United States of America than a trip to Adelaide. Despite saving every penny and putting every effort into his farming, he could not afford to marry until he was past forty. In 1887 he rented a four-hectare block near his father's old farm. There, he worked out his remaining sixty years in restless resignation.

Thomas Austin released some English rabbits on his property near Geelong in the early 1860s. He hoped to improve colonial life by hunting and shooting them. Twenty years later, rabbits were as far west as Fowlers Bay (SA), and had spread all over Tasmania and throughout the Barossa Valley. Their strongholds were the Riverina and the Mallee. By the end of the 1880s, one million hectares had been abandoned there because of them. Ten million rabbits were killed in New South Wales in the first eight months of 1888. As a single property contained thirty-six million, this slaughter made little difference. Ten years before, the NSW government had offered £25 000 for a successful method of getting rid of rabbits. Despite Louis Pasteur's suggestion of chicken cholera, no prize was awarded. The plague continued. One farmer went to town for a week to buy a binder to harvest his crop. On his return, not a leaf was standing. In 1892 Wilcannia was overrun by rabbits. As Eric Rolls puts it in his book *They All Ran Wild*:

> They ate the gardens and burrowed under the houses. Storekeepers had to wire-net their premises. The servants at the hotels brushed them off the steps. The inspector of stock hunted two or three from under his bed each morning.

Various methods of killing were tried. Ferrets and mongooses proved as useless as the hundreds of miles of rabbit-proof fences under which wombats dug and which emus trampled down. Poison was the most effective killer. In 1891 more than a million rabbits were killed on a property near Ivanhoe (NSW) with a mixture of arsenic to kill the rabbits, washing soda to dissolve the poison, and sugar to hide the taste of both. As with all methods of mass eradication, tens of millions of birds and small animals were also destroyed.

Since the gold rushes, colonial governments had needed loans from overseas to pay for public works. When these sources dried up during the 1890s depression, developmental projects were stopped and governments sacked employees in an attempt to restore prosperity. The dismissals created more unemployment, especially in country areas. In Victoria, injured railway employees (or their widows) had often found work as gatekeepers. During the 1890s their numbers were cut by over a thousand to a mere forty-five. At the end of the decade, 13 792 applications were received for 628 positions in the railways, more than half from country men. A fortunate few thousand rushed to the goldfields in Western Australia. Farming there was as hard as anywhere else. New settlers built huts from galvanised iron and divided them into four rooms with sacking. They made floors by pouring boiled redgum over carefully swept earth. The hard, shiny surface lasted about a week. All over Australia men repeated the cry of a Loxton (SA) settler, A. B. Murray: 'I came out with nothing; and was glad to get away'.

Although a depression, a drought and the rabbit plague were not the fault of individual farmers, many contributed to the severity of these disasters. Despite repeated warnings and bad experiences, pastoralists and farmers often overstocked their properties. Others pushed beyond 'the margins of the good earth' to cultivate semi-desert areas. To pay for this expansion, they borrowed from the banks and demanded that their governments do likewise to build railways to every nook and cranny of the colonies. When the crash came, there was no way of repaying either the private debt or the public loans. In poor or average years, sheep and cattle had to compete not only with rabbits but with each other for feed — an almost impossible task on overstocked pastures. Greed, ignorance and laziness tore the heart out of the soil. It was a rare farmer who could afford to nurse his land.

Public services edged their way into country towns. Wagga's four to five thousand citizens enjoyed their first gas streetlight in 1881, their first town water in 1885 and some kerbing and guttering by the end of the century. Sewerage did not start until 1916, which meant that digging household cesspools was a big and unpleasant job for which 'the standard charge was five sovereigns and a bottle of whisky, on which the tramp or out-of-work shearer, or whoever was too desperate to refuse, got drunk afterwards and nobody blamed him'.

Life in a country town could be as repressive as Norman Lindsay painted in his once-banned novel *Redheap*. When the Mt Gambier public baths opened in January 1898, objections were raised to their use by Indians and servants, and to the presence of the caretaker on ladies' days. Yet even Redheap (Creswick) had its inspiring character, Mr Bandparts. Several towns had free-thinking newspaper editors whose views on God, war and social issues did not please everyone. Moreover, country newspapers were often literary and informed in a way that few city dailies are today. Kalgoorlie's *Western Argus* was a fine example. Economic decline, the threat of an eight-hour day for bush workers, and tight city control of advertising and publishers' supplies helped to destroy these pockets of radical or independent thinking.

HEALTH

Belief in the 'germ theory' of infection transformed medical practice in the 1890s. The identification of a particular germ for the spread of each disease displaced the 'miasma' theory. The older view held that sickness was due to 'corrupt air', 'excessive sunlight' and 'foul odours'. Germ theory stimulated new medicinals and revived demands for public hygiene.

According to the Inter-Colonial Medical Congress, there was 'apathy in all matters of public hygiene'. This want of interest struck in 1889 when more than 400 people died in Melbourne's worst typhoid epidemic. In response, a Royal Commission examined the Sanitary Condition of Melbourne, the Public Health Act was amended, a Department of Health was established and the first full-time public health officer employed. Most importantly, a system of underground sewerage was begun. Other colonies improved their public health laws but there was no real effort because there was so little money. Progress depended on panic caused by epidemics.

Before the germ theory, most medicines had been either stimulants or depressants, or both. Alcohol was the favourite stimulant, with both doctors and patients. One consumptive girl drank seven bottles of rum, twelve bottles of brandy and sixty-one bottles of spa water during her first twenty-eight days in hospital. After doctors gave up their support for alcohol, they prescribed drugs which were no less dangerous, such as strychnine. Phosphorous was highly praised as a means of 'refreshing brain tissue'.

In a delightful account of childhood, *A Bunyip Close Behind Me*, Eugenie McNeil recalled that in the 1890s her mother's 'cure for most ills was bed with a glass of hot claret and a comforting linseed meal poultice on the spot where it hurt'. Two slightly more unusual remedies were a spider's web to heal cuts and the drinking of glasses of blood to cure anaemia.

Hospitals in the nineteenth century were very fussy about whom they would admit as patients. Their attitude was summed up in an 1872 by-law from Wangaratta:

> That no pregnant female, for the purpose of confinement, no child under five years of age unless for the purpose of undergoing a

surgical operation, no person insane or suffering from delirium tremens, no person whose case shall be considered by the Hospital Surgeon to be incurable ... be admitted.

The exclusion of each of these groups was necessary for the efficient running of a hospital. Expectant mothers were not admitted because childbirth was frequently followed by a deadly and highly contagious form of blood poisoning. An infected ward would be closed for a month while it was

thoroughly cleaned and scrubbed out several times. The beds washed and all the woodwork sanded or scrubbed with pumice stone. The linen and blankets were washed and fumigated and the straw in the mattress burned. Fumigation [involved] sealing up the ward and burning sulphur to produce sulphur dioxide fumes.

Of the 12 000 people who died of infectious diseases in Melbourne between 1860 and 1890, only 2 per cent died in a hospital and many of these had been admitted for some other reason.

Young children, the incurably sick, the insane and the dying were unwanted because hospitals depended upon charity. The very young required intensive care. Incurables and lunatics lingered for years, straining the hospitals' finances. The dying were turned away because a high death-rate lowered a hospital's reputation and thereby its public appeal for funds. Some hospitals improved their ratio of 'cures' by discharging and readmitting patients every fortnight, without the patient as much as getting out of bed. Others rushed anyone who appeared to be dying out their doors and into 'rest homes' next door. The very poor were especially unwelcome because the hospital had to pay their funeral expenses. Despite all these rules, most people looked upon hospitals as places where you went to die.

Steps were taken to find beds for those whom the hospitals rejected. Melbourne gained the Austin Hospital for Incurables in 1882, the Queen Victoria Memorial Hospital for women and children in 1899, and an infectious diseases hospital at

Fairfield in 1904. Money for building programs came largely from private sources. Catholic hospitals were kept going by the unpaid efforts of religious orders such as the Sisters of Charity who had opened St Vincent's in Sydney in 1857.

Patients were usually treated by 'honoraries'. The title suggests that the doctors who gave their services were engaged in charity work. In truth, they used their positions in a hospital for personal advancement. Doctors wanted to become honoraries because of the prestige it gave them in private practice. In addition, only in a large hospital could they find the range of illnesses that enabled them to improve their medical skills. Some doctors were so anxious to be elected honoraries that they spent thousands of pounds enrolling subscribers who promised to vote for them. Bookmakers took bets on the outcome. The honorary at one hospital took his pack of fox terriers on his rounds of the wards and kept his horse in the front corridor of the basement. The honorary system was abolished for a while in Launceston because it 'was rotten to the core': 'Patients were left unattended for days together whilst these "honoraries" were engaged in their ordinary practice'. The system was reintroduced under pressure from local doctors, who needed to train on the job.

Conditions in the wards were overcrowded but otherwise hygienic, thanks to gallons of carbolic cleanser. Bed bugs were universal until the introduction of iron bedsteads; the lavatories were earth closets at the end of each ward; both inconveniences made patients feel at home. Gas lighting was used in the cities and was spreading to country hospitals, reaching Mt Gambier in 1892. Hospital visitors were often charged admission fees and were allowed in for only two hours, twice a week.

Carbolic was used in Melbourne in 1865, just as the surgeon Charles Lister first published his ideas on antiseptics. Its application did not become general until the early 1880s. A doctor described the first patient he met as a medical student in 1878, who 'had an old burn, dressed with a linseed poultice'.

> The smell from it was indeed bad, and was easily understood when the poultice was removed and the dresser calmly proceeded to remove with forceps the numerous maggots crawling over the foul discharging surface.

Pus was seen as a sign that the infection was cleansing itself.

Theatre tables were only beginning to have their cushioned, and hence germ-infested, tops removed. Melbourne did not get a decent operating theatre until one was donated in the early 1890s. At that time, surgeons in Hobart were still operating in their old bloodstained frock coats. One leading surgeon wore diamond rings to impress the gallery which he filled with champagne-drinking friends. Others persisted in holding instruments in their mouths. A Sydney nurse recollected that when she began training in 1894,

> all instruments for each ward were kept in a cabinet with glass shelves covered with baize. All these instruments were sterilised once a day and put back in the cabinet. We were not taught to sterilise the nail-brushes the doctors used for their hands. Gloves did not exist.

Carbolic could kill patients as well as germs. In the late 1890s, carbolic (antisepsis) was replaced by steam and rubber gloves (asepsis). A few doctors nonetheless continued to ignore these advances all their working lives, some of which extended into the 1930s.

Operations for appendicitis became commonplace in the 1890s, as asepsis made stomach surgery less likely to lead to carbolic poisoning. This increased margin of safety, plus a fee of between thirty and one hundred guineas, saved many a Melbourne surgeon from going broke after the collapse of the land boom in 1893. King Edward VII gave royal approval to the humble appendix when his was successfully removed in 1902.

Not all cases were treated surgically, as leeches were still used. Less profitable operations removed adenoids and tonsils.

Lucy Osborn, one of Florence Nightingale's followers, introduced modern nursing methods to Australia while she was matron at Sydney Hospital from 1868 to 1884. Although a woman of great determination, Osborn retired before her ideas were widely adopted. Drunken nurses were still to be found in Sydney's Prince Alfred. Training was either non-existent or lasted less than a year. Nurses were expected to learn by doing. New drugs and operations began to force the pace of progress after 1890. For so long as wages were low and the hours long, no improvement in the quality of the recruits could be achieved. In the 1890s a fully-trained sister earned a pound a week, plus full board. Trainees got about eight shillings and their keep. For this, they worked a seventy-hour week.

The impossibility of a trainee finding time and energy for study is shown by this extract from the memoirs of Sister Harris, who joined Melbourne Hospital in 1886:

> Mrs McKie was then Matron, and a very fine capable woman in every respect, but not a trained nurse. The nurses were in the main elderly women with years of experience. The probationers who were employed to assist in the nursing were not bound to any period but could leave at will, which many did, finding the service too hard. There were no wards' maids and the probationers had to polish floors, etc. in addition to the probationers' work. We went on duty at 6 a.m. and worked until 8 p.m. one night and 6 p.m. the next, with half an hour off for each meal and half a day once a week. Many fell out, broken in health and disappointed.

Another nurse, this time from Sydney, recalls the skills she was expected to learn:

> There were detailed instructions as to how to give baths of various temperatures and how to make and apply linseed poultices, alkaline formats, starch poultices, bread poultices, mustard poultices

(or a mustard leaf), turpentine stripes, cantharides, plasters, poppy-head formentations. Leeches were used.

The setting-up by 1894 of at least one training centre in each capital city did little to improve this situation. The problems were overcome by the establishment of professional associations formed by the nurses themselves.

ABORIGINES

After a hundred years of contact with European civilisation, all the surviving Aborigines in Tasmania had mixed parentage. In Victoria, the numbers had fallen so low that the whites were hardly bothered. By contrast, New South Wales, Queensland, Western Australia and South Australia had what their governments called 'Aboriginal problems'. Concentrating on these four colonies does not mean that the other two were free from blame. Rather, their campaigns of dispossession had proved so complete that Aborigines remained politically unimportant for another sixty years.

Outside the south-east corner of Australia, Aborigines continued their defensive action against the European invaders. In 1888 the King Sound Pastoral Company (WA) lost over 7000 sheep as the Aborigines realised that livestock was the weak spot in the pastoralists' economy. In the early 1890s an Aboriginal leader, Sandamarra, appeared in the Derby district of Western Australia. He joined the ranks of the enemy as a police tracker. Once he had gained an understanding of his enemy's tactics, he killed the constable who was supposed to be in charge of him, captured some guns and freed a group of his countrymen whom he then led in a series of attacks. Attempts to undermine Aboriginal resistance by destroying their culture were also rebuffed. Church of England propagandists under the command of the son of the Bishop of Perth were driven out of the Forrest River area in 1898. Pastoral expansion in the Northern Territory doubled during the 1880s. By the end of the century, many cattle stations had to be abandoned because of Aboriginal struggle.

In South Australia, resistance showed another side when settlers encountered twenty-eight Aborigines early in the 1890s. This group had grown in thirty years from a male and two females who had escaped from a settlement on the Murray River. They were rounded up once more. Although perfectly healthy at the time of capture, they died out within a few years of contact with white civilisation. They had prospered for as long as they remained out of sight. As their numbers increased, so too had the likelihood of their discovery. When we read of twentieth-century Aborigines who had never seen a white man, we must realise that this was not the case: in fact, they had seen him coming and had kept out of his way.

Laws dealing with Aborigines came after their physical and cultural defeat. Thus, Victoria brought down its Act in 1869 when only a couple of hundred unmixed Aborigines were left. By 1897 Queensland's Native Police had murdered enough of their fellow Aborigines that the frontier was safe enough for the whites to pass laws for the protection and preservation of Aborigines. Western Australia followed in 1905, but South Australia waited till 1910–11 when its frontier in the Northern Territory was handed over to the Commonwealth government.

Queensland's Act became the model for the other states. It established a number of small reserves where Aborigines were to be sent. From these, pastoralists obtained labour. Persons liable to be sent were all 'full-bloods' and all 'half-castes' who lived with or often came in contact with full-bloods. No appeal was possible against being sent to a reserve. Western Australia and South Australia made exceptions for those Aborigines who had jobs. The Acts were designed to provide the whites with cheap labour, not to take it away from them. In

The Destruction of Aboriginal Society, Charles Rowley described the reserves as places 'where the Aboriginal family produced in safety the labourers of the future ... a subsidy to the pastoral and other industries'.

Some reserves were run by government officials and others by government-assisted missions. In many areas the local policeman became the Protector of Aborigines. This arrangement was rather like setting a hawk to watch over a chicken. An indication of how these police Protectors behaved is that those Aborigines who spoke a kind of Pidgin English divided Europeans into two groups, 'white-fella' and 'pleeceman'; those who knew no English used words from their own languages such as 'fierce', 'severe-looking', 'sour', 'salty', and 'the chaining horseman'. This last name came from the habit of chaining Aboriginal witnesses and prisoners when taking them in to the towns for trials. The police officer in charge of a party of witnesses was paid two shillings a day for each of them; one constable earned more than £450 in nine months in this way. When rations replaced cash, there was an increase in the number of prisoners shot while trying to escape. Some whites worried for fifty years whether it was kinder to chain Aborigines by the hands or by the necks. Others believed, in the words of a member of the West Australian Parliament, that 'It will be a happy day for Australia when the natives and kangaroos disappear'.

WHITE AUSTRALIA

A strike by European seamen along Australia's eastern coast against Chinese crews had lasted from November 1878 until January 1879. Riots erupted. Anti-Chinese feeling was still running high when the leaders of the Australian colonies met late in 1880 to work out a plan to bar Chinese immigrants. New laws were passed, except by Western Australia, which still did not have self-government. By the middle of the 1880s, the anti-Chinese movement was fading away because the restrictions were working. Then, in May 1887, two Imperial Chinese officials, General Wong Yung Ho and Consul-General U Tsing, arrived in Sydney as part of their tour of inspection of Chinese around the world. The very fact that China had sent two officials was taken as proof of a Chinese desire to swamp Australia. The anti-Chinese movement flared again.

Early in May 1888, alarms were sounded at the arrival of a ship, the *Afghan*, carrying 268 Chinese. Recent laws would have stopped all Chinese landing in Victoria and New South Wales. Those controls proved so much trouble to administer that another inter-colonial conference had to be held in Sydney in June. All the mainland colonies agreed to admit only one Chinese passenger for every 500 tonnes of a ship's cargo. Despite strong Chinese protests to Britain, these new laws were put into effect. While some colonies imposed tighter rules than others, their combined result was to close down Chinese immigration. A few still came, but fear of being overrun by Chinese slipped from sight.

The Australian colonies did not worry much about Asians again until the late 1890s. Queensland found itself in trouble because it had agreed to some of the trade treaties that Britain had signed with Japan. Japan — not China — became the main concern for the new Commonwealth in 1901.

One of the main reasons that people gave for being against Chinese coming to Australia was that they worked long hours for very low wages. Many Chinese were forced to do this, but so were large numbers of European workers. Like them, the Chinese did not want to work for next to nothing. They too joined unions and went on strike. In doing so, the Chinese were following the example of lots of other non-European workers who were good unionists. Aboriginal workers were active in the big shearers' strikes of the early 1890s. Islanders on the sugar farms of Queensland fought their bosses long and hard for higher wages. Afghans at Bourke (NSW) and Japanese in Perth also struck for their rights.

One of the most important of these non-European unions was formed in Melbourne by Chinese who worked in the furniture trade. In September 1885, about 300 Chinese workers went on strike against their Chinese bosses. Within three years, the Chinese Workers' Union had won a basic wage, a fifty-hour week, holidays, and jobs for union members only. When the depression hit Victoria in the early 1890s, the Chinese Workers' Union, like almost all unions in the colony, fell apart. It was not active again until 1897 when it opposed sackings and wage cuts. By the end of the century, the Union was back on its feet and had won a strike for higher wages. The Chinese formed their unions and withdrew their labour power for the same reasons that the Europeans did. While they could survive for a time on bowls of rice, they much preferred to eat duck and dried fish brought from China. Whenever the Chinese proposed joint action with European unionists, the latter refused in the rudest fashion. This rejection helped Chinese and European bosses to go on mistreating both lots of their workers.

VIEW OF THE WORLD

A New South Wales contingent had arrived too late for the Sudan campaign of 1885. Its tardiness was just as well, because the officers were incompetent and the men ill-equipped. During a public display on Sydney Harbour at Easter 1891, four engineers blew themselves up when they attached an electric wire to the mine on their boat instead of to the one on the harbour floor. A Royal Commission in 1892 found the military system 'very unsatisfactory' and called for extensive reforms. Five years later, the commanding officer dismissed the field artillery volunteers as a 'laughing stock':

The term 'Field Artillery' seems scarcely appropriate to apply to an aggregation of obsolete guns and cart-horses, even though the latter may be attached to the former by the usually recognised Field Artillery means. If force of circumstances compels Artillery men to use such horses, they at least should feel that if, by dint of spur, and whip, and strong language, they have got a gun into a suitable position, the labour ought to be repaid by seeing effective fire opened. This is scarcely possible with the present old muzzle-loaders.

More alarmingly, the officers in charge of the fixed batteries protecting Sydney Harbour had been declared medically unfit and professionally unequal to their highly technical tasks.

When war broke out in South Africa in 1899, the Australian troops strove to arrive in time. At first, some doubted whether Australians should go. Those dissenters saw the enemy, the Boers, as honest, God-fearing farmers, very much like themselves. Others felt that the fight was a bit unfair already, because the total Boer population was about the same as that of the Melbourne suburb of Collingwood. A few were against the war for political reasons. An even smaller number opposed all wars. Added together, these Australians were a tiny part of the population. Many quietly favoured Britain. A few wanted a stoush for its own sake.

This balance changed after 'Black Week', 10–16 December 1899, when the Boers won three battles. Shouts of joy in France, Germany and the United States stirred emotions here. Most Australians now saw the fight against the Boers as a struggle for the British Empire itself. Since Australians relied on Britain's navy, they backed Britain to win in South Africa. Sending troops there was no longer a blind act of loyalty, or a mad desire to kill, but a defensive tactic in the longer term. If the British Empire went down anywhere, what hope had Australia against Japan, Germany or Russia? South Africa became Australia's first line of defence.

Opponents of the war persisted, but they were limited to a few who were themselves divided as to why the war was wrong. The Professor of History at Sydney University, G.

Arnold Wood, was against the war because it was unjust. Some labour politicians were against it because it seemed part of a plot to send Asian labour into the gold-mines in place of white workers. J. F. Archibald, editor of the *Bulletin*, opposed the war because he saw it as a Jewish plot to take over those riches. Most opponents of the war shared the racial views of its promoters. They just had different ideas on how to protect the white race.

Before the war was over, 16 463 Australians had fought, 588 had been killed or died from fever, and six had been given the Victoria Cross. Two had been executed for shooting twelve Boer prisoners. These two were the well-known poet Harry Morant, 'the Breaker', and his friend from Bathurst (NSW), Peter Handcock. Their crime was only the tip of an iceberg. After 1900, the war became a mopping-up operation which went on for two years. The Boers fought in small guerilla bands. The British rounded up their families into some of the world's first concentration camps and burned their homes and farms. In the eyes of the Boers, 'every little village in Australia spewed up its foul vomit of contingenters. The war in South Africa gave your idle young men an opportunity to shoot and burn and destroy. South Africa was your criminal safety valve.'

Australians got a sharp reminder that there was a threat from Asia as well as from Europe. While the Empire watched South Africa, the Boxer Rebellion broke out in China in 1900. In China, crop failures enflamed the Boxers against Christian missionaries and foreign firms. One Boxer verse complained:

No rain comes from Heaven,
      The earth is parched and dry;
And all because the churches,
      Have bottled up the sky.

Some 460 sailors left Victoria and New South Wales to put

down the uprising, although there was little fear of Chinese forces attacking Australia.

The danger was seen as Japan. Most Australians had not known that there were any Japanese in Australia until a group of Japanese pearl divers won a Melbourne Cup sweep in 1891. Australians became aware of the growing power of Japan in 1895 when that country defeated China in a short war. The victory made Brisbane's *Courier* certain that, 'were Japan to turn her naval arm against what lies in Australian waters, we should go down against her'. Until atomic bombs fell in 1945, a majority of Australians would never be free of this fear.

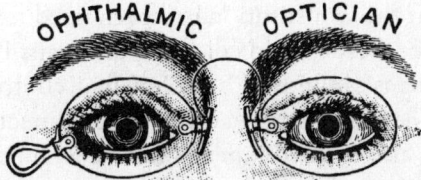

1901: A CONTINENT FOR A MARKET

Bernard O'Dowd won the *Bulletin*'s 1900 competition for a Federation poem with his sonnet *Australia* in which he interrogated the coming Commonwealth. 'Are you', he queried,

A new demesne for Mammon to infest?
Or lurks millennial Eden 'neath your face?

O'Dowd and his mates around the Victorian weekly *Tocsin* suspected that the Constitution had been fixed for the benefit of British bond-holders and colonial plutocrats. His group of radical nationalists opposed both imperial control and local capitalists. The dissenters wanted the continent to be one nation. They also wanted a democratic Commonwealth, not the monarchical model. Moreover, they attacked the Boer war as 'unnecessary and unjust'.

Federation of the six Australian colonies was one step in the newest era of globalisation. Globalisation Mark I had flourished around the Iberian seaborne empires, carrying Luis Vaez de Torres (1606) through the strait that bears his name. In our region, Mark II manifested itself in the East India Company and the Netherlands Indies Company. Mark II also saw James Cook claim possession in 1770 and a trading post under Phillip from 1788 to service the trade with China. A third stage came in the middle of the nineteenth century with free trade and the replacement of slavery with indentured labour.

In the context of globalisation Mark IV, Federation meant the creation of yet another nation-market-state. Australia followed the example of the United States, Canada, Germany and

Italy in the 1860s. Australia's first prime minister, Edmund Barton, declared on 1 January 1901: 'There is a nation for a continent, and a continent for a nation'. That slogan left out the crucial demand, namely, a nation-state to defend a market across the continent. That aim lowered trade barriers between the colonies-cum-States.

Federation also marshalled investments instead of squandering those resources in each of the six colonies. One example was the erection of BHP's iron and steelworks at Newcastle with ore shipped from South Australia. Without Federation, Australia might have had two or more inefficient works — or none.

The agitation to federate coincided with an economic contraction in the eastern colonies and a gold boom in the west. The London financial crisis in 1890 was followed by bank failures in Victoria and Queensland. Throughout the 1880s, Australia had attracted one-fifth of new issues on the London financial market. British investors became anxious to protect their funds. When London financiers refused to invest in an 1891 loan for Queensland, the *Economist* voiced the fears common among investors about the labour movement in Australia: 'Possibly the rates of wages in Australasia will suffer by a partial cessation of borrowing'. British bankers regulated the rhythms of economic life in the colonies by tightening the purse-strings.

Bank crashes in Australia encouraged an alliance between the colonies. Melbourne financiers argued that their counterparts in London would be more willing to lend if the debts of each colony were underwritten in a federation. A crisis in one part of the country could be met by the resources of the rest.

British capitalists and their political agents were keen to maintain appeals to the Privy Council in order to protect investments in government and corporate ventures. In 1897, the Colonial Office worried that loans may not be secure if suits for their recovery could be finalised in the High Court of

Australia. 'Is it likely', a high official wrote, 'that the House of Commons where such capital is largely represented will allow the appeal to be swept away?' Worse still, populist politicians might repudiate repayment.

To protect British investors, the Secretary for the Colonies, Joseph Chamberlain, conspired in 1897 with the Premier of New South Wales, George Reid, to amend the draft Constitution. The Adelaide Convention in 1897 altered the clause dealing with the Privy Council to allow unfettered appeals on non-constitutional questions. Another result of the Chamberlain-Reid discussions was that the Governor-General could act without the advice of the Executive Council.

Australian delegates went to London in the summer of 1900 to watch over their draft being turned into an Act of the British parliament. Federation almost stalled on the question of appeals to the Privy Council. As one of the delegates, Alfred Deakin, put it: 'The Conservative classes, the legal profession and all people of wealth desired to retain the appeal to the Privy Council' in every case. Chamberlain assured the House of Commons that he was protecting 'the private interests of investors, a very large class of British subjects interested in Australia'. In the end, the Australian representatives compromised to allow the Australian High Court the power to allow appeals on constitutional issues.

At the crux of globalisation Mark IV were larger businesses, then referred to as 'Trusts', which needed larger markets and stronger governments. The expansion of capitals had produced the modern corporation by the 1880s. The Colonial Sugar Refineries was a prime example in eastern Australia, spreading from New South Wales to Fiji, buying up cane farms and mills. Such a concentration of capital was like federation in the sphere of business.

Australia's federationists were alert to the United States situation and gave the new Commonwealth power to make laws for the control of 'foreign corporations, and trading or financial corporations'. One such giant was International Harvester. It had 90 per cent of world sales when, in 1905, it dumped machines here at low prices intended to bankrupt its local rival.

THE COMMONWEALTH

Starting the Australian Commonwealth at the beginning of a new century should have brought about a great outburst of nationalism. Yet the project seemed blighted. The people's interest turned towards the Empire's struggle against the Boers in South Africa. Public rejoicing turned to mourning with the death of Queen Victoria. The Governor-General made a mistake in choosing a prime minister. A commanding officer for the armed forces could not be found. Even before these difficulties, the people had shown little enthusiasm for Federation, voting against it or abstaining. Some were planning to break away even before it began. One rude fellow suggested that the Fathers of the Constitution could barely write English. And so it was that Australia had one nation for a continent, one continent for a market.

Queen Victoria went into a coma on Saturday 20 January 1901 and did not regain consciousness until noon the following Tuesday, when she asked for her favourite Pomeranian dog so that she might pat it. Later that day, she patted her relatives and died at 6.30 the same evening. Official pieties were put in the obituary in the *Sydney Morning Herald* which described her as:

> a good woman, a good wife, and a good mother. In her life and person she held up to the imitation of her countrywomen the true type of the womanly woman, which has made the life of the English home what it is, kept British domesticity sweet, and held society in all its grades together.

The republican-minded *Bulletin* lined its editorial pages

with heavy black margins but reproduced the *Sydney Morning Herald*'s opinion in simpler words:

> Victoria was simply an admirable woman and an admirable Queen, in an age and a country where any good woman of some education and refinement could be a good Queen. [Her] epitaph should be that she was a good woman of homely virtues, whom a mass of greasy knights and mayors laboured hard to bring into unmerited contempt.

Edward VII was far less the model of domestic virtue; his reign was noted for his ability to maintain the peace in Europe in the brothels of Paris. In 1896, a jury had acquitted John Norton, the editor of the Sydney *Truth*, of sedition when he had echoed the cry 'God Save the Queen' so as 'to keep her rascal of a turf-swindling, card-sharping, wife-debauching, boozing, rowdy of a son, Albert Edward, Prince of Wales, off the throne'. Ted Findley, Labor MLA for Melbourne, was less fortunate in 1901 when the Labor Party's weekly paper, which he edited, reprinted the same list of charges against the new King from an Irish newspaper. Findley was expelled from the Victorian Parliament.

Although the Commonwealth was to come into being on 1 January 1901, by the middle of December the only person certain of his future job was the Governor-General, the forty-year-old seventh Earl of Hopetoun. His first task was to install a caretaker administration until elections could be held and parliament could meet in Melbourne. Instead of sending for a leading federalist, the Governor-General asked the anti-federalist Premier of New South Wales, Sir William Lyne, to form the first government. By Christmas Eve it was clear that Lyne could not get enough leaders from the other colonies to join him. The queen's representative turned, at last, to Edmund Barton. Thus the smooth birth of the Commonwealth was upset by what the press called 'the Hopetoun Blunder'.

The Department of Defence seemed to be even more

ill-fated. Its first minister died nine days after being appointed. Indeed, there were to be ten different ministers for defence in ten years. The second minister told parliament that he had taken office with the hope 'that the Department would not give me a great deal of work or trouble'. This wish was not to be granted. The first problem was to appoint a commanding officer. Partly in order to avoid inter-colonial jealousies, it was decided to import another British officer. As the minister told parliament in July 1901: 'We want one of the best men in the Empire to start this machine, whatever we may do afterwards'. Difficulties arose in getting the best man. In September 1901 General Sir Reginald Pole-Carew, KCB, CVO, DL, JP, refused because the pay was too low. A few days later, General Sir Henry John Thornton Hildyard, GCB, former commandant of the Staff College at Camberley, also declined. In November 1901, Colonel Sir Edward Thomas Henry Hutton, who was on the half-pay list of the British Army, accepted at a salary of £2500 per year, plus expenses, and was made a kind of general. So it was that Australia got one of the best men in Europe.

Even the syntax of the Constitution Bill came under fire. In a pamphlet entitled *Ungrammatical Statesmen*, S. A. Rosa, a radical Sydney journalist, allleged that the authors of the Bill had used 'less' instead of 'fewer' when qualifying numbers; had made it appear that citizens would have to be both aged and invalid to obtain a pension; had forbidden the States to mint an unheard-of alloyed currency — 'gold and silver coin'; and had inconsistently followed 'not' with either 'or' or 'nor'. After listing sixteen pages of similar errors, Rosa wondered:

> When will Australians understand that a man may be puffed by certain newspapers, and helped, by cliques and societies, into lucrative positions, and yet be a pompous ignoramus, a shallow self-seeker, or a tricky intriguer partially concealing, under a veneer of a liberal education, a vulgarian's contempt for everything but the cult of the golden calf?

The man whom Rosa had in mind was about to become
Australia's first prime minister, Sir Edmund Barton, known as
'Toss Pot Toby' because of his addiction to the bottle.

DUNLOP
Hot-water
Bags

DUNLOP
HOT
WATER
BAGS
Last many Winters.

Winter
Comforts.

DUNLOP RUBBER CO.
Melbourne, Sydney, Adelaide, Perth,
Brisbane, Christchurch, N.Z.

2 1902–1913 FRUGAL COMFORTS

The early years of Federation pointed towards 'frugal comfort'. Commonwealth spending was limited for two reasons. First, the Constitution required the Commonwealth to return three-quarters of customs revenue to the States, which collected the only income taxes. Secondly, drought shrank the economy.

The 1900s cleared away dead wood to plan for later on. In parliament, the tussle became Labor versus anti-Labor. Orders were placed for an Australian navy. Universal military training was adopted. Policies that did not cost much money did slightly better. white Australia was enforced. Industrial Arbitration and Conciliation was given a trial run. More reforms followed in the early 1910s because so much had been on hold since the 1880s.

WORK

Every item on our meal tables has a trail of labour behind its progress from the wealth offered by nature. The application of human capacity can be traced in the story of table salt. Increasing saltiness of the soil upset farmers on South Australia's Yorke Peninsula until they realised that the lagoons could be worked as salt deposits in summer. Over 1000 men were employed, wearing coloured glasses and veils to protect their eyes and faces from the blinding glare off the beds of salt crystals. If the surface had set hard, a horse-drawn rake broke it up. Otherwise, the job was done by a man pushing a plough-like implement. The salt was then scraped up into piles by a flat board attached to long poles; these mounds were then bagged or stored in vast heaps. Some salt was exported rough. The rest had to be refined before it could be bottled for sale to households.

Women Workers

Twenty shillings a week was the smallest amount needed by an unmarried woman if she were to support herself entirely from her earnings, and keep healthy. People could, and did, live on less, but only by cutting down on food and by accepting poor housing. Few factory jobs paid more than 16 shillings a week. For packing pepper into 100-gram cartons by hand, a 23-year-old woman received twopence an hour; her forty-eight hours earned her 8 shillings. Many working women were young girls adding to their family's income.

Clothing was made largely by sweated labour; the sewing was sent out to women in their own rooms. This system spared an employer the costs of renting a building, or heating and lighting it. Outwork also avoided the factory inspectors. One woman received 11 shillings for six dozen bibbed aprons, which had taken her ninety-six hours to sew. Out of that pittance she had to pay 1 shilling and 9 pence for the cotton thread and 8 pence on tram fares to collect the material and return the finished goods. She had worked for a little more than a penny an hour. Another woman made up an order for twelve white underskirts to the following pattern: '48 pieces of lace insertion, all joined; 48 vandyke tucks put in; two frills, and beading to be attached; three tucks above the frill'. These fineries sold in the shops at £2 12s 6d each. She got 15 shillings for the lot.

No social issue troubled the well-to-do more than 'the

servant problem'. The problem arose because there were 150 000 domestic servants to clean 200 000 dwellings with more than six rooms. Some commentators recognised that 'the servant problem' was really 'the mistress problem'. One writer claimed:

> to know a doctor's wife who expects her cook to answer the door, and a wool broker's wife who *measures* the pudding left over which her maid must not eat; and a lady in one of the Victorian up-country homes who expects her cook to make all sauces, pickles, jams and bottled fruit whilst cooking for her ten servants and a family of twelve.

A maid wrote to the newspapers claiming that 'the servant problem' would be better understood if working conditions were given pride of place. At her previous house, she had been told to bathe in the laundry-tub, ate scrap food and got no space to hang her clothes. The live-in servants were upset by the long hours expected of them. A maid had to work from 6 am to 10 pm, her only time off being one night a week, one Sunday afternoon in three and one weekend a month. In return, she got 10 shillings a week and full board, 'full board' meaning cold leftovers and sharing a room with two others. Women accepted these conditions because they left them better than their sisters working in factories, and much better placed than those doing 'out-work'. Domestic service, even at its worst, provided enough to exist, which was not true of almost all other female jobs.

Conditions could be better for waitresses or shop assistants. By working from nine in the morning till seven at night, a waitress could expect a pound a week plus her meals. Many worked only part-time and so could not have lived on their earnings alone. Wages might be increased by tips from customers, while in some places waitresses were paid a percentage of their takings.

No job was more sought after than that of a shop assistant in an inner-city store. This appeal was surprising because the hours were long, the pay low and the conditions poor. Two explanations are possible. First, the work was looked upon as ladylike and refined, and so it attracted middle-class women in hard times and working-class girls trying to improve themselves. Secondly, a tiny minority of women in the high-fashion sections earned about £4 a week. The demand for jobs as any kind of shop assistant meant that employers were able to require long apprenticeships on low wages. Girls of fifteen worked from 9 am to 6 pm for 5 shillings a week. When 'trained', many would be sacked and another lot taken on. If a girl stayed till she was twenty-three, her wage would be £1 5s 0d a week. To earn this amount, she had to stand up all day. She had to wear all-black clothing, which was costly to buy and to keep clean. She was watched over by floor-walkers who delighted in insulting their staff in front of customers.

So few married women worked in New South Wales factories in 1910–11 that they were not officially recorded. Reasonable guesses indicate that there were about 1200 in the whole state; almost half were either widows or deserted wives. Even this small number caused alarm, because machine-work was said to destroy the physical strength and moral fibre of mothers-to-be. Treadle sewing-machines were seen as dangerous to child-bearing. The employment of married women was opposed because it increased the use of contraception, the incidence of miscarriage, bottle-feeding, neglect of the home and wild spending by husbands. Indeed, cries went out to end all female employment — except domestic service.

Working Men

Conditions in factories were not much better for men. A government inquiry into the Victorian starch-making industry found not a single firm offering wages or conditions to a decent standard. The evidence exposed the harshness of the work and the meanness of its rewards:

> I am in receipt of 30s per week of 54 hours and have been in the starch trade for 12 months. It took me about six weeks to learn the work I am doing. Working in the ranges my feet get wet, and after going into the stove I can wring the perspiration out of my flannels. The ranges are very low, and in a couple of them I have to kneel. For about two hours I am continually going into the stoves, where it is very hot.
>
> Afterwards, I stack the starch on racks in the crystallising stove. As the racks rise, I have to throw 5 lb, 6 lb, and 7 lb blocks as high as 20 ft. When taking them down another man throws them to me in parcels of 10 lb, or 12 lb [4–5 kg] weight. It is very severe on the wrists and fingers. In my daily work I handle packs weighing from 2 cwt to 2 ¼ cwt [100 kg], and am often on tiptoe.
>
> I have worked 48 hours at a stretch at coal-shovelling, and not felt as tired as after a day's starch work. Starch work has tired me so that I could not eat my tea, and coal-shovelling never did that. In the ranges, the solution of caustic soda lies on the floor, and destroys my boots. A pair of boots never lasted me more than five or six weeks. I provide my own clothes and boots. In other occupations boots lasted me six months.

This witness worked for Robert Harper who had just been elected to the Commonwealth Parliament. His wife was president of the Women's Work Association, which helped 'poor-but-unladylike' women to sell jam and needlework without the shame of revealing their names. Mrs Harper was also president of the Spinners' League, which made woollen petticoats for the 'deserving poor'. 'Hospital Sunday' in October saw the greatest yearly act of Harper charity when he gave a cheque on behalf of Robert Harper & Co. The '& Co.' was an attempt at honesty, since each employee had been obliged to give a penny a week to fund his employer's generosity.

Harper's instincts were equalled by those of E. R. Walker,

owner of the Tessellated Tile Company in Nunawading. When his employees turned out at the local railway station one morning in 1910 to mark his return from a world tour, he took the two hours off their pay for being away from work.

Before unionism was widespread and for as long as unemployment was pressing, public inquiries were compromised because employers bullied their men. A Melbourne cab-driver, for instance, was sacked for giving evidence about his working conditions to a parliamentary inquiry in 1907.

Any factory that had opened before the New South Wales 1896 Inspection Act did not have to meet its standards, no matter how bad the state of its lighting, air or sanitation. Many new factories were half-converted warehouses or were roofed with unlined galvanised iron. In summer, as the temperature reached 56°C, mass faintings and hysteria were all part of a day's work. A New South Wales Royal Commissioner in 1911 found that not even the rules about fire escapes were being kept. They were often narrow iron ladders fastened to the side of a building and could be reached only by climbing through a window.

Dreadful conditions continued despite stronger factory laws. Sometimes a model factory opened, such as at one Sydney tobacco firm, where a canteen sold excellent hot lunches for 2 shillings, as well as cheaper meals for poorer girls. The State Savings Bank operated a branch there. The company paid half the costs of a health and insurance fund for those it employed for longer than a year. A full-time matron visited the girls if they became sick.

LIFE IN THE CITIES

Improvements in city life could be a mixed blessing. Public health demanded sewerage. In Sydney, the laying of pipes meant cutting two-and-a-half metres through solid rock. Much of this work was done by hand. The men worked with their heads about fifty centimetres below the surface. The air was heavy with fine dust which got into their lungs, where it gave rise to a white fibrous tissue which slowly strangled them from the inside. Anyone who worked at rock-chopping for two years was certain to become ill and equally certain to expire, choking to death in a chair because it was too painful to lie down. Hundreds of strong young men suffered in this way. They were generally family men attracted by the prospect of steady work. A government inquiry in 1901 recommended a six-hour day and more fresh air. These reforms were slow in coming and not enough. Until the government introduced more costly digging methods, Sydney's drains were 'built with young men's lives'.

Cost Of Living

Home ownership was almost an impossible dream for most of the poorer families. Nonetheless, many were paying more in rent than they would have had to repay on a housing loan. The trouble was, as always, that the poor had no savings and so had almost no hope of getting a bank loan. They therefore paid rent all of their lives and passed this future on to their children. Those who could afford the higher rents also had far less trouble getting a loan: the better-off therefore spent a smaller percentage of their income on housing, as well as leaving their children valuable property.

To try to find out the cost of living, the Commonwealth government asked 1500 families to note down their incomes and spending from the year beginning 1 July 1910. Only 212 of the booklets came back in a useable state. The information is therefore of most use in drawing comparisons about the problems faced at different income levels. Families of more than four who were earning less than £200 p.a. spent about half as much on meat, fruit, vegetables and dairy products as the richer households. Both groups spent the same amount on bread, sugar and tea. Hence, the general health of the poorer families suffered because they were eating more starch than protein.

Even when a family could afford all the food its members needed, there was no certainty that they got what they had paid for. Impure food was widespread. Until after 1905 Australia had no laws able to deal with the fraudsters. Few if any soft drinks were pure, most being mixtures of sweeteners and dyes, which led the New South Wales government chemist to comment: 'With a little less sugar these liquids might be used as red ink'. Anti-drink campaigners were shocked to learn that their favourite drinks contained anything from 2 to 8 per cent by weight of alcohol. Wheat flour was mixed with other grains; glucose was added to honey; pepper was made from ground olive stones and rice, coffee from roasted wheat and toast, and tomato sauce from pumpkins, apples and flavourings. One imported batch of cream of tartar proved to be 30 per cent plaster of Paris, 16 per cent bone ash and 54 per cent starch. In 1908 the journal *Lone Hand* had a chemist examine sausages bought at seven different butchers; each 450 grams was found to contain an average of 210 grams of water; any meat was of very poor quality, with pork sausages containing no part of the pig whatsoever.

Between 1906 and 1912, pure-food controls came into effect in all six States, but they were all different, which made it difficult for manufacturers to sell their goods on an Australia-wide basis. After a series of conferences and Royal Commissions, an agreement on standards was reached. The Australia-wide market, which had been the basic aim of Federation, was possible.

Even if food was pure when bought, keeping it fresh was not easy. Refrigeration was in commercial use, but home models were not widespread until after the 1940s. Instead, in closely settled areas men delivered blocks of ice two or three times a week. These were placed in the top section of a lead-lined chest to cool the food placed beneath. In outlying suburbs and on farms, 'the only way of keeping food fresh was to put it in a hanging canvas safe, which had a bowl of water on top with cloths soaking in it and dripping water over the sides'. Because ice was not available, these districts were the first to have refrigerators, usually kerosene-powered. Town dwellers could see no reason to give up their low-cost ice-chests for costly refrigerators. Someone had to be home when the ice-man called to put the ice in the chest. That someone was usually the housewife. When wives started paid work, refrigerators were among the first durables paid off with their new wages.

Before vitamins were discovered, eating habits were quite different. Because energy was the main benefit that people wanted from food, more highly calorific breads and potatoes had been eaten. Unfortunately, new grinding methods, which gave a much whiter flour, were also taking away bread's major nutrient value, vitamin B1. Governments and the public thought that the purity of bread could be judged by its white-ness and lightness. Soggy black bread would have been healthier. Salads were almost unheard of, although crinkly tomatoes, sprinkled with sugar and scooped out with a spoon, were popular as a tonic for men and were called 'love apples'.

Transport

Hiring a horse-drawn cab in Melbourne in 1907 was a risk. Drivers did no test for their licences, nor was there a minimum age. 'The Chief Commissioner of Police complained that he engaged a hansom cab to drive him to the Crown Law Offices, and the Cab took him in the first instance to the Vienna Cafe; and in the next, when he told him to go to William Street, the driver took him to Spencer Street; and it was only after great difficulty he got to the place he wanted to go to.' Drivers also had a rough time of it. Many passengers refused to pay their fares. A driver on wages earned about a pound a week. At that moment, the High Court was deciding that the basic wage needed to keep a man, his wife and three children in 'frugal comfort' was more than twice that amount. Drivers for stables such as Mayne, Nickless & Co. were slightly better paid but had to be on constant stand-by and generally worked 90 to 100 hours a week.

Trams were pulled by horses or were driven by steam, electricity or an underground cable. Their versatility and low running costs brought them into widespread use. Electrification of Brisbane's tramway system after 1897 increased the annual total of passengers from nearly six million to more than sixteen million in three years. Not every town could afford to switch over all at once. Adelaide's horse trams continued running until 1917, partly because of their popularity with passengers. They stopped everywhere and anywhere; people jumped on and off while they were moving. They were deliberately derailed to allow other trams to pass, and also for the entertainment of the drunks on the last trip at 11 pm.

With the arrival of the motor car, trams had to fight for the right of way on streets which were rarely wide enough for double tracks plus two lanes for driving and another two for parking. Among the capital cities only Melbourne, with its broad inner-city streets, kept more than a token few.

Australia's first locally made horseless carriage was probably the steam-driven contraption that conveyed Lord Brassey, the Governor of Victoria, around Melbourne on 26 February 1897. One of the builders of that vehicle, Hartley Tarrant (1860–1949), went on to play a larger part in Australia's motor industry. In 1908 he gained the right to import Fords. He also made his own brand of cars, installed the first petrol bowser, and became Captain (later Colonel) in charge of the army's Volunteer Automobile Corps, after selling the idea to the army in 1909. A civilian use for trucks appeared in Queensland during the 1902 drought, when two steam lorries carried the wool clip to the railway, horse teams being unable to reach it because of the lack of roadside feed.

Before the Great War, motor vehicles were few and far between. Only 37 000 cycles, cars and trucks were registered in 1914. They were popular for their entertainment value at races and endurance tests. At Sandown Park on 12 March 1904 the fastest car of the day covered the 4.8-kilometre circuit in 6 minutes 55 seconds. Long-distance events were more of a challenge because roads were so bad. Grades over the Blue Mountains were so steep that races ending in Melbourne often started from Bathurst rather than from Sydney. Early in May 1900, the Bathurst to Melbourne trip took nine days. Fifteen years later, the drive from Perth to Sydney took a week; by 1929, that run could be completed in less than four-and-a-half days.

Newspaper accounts of the arrival of the first motor car in country towns recall the changes in attitudes. In 1902, the editor of the Mt Gambier *Border Watch* told his readers that a display of car driving had shown that 'There was no hard work in it like bicycle riding and it seemed freer than a buggy ride', while the automobile itself was as 'docile as an old family horse'. The idea that motor cars were really horses in disguise took a long time to disappear.

Motor cars changed women's clothing fashions. Dresses became narrower because sweeping bustles and flowing trains were out of place on the high cramped seats of a T-model. Not all adjustments to the 'motor age' were as simple, even for seasoned drivers. Those who had learned to drive on the original two-gear T-model were never really at home with three forward gears.

Governments were unsure how to control cars and their drivers. South Australia passed a Motor Car Act in 1904, making cars carry a disc showing the owner's name and address; respectable citizens protested at these 'dog tags' by driving along King William Street with black veils over their faces. Fortunately, another section of the Act had imposed a 19 kilometre per hour speed limit in the city. Until 1919, drivers in Western Australia were issued with their licences by the dog inspector. Victorian drivers roamed at will before 1910 because the Legislative Council believed that any form of control was an interference with the freedom of anyone rich enough to own a motor car. As late as 1924, one magistrate accepted drunkenness as an excuse for driving a stolen vehicle.

Sanitation

As mixed sea bathing and 'fresh air' became popular, Melbourne's citizens travelled by train to the beaches between Mordialloc and Frankston. From 160 000 rail passengers on this line in 1904–5, the number had leapt to 725 000 by 1913–14. Holiday-makers either camped along the foreshore or rented bungalows. In either case, few attempts were made to enforce standards of sanitation or building. Slops, garbage and human waste were dumped or buried freely in the ti-tree bush. Overcrowding at Wimbourne Avenue, Chelsea, was extreme. On one allotment, 14 metres by 45 metres, six bungalows housed twenty-five to thirty residents; a larger block of 15 metres by 90 metres, contained a house as well as nine bungalows made of white-washed hessian over wooden frames. Three earth privies served forty to fifty people. This state of affairs existed because the Central Board of Health had no power to deal with 'the calculated inertia' of the Dandenong Shire Council.

Although the 1890 Health Act empowered the Board to order a local council to carry out a piece of work, it gave the Board no means of dealing with a council that refused to do so. Nor was the Board authorised to carry out the work itself and charge the cost to the council. If the Board did so, it would have to take the council to court, a chancy action. Normally, the combined pressure of voters and the Health Board gained some improvement. In the Chelsea case, the people who suffered were visitors, not rate-payers. Melbourne's newest health resorts were turning into health risks.

LIFE IN THE COUNTRY

As if an economic depression and a plague of rabbits were not enough troubles, at the turn of the century country people suffered the most severe drought ever recorded. For eight years none of the inland subtropical eastern half of Australia had more than its average rainfall. When almost no rain fell in 1902, there were no reserves of feed or water to fall back on. Nearly one-third of the sheep in New South Wales died. The wheat crop was about one-tenth of the usual harvest.

The quest for water has shaped the human occupation of this continent. The Aboriginal paintings that Europeans call landscapes are often maps of water soaks. In the 1970s, for example, Papunya became a site for commercial art after the authorities established it as a bore-water camp. Its artists retold the rain-dreaming of the claypan at Kalipinypa across which storms sweep from the west. Water is as sacred to Aborigines as is their land, because the soil needs the power of rain-making to flourish. A Luritja rain ceremony involves copious blood-spilling and the term for lightning flash is 'rain penis'. Aborigines accepted that they were at the mercy of their environment. Their ceremonies were necessary adjuncts to the natural world, not the means to control it.

The European settlers knew enough science not to worship nature and they possessed enough technologies to defy its rhythms. The settlers would not accept that their new home could be barren. Explorers died of thirst seeking an inland river or sea. Faith that rain would follow the plough broke farmers and the lands they tilled. Bush women went mad watering their geraniums.

Europeans had also brought a commercial outlook towards the resources of nature. Land became another commodity. To dispossess the original owners, pastoralists fenced off waterholes. To exclude small farmers, the squatters grabbed the river frontages and billabongs. But neither the pastoralists nor the dirt-farmers could control the climate.

The years between 1895 and 1902 brought three consecutive *El Niño* effects. That rolling *El Niño* also ravaged a sweep of peoples from East Africa, through India and China, and on to Brazil. The ending of that prolonged *El Niño* sequence opened the road to other changes in Australia's environment. Prickly pear had been held back during the droughts, when it had been used to feed cattle. In 1900 it infested only 4000 hectares: by 1920 it had engulfed 25 million hectares.

The drought refocused attention on irrigation. Control of the Murray waters had been debated at the 1897 Federation Convention in Adelaide. One plan was to give the Commonwealth power over navigable rivers and their tributaries. New South Wales and Victoria refused to give in to South Australia on the use of those waters. Meetings dragged on until the next drought in 1915 resulted in the River Murray Commission.

The long dry revived fears that Australia would not be able to feed its population of five million. The search was on for high-yield grains. Crops per acre had been falling since 1860 because of stem rust in the higher rainfall districts closer to the coast. Grain had been imported in 1890. After fourteen years of cross-breeding, William Farrer named his 'Federation' strain in 1900. This early maturing and drought-resistant type expanded the wheat belt far past the Great Dividing Range. The western plains changed colour from golden to brown.

New strains could not prevent the return of *El Niño*. In 1914–15, the wheat crop was back down to the 1902 level. Next year, the harvest was the biggest ever, leaping from 25 million to 179 million bushels. The surplus fed the allied troops. The promise to aid the Mother Country to 'the last man and the last shilling' was extended to 'the last loaf'.

In the worst years farmers worked in the towns, leaving their families to battle on with an endless diet of pie-melon jam and rabbits. 'Underground mutton' always had to be eaten boiled because it contained not a grain of fat. A tin of dripping became a rare treat.

The memoirs of George Ashton, who worked near Braidwood around 1912, left a dismal picture of living in the country. The fourteen families whom he visited regularly were almost unable to read and write; none bought newspapers, but if an outsider turned up he was passed from family to family to recount the latest news. Money was largely unknown and a barter system operated through wandering 'Syrian' traders who brought in tea, sugar, salt and 'cocky's joy' (golden syrup), as well as luxuries such as cloth, condensed milk and patent medicines. These extras were exchanged for the skins of rabbits and the occasional fox. Houses were built from split timber neatly fitted into logs and roofed with bark, while the floors were usually beaten white-ant bed.

Public services in country areas grew, partly because the new entertainment of moving pictures needed electricity. This power was supplied by the local theatre operator. Telephones were another innovation which cut the social barriers between country and city. Despite the arrival of cars, water supplies, street lighting and postal services, country people continued to move to the cities in search of comforts.

Railways both weakened and strengthened country towns. The trains that helped farmers send their produce to market also let city businesses take trade away from local firms. In 1918, a Victorian Royal Commission looked into why nearly 170 000 people had left districts outside Melbourne since 1901. The greatest loss was in the gold districts, where the number of miners had fallen from 26 103 to 6609. More and more, the smaller towns were kept going by government employees such as policemen, teachers, post-masters and railway officials whose wages were an important boost to local traders. Because so many farms were too small to split up among all the sons, boys moved to the city to work in unskilled jobs with the railways and tramways. Country girls took jobs as shop assistants in the suburbs; their bush manners kept them out of the larger city stores.

No one in the bush worked harder or suffered more than the wife of the small farmer. An article in the Melbourne *Argus* early in 1902 detailed her drudgery. Her day began before dawn. After milking the cows, she fed the calves, pigs and fowls. Then she

> got breakfast, consisting of cold salt beef, porridge, and tea; washed up; sent children to school; carried water in kerosene tins for the day's use, set the house in order, made bread, scrubbed and washed. Dinner must be prepared — mutton, potatoes, rice and tea. Then she must help outside with planting potatoes, or with finding the pigs that have escaped. Then milking time, then tea-time — cold beef, bread, butter and tea, but if times are bad, merely bread, dripping and tea. After tea, clothes to make, or maize to shell, or potatoes to cut for the morrow's planting.

It was a cruel fact that milk and butter were scarce on dairy farms and meat was of poor quality because the produce had to be sold. One farmer explained how his wife

> did as much as a man until the youngster arrived. She helped with the clearing; can work a lever with anybody, I've seen her shift a four-foot log and get it in position on the pile. She helped with the fencing. She did most of the 'picking up' on the piece I'm plough-ing now. And last year when I am bad with the influenza for nearly a fortnight she went on with the ploughing as well as I'd do myself, the kid in a big box at one end of the paddock watching her.

In 1903 the Melbourne artist Fred McCubbin immortalised this life in his huge, three-panel painting, *The Pioneers*.

The mother on a well-to-do farm exclaimed: 'We are just white slaves'. Another pointed out that, although the only time she had for sewing and mending was when she was preg-nant, she had made all the family clothes, and without a sewing machine.

If farmers' wives are added to the women who took in washing and ironing to support their families, the post-1960 increase in working wives would appear smaller than indicated in official figures: from 6 per cent in 1901 to 32 per cent in 1971. Lots of wives have always had to work at more than their own housekeeping. What changed were the numbers who were paid wages.

HEALTH

Bubonic plague struck Sydney in 1900. That assault panicked the three eastern mainland States into strengthening their Health Acts. However, local government bodies could still block those reforms. Unless council inspectors were appointed and prosecutions carried through, laws were so much waste paper. Public health measures were limited, according to Queensland's Director-General of Health, to 'abolishing stinks, clearing choked drains, removing dead animals, and cleaning up backyards'. Positive steps such as inoculation campaigns and special care of children were mostly left to individuals. These protections were available to those who could afford to pay for them.

Commonwealth power in regard to health matters was limited by the Constitution, although invalid pensions and maternity allowances were introduced. The most effective Commonwealth activity was the setting up of a Quarantine Service after 1911.

The birth-rate fell from thirty-eight per thousand in 1870 to twenty-seven per thousand in 1900. That decline alarmed governments anxious to build up Australia's population for war. Explanations for this fall included the increasing use of contraceptives, which were described as 'race suicide'. The government report of the 1903 New South Wales inquiry into the birth-rate was destroyed as an obscene publication. The advertising of contraceptives was made illegal. Since it was not possible for governments to force women to have babies, the next best thing was to make sure that as many babies as possible were kept alive. Some free health services for mothers and children were started.

The authorities became concerned that the children of the poor would turn into drunks, criminals or socialists. As a preventive measure, the middle-class improvers adapted an idea from early nineteenth-century Germany. Children of pre-school age were to be placed in an environment of play and kindness, which would help them grow into good citizens. They would be tended like flowers so that they would not drink, gamble or strike. The movement acquired its name from the German words for children and garden: *kinder* and *garten*. When the movement got under way in Adelaide in 1905, the working-class families slammed their doors. They feared that the government wanted to steal their children. After they saw the benefits of the kindergarten, the poor women around Franklin Street went to their neighbours in Bowden and offered to mind their children so that the Bowden mothers could spend a morning at the Franklin Street centre. The kindergartens were not to help poor families by minding their children while the mothers earned enough to feed them.

Because cows' milk was so often impure, doctors encouraged breast-feeding. Few babies were born in hospitals because of the danger of mothers getting blood poisoning. Medical information therefore had to be taken into the home. Between 1904 and 1914, child-care officers visited 29 000 mothers. Books on mothering were sent to every address where a birth had been recorded within Sydney.

Classrooms were used to investigate the health of the nation's young. Between 1906 and 1913, all States set up some kind of school medical service. The results from these inspections were startling. In Queensland, for example, 30 per cent of the children examined had a physical defect which would interfere with their learning; 97 per cent had bad teeth. In New South Wales, more than half of those children who had been described as dull were in fact suffering from adenoids, deafness or poor sight. There were even cases of undetected heart troubles and cancers. These surveys examined children but did not treat them. The examinations probably forced parents to get attention for their children. However, without follow-up services, or changes in food and housing, inspections once every four years were of no real help. They showed what was wrong but did little to fix it. Compulsory military training provided more information about the physical condition of Australia's youth. In 1912 the average fourteen-year-old cadet was about 150 centimetres tall and weighed 40 kilograms; eighteen-year-olds were 15 centimetres taller and almost 19 kilograms heavier.

Dentistry

Teeth are the only part of the body that doctors have not claimed the right to treat. Before 1890, many dentists were untrained and only a handful had been professionally educated. Casual apprenticeship was the rule. The extraction of teeth was almost the only treatment available. Amateur dentists usually worked in their own homes and the patients sat on boxes with the back of their heads pushed against a wall. Since no anaesthetic was used, the main qualification was the brute strength to yank the tooth out as quickly as possible. Blacksmiths were in great demand.

Of eighty dentists in Adelaide in 1902, only eight held diplomas. This lack meant that laws to improve dentists and their education could not be enforced overnight. Patients could not be deprived of almost all dental services until enough fully qualified dentists were trained. Victoria opened a dental college in 1892, followed ten years later by New South Wales. The backwardness of dentistry gave that profession certain advantages over medicine. Dentists were less bound by the past, so modern techniques, usually from America, were welcomed by the new graduates.

Several old treatments, such as the filling of holes, now

became widespread. Local anaesthetics, introduced in the 1890s, made drilling easier. Holes were plugged with soft gold, tin foil or melted-down threepenny bits. False teeth ranged from those specially carved in ivory and mounted on a gold base to mass-produced sets bought over the counter. Tooth-pastes, known as dentifrices and made from charcoal, chalk and cinnamon, were advertised but not widely used. When medical inspection of primary-school children started around 1910, 90 per cent of all pupils were found to have decaying teeth. Community standards and attitudes can be seen in the fact that, although large numbers of volunteers for the Great War were rejected because of poor teeth, the army's first reg-ular dental surgeons were not appointed for almost a year.

By the early part of the twentieth century, most of the infe-rior dental work was no longer done by totally untrained 'quacks' but by second-rate qualified men who offered cheap services and gave something below second-best. Usually these dentists advertised a list of charges based on the false view that all fillings took exactly the same amount of time. The best way of making sure that their prices matched their costs was not to waste time cleaning out the cavities. This crudeness meant that fillings fell out, or that decay continued inside the tooth, resulting in an abscess.

Nurses

Working conditions for nurses continued to be bad despite efforts by the nurses themselves to establish govern-ment-backed registration boards. Although doctors depended on the nursing staff for the recovery of their patients, medical honoraries continued to treat them as inferior beings. A Bendigo doctor described the perfect nurse as possessing 'the three R's, sound serviceable teeth, absence of varicose veins and flat feet, no squint, a tidy head of hair and a short back'.

A retired nurse was quoted in the Victorian Parliament in 1918 on the daily pattern of her old job:

It must not be forgotten that nurses' work is strenuous physical work. During her day, beginning at six a.m., she is only off her feet during the two half-hours allowed for the two meals, breakfast and dinner. The rest of that time she is taking arduous physical exercise, walking quickly, scrubbing, washing and lifting heavy patients, making beds, &c. She cannot slacken, because, when the actual nursing does not take all her time, she must clean the wards. A nurse's work consists in — Making beds and washing patients. Carrying out technical medical treatment. Preparing for operations. Doing dressings. Carrying meals to patients. Giving medicines, &c. Scrubbing chairs, lockers, tables, cupboards, windowsills, doors, enamel ware, &c. &c. &c. Looking after stock.

In many country hospitals the situation was worse. At Wangaratta in 1909, for instance, day nurses worked a 77-hour week, while night nurses worked almost as long. They did not get a night off until they had completed a two-month roster. Wages remained very low. A three-year-trained nurse started on £40 a year in 1918.

The sick, no matter which illness they had, faced the threat of pneumonia. Recovery was possible only with the most careful attention, described by a Sydney nurse:

Pneumonia patients were kept sitting upright, tied, by means of a pillow under the knees, to the back of the bed, to maintain position. This was not easy. They were usually big solid men, they were very sick, and they slipped easily or sagged over to one side. They coughed and spat up thick sticky sputum which they found difficulty in getting out of their mouths and into the spittoons. They had to be helped to reach the spittoons on their lockers. They had to be lifted back into position frequently and the poultices and wrappings made them heavy and awkward to handle. What with four-hourly linseed poultices (mixed at high speed in the day-room where the kettle of boiling water was, and rushed to the bed at the double), brandy, rum, egg-flips, spongings and morphia; even those with the brightest prospects required constant hard nursing; delirious ones had to be coaxed into subjection and persuaded to remain in bed, even to the extent of being confined by bed-rails and manacles, lest they escape altogether.

Treatments

In country districts, the chance of recovery was no greater and the treatment even more makeshift. At Loxton (SA), as in so many small Australian towns, there was no doctor; health matters were handled by an untrained midwife who eased the thirst of pneumonia patients with juice scooped from a water-melon hanging from a tree.

Diphtheria remained a major child killer. Before the intro-duction of Behring's anti-toxin in the mid-1890s, doctors had tried all sorts of cures, including successive doses of 'an emetic, an aperient, quinine, champagne and spa water'. The autobiog-raphy of a leading politician contains this account of the treat-ment he received for diphtheria in 1901:

> I had a tube down my throat for three days and three nights. I can remember being held at the front window of the cottage by rela-tives in turn for those three days and nights so that I might be able to get some air. My hands were held to my sides inside blankets.

Although anti-diphtheria injections were available at the turn of the century, several deaths from anti-toxin poisoning occurred before a safe method was developed. The dangers from the preventive frightened off parents. As a result, the infant death rate from diphtheria did not decline very much until the early 1940s.

With so many simple illnesses beyond the power of doctors to cure, patients turned to 'quacks' and patent preparations. Some of these were harmless, such as Mrs Terry's Tablets which were 98 per cent sugar and 2 per cent salt. Others were as dangerous as Mrs Winslow's Soothing Syrup, which used morphia to put children to sleep, or Dr Williams' Pink Pills for Pale People, which cheered you up with a little arsenic. Herbs were widely recommended: Southern Wood for poor beards, strawberry leaves for the blood, and mint for headaches.

Far more harmful in the long run were nostrums that

claimed to cure everything from syphilis to bubonic plague, from indigestion to cancer. These were advertised with complete dishonesty, and cost money that would have been better spent on wholesome food. The Commonwealth government used its customs powers to control the entry of these products but it could not stop their production inside Australia. Without uniform laws across the six States, the US-based 'Toadstool millionaires' found ways around the law. Of course, these worthless products remained popular until doctors could do better.

As long as open paddocks remained, Australians had fresh milk. The spread of the cities separated the cow from the consumer. In the 1880s, milk carried by train from Gippsland was not sold in Melbourne until thirty hours after its production. The wealthier people with large blocks of household land kept their own cows, as did the hospitals. One leading citizen kept his cow on Melbourne's Domain up until the Great European War.

Some enclosed dairies remained in the inner suburbs. Most of them were little more than cesspools for breeding typhus. Collingwood's health inspector found that one four-roomed 'dairy' housed fourteen people as well as the cows. Only half of the milk samples that he tested were pure. One-quarter of them contained up to 40 per cent added water. The call went out for local governments to regulate the supply through council depots. In 1907, future prime minister William Morris Hughes expostulated: 'If private enterprise cannot sell fresh milk, what in the name of all that is manly and independent can it do?'

Milk from country districts was not often any purer. Australian dairymen passed by Pasteur's discoveries of the 1870s. They carried on in their slap-dash ways for another sixty years. In 1930 the standard textbook on Australian dairying reported that dipping one's hands into the milk before starting on a new cow was 'very common'; the writer also regretted that '90 per cent of our dairy farms have long ago abandoned any effort to rid their dairy premises' of flies. Even when milk had left a farm pure, it was deposited on the doorstep in a billy can which the milkman filled in the street.

Despite these sources of infection, almost no public funds were spent on new city hospital buildings in the fifteen years before the Great War. Hobart hospital did not get flyscreens until 1919. Melbourne Hospital was rebuilt in 1913, but only because of a private gift of £120 000, and after a delay of twenty-five years. The average hospital was small and privately run. In 1911, New South Wales had 426 private hospitals, of which 250 held fewer than four beds. The nature of such institutions can be viewed through the eyes of a doctor:

> On arriving [in 1903] I found I had been appointed to the Tambo [Queensland] District Hospital which was built in 1872. It was called a hospital, but it consisted only of several large rooms, in a galvanised iron building, built flat on the ground with a veranda all round. I imagine it is called a hospital because one small room was fitted with shelves, upon which were bottles containing drugs, and was labelled the dispensary. There was no operating table, no surgical instruments of any sort, a matron who had many good points and some experience, but had not been trained.

The Tambo saddler was the local anaesthetist because he had given chloroform to horses and to women in difficult births. A few larger country towns, including Wagga (NSW) and Mt Gambier (SA), were more fortunate and had new hospital buildings just before the Great War.

ABORIGINES

In 1904, in Western Australia, two Aboriginal station workers were overheard talking about plans for a revolt to kill all the pastoralists in the Roebourne and Port Hedland districts. The police were informed. All the whites were issued with rifles. The Aboriginal workers changed their plans from a general attack to tactical engagements. Economic warfare expanded as thousands of cattle were speared. Further expansion by pastoralists was opposed. Indeed, when the Canning stock route opened in 1911, its users were attacked in a series of raids. Attempts by missionaries to destroy Aboriginal culture were repelled. Attacks on the newly established Benedictine Mission in the Kimberleys followed in 1910–11.

Pastoralists faced a dilemma: they had to defeat the Aborigines but not kill them off entirely because the stations depended on their labour. Hence, sending the blacks to prison was also not satisfactory. Castration, which was also suggested, would have deprived the pastoralists of a long-term labour supply. Some fathered their own workforce. Most paid baby bonuses to Aboriginal mothers.

In these distant regions the Aborigines were not killed off. Their land was stolen, but their labour was essential to the invaders. As Peter Biskup pointed out in his book *Not Slaves, Not Citizens*, 'there developed an almost classical colonial situation: political and economic power was in the hands of the Europeans, while the Aboriginal societies retained much of their traditional characteristics'.

During the twentieth century, this colonial relationship changed a good deal because of resistance by the Aborigines. Realising that only a large-scale army could defeat the black patriots, the whites gave in by declaring vast areas in the Kimberleys and Arnhem Land to be reserves, hoping to confine the more militant Aborigines to these zones. This tactic cut down the supply of labour and so new laws were needed to drive Aborigines out of the schools, off the lands they were farming, away from the towns and into the arms of the pastoralists.

Before the 1905 Act in Western Australia, a goodly number of Aborigines had set up farms under government schemes intended to assist Europeans. Aborigines had not been prevented from applying. In the Newcastle (WA) district, an

Aboriginal man named Ryder had thirty hectares under wheat, a one-hectare vineyard, twelve hectares ringbarked, and was buying more land for his son.

After a few protests from white parents, the Minister for Education expelled Aboriginal pupils from state schools even though they had been passed clean and healthy by the medical officer. In August 1918, the Aboriginal farmer John Kickett protested to his local Member of Parliament:

> I want a Little Fair Play if you will be so kind Enough to see on my Beharfe. I have five of my People in France Fighting. Since you were here for your Election one has been killed which leaves four ... as my People are Fighting for Our King and Country Sir I think they should have the liberty of going to any State school.

Education was not needed by stockmen or unskilled labourers, which were the jobs that the government wanted Aboriginal workers to fill. John Kickett's plea was ignored.

Under the 1905 Aboriginal Act, Kickett and all his children could have been taken from their farm and sent to a reserve. The fact that they were well-off farmers and well-educated would not have saved them, because the law covered any half-caste who looked under sixteen years of age or who was in close touch with Aborigines.

As well as keeping up a regular supply of labour, the 1905 Act permitted the removal of Aborigines with venereal infections. Two barren islands off Carnarvon were set up as dumping grounds. The death rate was so high that in 1910 the officer in charge asked for a bone-crusher to 'utilise all available organic matter for the object of improving the nutritive value of the soil'. Medical services for Aborigines were intended to protect the Europeans from cross-infection. Doctors refused to drive out to see them. In 1911 the nursing staff at Geraldton (WA) went on strike rather than tend to Aboriginal patients.

Racist practices in health, education and justice were bolstered by racist ideas openly voiced in official and respectable publications. A 1906 booklet promoting Western Australia overseas claimed that the Aborigine was 'brutish, faithless, vicious, a natural liar and a thief'. To celebrate the new Commonwealth, the *Sydney Morning Herald* ran a series of articles on Australia's past, including one on the Aborigines by Ernest Favenc, an amateur investigator. Favenc denied that Aborigines were cannibals and said they had some brains. Yet he backed the view that they were 'decidedly treacherous', bound to die out and doubly wicked when civilised.

New South Wales pastoralists wanted Aboriginal labour as much as did their northern counterparts. Once again the government obliged. The Course of Instruction for Aboriginal Schools told teachers to 'direct the whole of the school work with the object of assisting the boys to become capable farm or station labourers, and the girls useful domestic servants'. Because moral discipline is necessary in a useful worker, the Aboriginal children were to be taught 'a love and reverence for the Creator' through a course in nature study. Before taking their pupils on a bush walk, 'A short quotation from Kendall, illustrating the Charm of the Australian bush, should be memorised'. Presumably, the choice was not 'The Last of his Tribe'.

On Christmas Day the Aborigines Board in New South Wales gave Aborigines 'the usual ingredients for plum pudding' and bought sports day prizes to keep them 'away from the adjoining townships'. Separation of children from their parents became an important part of the Board's scheme for assimilation. A 'Home Finder' encouraged Aboriginal parents to apprentice their children as domestic servants. Despite all these good works, the Board complained that it could never make Aboriginal parents understand that its 'one aim is to make the lot of the children better and easier'.

WHITE AUSTRALIA

Two of the earliest laws passed by the new federal parliament were designed to keep Asians out of Australia and to send Pacific Island labourers back home. The debates on these Bills were very long, although hardly anyone spoke against them. On the face of it, both laws should have been very simple to write, but there were lots of traps. The law to stop Asians coming to Australia had to be phrased in a way which would not insult them. The law to send home the Islanders from Queensland's sugar farms ran into trouble as it was being put into practice.

Strong supporters of white Australia wanted a law which said that non-whites would not be let into Australia under any conditions. These champions of racial purity usually saw non-whites as anyone who did not come from Britain or from northern Europe. A law voicing that prejudice would have been passed had the British government not been against it. In 1901, Britain did not have a powerful ally. Germany, France, Russia and the United States were all less than warm friends of the British Empire, although none of them was its bitter enemy. Britain was still frightened of Russian moves around north-west India. London, therefore, was trying to make friends with Japan, which opposed Russian actions near China. If an important part of the British Empire, such as Australia, insulted the Japanese by treating them as less than human, Britain's hopes for a treaty with Japan could be upset. So it was important to write an immigration law which kept both Australia and Japan happy.

The way out was found in a 'dictation test'. Under this device the government could ask anyone coming into Australia to write fifty words in any European language that the government cared to pick. This test was given only to people whom the government did not want. While a German would be admitted without being tested, it was certain that an Asian

would be asked to write fifty words of Dutch, Polish, Roma-
nian, or any language that he would not be likely to know.
Japan was not happy with this trick but at least the law was not
openly racist. Australia would be 'white', Britain could have
her treaty, and Japan would go to war with Russia. The law
was changed in 1905 to meet some of Japan's wishes. The 'dictation test' could now be in any language, not only a European
one. Businessmen, students and important people from Asia
could visit Australia for limited periods.

What was the government to do about the Asian men
already in Australia, some of whom had been born here? Were
they to marry European girls? Or were they to be allowed to
bring in Asian wives? Here was the rub. If they married Europeans, they would do what the supporters of white Australia
feared most, that is, they would breed a race of 'mongrels' with
the worst features of both races. If they brought in Asian
wives, this remedy would increase the non-European part of
the population. If they were not allowed to do either, they
might use white women as prostitutes. The government could
find no ready answer to this problem and shifted between one
view and the other for a further twenty years. By 1920 the
problem of Asians coming to Australia no longer existed. The
'dictation test' had made it clear that they would not be let in.
They did not waste their time trying. Socialists were among
the very few Australians who opposed White Australia on
principle. When one of their leaders was asked if he would let
his sister marry a Chinaman, he replied that he would rather
that than her marriage to a capitalist.

Queensland's sugar farms had employed Pacific Islanders
for nearly thirty years when the new Commonwealth passed a
law to send most of them back to their homes. Recruiting had
to stop by 31 March 1904. Almost all were to be deported at
the end of 1906. Those who had been born here, and those
who had lived here since 1879, would be allowed to stay. Many

Islanders did not have homes to go back to. Most wanted to stay in Queensland.

Not all the Islanders had been forced or tricked into coming to Queensland. Quite a few had wanted to come because they were in trouble with their own people. One of these wrote to the government official in charge of Islanders in June 1907:

> *Dear Mr Brennan*
> *I am writing to let you know if you want to send me home or not but I am frightened to go home. I got trouble in my country if I go home to my passage I might get kill because they are waiting for me all the time the best for me to stop with my brother Dick Assie and Tom Sulla. Dear Mr Brennan you will let me stop in Queensland because I will get kill that is all I ask you. I remain your truly son*
> > *Peter Janky*
> > *Malayta*

Islanders in Queensland had farms or shops of their own. Some had been away from their island home for so long that their families were dead. Others feared that the old life would be dull after years in Queensland's sugar towns.

The Islanders organised against being sent away. As well as writing to the King and to the Governor of Queensland, they formed the Pacific Islanders' Association in 1904. The chairman was Henry Diamur Tongoa, a New Hebridean, aged about thirty. Tongoa had been in Australia for twenty-six years and ran a boarding house in Mackay (Qld). He wrote and spoke forcefully. In 1906 the Association sent a plan to the prime minister, Alfred Deakin, asking for an area of land which the Islanders could farm, instead of being sent back to their islands. This idea was not accepted by the government but an investigation suggested changes in the deportation law. These amendments made it a little easier for Islanders to remain. Others were allowed to stay if there were very special reasons such as leprosy on their home island or fear of being killed on return.

By the end of 1909, 4269 islanders had been sent away and only 1654 remained. A few who went home were killed as they had feared. Two armed ships stayed in the Solomon Islands throughout 1906 and 1907 to stop more murders and robberies. Almost all returning Islanders were sick for a few months, with malaria and stomach upsets caused by the change in food. Those who were allowed to live in Australia worked in the sugar fields or on other farms.

Even at the height of this passion for white Australia, governments let Asiatic divers work in the pearl-shelling industry around Broome (WA). Pressure to make the industry 'white' resulted in a Royal Commission which, in September 1916, agreed 'that the White Australia Policy will be neither weakened nor imperiled by allowing the pearl-shelling industry to be worked by Asians'. Nonetheless, the commissioners voiced the racist attitudes that were the basis of some opposition to White Australia:

> diving for shell is not an occupation which our workers should be encouraged to undertake. The life is not a desirable one, and the risks are great, as proved by the abnormal death rate amongst divers and try divers. The work is arduous, the hours long, and the remuneration quite inadequate. Living space is cramped, the food wholly preserved of its different kinds, and the life incompatible with what a European worker is entitled to live. Social life is impossible and enjoyment out of the question.

This hole in White Australia lasted until the first Pacific War closed down the pearling industry in 1941. The industry opened again in 1945, but by then some of the Asian divers would not accept the sub-human jobs. Two ex-servicemen divers from Indonesia formed a union to fight for higher wages and better conditions. As a punishment, both were deported by the Labor government in 1948.

VIEW OF THE WORLD

During the 1890s, Australians had became aware of the importance of Japan. Attention turned to alarm early in the twentieth century. Britain signed a treaty in 1902 which made Japan Australia's closest ally in the Pacific. In 1905, Japan crushed Russia in a major war. These two events changed Australian views towards the United States and Britain, as well as towards Japan. People who had been against any preparation for war now advocated an Australian navy and compulsory military training for all boys. More Australians were convinced that they would have to fight Japan, probably sooner than later.

The initial alliance between Britain and Japan covered only China and Korea. This arrangement was widely supported in Australia although it worried some people. In Victoria, the Labor Party's weekly paper, *Tocsin*, saw Britain saying to Australia:

> You are not to attempt to hold the fort for your own race, because Downing-street relies on the aid of Japan to enforce opium trade on China or to see that English Lords' sons instead of Russians get billets bossing it over the natives of Manchuria.

When Japan went to war with Russia in 1904 most Australian newspapers looked forward to a Japanese victory. By the time that triumph was complete, the Press was concerned at what would happen next. A visit by a Japanese fleet in 1906 gave Australians a chance to see their probable enemy, and current ally, at first hand. Some refused to accept invitations to visit the flagship. Labor's Senator Dawson, a former Minister of Defence, told Rear Admiral Shimamura that he feared 'the day will dawn when Australia will rue the gush it showered on you'.

Britain had made its alliance with Japan because it shared Japan's fear of Russia. After Russia was defeated, London saw less need to keep so many of its warships near China. Five British vessels left the Pacific. The naval defence of Australia was passing to the Japanese. Since Australians feared Japan more than any other country, this policy was not welcomed here. Australia decided to build its own navy. When the Great European War broke out in August 1914, the Royal Australian Navy had a number of smaller craft, two submarines, three destroyers, two light cruisers and the battle-cruiser HMAS *Australia*.

If Britain appeared to be leaving Australians to the care of Japan, another white nation might take them under its wing — the United States of America. Important Australians called for an alliance with the United States from 1905 onwards. Prime Minister Alfred Deakin arranged for a US fleet to visit Australia in 1908. He used the threat of an alliance with Washington to strengthen his bargaining hand against Britain.

Australia faced a tricky problem. It could not break away from Britain, for a range of economic, military and sentimental reasons. Yet it could no longer rely on Britain completely. Australia did not like Japan as an ally, but this connection was better than having Japan as an enemy. So Japan had to be kept at arm's length without being insulted. The United States might be a valuable friend in the future but for the time being it was not willing to shift its full strength from the Atlantic Ocean to the Pacific. Australia's leaders had to juggle friendship with Britain, Japan and the United States. Equally, those three countries had to be kept friends with each other for as long as possible. In the meantime, the new Commonwealth had to build up Australia's own army and navy. Some even saw the need for an air force.

The German threat to the British Empire came from Germany's successes in scientific and technical training. Strategists argued that similar methods would have to be developed in Australia. One obstacle to the growth of secondary education was the lack of qualified teachers. Of the 867 registered secondary school teachers in Victoria in 1911, fewer than 1 per cent held qualifications that would have let them teach in Germany.

Kitchener's Report

Because the Commonwealth government would have more money to spend after 1910, officials began plans to improve Australia's defences. Expert advice was sought. Lord Kitchener, who was leaving his position as Commander-in-Chief in India, was asked to return to England via Australia. He arrived at Port Darwin just before Christmas 1909 and finished his report in Melbourne on 12 February 1910.

Despite this brief visit, his observations were very detailed. He summed up the poor state of Australia's defences in his introductory remarks. After praising the 'young manhood of Australia' with whom he had fought in the Boer War, he added:

> In these days, however, excellent fighting material and the greatest zeal are not of themselves sufficient to enable a force to take the field against thoroughly trained regular troops with any chance of success. The training I saw in the camps indicated that there was a distinct tendency to go too fast, and to neglect essential preliminaries of training for more advanced studies which the troops engaged were not capable of carrying out properly. The conclusion I have come to is, shortly, that the present forces are inadequate in numbers, training, organisation, and munitions of war, to defend Australia ...
>
> I would also mention that railway construction has, while developing the country, resulted in lines that would appear to be more favourable to an enemy invading Australia than to the defence of the country. Different gauges in most of the States isolate each system, and the want of systematic interior connexion makes the present lines running inland of little use for defence, though possibly of considerable value to an enemy who would have temporary command of the sea.

Kitchener called for a wide-ranging system of part-time compulsory training for all males between the ages of twelve and twenty-five. The most important achievement would be the 80 000 infantry, light horse and artillery men aged between eighteen and twenty-five.

The Labor Party made the running on militarism because it was the governing party from 1910 till 1913. Kitchener's program fitted with its enthusiasm for White Australia and its calls for National Sentiment. The ALP showed little sign of the international solidarity needed if workers of the world were to unite to prevent war. Those attitudes were confined to a fringe of Socialists. The greatest illusion was that fighting would strengthen the combatant countries, morally and economically.

3 1914–1919 THE GREAT EUROPEAN WAR

'War is nothing but a continuation of politics with the mixture of other means.' That maxim of the German general Karl von Clausewitz (1780–1831) is as true for domestic affairs as for international ones. In 1914 the British feared that their Russian ally faced social revolution, as it had ten years before when it had gone to war against Japan. To keep the Czarist autocracy in place, a year-round supply route had to be secured. Hence, on 25 April 1915, Imperial troops, including the Anzacs, were sent to break through the Dardenelles, conquer Constantinople and storm into the Black Sea.

War is also a continuation of economics. The Australia of 1918 was very different politically and industrially from the Australia of 1914. The Labor Party had won the federal elections in September 1914 with the borrowed slogan of fighting the war to 'the last man and the last shilling'. It split apart in 1916 over conscripting the last man. Divisions in the Labor Party had been shaping up over other issues before the war and would have intensified anyway. Wartime shortages and new production methods altered the shape of Australian industry. Most important of the changed economic structures was the BHP iron-and-steel works at Newcastle where construction had started in 1913. The rolling of the first steel there on 24 April 1915 has as much claim to be called the event that gave birth to an Australian nation as the landing at Gallipoli a few hours later. So the war speeded matters up, twisting them to its needs.

WORK
Training for war

Australian children were prepared in both body and mind for the Great War of 1914–18. At the urging of Lord Kitchener, voluntary school cadet corps, which had existed since the 1870s, were replaced with various forms of compulsory training for all males between the ages of twelve and twenty-five. This enforcement sparked opposition from working-class lads who did not want to give up their only free afternoon to attend drill parades. The children of the rich did their training in school hours.

Although a Labor government had brought in military training, sections of the trade union movement opposed it from the start. Coal-miners on the northern New South Wales fields voted 3359 to 1882 'against the hare-brained scheme of the so-called Labor Party' and promised 'to oppose the brutal measure to our utmost, seeing that the workers of this country have nothing to defend'. This anger fed into the Labor split.

The miners' attitude was close to that of the best remembered Anzac, Simpson, who used a donkey to transport the injured away from the front line. His full name was John Simpson Kirkpatrick. He had jumped ship in Newcastle in 1910 to hump his bluey from Cairns to Kalgoorlie as a labourer. In 1912 he wrote to his mother back in England:

> I often wonder when the working men of England will wake up and see things as other people see them. What they want in England is a good revolution and that will clear some of these Millionaires and lords and Dukes out of it and then with a Labour Government they will almost be able to make their own conditions.

Unable to get work in Australia, Kirkpatrick joined the

army to get a free passage home. Instead he was shot through the heart at Gallipoli on 19 May to become a mythic figure, shorn of his radicalism.

Not all opposition was political. Quakers objected on religious grounds. One sixteen-year-old Quaker was kept in solitary confinement on half-rations because he refused to violate his conscience. More common were the hardship cases, such as this one reported in the Adelaide *Advertiser* in October 1912:

> David William Fitzgerald was 44½ hours in arrears with his drills. He said he lived about four-and-a-half miles out of town and had no horse to bring him in. He worked from daylight until dark, and when he finished he was too tired to drill. The Stipendiary Magistrate: 'If there was a football match on, you would soon walk in'. The father of the boy said it was impossible for his son to attend the drills, as he had no way of getting into the Port and it was too far to walk. The Stipendiary Magistrate: 'You must get him a horse then'. A fine of £5 and 15/- costs was imposed, in default six weeks in the reformatory.

David was one of 6000 boys gaoled in a period of four years.

This cadet training was more than a preparation for war. At a time when most boys left school aged about thirteen, the army was a way of keeping up the discipline needed in factories. For those who stayed at school, the parade ground backed up classroom lessons in 'obedience, respect for authority, self-control, order and method, alertness and responsibility, self-respect, and the conception of service for the public good'.

The syllabus also prepared children for war. The 'School Papers' were full of praise for a British Empire which protected 'the dignity of manhood, the virtue of womanhood, the innocence of childhood'. Students were taught never to forget that they too had a 'share in guarding most zealously the honour of their country's flag'.

War was pictured as a game in which the strength of nations and the manliness of boys would be tested. Indeed, Germany's defeat would be attributed to the Britisher's love of sport, which let him fight the war 'as the greatest game their race has ever played'. Sport made the British armies brave, fair-minded and resourceful. When public examination papers asked students 'Why is Australia at war?', and 'How would you answer a boy from a foreign country if he were to ask you why you are proud to belong to the British Empire?', the answers were not matters for debate.

This propaganda proved effective. Between 1914 and 1918, 300 000 Australians volunteered to fight the Empire's battles. School teachers were prominent. From the 1500 in Victoria aged between eighteen and forty-five, more than half joined up, of whom 146 were killed.

Education departments set up war relief organisations to supply soldiers with socks, gloves and shirts, and the military hospitals with food. Pupils raised money by collecting leeches, making straw brooms, and growing and harvesting table-raisins. These seemingly small actions were repeated by schools across the country and produced hundreds of tonnes of food and clothing, and hundreds of thousands of pounds in war savings certificates.

At the war

At first, almost all the volunteers were eager to fight, and left home with hearts filled with hope rather than fear. A 24-year-old printer from Fitzroy described his departure:

> relatives and friends of the boys were allowed on the pier; guess there was about 2000, then began the fun, the boys on the boat catching sight of a friend would call out, then a streamer could shoot by your head, everywhere was excitement, the chaps struggling for positions, and getting mixed in the streamers. As the boat moved out the streamers crossed and uncrossed looking not un-like a silkworm cocoon. When we had steamed out of sight, we settled down to a good dinner.

The front-line fighting killed this innocent joy. The popular author Ion Idriess reported on his time at Gallipoli:

> Immediately I opened my tin of jam the flies rushed it, all fighting amongst themselves. I wrapped my overcoat over the tin and gouged out the flies, then spread the biscuit, held my hand over it, and drew the biscuit out of the coat. But a lot of flies flew into my mouth and beat about inside. I nearly howled with rage. Of all the bastards of places this is the greatest bastard in the world.

Turks who overheard Australians talking came to believe that Australians called upon the Great God Bastard as Moslems did upon Allah.

It was not only what the soldiers suffered that brought about changes in their attitudes. It was also what they did. One wrote home:

> up the hill we swarm; the lust to kill is on us, we see red. Into one trench, out of it, and into another. Oh! the bloody gorgeousness of feeling your bayonet go into soft yielding flesh — they run, we after them, no thrust one and parry, in goes the bayonet the handiest way.

An ambulance man summed up his fighting mates:

> I am inclined to think they make it too willing bayonetting and killing when mercy should be shown and prisoners taken. There is no doubt that our men are hard and even cruel.

The worst was still to come in the trenches of France, but the Anzacs got a glimpse of hell between 4.30 and 5.15 am on 7 August 1915 when 234 Light Horsemen fell dead in an area no larger than a tennis court. Yet all through the Gallipoli campaign, the desire to get back to the fighting remained. A journalist wrote:

> I used to think the desire to be in the thick of things was a pose, or make-believe, but I know differently now. They are actually angry when told they must remain in hospital for a few weeks.

That comment was made in a private letter, not for his newspaper.

France changed all this. Every soldier came to want, indeed was anxious for, a wound that would get him a 'blighty', a couple of months in England. The wounded courted bullets rather than slowly rot with thirst and gangrene in no-man's-land. The light-heartedness was also gone. On 18 July 1916, an officer wrote before the battle for Fromelles:

> one or two of the chaps got shell shock and others got really frightened it was piteous to see them. One great big chap got away as soon as he reached the firing line and could not be found. I saw him in the morning in a dug-out, he was white with fear and shaking like a leaf. One of our Lieuts got shell shock and he literally cried like a child, some that I saw carried down out of the firing line were struggling and calling out for their mother, while others were blabbering sentences one could not make out.

During the following night, 5133 Australians were killed. A shop manager from Toorak declared after seven days under bombardment in Pozieres:

> God the whole chaos is too terrible for my pencil. Take it from me none of mine will ever tackle this job again. If men refuse to fight all the world over war will cease.

Eight million soldiers died in battle. Of the 300 000 Australians who left Australia, 60 000 were killed and another 120 000 wounded. Some of the survivors stayed in hospitals for the rest of their lives. Others were bedridden for long periods throughout the next thirty years. Everywhere in Australia were armless, legless or blind men. No one who fought could ever be the same. Some saw that war had given them their only chance to be socially useful and they became strongly pro-war. A tiny handful helped to form the infant Communist Party. About half joined the Returned Services League. What of the other half? Were they the ones whom the poet J. A. R. Mackellar had in mind when he wrote:

> *Our brothers speak few words, who have come back;*
> *They snarl, sometimes, like wounded beasts at bay,*

> But most they sit in darkness, whimpering,
> Or grimly smiling answer: 'Not that way',
> Pointing a shaking finger whence they came.

Sixty years later, Albert Facey voiced similar anti-war sentiments in *A Fortunate Life*.

War had been pictured in the nineteenth century as a game.
Experiences on the battlefield affected how team sports were
played. Parade-ground drill brought more discipline to
sports training, itself a novelty for Rugby League. Plotting
plays on a blackboard was like preparing for a sortie into
no-man's-land. When North Sydney won the premiership in
1921, its officials praised 'systematic organisation, sound
administration and scientific coaching'. Those elements paralleled changes in civilian workplaces where time-and-
motion studies aimed at the maximum effort in the shortest
time. The introduction of time-cards in the New South Wales
railways provoked a major strike. Men refused to be treated
like machines.

LIFE IN CITY AND COUNTRY

Wartime enthusiasm found another outlet in anti-German
propaganda and actions. The federal government encouraged a
journalist, Critchley Parker, to make up atrocity stories. The
public responded by adding 'Beheading the Turk' to horse-
riding competitions and by renaming coconut shies 'Hitting
the Kaiser'. These games were the lighter side of the persecu-
tion of Australian citizens of German descent. Frederick von
Drexel was forced to resign as Mt Gambier's scout master. In
Tasmania, Gustav Weindorfer had his dog poisoned and was
reported by neighbours for owning 'heavy machinery' and
'wireless aerials', which turned out to be a kitchen stove and a
clothes line. Ludwig Kugelmann, general storekeeper in the
Melbourne suburb of Canterbury for more than thirty years,
felt obliged to change his surname to 'Love-Wisdom-Power'.

Elsewhere, the government changed German placenames to honour British generals — Blumberg became Birdwood and Kaiser Stuhl became Mount Kitchener.

Conscientious objectors were another group against whom hysterical patriotism could be turned. In 1916 a Glen Innes man wrote to the *Sydney Morning Herald* suggesting that 'the first shot from each and every soldier's rifle should find its home in a conscientious objector'. White feathers fluttered freely to shame men into joining up. Men who had volunteered but were rejected wore buttons to show their patriotic manliness. One poet pictured the response to 'What did you do in the Great War, Daddy?' in this way:

> And what shall you say, and how shall you lie,
>   Dalliant and dandy and dancer,
> When the lad with the truth on his lip and his eye
>   Searches your soul for an answer?
> Unblushing you face the man middle-aged,
>   Or the woman who's married a hero;
> But when a babe asks you what warfare you waged
>   You'll find yourself sagging to zero.
> By a babe you'll be branded unclean at the core
>   Who helped not to win us the war.

As the conscription plebiscites were fought about in 1916 and again in 1917, and Irish-Australians became angry at the repression of the Easter rebellion in Dublin, a torrent of anti-Catholicism erupted. In Victoria, an advertisement for parlour-maids at Government House said that only Protestants need apply. During the influenza epidemic early in 1919, the government withdrew its acceptance of Archbishop Mannix's offer to staff the emergency hospital in the Exhibition Buildings with nuns. One Protestant parson had claimed that the vision of nuns in black habits would lower the recovery chances of non-Catholic patients.

The unexpected end to the war in November 1918 let the clergy concentrate their 'peace' sermons on the need for gratitude for a speedy deliverance after more than four years of slaughter. Others cheered their congregations with the text, 'Without the shedding of blood, there is no remission of sins' (Hebrews ix, 22). Sunday school children were told to imitate the Russian peasant who, when his hand was branded 'N' by Napoleon's troops, cut it off and gave it to his conquerors, saying, 'There, this belongs to Napoleon. I am a Russian, and there is not a bit of me that does not belong to the Czar. If I have to die, I will die a Russian.' 'Uncle Will', in the Presbyterian *Messenger*, explained that this mutilation was 'loyalty and patriotism of the very best kind'. During the next twenty years, more and more Australians came to doubt the truth of this savagery.

HEALTH
Venereal disease

Public health measures against venereal diseases were stopped by religious feelings almost until the Great War. Then, the prime minister asked the States to make notification of all cases compulsory and gave a pound-for-pound subsidy towards treatment. Detection of syphilis had been made easier with the 'Wasserman test'. Although treatment was improved by a German chemical, Salvarsan (606), a complete cure was difficult, if not impossible. Babies who inherited syphilis were born with old, lined faces and enlarged heads.

Medical inspection of the half-million volunteers for the army showed up the seriousness of venereal infection in Australia. Because venereal disease reduced the fighting strength of the army, it had to be prevented. After a deal of soul-searching, army doctors in Egypt set up washing tents for men returning from leave. The authorities argued that their job was to prevent or cure illness, and not to behave as if God had invented venereal disease in order to force purity on men 'in the prime of life, 12 000 miles from their homes, under conditions of great danger and hardship'. Despite the doctors' efforts, and lectures on the manliness of not having sex, one in ten of the Australian Imperial Force (AIF) reported sick with what was called 'a self-inflicted wound'. Pay was stopped while the men were infected — a fact which would have been noted by wives in Australia.

Facey's memoirs show that even the most virile young men could remain virgins, in thought as well as deed. Similarly, same-sex activities need not have been as widespread in the AIF as novelists have made them appear in the British and German armies. Australia's official war history noted that the records revealed almost 'no evidence pointing to any significant homosexuality in the force'. The physical affection that pervaded the British officer corps found its expression in the AIF around the social bonds of mateship. After the war, the returned diggers distanced themselves from anyone who had not gone through hell with them, other men as well as women.

The war produced many advances in medical practice. The very existence of so many seriously wounded soldiers meant that doctors had to experiment. Risks that could not have been taken in a peacetime hospital became everyday events for field surgeons. Blood transfusions became common, though not regular. Chest surgery was undertaken for the first time, plastic surgery was spurred on, and all forms of surgery improved by new methods of draining wounds. Teamwork and specialisation were two other innovations from the battlefield.

Within Australia, the war produced a shortage of doctors and drugs. About one-third of the doctors joined up, which meant that those who remained were both elderly and in greater demand, a combination which did nothing to improve the standard of care. The difficulties in consulting a doctor drove more and more people to seek the advice of 'quacks' and to rely on patent medicines.

'Aspro'

Even doctors could not get well-known drugs as easily as they had before the war. The disruption of world trade stopped their shipment to Australia. An outbreak of meningitis at the Broadmeadows Army Camp late in 1915 highlighted the shortage of vaccines. The government set up its own Serum Laboratories, which blessed Australians until sold by the Keating ALP government in 1994.

In addition, many medicines were made under German patents. The best example of this was Bayer's aspirin. The ingredients of aspirin were obvious, but the method of blending them to produce a safe pain-killer remained a company secret. Allied governments around the world offered vast rewards for anyone who could supply an alternative. The solution came from Australia.

The story of how this happened was told by Frank Anstey, a Labor member of the Commonwealth Parliament. After speaking to a socialist rally one Sunday evening in Melbourne in 1915, Anstey was asked to visit a chemist in St Kilda Road where he would learn something of national importance. In the shop he met two researchers who claimed to have discovered the secret of Bayer's aspirin. They could not get government support because the officials thought them incapable of solving a problem that had baffled big companies overseas. Anstey used his political influence to have the chemists' claims tested. Within a few months their product was being sold under the brand name of 'Aspro'. At first, other chemist shops would not stock the new product because of their tie-ups with the international drug companies, who disliked any competition. So 'Aspro' had to be sold through newsagents and tobacconists. By the end of the war, the makers of 'Aspro' became the founders of one of Australia's largest companies, Nicholas Pty Ltd.

The biggest medical change brought about by the war was that so many men who would never have gone near a doctor even when ill were treated by leading doctors who were also in the army. Nonetheless, in the words of Sir James Barrett, a teacher of medicine at the University of Melbourne, the important question was what the purpose of this treatment was. His answer: 'To determine whether a man receiving a few pence a day was fit to take his place in the front line'. Barrett went on to point out that the ordinary soldier was not slow to see the strangeness of this situation and to wonder, 'If all this can be done now, why should not some similar arrangement be made in civil life?' Throughout 1919, support for the nationalisation of medicine came from papers as politically different as *Labor Call* and *Punch*. The *Bulletin* wondered whether the best thing would be to hang a doctor every now and then, in order, as it said, to encourage the others.

WHITE AUSTRALIA

When the Great European War broke out in August 1914, 50 000 joined the Australian Imperial Force within five months, and another 160 000 during 1915. After a very strong start in 1916, the number of men volunteering slumped. During the last two years of the war, the total never rose above 5000 a month.

Several forces contributed to this decline. First was the simple fact that most of those able and willing to go had already done so by the end of 1916. Secondly, Irish-Catholics in Australia were angry at the way Britain had put down the uprising in Ireland. If the war was for the freedom of small nations, why was Britain shooting fighters for Irish independence? Thirdly, the working people were suffering. War profits were high and prices had gone up but wages stayed the same. The governments failed to control prices and profits. Fourthly, because Australia had so much farming and grazing, large numbers of men were needed for harvesting and shearing, and for transporting wool and wheat to the cities and to Britain. Farmers who had let one or two sons go to war in 1915 and 1916 could not afford to have more men leave. Fifthly, the mass deaths in the trenches of France made the war less attractive than it had been at the start, when it was seen as a series of quick charges and dashing battles. Men were not as ready to throw their lives away in mad attempts to storm the enemy trenches.

The Labor government could not force men to go overseas because most Labor senators would have blocked the necessary legislation. So the prime minister, W. M. Hughes, talked the Labor Party into asking the people what they thought about compelling men to fight overseas. After the plebescite was defeated, the Labor Party split and Hughes stormed out. He stayed on as prime minister until 1923 by coming to terms with the non-Labor party.

Japan and conscription

Why was Hughes so anxious to have conscription? Some of Hughes' opponents at the time claimed that he had been tricked by the British into throwing away Australian lives. They said Hughes was betraying Australia. Rather, Hughes was defending White Australia. He wanted to send more Australian soldiers to fight in Europe in order to keep the Japanese out of Australia after the war. He made this aim clear in a letter to his Minister for Defence, George Pearce, in April 1916 during a visit to England:

> The position is aggravated — I will not say it is critical — by the fact that Britain has approached Japan with a view to obtaining naval (and, or, military) assistance — say in the Mediterranean — and that the Japanese Government, while ready to grant this, asks for some evidence of Britain's friendliness to her in order possibly to justify her action or placate the opposition. And, as Grey [Foreign Secretary] says — if we say: Well we are very friendly towards you and we want your aid to win this war — but (1) you must not get any concessions in China: (2) your people cannot come to Australia: (3) you are not to be allowed most favoured nation

treatment with Australia (or other parts of the Empire), Japan can hardly be expected to treat our protestations of friendship very seriously.

Grey therefore had asked Hughes to agree to the Japanese having some reward in return for their support. Hughes replied that Australia would give Britain extra support so that it would not have to give in to Japan. His letter to Pearce went on: 'I told Grey that Australia would fight to the last ditch rather than allow Japanese to enter Australia. Upon that point we were adamant.'

When he campaigned in Australia, Hughes had to fight with one hand tied behind his back. He could not come straight out and say that he thought that his Japanese ally was a bigger danger to Australia than Germany. This opinion might so insult the Japanese that they would go over to the other side. Germany was already trying to arrange for this switch and the opposition party in Japan was very pro-German. Although the British alliance with Japan upset Hughes, to have Japan as an enemy terrified him. So he battled to save white Australia by removing Britain's need for Japanese help through the conscription of Australians.

1919: THE MOODS OF VIOLENCE

Although 1919 saw the official end of the Great War, it was not a year of celebration in Australia. The move back to peace was neither easy nor comforting. At home and abroad there were signs that the war had been merely the start of greater disasters. The influenza pandemic had already killed twice as many people as had died in battle. Revolutions sparked back and forth. To many it appeared that the Four Horsemen of the Apocalypse had been let loose, as war, disease, famine and death raged through the world.

Externally, the picture was red with blood and white with terror. Bolshevism not only survived in Russia but Soviet-style governments had been proclaimed in Hungary and Bavaria. Vast strikes broke out in England, Canada and the United States; civil wars occurred in Mexico, Ireland and Italy, and rebellion in India and China. Strife had not ended. New and no less violent forms erupted.

With the world in turmoil, Australia could not remain the quiet continent. The bitterness surrounding the conscription campaign and the strikes of 1916–17 remained keen. Into this situation came 200 000 returning soldiers — armed, used to fighting, and hard to control. Would they follow those soldiers in Russia, France and Germany who had turned their guns on the capitalists? Or would they be ultra-conservative and shoot down the socialists? No one could be certain how the diggers would line up as they cast a shadow over all political groups.

The first sign of the anti-socialist outlook of a majority of the returned servicemen came in Brisbane in March after a red flag had been carried in a parade. That evening, some soldiers marched on the Russian Club. They turned back after a shot was fired over their heads. They decided to come back the next night to finish the job. True to their threat, several thousand ex-soldiers tried to storm the clubhouse, which was protected by police, nineteen of whom were hurt in a three-hour battle. Conservatives were delighted and their paper, the Brisbane *Courier*, rejoiced that 'The first blow had been struck by the returned men for the honour of the flag for which they fought and suffered'. The Labor Party's *Daily Standard* sarcastically noted that 'War, glorious, enobling, uplifting, delightful war is having its influences on peace'.

In May, rioting in Fremantle arose from a longstanding local dispute, but, like the more spontaneous violence in Melbourne in July, it found ex-diggers fighting against the forces of law-and-order. The capitalists' fear of 'Bolshie' soldiers was fulfilled for a moment.

If rioting soldiers in Melbourne were suspected of being under Communist influence, there can be no doubt of the anti-Communist ideas of the small group of officers and gentlemen who assaulted a past Labor member of the federal parliament, J. K. McDougall, at Ararat on 6 December 1919. The five attackers drove up from Melbourne on Saturday morning. Two of them went into McDougall's farmhouse pretending to need help with their car. When McDougall went to assist them, they kidnapped him, then tarred and feathered him. His offence was that twenty years earlier he had written a poem in which he criticised the Australian soldiers in the Boer War:

> Ye are the sordid killers,
>   Who Murder for a fee;
> Ye prop, like rotten pillars,
>   Trade's lust and treachery.

In the 1919 federal election campaign, the anti-Labor

parties misrepresented this verse as an example of the Labor Party's attitude towards the Anzacs. When the five men were brought to trial they were each fined £5. They had the sympathy of the judge who thought that they had been provoked by McDougall's verse.

More sensational and successful than any of these incidents was the Darwin rebellion. In 1919 the local residents arrested and deported the Northern Territory's Administrator, Dr Gilruth. Trouble had been brewing for nearly ten years. In 1914 Gilruth had nationalised the hotels, sacked the union barmen, and raised the price of beer by a penny a glass. A beer strike was called. In reply, Gilruth closed the hotels altogether and stopped the sale of alcohol even to hospitals. Three or four old Territorians who drank a bottle of gin a day took sick and died. The editor of the *Northern Territory Times* accused Gilruth of murdering them.

Gilruth's next error was to introduce daylight saving during the war, which meant that everyone had eight hours solid drinking time after work. Other scandals included the sale of opium, blackmail, and the opening of private mail. Gilruth and his secretary were accused of hoping to receive £20 000 in bribes in return for a land deal on behalf of the British cattle firm of Vesteys. That matter led to Gilruth's arrest and deportation. A Royal Commission found the rebels justified in their action.

Violence was not the only response to the war. Many were sick in body and spirit — broken men like Dominic Langton, the hero of Martin Boyd's novel *When Blackbirds Sing*. For as the *Medical Journal of Australia* wrote in July 1919: 'The world has millions of citizens to-day whose mental outlook has been warped and deteriorated by the terrible experiences of the battle field'. Before 1914, most people had hoped for the best. After 1918, many just hoped that the worst would not ensue.

4

1920–1927
THE TERRIBLE
TWENTIES

The 1920s are often looked on as an interval between those two acts in the drama of life, the Great War and the Great Depression. Certainly, there were barren patches. Nonetheless, important additions were made to Australian society: the Country Party emerged as another voice for rural people; manufacturers gained substantial tariff protection; both town and country benefited from the growth of the Council for Scientific and Industrial Research (later to become the CSIRO). The working class produced new organisations in the Communist Party (1920 and 1922) and the Australian Council of Trade Unions (1927). To this list it is possible to add radio and repatriation, the move of the national parliament from Melbourne to Canberra, a 44-hour week, child endowment in New South Wales, the Balfour Declaration offering greater independence within the British Empire, and the Loan Council. Film-makers flourished against the power of Hollywood. Modernism enlivened painting and poetry. Lists do not prove much, but these items established the 1920s as a period of seeding, if not a rich harvest.

WORK

Secondary schooling continued to expand during the 1920s, although it came under challenge from politicians of all persuasions. The usual form of training for boys was an apprenticeship. Girls paid to learn shorthand and typing. Employers thought post-primary education for everyone was dangerous and wasteful. Politicians, encouraged by employers, tried to limit the access of working-class boys to state high schools by the reintroduction of fees.

An editorial in the *Sydney Morning Herald* in June 1930 spelt out these views:

> Most people are destined to earn their bread in vocations in which no great degree of book-learning is required, and curricula which devote too much attention to purely cultural studies are apt to produce misfits discontented with their lot. In many countries, of late, there has been a reaction against the practice of 'over-educat-ing' the rank and file, that is to say, of equipping them, irrespective of their tendencies and aptitudes, with knowledge which is useless to them in after life and is quickly forgotten.

That attitude was part of a fear that working people every-where were on the march. Civilisation had to defend itself against the revolt of the masses. They were organised, politi-cally and industrially. Right-wing professors advocated eugenics to limit the birth-rate of the lower orders.

Schoolteachers battled the system on behalf of their poorer students. Between 1922 and 1944, the novelist Dymphna Cusack taught at Broken Hill, Goulburn, Newcastle and Parramatta. She favoured sex education, opposed corporal punishments, disapproved of IQ tests, and supported equal pay for women teachers:

> Since most of us went into the teaching profession inspired by high ideals, it took a long time to corrupt us. Neither our univer-sity course nor our Diploma of Education course did so, but the years we spent as victims of an Education Department that was fifty years out of date did their worst with those fine human quali-ties with which most of us started.

She crafted all her classroom teaching around drama, linking the subject matter with the lives of her students.

Despite the upsurge in scientific discoveries, most education in Australia went back to the idea that the 'essential work of the primary school is to teach the children to read, to write, to count, and to speak correctly'. History and geography, as well as science, were sidelined. Even the movement towards manual arts and physical training was halted in the drive back to the three 'Rs'. Lessons were dull and exam-oriented, largely because teachers were ill-trained. Classrooms were often in a poor state. Teaching methods that looked bright and new were often worse than those they replaced. School radio broadcasts, which started in Sydney late in 1924, were given as dead-pan talks without any sound effects or student activities. Children had to sit up, fold their arms and listen.

The closest most women got to a career was as primary school teaching. A few more women had gone out to work during the war but nowhere near as many as in Britain. A handful found jobs in otherwise totally male areas. These were exhibition females to be pointed to as proof that there was no discrimination. Their existence confirmed the rule that males were supreme. Sydney had its first two policewomen in 1915 and Western Australia its first woman architect in 1924. Five out of eight doctors employed by the Victorian Education Department were women, which suggests that they were not accepted as general practitioners. More could have been sent to protect female factory hands.

Job safety

While accidents are always possible, most injuries at work are not a matter of chance but are caused by the failure to keep safety rules. In some cases, deaths are a direct result of working conditions. For example, in order to collect fares on Sydney trams, conductors had to walk along footboards on the outside. Between 1911 and 1932, nearly 4000 conductors were injured in falls, collisions or side-swiping incidents, although the total employment at any one time never exceeded

5000. Because conductors were stuck outside in all weathers, the TB rate among them was twice the average for all male workers. A government report showed that 'the nerves of tramwaymen were in a worse state than those of explosives manufacturers, due to the ever-present danger'.

Very little attention was given to treating work accidents on the job. Evidence to the 1925 Commonwealth Royal Commission on Health showed that across Australia only fifty-two companies made any attempt to provide immediate medical treatment for sick or injured workers. This help was usually no more than a first-aid room. Of all Australian workplaces in 1925 only one employed a full-time doctor, twenty-one had part-time doctors, twenty-two had qualified nurses and six had unqualified ones.

Some idea of the employers' outlook can be gained from this memory of conditions at Broken Hill. A retired miner recalled:

> They used to have horses in the mines in those days. Real beauties
> — little draft horses — champions. One day the winder driver
> made a blue. Instead of stopping at the one thousand level he went
> to the one thousand one hundred level and four fellas were in-
> jured. Did not do anything, just bad luck. Three weeks after the
> fellas' mate on the other shift went through and killed the horse
> and got the sack on the spot. A horse was more valuable than a
> man was!

In the Hunter Valley, the coal baron John Brown kept a stable of 250 racehorses while the miners starved.

Australia was dependent on rural industries in need of workers at different times of the year. Large bodies of men were always on the move from one job to another. Although these workers might be employed almost every week of the year, they would travel long distances to find work. Two such wanderers were Bill Cupland and Jack Pickles who travelled through north Queensland in the early 1920s. Growing tired of sweating for eight hours, six days a week at building a railway line in the tropical sun, they decided to try their luck by walking to the meatworks at Alligator Creek, outside Townsville. After a thirsty tramp, they arrived in time for a hearty tea of meat, potatoes, pumpkin, prunes and rice, with as much bread as they could eat. Their room was plain but clean. Breakfast the next morning was more meat, potatoes, bread and black tea. They started work shortly after nine and found it much easier than railway labouring, though they now worked a ten-hour day. Their wages were thirty shillings plus keep, which gave them a chance to save, as the only distraction was a fruit and soft-drink store at the settlement run by a Chinese. The men put on weekly concerts and paid for a library of newspapers and bushranger yarns. So far as Bill and Jack could tell, everything was fair enough, providing they did not want to join a union. The other skill was to keep out of the way of the works manager during one of his rages when he would invest anyone he bumped into with the order of the sack.

LIFE IN THE CITIES

Many hotels had been places of social, political and business life, until the introduction of early closing during the Great War turned them into five to six o'clock pig swills. Between 1907 and 1914, temperance advocates had forced over 1300 licensed premises in New South Wales and Victoria to close. As many of these outlets were little more than plonk shops, their disappearance was good for the drinking public.

But reform was not enough. Nothing less than a total ban would satisfy those Protestants who told ten-year-old children that their youthful desire for wine jelly could lead to rum and ruin. War, bloody and intemperate, gave the prohibitionists their chance. On 14 February 1916, soldiers from the Liverpool (NSW) training camp rioted in Sydney. Four months later, New South Wales voted for six o'clock closing. By the end of the year, Victoria and South Australia had followed suit.

As a result, 90 per cent of the beer drunk in the 1920s was sold between five and six o'clock. To cater for this rush-hour trade, public bars took over at the expense of parlours with their darts and billiards; in short, civilised, social drinking was destroyed. Vast volumes of that previously disliked mixture, bottled beer, were sold across linoleum counters to speed up service and to cut down on breakages. After the troops came home in 1919, six o'clock closing was still in force. Special permits for after-hours drinking at licensed clubs helped the Returned Services League recruit members.

For sixty years, Melbourne's newspaper buyers had a choice between the conservative *Argus* and the somewhat more progressive *Age*. Other papers, particularly evening ones, came and went but the *Argus* and the *Age* seemed unchallengeable. Then in 1921 Keith Murdoch became editor of the failing evening daily, the *Herald*. Within four years, he had built its sales from 98 000 to 175 000. Two things helped him. First came financial support from the Baillieu family, who had interests in mining, investment and manufacturing. Secondly he played up the 'Gun Alley Murder'.

Twelve-year-old Alma Tirtschke's naked, raped and murdered body was found in Gun Alley, off Little Collins Street near Exhibition Street, late in the afternoon of 30 December 1921. Colin Campbell Ross was hanged for this crime on 24 April 1922. During those four months, Murdoch tried and convicted Ross on the front pages of the *Herald*. A leading lawyer said that 'Public opinion was inflamed as it has not been inflamed within the memory of this generation. Ross was tried for his life in an atmosphere charged and overcharged with suspicion. Whether guilty or innocent, he entered the dock in circumstances under which few men are compelled to enter it'. The *Herald* added its own reward to that of the government for information leading to a conviction. The greatest rewards were gained by Murdoch and his backers. When the *Herald* moved to a larger building in Flinders Street, it was popularly known as the 'Colin Ross Memorial'.

In addition, Murdoch ran a new kind of newspaper, the *Sun-News-Pictorial*, a morning tabloid which grew from 93 000 sales at its launch in 1925 to 166 681 by 1928. With its emphasis on sport and features, the newcomer appealed to working people. Its shorter articles suited the quickening pace of their lives. The idea of the 'News' as up-to-the-minute appeared. The Press put news onto their front pages and added 'Stop Press' items. Printing technologies allowed for more photographs in the daily papers. Commerce exerted greater influence. The editor of the *Age* declared in 1928: 'Often against heavy pressure, independent papers which value a high literary policy and spiritual standard resist the invasion of advertisements onto some of their pages'.

The monthly journal of the newspaper industry surveyed the changes:

> Australian journalism has been considerably influenced in the last decade or so by American conceptions of news and display. Australian readers have been taught to read while they run — to grab their impressions of the news-article from the heading and the lead. The method of presentation is held to be as important as the news itself. The underlying idea is that the eye of the reader shall be led quickly along an easy typographical pathway, so that he may absorb the sense of the news with the least possible mental effort. People are being asked to judge newspapers according to the ease with which they may be read, as well as the quality of the news which they purvey.

The popularity of the cinema was adding to the attractions of the visual, just as radio would speed up the pace of information. In the age of aviation, the automobile was beginning to seem a slowcoach.

Transport

During the 1920s, the number of motor vehicles registered in Australia increased tenfold to more than 650 000 cars, trucks, buses and motorcycles. Because of the size of the vehicles, and because of government policy, it was not profitable to import tens of thousands of ready-made cars each year. It became usual to import American chassis, assemble them here, and then fit them with Australian-made bodies. In 1917, E. W. Holden's South Australian firm erected an assembly-line capable of producing 6000 bodies a year. In the first month, its skilled tradesmen produced two car bodies. Holden recognised that all of Australia did not have enough skilled tradesmen to make his modern plant profitable. The union officials agreed to divide the work of coachbuilders between 'assemblers, oxyacetylene welders, sand blast operators and glazers'. The rest was given to workers trained in only their one task. The workmen complained at this dilution of the trade:

> Under the old order of things a man built the vehicle from start to finish, and naturally he was interested in his job. Today in the standardised part of the industry it is not so. It is all in sections and one man simply does a part. In the motor trade, you are compelled to stand and work in one position all day long and it becomes more wearing than the heavy lifting. It is the most harassing work I have met with.

In 1922, Holden moved to a four-hectare plant at Woodville (SA) where production leapt to nearly 13 000 car bodies a year. He signed a contract with General Motors, under which 36 000 came off the assembly line in 1926. Dunlop started mass producing air-filled tyres in 1923. In 1925, Ford opened its own plant at Geelong. All expansion halted in 1931 when Holden made only 1651 bodies before being taken over by its American partner.

Improvements in design allowed more people to drive. Self-starters did away with the need for cranking, opening the road for the frail. Most motorists, however, were still men. Smoother rides came with shock absorbers and low-pressure balloon tyres. Removable wheels made punctures easier to fix. Prices were also falling. In 1920, a Chevrolet cost £545 but in 1926 a much better model cost only £210. About half the cars bought in the 1920s were on hire purchase, which lent two-thirds of the total price at 6.5 per cent interest.

Although most private cars were owned by the well-to-do, they were not the 'visible symbols of the selfishness of arrogant wealth' that they appeared to be to the British working class. Instead, Australians saw the car more in the way that North Americans did. Here, the motor vehicle brought better roads, faster medical attention, cleaner streets, improved bush schools, and wider chances for pleasure and holidays. The sealing of main streets did away with dust when it was dry and mud when it rained. No longer would horse-dung be mixed in with both. The cost of making roads was very high. By 1928, their construction took more than one-quarter of all public investment. It was a major cause of the overseas debts hobbling the economy.

Suburban spread

After the Great War, the War Service Homes Scheme gave loans only for separate houses on individually owned blocks. That policy speeded up the move to the suburbs. At the same time, the bus and the motor car contributed to the sprawl. Before the war, public transport had been provided by trams and trains. They encouraged housing alongside their tracks, making suburbs spread out from the inner-city areas like spokes on a wheel. In the 1920s, the unoccupied areas between these spokes were filled in because of a new form of public transport, the bus, which could go down most roads since it did not need steel tracks. A similar impact was made by the private car.

The private car altered the shape of suburbs as well as their expanse. Until the 1920s, the frontage of an average household block had been about thirteen metres. Then came two changes. First, Australians borrowed the bungalow-style house from California: flat on the ground, one storey and straightforward in its internal design. This simplicity made it easier to clean. Hence, a middle-class housewife could get by without full-time live-in help. However, the rectangular shape of the bungalow worked most effectively with its long face to the road. This preference meant adding another three metres to the width of a house block.

At the same time, more suburban dwellers were buying cars, which had to be kept in garages around the back of the house. Their off-street parking meant adding a further three metres to the width of the block to allow for a driveway along one side. Garages were kept separate from the house for two reasons. One, after the car replaced the horse, many people took a long time to realise that cars did not have the health dangers that made it necessary to stable horses away from living areas. Two, because there were so few petrol stations, every motorist kept at least one four-gallon (eighteen-litre) drum of petrol at home. Fear of fire and explosions led councils to bring in strict building laws for private garages.

It was not simply the average Australian's desire to expand their blocks of land which made our major cities stretch as far as they did. Government policies, labour shortages, housing styles, private cars and council rules all helped.

Trains

Sydney needed a train service to bring in large numbers of workers and shoppers. Electric trains were not quicker than steam trains at top speed but they had faster acceleration, and this was essential for suburban lines, which had many stops. An above-ground system would have been too expensive because of the great price of inner-city land. So the trains had to go underground. But underground steam trains would have created impossible pollution problems; the smoke and soot would have become unbearable for the passengers. Electric trains came to the rescue.

Sydney's underground lines were built during the 1920s. March 1926 saw the first electric train and in December the line from Central to St James opened. Work for the Harbour Bridge started at the same time. When the bridge was finished, the route extended to Wynyard and across the bridge to Waverton on the North Shore. This connection changed the whole shape of Sydney. The harbour, which made Sydney such a perfect site for a city, cut its natural line of development in half. Until 1932 the city had spread only south, east and west, with a fringe of northern harbour suburbs served by ferries. With the opening of the bridge, Sydney started on its long march north to Gosford. That it did not arrive at Newcastle was due partly to the fact that the electric trainline stopped at Gosford.

Much of Sydney's underground system was built by excavating a strip of land before covering it to form a tunnel. In some places, the workers blasted through sandstone. Most of the underground lines followed existing roads or parkland. Around Wynyard station, the digging went on beneath buildings. Work on the Eastern suburbs extensions restarted in 1947, but a truncated line did not open until 1979.

While Sydney pushed northwards, its business district shuffled south. Shops around Circular Quay that had sold to ferry passengers slowly went broke because the trains' first stop was now a kilometre away at Wynyard.

When the Harbour Bridge opened in 1932, Australia was in the grip of a great economic depression and many people saw the bridge as a waste of money. The *Bulletin* said it was a good symbol of 'the vampire city sucking the life-blood out of the suffering country'. From the other side of the political fence, the communist *Workers Weekly* noted that 'Despite all the technical skill and science which the bridge typifies, the Capitalist system cannot find work and proper food and housing for its wage-slaves. There is the huge bridge, and on the opposite side of the street, the slums created by Capitalism!' In the months after its opening, the bridge became popular with those unemployed who put an end to their suffering by jumping from it to their deaths.

LIFE IN THE COUNTRY

As motor vehicles began to replace horses, the demand for artificial fertilisers increased. Australian control over the phosphate deposits at Nauru became more important. Pastures could be improved with subterranean clovers after a means had been found to separate the burr from seed. 'Sub and Super' were a powerful combination, as C. E. Prell showed when he used them to treble the sheep numbers on his Goulburn property, 'Gundowringa'. Yet those improvements could not get rid of the twin evils of rabbits and prickly pear. Both had spread during the war because so many young men were away from their farms.

Unusual methods of killing rabbits were tried: pastoralists used gases from motor-car exhausts; an Armidale company sold a secret substance to make strychnine tasty to rabbits; quince jam, lightly cooked and heavily sugared, was the decoy they liked best.

Prickly pear had been introduced as food for the cochineal beetle from which the dye for soldiers' red coats was made. Later uses included hedges and stock feed. Wartime experiences led returned farmers to try tanks and flame throwers to get rid of prickly pear. By 1925, the exotic plant covered 24 million hectares in northern New South Wales and southern Queensland.

Queensland's prickly pear was eventually killed off by biological control when several chemical methods failed. After years of experiments all round the world, in 1926 scientists released the eggs of an Argentinian moth, *Cactoblastis cactorum*. Its larvae bore into the plant, which then collapsed since it is 90 per cent water. Unfortunately, the moth does not flourish in the cooler and wetter parts of New South Wales where millions of dollars a year went into spraying the pest.

Like Banjo Paterson, comfortable city dwellers never lost their faith in the value of farm life for other people. Writing about the 1922 Royal Easter Show, the *Sydney Morning Herald* reminded its readers that:

> the soil is permanent; the soil is always there; the soil, if provi-dently treated, is inexhaustible. The soil is the beneficent foster mother which nourishes us all and will never fail us. Empires rise and fall; cities decay; but the soil remains whereby man lives. Ur-ban industries, great towns, mines are all very well. But they are in a sense, superfluous.

Three years later the *Bulletin* editorialised in favour of the anti-communist and patriotic results of scientific farming. Meanwhile, down on the farms, discontent was bubbling up.

With so many country dwellers, especially the youngest and most active, away at the war, it was not surprising that the 1918 inquiry into Victorian country life should have noticed 'a great lack of community loyalty [and] a want of leadership'. Fresh ideas were needed. Some of these innovations came from the professors of agriculture who had been appointed to the universities of Sydney, Melbourne and Western Australia just before the war. Good advice requires a receptive audience. The emergence of the Country Parties showed that commu-nity loyalty and leadership were rebuilt by the return of ex-servicemen.

In 1916, 25 per cent of all the Australian Imperial Force (AIF) had hoped to become landholders. Half of these had some farming experience, but only 13 per cent had any sav-ings. To fulfill this desire for land, Australian governments sponsored soldier settlement schemes. With little or no training, thousands of ex-diggers were expected to produce eggs, fruit or wheat from holdings too small to be profitable, especially once world prices for farm products fell. By June 1927, one-third of the soldier settlers had walked off their land.

The failure of such settlements in the eastern States did not stop Western Australia starting her own scheme for British immigrants. Government advertisements told the success story of P. Rees who had left England with no money and no experience in 1913. By saving, and with the aid of a bank loan, he bought 340 hectares for £7000 in 1920. Four years later, he grew the State's champion wheat crop, worth £4000. Interested migrants who wanted to be like Farmer Rees were advised to contact Australia House, London. The publication that carried the Rees advertisement also had the following much more accurate account of pioneer farming in Western Australia:

> ... at the outset, the man on the land lives in the crudest dwellings. The walls are of rough timber, the crevices being plastered with mud; the roof, sheets of bark or galvanised iron; the floor, *terra firma*; bed, furniture and household utensils just what the settlers' ingenuity can devise out of packing cases, sacking and — that priceless boon to all rural pioneers — the kerosene (or petrol) tin.

This dismal account did not convey the heartbreak felt by the thousands of young wives who had never doubted the government's story until they arrived in outback Australia. Forty years later, one of them recalled her first months in the west:

> Children became ill with dysentery, both my baby daughter & little son were very ill; the foreman advised us to give them hard lumps of red gum to suck from the trunks of the trees. Then 'barcoo rot', as it was called, broke out, & the children became covered in sores through improper & insufficient food. Our shack now became flooded continually, and finally the supervisors found that our shack had been erected over a small running stream: it had to be pulled down and re-erected — the whole of the camp assisting.

By this time the floor boards began to arrive: but my husband became dangerously ill with pleurisy & pneumonia, it was a miracle he pulled through in the awful conditions. No wonder drugs in those days, not even a drop of milk: & only a drunken old doctor who called every few days: my husband was ill for 4 months. Thereafter, through all those terrible months, the Red Cross saved us: they sent enough money by cheque each week, & medicine, to keep us until my husband eventually got back on his feet.

The rural districts were no better off for schools than for hospitals. Bush children had been starved educationally for more than a century. In the 1920s, they gained a little from correspondence teaching. Victoria had introduced this system in 1914 when a mother travelled over three hundred kilometres to Melbourne to seek help to teach her children at home. Twenty years later, Victoria had 2000 correspondence pupils of whom almost half were taking secondary subjects.

One-teacher schools were either very good or very bad. Their bright side was that a teacher could be more open in her methods because she was her own headmistress. In a classroom with fewer than twenty pupils spread over six grades, it was possible for children to learn at their own speed rather than being controlled by the lock-step method of yearly promotion from grade to grade. Some bad features were the high turnover of staff. One South Australian town, Appila, had twenty-seven teachers in thirty-seven years. On the other hand, if a bad teacher stayed for years, students could not be promoted to a more stimulating environment.

Native bears

The settlers' need to eat stopped most nineteenth-century Australians from working in harmony with nature, no matter how much they admired its splendours. In a new and largely rural economy it is not surprising that native flowers, birds and animals should be destroyed. Occasional attempts were made to protect particular places or species. But, as the *Sydney Morning Herald* had noted in its Federation issue: 'It cannot be said that any adequate provision has been made, and thus it is certain that in a decade or two many of our most valuable and interesting forms of animal and bird life will be extinct'. Of all the species of native animal, the least offensive was the native bear. It did not compete with sheep or cattle for feed. It could not injure property or stock. It merely sat munching gum leaves awaiting its doom. By the 1920s only Queensland still had large numbers of koalas, despite a six-month open season in 1919 when over a million were killed. So great was the outcry on that occasion that shooting was not allowed again until 1927.

Country people were split on the issue. Landless workers and small farmers wanted an open season because it gave them a chance to increase their incomes by selling the fur. One of them wrote to the government:

> *Dear Sir,*
> *I have asking of you again to open yous bears or possums all to-gether as I have asked you as to do it does not make any differs to you or any other man. All I opjet to is to protect a animail for its hide and I do not uphold you or any other man that is off you shanto opened it.*
> > *Yours*
> > *Trapper*

Pastoralists and well-to-do farmers opposed open seasons because of the damage done to fences and stock by 'Trappers' with the outlook quoted above. For the wealthy, an open season meant a financial loss. Others were horrified at the methods used to kill the animals:

> If by cyanide, a jam tin of water with this in solution, is placed at the foot of a tree or a near-by hollow log, and the morning shows the agony passed through before death gave the animal release. If shooting, the acetylene search light brought to view the 'possum crouched peering with light lit, frightened eyes from some

outstretched branch, or forked limb, a crash! an horrible thud, and there lies one more to be skinned and its white body slung to the dogs or ants. If snared, trappers place slanting saplings against the likely trees, and arrange on each the deadly wire noose through which the opossum will thrust his head coming down. In the early morning, before dingoes and crows have disturbed the carcases the trapper does his rounds to collect the strangled 'possums and bears. All 'joeys' are torn from the pouches, the young ones being thrown to the dogs, and the more developed ones sometimes, and if alive, are liberated for future gain.

During the open season of 1927, another half-million koalas were killed. There has not been an open season since. After 1927 the fur frontier moved further west, away from farmers whose property the trappers endangered, and onto land where graziers welcomed those hunters as allies against the wallaby and kangaroo.

HEALTH

The discovery of vitamins A, B, C and D between 1915 and 1919 brought almost no changes to Australian eating habits, not even in hospitals. A Sydney nurse recalled that though vitamins were being discussed 'we were taught that they were accessory food factors, but it was a long time before they were consciously incorporated in our diets. Some of the nurses, about 1933, were asking if salads and fresh fruit could be served in the dining room.' Melbourne Hospital appointed its first dietitian in 1928; even there, the quality of the food served to staff and patients depended on hospital finances. Some idea of how little attention was paid to vitamins and how much importance was given to calorie-producing starches is clear from this 1922 menu from Ballarat Grammar:

Breakfast: porridge, toast, bread and hunser (a mixture of honey, golden syrup and left-over jams);
Lunch: choice of two meat dishes, vegetables, steamed pudding or sago, water to drink;
Tea: soup (only every second day in summer), bread, jam and hunser and tea.

The soup and vegetables would have had all the vitamins boiled out of them. The lack of fruit, eggs and dairy products is obvious. The Ballarat Grammar kitchen was no better or worse than thousands of other big kitchens across Australia.

Family meals were usually not very different. In very large families they could be a great deal worse. In evidence before the 1925 Royal Commission into Health, Dr Richard Arthur, MLA, claimed 'that the staple food [in large families] consists of white bread with either dripping, jam or treacle, and tea. There is a certain amount of meat scraps and potatoes, perhaps rice occasionally, but the staple diet the children get, two or three times a day, is such as I have described. Milk is almost an unknown quantity'.

One notable exception was the introduction of raw liver sandwiches (soon replaced by injections) for pernicious anaemia.

Despite advances in surgery during the war, there were hardly any changes in treatments for the most common diseases. Several other discoveries were made but did not gain widespread use in Australia. Consequently, many people continued to trust patent medicines, quacks, herbalists, or their own abilities. Writing in the *Medical Journal* of 3 April 1926, a doctor reported that, 'Even at this present day there are some men in outlying sheep runs who take sheep droppings as pills'. In Adelaide, some four years earlier, a man had cut off his right testicle two weeks after an accident to it; he had sewed up the wound with black cotton but was forced to seek medical advice shortly afterwards. The official report of the case recorded: 'The patient was of normal mentality, had a knowledge of first aid, and had castrated animals'. Because medical treatments were often useless, the general belief was that you either got well or died. A twelve-year-old boy who died of pneumonia in 1920 had had the complaint each winter from birth; he had never seen a doctor because his family thought he had caught it from his mother who had had it while she was breast-feeding him. Their view that he would either die or grow out of it proved correct.

Public health

Queensland was the scene for two health scares. Early in the decade, the link between lead paint and blindness in children was shown. Nonetheless, paint manufacturers prevented a complete ban on lead-based paints. The cause of blindness had been a puzzle for a long time because of the strange pattern of illness. Only children in Queensland cities were affected and then generally only one member of the family. The explanation was straightforward enough once the pieces were put together: poisoning was more likely in Queensland because the sun there was hot enough to crack the paint on veranda railings; poisoning was confined largely to the cities where the houses were on high stumps, which required railings all around for safety; poisoning affected only those children who bit their fingernails or sucked their thumbs after picking at the dried paint peelings on sun-baked verandas. Like so many medical discoveries, this piece of detective work had no immediate results because the researchers lacked the laws to back it up. Blindness from lead paint poisoning remained to blight lives until well into the 1950s.

Diphtheria was at the centre of Queensland's other public health tragedy. Twenty-one children in Bundaberg were injected with impure toxin-antitoxin in January 1928. Twelve of them died. This mistake stopped some parents from having their children injected, even though a safe method quickly came into use.

Veneral diseases continued to be both a major problem and *The Forbidden Subject*. Treatment methods did not alter until the arrival of the wonder drugs in the late 1930s. At the 1925 Royal Commission, experts claimed that 'At some hospitals the treatment is no better than patients used to get, and still get, from chemists and unqualified persons, and at some hospitals they have to turn patients away'. Some attempts were made to bring the topic out into the open. In 1930 a local doctor wrote a three-act play, *Just One Slip*, dealing with venereal disease. A film, *Damaged Lives*, also screened around Australia. This drama had several performances in Sydney where it was followed by speeches and preceded by a girls' choir singing songs from Gilbert and Sullivan operettas.

After the 1900 outbreak of bubonic plague, the government had set up a 'rat intelligence service' in Sydney. By 1922, some 330 000 rats had been caught and examined. Another plague scare in 1921 brought in 40 000 rats in less than six months. A year earlier, the *Sydney Morning Herald* advised the new Minister of Health and Motherhood that:

> ... if he wishes to find an all-pervading evil waiting to be eradicated, let him tackle the rats which have grown in numbers to a most alarming extent of late. Perhaps the overcrowding of the houses by human residents is pushing out the rats which cannot now find house-room in their former haunts, or perhaps a strike is on among the rodents, who have stopped work, and can find time to stroll about the city streets.

Household water supplies continued to be a danger. The doctor employed by Sydney's Water and Sewerage Board explained:

> The water supply is delivered to consumers in an unfiltered condition. The only treatment it receives is sedimentation in the storage basins and the screening of a rough character on its way from the last storage reservoir to the consumers. This screening takes out a large amount of the vegetable matter which is floating in the water.

Sterilisation of water supplies was a long time coming to Australia. Swan Hill (Victoria) took the lead in 1926.

Birth-rates

Male concern at the falling birth-rate made politicians willing to pay for health services for mothers and babies. Education of mothers remained a central issue. In the 1920s, a specially fitted-out rail carriage took the message of breast-feeding to Queensland's outback. Like so many other worthwhile activities, this program did not operate from 1930 to 1934 when it would have done more good than ever. By the mid-1920s, 80 per cent of births were attended by a doctor, and about half took place in hospitals. Nonetheless, the death-rate among mothers and babies declined hardly at all. The 1925 Royal Commissioners on Health concluded:

> All the witnesses we have examined concerning this subject agree that up to the present the conditions of maternity hygiene have not been satisfactory. It is admitted that the results of obstetric practice have not improved proportionately to the scientific advances that have been made in general medicine and surgery.

To improve survival rates, District Nurses were 'sent to deliver babies at home. In some slum houses the patient lay on bags on a dirty floor. Some would be irritable, having been dosed with spirits to ease the pain'. Australia had the second-lowest infant death-rate in the world, largely because of the popularity of breast-feeding. Mortality during the first month of life had stayed the same at thirty per thousand. Most of these deaths were preventable. From one to twenty-four months of age, deaths were due mainly to poor food. The real danger period was between two and five years when a child was likely to get diphtheria, TB, whooping cough and measles. This age group was almost entirely overlooked. Once at school, children received three medical examinations before their teens. During that time their major health difficulties were the result of poor diet, untreated sight and hearing weaknesses, or rotten teeth.

Nurses

Working conditions for nurses were changing, but slowly. In Victoria, they still worked up to twelve hours a day for less than ten shillings a week; trainees paid their own fees. Just after the Great War, Elsie Allenden started her training at the old St Margaret's Hospital for Women in the inner-Sydney suburb of Paddington. With eleven other nervous beginners she was 'shown around the wards, and our sleeping quarters':

> Six iron beds stood on either side of a long dormitory. Sheets served as quilts. Between each bed was a chair and a locker, and at the end, a community wardrobe. The floor was bare, and the boards rough.
>
> Next morning, we assembled in our new uniforms — long dresses almost to the ankles, a stiff, starched apron, a hard, stand-up collar, long sleeves and hard cuffs, a cap covering every bit of hair, black stockings, and rubber-soled nurses' shoes. Studs fastened collar, cuffs, and belt. We were hungry, too. The food at the hospital was not plentiful, and many a dish of gruel on its way to a mother was attacked and partly demolished before arriving.

Standards were low throughout the hospital. The operating theatre was on the second floor. Patients were carried up a narrow spiral staircase on stretchers, 'a tall nurse at the feet, a short one at the head'.

Further medical advances needed nursing to be recognised officially as a profession. By 1927 all States had Nurses Registration Boards. Nurses organised themselves into the nationwide Royal Australian Nursing Federation. Although these organisations improved the standard of nursing, they did little to alter nurses' working conditions. Pay remained low, the hours long, and the tasks uninteresting.

ABORIGINES

Aborigines were working out new ways to resist occupation. In Western Australia, they formed a union to put an end to 'being robbed, and shot down, or run into miserable compounds'. Their spokesman was William Harris, a farmer from the Morawa district, who had been writing letters of protest to the newspapers since 1906. Early in 1928, Harris led a group to the premier to demand full legal equality. From these beginnings came the idea that Aborigines had to run their own organisations. Most welfare associations were controlled by whites who thought that the Aborigines were not able to help themselves. From the early 1920s, the Maynards on the New South Wales north coast led the Australian Aboriginal Progressive Association. At its 1925 convention, speakers used 'language' to urge their people to reclaim their land. One family used spears and shields to drive off the police who had come to steal their children. Armed resistance was not over. Indeed, the shooting parties that followed the spearing of two whites late in the 1920s put Aboriginal affairs onto the front pages of newspapers around the world.

When the Western Australian government got reports of killings of Aborigines in the north-west of the state, they appointed a Royal Commissioner, T. G. Wood, to look into the matter. Wood's inquiry lasted two months and he visited the sites of the killings. His report accused the police of killing at least twenty Aborigines, but he accepted that there was no evidence on which to lay formal charges. Wood was highly critical of the failure of the Wyndham police and public to provide him with help. The thoroughness of Wood's inquiry was in complete contrast to the Board of Inquiry into the Coniston massacre in the following year.

On 7 August 1928, a white man named Brooks was killed near Coniston in the Northern Territory. Five days later, Police Constable Murray arrived and set out with a party of eight. After travelling fourteen miles, they came upon twenty-three Aborigines of whom they shot five, including two women, in self-defence. Three days later, they surrounded another camp and killed another eight. During the next week, three more blacks were shot while attempting to escape. Another then died from wounds received during the first shootings. Constable Murray returned to Alice Springs and reported killing seventeen Aborigines. Two days later, he set out again to investigate a reported cattle-spearing and attacks on a settler. After returning to Alice Springs with two prisoners, he went off once more. During the next three weeks, he shot fourteen Aborigines at three different places. In less than two months, Murray had been responsible for the deaths of at least thirty-one Aborigines. At no time did he deny this. He argued that the killings were necessary.

While Constable Murray was away on his second expedition, his case had started to come unstuck. The two Aborigines charged with Brooks' murder were let off because of lack of evidence and because the magistrate had bungled their first trial. This outcome was serious for the police. If the two captured men were innocent, then so presumably were the thirty-one whom Murray had shot.

The federal government reluctantly agreed to a Board of Inquiry but selected its members carefully: the chairman was the police magistrate at Cairns, while the other members were the police inspector at Oodnadatta and the Government Resident at Alice Springs. The secretary to the Inquiry could not take shorthand. The hearings lasted three weeks and included inquests into the deaths of eighteen of the dead. A final report went off within two days of the hearings. The trio of officials concluded that the shooting of the thirty-one Aborigines had been necessary.

This cover-up did more good for Aborigines than almost any other investigation. So upset did southern whites become at the Coniston killings that police were never again keen to go on shooting parties. Its impact would have been greater had the economic depression not swept every other issue from the political stage.

The concern of city-based groups sympathetic to the Aboriginal cause could not overturn the attitudes of white Australians. In 1928, Katharine Susannah Prichard's novel *Coonardoo* won the *Bulletin* competition and was serialised. Sales of the weekly magazine increased, exceeding a million for the month of October. Some people must have bought copies in order to be outraged. The outcry against this story of a white man's love for a young Aboriginal woman was so great that the *Bulletin*'s editor wrote to another writer, Vance Palmer, to tell him that his novel had been rejected:

> On re-consideration, we have decided that we can't print *Men are Human* — at any rate in its present form. I am sorry, because it is so well done, but our disastrous experience with *Coonardoo* shows us that the Australian public will not stand stories based on a white man's relations with an Australian aborigine.
>
> We would have notified you earlier, but it has taken us some months to ascertain the full extent of the feeling.
>
> There is no chance, I suppose, of your white-washing the girl?

A story about the love of a white woman for a black man was unthinkable.

WHITE AUSTRALIA

Prime Minister William Morris Hughes had split his own Labor government in 1916 by trying to introduce conscription for military service in Europe in order to protect white Australia. He was not about to give restrictive immigration away at the Peace Settlement. He blocked several moves by his Japanese ally to have a racial equality clause adopted by the League of Nations. On 13 February 1919, the Japanese delegate moved a detailed motion calling on all members of the League to 'accord as soon as possible, to all alien nationals, equal and just treatment in every respect, making no distinction, either in law or in fact, on account of their race or nationality'. This motion was talked out before the Japanese withdrew it. Then, on 11 April, they moved a more general motion calling for the 'endorsement of the principle of the equality of nations and the just treatment of their nationals'. This proposal was carried by eleven votes to five. The US President, Woodrow Wilson, however, declared it lost because everyone had not agreed to it.

Hughes considered the defeat of the Japanese proposal 'the greatest thing which we have achieved'. In a long book about the Peace Settlement, the British Prime Minister, Lloyd George, gave only a very brief paragraph to the dispute. In the margin of Hughes's personal copy, he wrote beside that paragraph: 'To him, a molehill — to us, Everest'.

To have won on paper was one thing. To populate the north was another. The most constantly argued aspect of White Australia became whether Europeans could live in the tropics. Once it was agreed that Anglo-Saxons could live in tropical Australia, the argument turned to asking whether they could 'settle, thrive, increase and multiply, maintaining [their] physical and mental qualities unimpaired'. This formulation, in turn, meant asking whether white women could breed in the tropics.

Death-rates were talked about until there were good reasons for believing that 'the people born and reared in Queensland are less vigorous than those born elsewhere and who come to Queensland as settlers'. This opinion gave rise to a demand for better living conditions. Clothing, diet, housing and sanitation had to be changed for the tropical climate. In addition, tight control over the type of new settlers was suggested. 'Domestic servants' were not to be encouraged because their 'descendants became shiftless "poor whites" '. Those people who were against white settlement argued that skin colour darkened the closer a race lived to the equator. Hence, the fall in strength and birth-rate of whites in the tropics was caused by the sun's rays. This supposition led them to support the introduction of southern Europeans whose skins were already darker than those of Anglo-Saxons. Men were encouraged to wear black underpants to prevent sterility.

Even more complicated solutions came up in discussion. Some doctors suggested that a 'scientific colour line' be drawn across Australia. Non-Europeans would be allowed to the north of it to work for white Australians. A supporter of this idea called for 'a well-drilled and disciplined native army, officered by Australians, with a few regiments of Australians' to patrol the border and to keep the peace within the northern areas. In 1924, the former Director-General of Medical Services, Major-General Sir Neville Howse, MHR, said that the Northern Territory could be developed 'by allowing sterilised black labour in for a certain period'.

Although much of this debate was carried on by scientists, they got most of their information from doctors, who were as confused as everyone else. For example, the results of different races breeding were hotly contested. One doctor alleged that because Europeans think that sex is evil and Asians think of it as heaven, a breakdown of White Australia would lead to legalised prostitution. Others discussed the relative vitality of black pigs and white pigs before drawing comparisons with people. Finally, the 1920 Medical Congress agreed that European settlement in the tropics could expand only if lavatories were improved.

The political world was equally in turmoil. The Australian labour movement had first come in contact with ideas about the international working class sticking together in 1903, when the English trade union leader Tom Mann started his work in Victoria. At the 1905 Labor Party Conference, the only opponent of the 'racial purity' objective was Harry Scott Bennett who was Mann's left-hand man. Discontent during the Great War helped to puncture some of the Imperial patriotism among the working class. The Bolshevik revolution in Russia in 1917 brought the policy of racial prejudice to the fore. A headline in a 1920 issue of the *One Big Union Herald* showed the changing attitude:

WAKE-UP WHITE AUSTRALIANS; TURN RED AND FOLLOW THE EXAMPLE OF YOUR DESPISED YELLOW BROTHERS.

The idea that the workers of the world should unite gained another boost in the 1920s when sections of the Australian trade union movement joined the Pan-Pacific Trade Union Congress. The August 1928 issue of the Sydney-based *Pan-Pacific Worker* asked Australian workers whether they were being robbed by white capitalists or by Asians. The answer was that Australian workers should join with Asian workers to fight against capitalists everywhere.

VIEW OF THE WORLD

When Prime Minister Hughes left Australia for Britain in April 1918, he thought he was going to plan how many more million men the British Empire could afford to have killed. He had no idea that he would arrive in Europe in time for the Peace Settlement. In November, Hughes opposed the Armistice proposals for three reasons: Australia had not been asked about them; Germany may not have to pay for the war; and the Australian takeover of German New Guinea was not stipulated. Australia suffered the status of a minor ally. Actually, Australia had the advantage of two voices because she could also influence Britain. Hughes later argued that Australia had become a nation at the Peace Conference because she had been given separate representation. This claim was wishful thinking, because the United States continued to see Australia as just another part of the British Empire. As shown already, Hughes scored his biggest successes in keeping the White Australia policy and in taking over German New Guinea.

New Guinea

Australian troops had taken over German New Guinea by mid-September 1914. They then left the German settlers to get on with business as usual. The big exception was that the Australian firm of island traders Burns Philp moved across the border from Papua. This intervention proved decisive in the future of the German Territory after the war.

Two Scottish migrants, James Burns and Robert Philp, had rejigged their partnership into the Burns Philp Company Limited in Sydney during 1883. Their ambition was to develop shipping, mining and other interests in the Pacific islands, especially New Guinea. Their ships collected indentured labourers for the canefields. Both men became active politicians. Philp was Premier of Queensland between 1899 and 1903. By the end of the 1890s, they were the largest landholders in British New Guinea. Their economic and political power continued to grow. Late in 1917, the Lieutenant-Governor, Hubert Murray, complained: 'That firm has a weird sort of pull somewhere, but I cannot quite locate it'. Within two years it was plain for all to see that its influence was in the Prime Minister's Department.

At the Peace Settlement, Burns Philp was not important in Australia's determination to gain German New Guinea as an Australian territory. As the Prime Minister, William Morris Hughes, put it on 28 January 1919: 'No nation would be threatened by Australia's possession of those islands, but the acquisition of them by another nation would constitute a menace to Australia'. In an effort to win support from the three main victorious powers, Hughes told the Peace Conference that 'As Ireland is to the United Kingdom, as Mexico is to the United States of America, as Alsace-Lorraine is to France, so was New Guinea to Australia'. Unfortunately for Hughes, the American President, Woodrow Wilson, was against outright takeovers because they would block US firms from trading there.

The battle between Hughes and Wilson went on for months. The solution was to place German New Guinea under a special 'C' class mandate from the League of Nations. The category put Australia 'under no obligation to grant equal rights in the mandated territory to the trade and commerce of other states'. This proviso kept the Japanese north of the equator.

Although the 'C' class mandate was not an outright take-over, it was an annexation for all practical purposes. President Wilson opposed it till the very last. Hughes's resolve to control German New Guinea did not get in the way of his sense of humour. When Wilson made one last attempt to have his own way by demanding to know Australia's final offer, Hughes played with his hearing aid — a large box — and said he had not heard the question. Wilson, never put off by other people's amateur dramatics, came back:

> 'Mr Hughes, am I to understand that if the whole civilised world asks Australia to agree to a mandate in respect of these islands, Australia is prepared to defy the appeal of the whole civilised world?'
>
> 'That's about the size of it, Mr President.'
>
> Defeated, Wilson grasped at straws and asked if American missionaries would be stopped from entering New Guinea. 'Certainly not, Mr President', Hughes replied. 'I understand that those poor people often go for months at a time without enough to eat.'

Having gained German New Guinea for Australia, Hughes had to decide what to do with it. As early as 8 February 1919, an editorial in an important Melbourne weekly, the *Australasian*, felt 'no reason to doubt that Australians, being of British stock, will in due time develop the genius for ruling others which the race has constantly displayed'. Pride was no substitute for detailed policies. As was ever the case when governments had no idea what to do, Hughes set up a Royal Commission. Its three members were Hubert Murray (the Lt-Governor of Papua), Atlee Hunt (Secretary to the Prime

Minister's Department) and W. H. Lucas (islands manager of Burns Philp). Murray suspected 'that the scheme was planned out long ago, and that I was put on the Royal Commission to German New Guinea merely as a blind — the other two being safe men for the capitalists in general and Burns Philp in particular'. Hunt and Lucas wanted a completely separate administration so as to avoid the pro-native policies of Murray. Murray wanted both Papua and New Guinea under his control. Hunt and Lucas wanted the German firms sold to private Australian companies. Murray wanted the government to take over the biggest ones. Murray failed. Burns Philp got what it wanted. An Expropriations Board sold the German companies. Its chairman was W. H. Lucas who had just resigned from Burns Philp.

Yanks and the Reds

The United States way of life and its international trading policies upset most Australians. Hollywood films were proof of the corruption and violence that Austral-Britons found unpleasant. The *Bulletin* editorialised against motion pictures in which 'the spread-eagleism of Jefferson Brick mingles with the manners and argot of the Bowery, the sensationalism of the Hearst newspaper and the morals of the Barbary Coast'. Western Australia's Premier Collier was so alarmed by the influence that American 'talkies' were having in Sydney that he wanted to ban them. Hollywood studios controlled cinemas throughout Australia, making it hard for local film-makers to exhibit their products.

If all social classes were offended by the vulgarities of the Jazz Age, the workers were horrified at the time-and-motion study methods of the assembly-line, and at the anti-working-class violence of US businesses and governments. Tens of thousands protested in 1927 against the execution of the Chicago anarchists Sacco and Vanzetti. Most local capitalists were either frightened by American business methods or so tied to British markets and companies that they opposed American investment. In 1926 the very conservative Prime Minister S. M. Bruce made a bitter attack on American oil companies, which are trying once more to get their grip upon this country'. He continued:

> The impudence of their demands is an indication that they are endeavouring to take over the government of this country. I refer to the Vacuum Oil Company, which is the child of the Standard Oil Company — one of the great monopolistic institutions that control the oil market — and the British Imperial Oil Company, which is controlled by the Royal Dutch Group.

Anti-Americanism was economically necessary, morally uplifting and highly respectable.

Throughout the 1920s, Australians argued over who were our friends and who were our enemies. For the conservatives, our friends were Britain and the Empire: our enemies were all those who sought to weaken the Empire, whether they were the United States, Japan, Germany, France, the Russian Bolsheviks, or Indian and Irish nationalists. When Germany was admitted to the League of Nations in 1926, the *Bulletin* identified four dangers: the Sovietised Russian, the Bolshevised Chinaman, the Prussian, 'And Uncle SAMUEL, in his persistent search for his pound of flesh'. Radical workers saw Australia's enemies as Imperialism — British, Japanese and American; many accepted that Ireland should be free, that Russia should be left alone to get on with its 'great experiment', and that Germany should be treated less harshly. Between these two extremes were many and varied attitudes. What is remarkable about Australians' outlook on the world at this time is its lack of agreement. For the first time, Australians were seriously divided on this vital issue.

Australian conservatives had two reasons for hating the Russian revolutionaries. First, they were a threat to their wealth and power. Secondly, they had signed a separate peace agreement with Germany in March 1918 which had almost let the Germans win the war. The press made no attempt to get at the truth about Soviet Russia. The Bolsheviks were always wrong. Tales of horror were reprinted, no matter how self-contradictory. So silly did the reports become that a Brisbane paper printed this spoof:

> Envious of the startling newspaper 'copy' the morning dailies were getting from Russia about the Bolsheviks, *Truth* cabled for despatches to Mr Hustleovitch Tellieski, the well-known Russian journalist, who, unable to see eye to eye with the bad Bolsheviks, is seeing them from afar, so to speak, and while himself residing at Stockholm has a direct sleigh service between that city and Moscow. His couriers, who travel disguised as blocks of ice, have brought him the following items, which may appear to be a little contradictory, but are, nevertheless, authentic:
>
> Monday — Grand Duke Gotofftheroofsky has been foully murdered by a Social Revolutionary.
>
> Tuesday — A Social Revolutionary has been killed by the Grand Duke Gotofftheroofsky.
>
> Wednesday — All the Social Revolutionaries and all the Grand Dukes, including the famous Gotofftheroofsky, have been slaughtered by the Bolsheviks, who cut their bodies into small pieces for use as horse-feed during the winter months.
>
> Thursday — The Bolsheviks have outraged 3 000 000 Lettish women.
>
> Friday — It now transpires that Archbishop Rasputoffski got all the women out of the Lettish province before the Bolsheviks entered, knowing that they would outrage them.
>
> Saturday — The ex-Czar is officially stated to be dead.
>
> Sunday — The ex-Czar is not dead, but has been elected shop delegate for the Deposed Despots' Union, now engaged in making false teeth for the Bolshevist members.
>
> No further news has been received.

"LOST MY JOB!"

5 1928–1933 THE GREAT DEPRESSION

The whole of the inter-war period could be seen as a depression in Australia. Real wages did not return to their pre-1915 level until the end of the 1930s. Unemployment was never lower than 7 per cent and more often was around 10 per cent. The difference in the period 1928–1933 was that more people were unemployed and for longer periods.

Although economic collapse affected all the capitalist countries, particular reasons made matters worse in Australia. In the 1920s, Australian governments borrowed heavily on the London loan market, which had dried up by 1929. This constraint meant Australia had to pay the interest on earlier loans but could not borrow much new money. When Nightmarch beat Phar Lap for the 1929 Melbourne Cup, people said that, like Australia, Phar Lap was carrying too much weight.

The result was that all the money for government services had to come from within Australia or from export earnings. Governments cut their spending and increased customs duties in order to pay back the London bond-holders. These policies reduced the spending power of the community, thus causing more unemployment. Wages were cut by 10 to 20 per cent. Unemployment approached 40 per cent of the workforce in 1932.

WORK

By the 1933 census, unemployment in the wage-earning class was down to 23 per cent. In New South Wales it was still nearly 27 per cent, but in Western Australia it was not much more than 18 per cent. Equally important was the length of time that people had been out of a job. Almost all the jobless had been without paid work for more than three months. Two-thirds had not worked in the past year; one-third had been without a job for more than three years. The figures for women workers were not as high, partly because their lower wages gained them preference over men. In addition, they withdrew from the workforce and turned to their families for support.

At the time, the basic wage for a family of four was over £3 a week. Victorian government aid was 7 shillings for a single man, 14 shillings for a married couple, and 7 shillings extra for each child. Relief work paid 35 shillings a week for a married man, but work was rarely available for a full week. The census taken on 30 June 1933 documented breadwinners' incomes for the preceding year. Twelve per cent had earned nothing at all; a quarter brought in less than £1 a week; another 17 per cent made under £2. Added together, a total of 54 per cent of the families got by on incomes of less than two-thirds of the basic wage. Savings bank deposits dropped from £226 million in the middle of 1929 to £193 million two years later. Total deposits did not return to their 1929 level until 1936. When the New South Wales State Savings Bank closed in April 1931, thousands of small depositors needed money urgently to survive. Many sold their bankbooks to shopkeepers and speculators for much less than their face value; their balances were paid in full to the buyers when the bank was taken over by the government-owned Commonwealth Bank at the end of the year.

To maintain themselves and their families, unemployed men tramped from town to town, slaved for next to nothing, struck for union rates, rioted, accepted insults — any and every response in order to exist. Because men needed to walk miles around a city following up rumours of work, and because money could not be wasted on fares even when a few days work was found, a man's boots became very important. If he were sleeping in a hostel or by the road he would tie them around his neck to prevent their being stolen. Men cycled after trucks to offer assistance with unloading. They fainted from hunger standing in queues at employment offices. An advertisement in the Adelaide *Advertiser* for four strong men to clear land brought men from hundreds of miles around only to find it was a cruel joke. One man recalled chopping wood for two hours to earn enough for a tin of powdered milk for his children. Bosses began by spreading work around their workers on the basis of three days each a week, but businesses often closed nonetheless. With the end of the motor-car industry, E. W. Holden turned his bodybuilding works into the biggest maker of fruit cases in the country, along with a multitude of items from filing cabinets to golf clubs.

One of the hardest hit groups were youths who had been trained for office jobs. A father reported that he had offered the services of his partly qualified seventeen-year-old son for six months on no wages to seven firms of accountants. No one would accept him. Even very young children had their share of suffering. Early in 1931, seven- and eight-year-olds in 'fancy dress' were begging in Melbourne's streets. A few died of starvation. Many others, to quote a Launceston report, were 'half-starved, half-naked'.

Books about the depression emphasise how bad things were for the unemployed and for the evicted — as indeed they were. But this misery is only a part of the story. Some other groups were better off. Despite talk about 'equality of sacrifice', the impact of the depression fell unevenly. British investors, often large banks, were paid the full rate of interest on the money that they had lent to Australian governments. To do this, wages and pensions, as well as interest rates for Australian investors, were cut by as much as 22.5 per cent. Inside Australia, these cuts did not hurt everyone equally. The Western Australian Attorney-General pointed out that 'if we cut the salary of a man earning £2000 per year he still has a pretty decent income. A cut of 20 per cent on a man on the basic wage is a different thing'. A few weeks later a Stawell woman wrote to the papers:

> When my husband died, I was strongly advised to put my money into Commonwealth bonds. Last July when the government called for help I put in all I had. Now I am wondering what is going to happen. Is a widow to be treated as a company that has thousands of pounds in bonds? It seems hardly fair.

The rich continued to employ servants, have lavish weddings and go on overseas holidays, as illustrated in the pages of *The Home*.

One of the strangest novels of the depression was Reginald Gellibrand Jennings's *Threads of Yesterday*, which told of Captain Oakley Flames and his manservant Jorrocks. Ruined by the depression, Flames resigned from his Melbourne club but dressed for dinner each evening and drank a glass of port to 'the old days'. To everyone's relief Flames is finally rescued from this poverty and from the snares of the rich and snooty Cynthia Selwyn.

One result of the depression was the closure of small businesses. Profits of large firms either rose, or fell only slightly. For example, the giant Colonial Sugar Refining Company reported in May 1931 that it 'has not been affected by the financial trouble in Australia'; Melbourne's Metropolitan Gas Company increased its profits for 1930–31 by one-third over those of the previous year. The retail chain store of G. J. Coles had a fall in profits of about 6 per cent, which was about half the rate of the fall in wages.

The depression meant more than unemployment, evictions and lower wages. There were also full interest payments to

British bond-holders, and good profits in Australia, both of which were paid for out of the sacrifices of workers, farmers, pensioners, small business people and small investors.

LIFE IN THE CITIES

Keeping a roof over your head was almost as important as finding work. Unemployed families lost homes that they were paying off. More were dumped onto the street when they could not pay their rent. Half of the buyers of War Service Homes were behind in their repayments in June 1932 to the tune of £432 350. They had a friendly landlord in the government. For the 60 per cent of working-class families who did not own their own homes, the threat of being turned out was as real as it was terrifying. Battles, often organised by the Communist Party, were waged to stop evictions. Two of the biggest struggles in New South Wales were at Bankstown and Newtown in the middle of 1931 when the police shot and wounded several defenders. Fires in a few of the houses from which families had been evicted soon convinced landlords that it was more profitable to have non-paying tenants.

Once a family was evicted, it faced the awful decision whether to split up, to sleep out, or to build a shack. The 1933 census showed that 33 000 people were on the road in the middle of winter. A further 400 000 were sheltering under iron, calico, canvas, hessian, bark and other makeshift materials. Homeless families often came together to set up camps, like the so-called 'Happy Valley' near Botany Bay. After a visit there in June 1931, the State Governor's wife, Lady Game, said she saw one little home in which she would not mind living herself. 'Happy Valley' became a showplace slum. Most camps were totally miserable, unhealthy and police-harassed dumps. When Alfred Byfield, father of seven children, dropped dead in the Mudgee Police Court during his family's third eviction case, his death was almost a happy release. While all these families went homeless, 4 per cent of houses in Australia remained empty.

Homeless single men were herded into army-style camps in Victoria and made to work for very low wages, which many of them refused to do. The camps became so radical that they were closed as 'destructive of morale'. Other schemes were started by private and church bodies. The Unemployed Housing Fund hostel in Darling Harbour sheltered 400 men. It was run like a cross between a gaol and a boarding school: lights were out at 9 pm, and late passes till 11 pm were available for only two nights a week. The men had to be out of the hostel by 9 o'clock each morning, unless it was raining. Anyone breaking the rules was thrown out.

Classrooms became centres for helping the children of the unemployed. In 1930 alone, 60 000 meals, 7000 pieces of clothing and over 2000 pairs of boots were given away in Victorian schools. Because so many families took to the road looking for work, 'schools on wheels' were set up to follow the harvest.

These children were lucky in that they were still being supported by their relations. Less fortunate were the babies and infants whose mothers could not afford to keep them. Others were separated from their mothers at birth because their mothers were unmarried. These children were branded as illegitimate and abused as bastards. Religious bodies took in these 'fallen women', punishing them for their sins. Dymphna Cusack's *Jungfrau* (1936) told of a young woman whose ignorance trapped her into pregnancy and who took her own life when she was unable to arrange an abortion. This problem also confronted married women who could not afford raise another child while their husbands were out of work.

Everyday experiences show the force with which the depression tore through old ways of living. Beer drinking fell from 12.5 gallons (57 litres) to 7 gallons (32 litres) per head, and 5 per cent of all hotels closed. Counter lunches came back but were no longer free or grand. The pubs charged threepence for bread, cheese, boiled mutton and German sausage. Even Sydney's Carlton Hotel had a half-crown businessmen's luncheon 'to meet the times'. The number of visitors to Sydney's Easter Show in 1931 was down by 25 per cent. People turned to cheaper entertainments: singing in parks rather than a visit to the talkies; greyhound races along a rough track, often in a gully, instead of the sport of kings. Of course, if sixpence was all there was between you and starvation, then a beer, the flicks or a flutter was a fair toss of the coin.

Even workers could be better off during the depression, but only under unusual conditions. Anyone with a constant job had an increase in real income because prices fell more than the 10 per cent wage cut. Although a number of families were in this situation, most had to help relatives. Men in their fifties and sixties were kept by their sons; women took their children to stay with in-laws; some children stayed at school longer, while others left before their time. Though a family's buying power might increase, so too did the demands upon it.

LIFE IN THE COUNTRY

The severity of the depression in Australia derived from falling world prices for primary products. In 1929, only two-thirds of the wool clip was sold, and that at only two-thirds of the 1928 prices. World prices for wheat fell from between five and six shillings a bushel in 1929 to less than three shillings in 1930.

The decline in wheat prices was felt most in Western Australia, where as late as 1930 the government was encouraging farmers to expand their acreage; it was also still settling new immigrants on agricultural blocks. These growers faced disaster. The 1931 report of the Agricultural Bank listed 631 farms that had come back under its control, plus another 226 properties that had been sold at a total loss of almost £40 000.

Those who hung on faced a tough time. 'The staple dish was

boiled wheat and treacle — known as "cocky's joy" — with rabbit, kangaroo or emu to supplement the ration. Golden syrup, 3d more for a 2 lb. tin, replaced treacle as a special treat for Christmas.' Galah pie was a cause for celebration. When the inner tube of a car tyre wore out, the tyre was packed tight with dried horse manure.

In the early months of the depression, farmers heavily in debt to private firms were declared bankrupt and their goods put up for auction. From the start, the Wheat-growers Union organised the resistance to these auctions. Farmers turned out in their hundreds from miles around. One of them recalled that 'any strangers there were taken to one side and told to go or stand outside or shut up'. The items that had been put up for sale went for next to nothing and 'were given back to the [owner] and he simply continued on'. A couple of years later, the wheat farmers organised a 'strike', refusing to sell their wheat unless the government paid them a subsidy.

Conditions were not much better in the eastern States, where many soldier settlers walked off their farms empty-handed. One called on a neighbour to say farewell: 'Look at me, Missus, look at what I have to show for ten years' work. Even in the army I was dressed better than this'.

Despite the disaster on the land, some Australians went on seeing the opening of more farms as the way out of the depression. City capitalists disagreed about the cure for the depression. They were split between the retailers who wanted more sales versus the manufacturers who wanted lower wages. In August 1931 the chairman of BHP called for 'lower wages generally, a reversion to the 48-hour week and the suspension of all Awards'. He hoped to take advantage of the high demand for jobs to force wages and conditions down as far as possible. While BHP did not get its way entirely, its leaders went on pushing industrialisation as the way to Australia's recovery.

After Britain and Australia came off the gold standard in 1931, the price of gold rocketed. A Burnie bank manager accepted a customer's gold-studded false teeth as a deposit. Gold regained its magical ability to take men on vast treks with only the promise of a lucky strike. Lasseter's lost reef tempted more than one man to his death. The discovery of the 'Golden Eagle Nugget' in Western Australia raised the hopes of the 16 000 men who had accepted the Victorian government's offer of a swag, a pan and a printed guide to fossicking. By the late 1930s, gold-mining had become an important part of Australia's economic revival. The volume of gold production trebled, its value increased sevenfold, and its share of Australia's export earnings quadrupled to 11 per cent.

HEALTH

Public health standards fell during the depression largely because local governments were unwilling to enforce laws that many ordinary citizens could no longer afford to observe. When families were evicted from their homes, they built shanties that did not meet the building regulations. Rather than have homeless families polluting creeks and parks with their waste, councils sometimes helped campers onto grounds which could be inspected and kept in order. Where an evicted family moved in with relatives, greater demands were placed on the sewerage and on the cooking and sleeping arrangements so some lowering of standards followed. Unemployed workers would sometimes set up backyard industries. These worksites were often unhealthy and created stinks in the suburbs. Another problem arose because people could not afford to have garbage removed and tended to dump it on public lands. A Victorian health inspector noted some side benefits:

> Manure (the best breeding ground for flies) is seldom allowed to accumulate now, being very much in demand by the many unemployed who now grow their own vegetables. Back yards and vacant allotments have in numerous instances been cleared of noxious plants and in their stead a nice vegetable or flower garden

has been laid out and maintained. Whilst quite a number of houses have fallen into a state of disrepair to compensate for this, many unemployed or rationed owners and occupiers have renovated their homes and tended to the grass plots on the footways.

These improvements could not outweigh the harm that occurred because of the disaster of capitalism's collapse.

The depression widened the gap between those patients who could afford to pay for their own doctors and those who could not afford any treatment. A few radical doctors set themselves up in the poorer districts to run virtually free health clinics. Most doctors increased the number of people to whom they did not bother to send a bill. Others needed to be chided by an editorial in the *Medical Journal*:

> [unless doctors] remember that they are first of all members of a scientific profession, their efforts will be sterile. The acquisition of wealth and even the leading of a comfortable existence must always be secondary considerations. However unsavoury this may be to some, it is nevertheless true.

For many middle-class Australians, poverty was an alien experience, as foreign to their character as the acceptance of charity. Some failed to seek treatment for cancers, tuberculosis and heart complaints, until it was far too late for anything to be done about them.

ABORIGINES

A global depression made little difference to most Aborigines. Yet they were among the first to be sacked. Governments spent even less on their welfare. Churches had ever more demands on their shrinking resources. German missionaries had moved into Central Australia from the 1870s, learning the local languages to preach the Gospel. Although these Lutherans made few converts, they protected the local people from white marauders, whether policemen or pastoralists. Early in 1926, in the middle of a seven-year drought, Pastor

Albrecht arrived with his wife at Hermannsburg Mission, south-west of Alice Springs. The couple studied the languages and tried to adjust their Christianity to Indigenous beliefs. According to one Aboriginal:

> Old Albrecht, he didn't understand life of families, not really. I don't think he understood everything, like inside feelings, or inside work with the community. There was not too much trouble. Albrecht was alright. What he wanted done, we tried to do, even if it made a bit of trouble. That's why we like old man, because old man do right thing for us, so we do good for old man. Mistakes don't matter. He tried very hard, he had to learn everything.

Albrecht's major achievement was to organise the piping of water hundreds of metres uphill from Kaporilja springs into the mission. The water sustained two hectares of vegetable gardens, which reduced the death rate.

To raise some money, the missionaries encouraged the Arrernte and the Luritja peoples to produce craft items, such as poker-work on mulga wood, for sale in Adelaide. Tour parties of whites began in the winter of 1928, often including artists. After Rex Battarbee exhibited his paintings of the area at the mission school, Albert Namatjira asked Albrecht how much Battarbee got for his paintings. On being told that they would bring as much as £20, Namatjira said: 'I think I can do that too'. With Battarbee's help in applying watercolours, Namatjira held the first of his sell-out exhibitions in 1938 to become the best-known Aborigine in the country.

VIEW OF THE WORLD

In 1928, the Australian government signed a pact to outlaw aggressive war. This agreement came ten years after the end of the war to end wars. Its sentiments represented the high point of pacifism among the major powers. The only conflicts then being waged were by those empires against their colonies. In China, Japanese troops clashed with communists and other nationalists. In 1931, the Japanese expanded their military control of Manchuria.

The incoming federal Labor government abolished what remained of compulsory military training in October 1929. This move had more to do with bitterness left over from the Labor split over conscription in the Great War than any assessment of military needs. The collapse in the economy brought cuts to defence spending. Strategists recognised that air forces would be central in any future war. Aviators brought about a shift in the way Australians viewed their place in the world. In June 1928, Sir Charles Kingsford Smith and Charles Ulm flew *Southern Cross* across the Pacific; the next year they made it to England in thirteen days. Two of the five postage stamps issued between 1927 and 1931 celebrated flight. The de Havilland company started aircraft construction near Melbourne in 1928. An overseas air mail service began in 1934.

Economic relations with the outside world were more pressing than military or diplomatic links. Governments had to meet interest payments and adjust imports in line with the loss of export income. Canberra pushed up tariffs and devalued the Australian pound. The Bank of England sent Sir Otto Niemeyer to Australia in July 1930. He told the elected governments to balance their budgets and cut wages before they could expect more loan monies. The Labor leader in New South Wales, Jack Lang, won 55 per cent of the vote in October 1930 by promising to resist the British bond-holders. His supporters declared that he was 'Mightier than Lenin'. The dream of a strong leader was testing Australia's democratic temper.

Throughout the 1920s, the respectable middle-classes had admired Mussolini and Italian *fascisti* for keeping the workers in order. In November 1930, a group of businessmen appealed to General Sir John Monash to head a movement to save Australia from Labor governments. The General replied: 'I have no ambition to embark on High Treason'. To celebrate the tenth anniversary in 1933 of the fascist march on Rome, a black-shirted honour-guard welcomed the Roman Catholic Archbishop of Brisbane, James Duhig, to St Stephen's Cathedral where His Grace blessed the fascist banners. On the other extreme, Stalin appeared as 'the man of steel'. The Soviet Union appealed because its central planning promised the efficiency that capitalism had lost.

The interest in foreigners was but a glance. The Empire remained the focus of attention. In 1931, the Statute of Westminster gave legal form to the calls from Canada, South Africa and the Irish Free State for greater autonomy. The Australian government did not ratify this arrangement until 1942. The conservative government that came to office at Christmas 1931 feared that the new system would deprive the Queen's Representatives of the power to dismiss elected governments as NSW Governor Game had done to Jack Lang in May 1932. Meanwhile, Australians voiced their resentments, on either class or nationalistic grounds, during the 1932 Ashes cricket test. The 'bodyline' tour had shown that the Britishers did not always play fair. As the visitors brushed the flies away while playing at the Sydney Cricket Ground, a voice from the outer cried: 'Leave our bloody flies alone!'

Hostility towards touring Poms did not dislodge the belief in the superiority of Anglo-Celts. The worst fears of the advocates of White Australia were confirmed early in 1928 during the tour of the first Negro band, Sony Clay's 'Colored Idea'. These jazz musicians had released their 'Australian Stomp' as their calling card. After headlines of 'Nude Girls in Melbourne Flat Orgy', the players were deported. At the same time, *The Jazz Singer* became the first talkie screened here, starring the blackface Al Jolson.

With almost no immigration to restrict, the authorities imposed quarantine around ideas. They banned subversive literature, which meant communist pamphlets. Anti-war novels were at first popular. For example, *All Quiet on the Western*

Front (1929) by Erich Maria Remarque sold almost 50 000 copies in the six months after its release here in March 1929; it was well reviewed, even by the magazines of the returned servicemen. That welcome disappeared in 1930 with the arrival of Robert Graves's *Goodbye to All That* which recounted how an Australian solider had murdered his prisoners.

Governments tightened moral censorship until 5000 titles were denied entry, including some of Shakespeare. James Joyce's *Ulysses* was banned in April 1929. These controls also applied to Australian novels, most of which were then published overseas. In 1930, Norman Lindsay's *Redheap* became a prohibited import. The following year the New South Wales police prosecuted as obscene a special issue of *Art in Australia* devoted to Lindsay's drawings and watercolours. A few weeks later, he cabled a message from the ship taking him to New York: 'Goodbye to the best country in the world, it if was not for the Wowsers'.

6 1934–1938 VERY SLOW RECOVERY

The depression did not end until after the start of the First
Pacific War, although recovery began from 1933. The collapse
strengthened the monopolisers by getting rid of less efficient
firms. For example, BHP absorbed the Wollongong plant of
Australian Iron and Steel. After the turmoil of James Scullin's
Labor government (1929–31) came six years of stable
anti-Labor rule. The world drifted to battle stations when
Japan invaded China in 1931, Italy stole an empire in Abys-
sinia from 1935, after which Nazi Germany bullied its way
into central Europe as Spain was butchered into fascism. Dictatorship, wars and the depression offered few reasons for
optimism, although some Australians looked towards Soviet
Russia as the future civilisation.

WORK

Poverty, unemployment, lost chances, anger and lack of hope
persisted. The teenage boys who had left school early and
missed out on an apprenticeship or training worsened a longstanding problem. One-fifth of all male school leavers in New
South Wales at the end of 1932 could not get work. Governments were half-hearted and private organisations limited in
what they could attempt or achieve. In Victoria, forestry
camps were set up to take in boys for six months before

dumping them back on Melbourne's streets. Once there, they were subject to the Vagrancy Law under which they could be gaoled for a month for the crime of being out of work during a depression. In an effort to improve their situation, the Anglican Brotherhood of St Laurence opened a hostel in Fitzroy in 1937. This building could only scratch the surface of the problem since it could take only thirty-eight boys, most of whom had jobs anyway.

In the search for long-term solutions to unemployment, governments pushed post-primary education further towards technical training. Trade union leaders believed that skilled tradesmen were less likely to be sacked, and support came from some of the bigger firms. By 1935, BHP dominated the Regional Education Board in Newcastle which lobbied the government into a review of New South Wales technical education.

In most States, secondary school curricula remained virtually unchanged during the inter-war period. One exception was in the New South Wales geography course, where W. Griffith Taylor's *Australia* ceased to be the set text because his view of Australia's potential did not suit the optimistic pronouncements of the government.

Unemployment started to fall in 1933 but a large body of men was still on relief work. Typical jobs were in a government forestry camp under makeshift conditions and for low wages. A worker at Belanglo, via Sutton Forest in New South Wales, reported that there was no water tank in his camp, that the nearby stream was useless in heavy rain and that there was nowhere to have a bath:

> Our tents are 8 by 6 feet, just room to sleep in. We have four kerosene lamps, which cannot be used in the tents, but only to guide us to the lavatory. Touching on lavatories, they are built on the army style, a hole dug, a cross bit of timber to sit on, no covering from the rain, and when not raining we have to contend with heavy frosts.

In reply to a plea for extra blankets the men were told that the cost would be deducted from their £1 a week wages. 'Needless to say the men did not order any, remarking they would sooner buy bags'.

On 22 January 1931, the Commonwealth Arbitration Court had cut the basic wage by 10 per cent. The judges argued that this would not reduce the people's spending power because prices had fallen. The savings to the bosses could be invested to create more jobs. This decision was another of the policies that were supposed to 'cure' the depression, but which made matters worse. The need was for greater consumption, not less. Three years passed before any of this income was given back. This delay turned out to be a roundabout way of making the cut in wages permanent for the vast majority.

Wonthaggi

In 1934, the working class began to regain its strength: trade union membership as a percentage of the total workforce grew for the first time in five years. Strikes increased for the first time in four years. Indeed, they increased by 60 per cent in both the number of disputes and in the number of workers involved. Of the 155 strikes in 1934, the most important was that of the Wonthaggi coal-miners, which lasted for four months and which the workers won.

Wonthaggi was a Victorian government coal-mine which supplied the Department of Railways. Workers at the mine had been badly hit by the depression. While the rest of the working class had their wagers cut by 10 per cent, the Wonthaggi miners had theirs slashed by as much as 40 per cent. This assault devastated Wonthaggi's economic life. The weekly payroll at the mine fell from £20 000 to £12 000. Some of this drop came from sacking 20 per cent of the miners.

Early in 1934, the Railway Commissioners asked for yet another wage cut at the mine. Its general manager started a policy of sackings aimed at frightening the miners into accepting a new 20 per cent wage cut, which he said was needed to keep the mine working at a profit. On 6 March he sacked seven miners. A stop-work meeting called for a strike. The manager tried to bluff the strikers by sending the rolling stock away, by clearing tools from the mines and by turning the pit ponies out: steps intended to show that he was ready for a long battle.

Meanwhile, the strikers were moving away from their usual form of strike action to seek community support. New kinds of defence activities were put into effect. In order to live, the strikers and the other people in Wonthaggi set up a self-supporting town. The basis for this achievement already existed because the major store was a cooperative, as was the local picture theatre.

The strikers bought cattle and set up slaughter yards. They went on trips to Pakenham where fruit could be had for the picking. Being close to the sea, they organised fishing parties. Free coal was taken from disused mines. Community gardens were dug for basic crops such as potatoes. A free barber shop opened and had 2500 customers. Similarly, over 1500 pairs of boots were mended free of charge. These actions succeeded only because the women of the town were involved. They raised money locally and managed most of the free goods and services. They also went on speaking tours to other States to demonstrate the town's solidarity.

By the middle of June the strikers were secure. They had the support of a wide section of the labour movement. So confident were they that they offered to hold a secret ballot over the conduct of the strike. The government declined. In the annual union election at the end of June, militants won all six positions. Within a fortnight the government gave in.

Over and above the victory at Wonthaggi came the encouragement for the working class as a whole. The miners had shown that wage cuts were not final even with unemployment at 20 per cent. Their victory gave hope to other unionists who wanted to win back conditions lost during the late 1920s and early 1930s.

LIFE IN THE CITIES

Radio had been used for some time to send messages 'point-to-point'. The first demonstration of broadcasting in Australia was in 1919 when a Melbourne audience stood to attention for 'God Save the King'. Public broadcasting started in 1923 under a 'closed set system'. People had to buy a receiver which they could tune to only one station. Only 1200 people had bought licences before the system was replaced by 'open-set' receivers in July 1924.

The open-set system brought two types of commercial radio: A-class stations got some of the licence fee and were allowed only fifteen minutes of advertising each evening; B-class stations were fully self-supporting and could have unlimited advertising. While B-class stations continue to operate in this way, all A-class stations were bought out by the government in 1929, and placed under the Australian Broadcasting Commission (ABC) by 1932. By then, there were fifty-five stations and nearly 370 000 radios. Within another three years, the number of licence holders had doubled.

Sport brought hundreds of thousands to radio as they listened with rising anger to the 1932 'bodyline' cricket tour. So popular did sporting programs become that, in 1934, the ABC put together a ball-by-ball description of the cricket from England. Details of play were cabled to Australia so that there was only a minute or two's delay before the studio announcer gave his lively account. Commercial stations used sound effects for bat and ball hitting. One made the sound of a falling wicket with a machine known as 'Ricketty Kate'. Some people tuned in just for the sound effects.

Radio stations saw the need to win over the young. When 3DB opened in 1927, the first words were from 'Winnie

Wattle' on her children's program. The ABC followed with more educational sessions. Its Argonauts Club, founded in January 1941, had 7000 members within six months.

Music, plays and religion were three areas of life that people experienced differently through radio. Broadcasts changed the lives of lovers of classical music. No longer did they have to stop in the middle of an *andante* movement to turn over their 78 r.p.m. records. The ABC built up the first full-time orchestras in each State and took music to the people with its concerts. In the late 1930s, ABC broadcasts also gave most Australians their first taste of anything like a live performance of great plays.

Although religious broadcasting had started as early as 1923, some churchmen asked whether this was the right path to follow. Would sermons over the airwaves let people stay at home to listen instead of going to church? Would Catholics tune in to Protestant sermons? Protestants gave way in August 1924 when a Sunday service was broadcast from Sydney's Pitt Street Congregational Church. Catholics took to the air in force with Dr Rumble's Radio Replies over 2SM, at first to explain that their 1928 Eucharistic Congress was not a cannibal feast.

Most people listened to commercial radio, which began round-the-clock programs in 1935; the ABC was on the air for less than fifteen hours a day. 'Soap operas' came from the United States in the 1930s. The 1940s saw the growth of quiz shows, to which Jack Davey and Bob Dyer called up their followers with 'Hi Ho, Everybody' and 'Happy Lathering, Customers'. As early as 1932, a writer in the *Sydney Morning Herald* complained that radio was nothing but 'jazz and sports advertisements for shaving soap and silk stockings and the latest crime'.

The voice that radio gave to retailers was part of a reorganisation of marketing. One effect of the depression was the expansion of chain stores and 'cash and carrys'. These shops had existed since the turn of the century, but they were better able to survive the economic strains of the early 1930s than were independent traders. Sometimes, these shopkeepers joined together in chains to get cheaper prices through bulk buying. Just as often, they resulted from one firm's takeover of others.

'G. J. Coles' is an example of the expansion of chain stores. George Coles had been born near Horsham, Victoria, in 1885. At sixteen he started work in his father's shop. After gaining experience in a Melbourne warehouse, he returned home and bought his father's business. A little later he went to the United States to look into '5 and 10 cent stores'. Back in Melbourne late in 1913, he opened Australia's first '3d, 6d and 1/- store' in Smith Street, Collingwood. His first day's sales totaled £100. When he returned from the Great War, he went into partnership with his brother, this time with the slogan 'Nothing over 2/6', a sign of how prices had risen during the war. Two years later, the brothers opened shops in Prahran and Brunswick before moving into the inner city with a shop in Bourke Street, opposite Myer's. By 1928, the brothers owned ten stores with a yearly turnover of more than £1 million. By 1936, they employed nearly 3000 shop assistants in forty-three shops, with plans to open ten more.

LIFE IN THE COUNTRY

'Insecurity is one of the most dominant emotions in country towns. In no town is there the feeling that it has a continuing function in a stable society. For fear it might go back, as it has seen others do, each town wants to go forward.' These conclusions came from two social scientists, Jean and Alan McIntyre, who examined 180 Victorian country towns in 1941 and 1942. Most of their information dealt with the decade leading up to the First Pacific War.

Many country towns were kept alive by people who

worked for the government as public servants, teachers and railway workers. In some places, pensioners made up 15 per cent of the population. During the 1930s one-third of the towns had increased their population, 46 per cent stayed the same and one-fifth, usually the smallest ones, had dropped back. The decline in population was caused by the near impossibility of finding work in the smaller settlements. Of the sixty-one flour mills that had been working in 1913, only thirty-six remained in 1940. Prices for all farm products in 1938–39 were only two-thirds of what they had been in the 1920s. Dairy prices remained almost the same, but wheat and wool were badly hit. Victoria's wheat acreage fell by a quarter, although this shrinkage was partly made up for by fertilisers which gave higher returns per acre.

Two-thirds of the towns were short of houses: half needed better homes, but the other half needed homes of any sort. Water supplies were neither adequate nor pure. Twenty-six towns had no public supply while six others used bores. In autumn, the water at St Arnaud was mainly mud; at another place, the McIntyres' toothbrushes sprouted green algae overnight. Only one-tenth of the towns had sewerage and six had no collection service at all; the vast majority used a pan service. Wherever sewerage was provided, farmers moved into the towns. At one large country hospital, grasshoppers found their way into the operating theatre, where the cooling system was a fan over a block of ice. The main street was likely to have paved footpaths, trees and a public park, but unlikely to have public lavatories or to be sealed from kerb to kerb. Twenty of the larger towns had horse-drawn cabs and a third had one or more chain stores. Country towns were a jumble of sewerage and shops alongside horses and carts, of flashes of progress and pools of stagnation.

Time and time again the McIntyres heard people say 'farmers can't co-operate'. Although this allegation might have been true in business, most towns had social clubs which grew on the support from farmers. Yet their communities needed outside leadership. Towns were full of memories of organisations that had closed 'when the Smiths moved to Melbourne', 'when the school teacher left' or 'when the bank teller went'. In Tasmania, one bank manager told his head office that:

> Since I have taken charge of the Branch I have connected myself with all the Social, Sporting, and all movements pertaining to the welfare of the town, and have become very popular, which is a big factor in obtaining business in these country towns.

The arrival of talking pictures ended a number of the entertainment groups such as the Skipton (Vic.) Dramatic Association, which closed in 1931 because of competition from fortnightly films shown by the Western District Touring Talkies. In some places, the company showing the films would book all the halls in town to stop competition.

The most usual kind of private fun was a combined dance and card party, euchre being the most popular game. These gatherings were often held every week. The old people would play cards until ten o'clock, by which time one or two couples would break the ice and dance. Sport also brought people together. Australian Rules had the largest following. 'Throughout the winter, it is continually present in most people's minds. Not that all these people play, but they identify themselves with their team, and take its wins and losses to heart.' Almost every town had its own tennis courts and football and cricket grounds. There were golf courses in 158 towns and a swimming place — not always a pool — in 128 of them.

Most of the larger towns had their own commercial radio stations. The most popular programs, in declining order, were: hillbilly songs and yodelling, serials such as 'Dad and Dave' and 'Martin's Corner' (when one station stopped broadcasting 'Dad and Dave' it got 1000 protests in two days), sport on Saturday, old-time dance music, light music, quizzes and competitions, plays and talks. People came into the studios just to watch the records go round.

Country newspapers were generally of a poor standard: 'The comments of the local people usually show a lack of satisfaction with their paper: "No news is good news, so our paper wins easily." "It can hardly scrape up enough news to get itself into print".' Sometimes a lively editor would appear and chase up local news, but the best reading was the advertisements, poems and stories bought from Melbourne papers. Prices at the Melbourne pig market were sometimes put into verse:

> *George Henry's £10/1/2 A. Baker's £10/4,*
> *£9/1 R. Retallacks, £8/11 a few more,*
> *£5/11/6 John Campbell's, £5/10/6 F. Jervis*
> *£5/8/6 F. Muzo's 10, Shaw Logan for service.*

Libraries existed in almost all towns but few were well stocked. Alongside an out-of-date encyclopedia and dictionary, they usually offered westerns, light romances and detective stories. Any other books were likely to find themselves on a shelf labelled 'Heavy'. 'Heavy' reading was more common in the industrial and mining towns where the workers 'read them quickly, too, always coming back for more'. This was true at Broken Hill where the librarian had worked underground for thirty years: 'When he found someone with a thirst for reading he threw open his most precious bookshelves and joined in passionate discussions with the readers'. One purpose of the library was as a place to chat on market days when it was too cold to stand in the street.

'The over-all impression' that the McIntyres took away from country towns was of a mixture of 'kindliness, bitterness, generosity, meanness, community effort and struggling for individual gain', and 'of anxious and to some extent thwarted people' who needed to earn a living but were never sure if they could. The McIntyres concluded that, while life in country towns was neighbourly and satisfied many people, 'the anxiety and frustration springing from economic insecurity tend to make it also small-minded'.

Bushfires

Twice in Victoria's history have fire-storms given the superstitious proof that human cataclysms are preceded by natural ones. The first was on the eve of the gold rushes; the second on Friday, 13 January 1939:

> On that day it appeared that the whole State was alight. At midday, in many places, it was dark as night. Men carrying hurricane lamps worked to make safe their families and belongings. Travellers on the highways were trapped by fires or blazing fallen trees, and perished. Throughout the land there was daytime darkness. At one mill, desperate but futile efforts were made to clear of inflammable scrub the borders of the mill and mill settlement. All but one person, at that mill, were burned to death, many of them while trying to burrow to imagined safety in the sawdust heap. Horses were found, still harnessed, in their stalls, dead, their limbs fantastically contorted.
>
> The speed of the fires was appalling. They leaped from mountain peak to mountain peak, or far out into the lower country, lighting the forests 6 or 7 miles in advance of the main fires. Blown by a wind of great force, they roared as they travelled. Balls of crackling fire sped at a great pace in advance of the fires, consuming with a roaring, explosive noise, all that they touched. Houses of brick were seen and heard to leap into a roar of flame before the fires had reached them.
>
> Seventy-one lives were lost.
>
> Men who had lived their lives in the bush went their ways in the shadow of dread expectancy. But though they [had] felt the imminence of danger they could not tell that it was to be far greater than they could imagine. They had not lived long enough.

This picture of 'Black Friday' comes from the introduction to the report of Mr Justice Stretton, the Royal Commissioner on the disaster. Stretton's report was surprising for the liveliness of the writing. More amazing still was the almost unheard-of honesty with which he condemned the selfishness of sawmillers who had refused to provide underground dug-outs, to keep their surroundings cleared, or to remove off-cuts and sawdust. He pointed out with equal force that the government had gone along with the failure of the Forests Commissioners to enforce the necessary standards.

Stretton had something important to say about Royal Commissions in general and his experience is worth quoting for what it tells us about other reports on which historians rely:

> The truth was hard to find. Much of the evidence was coloured by self-interest. Much of it was quite false. Little of it was wholly truthful. The timber-workers were afraid that if they gave evidence they would not be given future employment in the mills. The Forest Officers were afraid that if they were too outspoken their future advancement in the Forests Commission employ would be endangered. Some of them had become too friendly with the millers whose activities they were set to direct and check.

Five years later, when Stretton investigated a smaller disaster at Yallourn, he must have recalled the truth of his 1939 fear that his reform ideas were not likely to be put into practice in the immediate future.

The Yallourn fire gave Stretton a chance to investigate another feature of Australian life, the company town. Yallourn was the property of the State Electricity Commission (SEC) of Victoria. Stretton saw that the town's failure to defend itself against the fire was a direct result of the way the SEC treated its employees. After praising the cheap housing, well supplied with essential services, Stretton observed:

> Here indeed the townsman enjoys all that the heart of a man may desire — except freedom, fresh air and independence. He has no authoritative voice in the management of the town. There is no public library. There is no hall where the townspeople may publicly assemble as of right. There is no place where refreshment of any kind may be obtained after six o'clock in the evening. There is a cinema. There is no municipal democracy.

Stretton considered life in Yallourn was a 'positive, provoc-
ative denial' of the social needs fundamental to the preservation of any people. Put more bluntly, Yallourn burnt because
its citizens believed it deserved no better.

HEALTH

Between the wars, Australia's hospitals were crippled for lack
of government money. They scraped along with private gifts
from the wealthy, and with all manner of small-scale fund-
raising. There were egg days and wood days, hospital Sundays
at churches and collection boxes in hotels. Important items of
equipment, such as X-ray machines, had to wait until some
rich person donated them.

Hospitals were hit by financial cuts, as governments and
patients alike found it hard to meet their bills. One man wrote
to Melbourne's Prince Henry's Hospital in 1931 saying that
because he could not pay his account he would give the hospital all royalties from his poetry if the hospital published it.
Another sign of the worsening economic situation was the
employment of almoners whose job it was to see that
ex-patients found good homes and care, and that the families
of patients were not in too great a need. In the second half of
the 1930s, several States started their first big hospital buildings, partly as one way of reducing unemployment through
the form of public-works spending for which there would be
wide approval. After long and almost criminal neglect,
Queensland's public health and hospital services were boosted
after 1934 with a new Medical Act, with the first signs of
replacing honoraries in public hospitals with salaried doctors,
and a medical school at the university. Another cause of the
difficulties was the long time that patients had to stay in bed
even after small operations: ten to seventeen days for the
removal of an appendix.

Hospitals came under extra pressure during epidemics.

Infantile paralysis, as poliomyelitis was then known, returned to Melbourne in June 1937. In what was to be Australia's worst-yet polio epidemic, the disease spread to three neighbouring States. Victorian schools were shut and by the end of the year nearly 70 000 pupils were getting special correspondence education. A former editor of the Melbourne *Herald* claimed that his managing-editor, Keith Murdoch, played down the outbreak. If people had known how bad things were, they would have stayed out of the shops, which would have hurt the paper's advertisers.

With the increase in car ownership came a new disease, popularly misnamed car accidents, as if the cars themselves accidentally ran into each other. Total deaths in cars leapt from 400 a year in 1924 to 1433 in 1939; total injuries rose from 7671 to 25 653. These figures were a far cry from pre-war motoring days when the most common motoring injury was a broken wrist from an obstinate crank handle. Because treatments took so long, great strains were placed on hospitals. As early as December 1922, one-tenth of all patients in Royal Melbourne Hospital were there as a result of motoring injuries. Ten years later, the Victorian government brought in compulsory third-party car insurance so that hospital bills would be paid some time.

Traffic accidents increased the number of emergency operations and the demand for blood during surgery. City blood banks were set up in the late 1930s, after which blood transfusions became widespread. Before this service, a close relative would be tested and, if suitable, placed on a stretcher beside the patient's bed so that blood could be given directly. Well into the 1950s, country hospitals had people who agreed to be called upon to give blood at any hour of the day or night. Because of the Red Cross Blood Transfusion Service, Australia was one of the few capitalist countries in which blood donors were not paid by the litre. A gift relationship prevailed.

Indeed, town and country equally depended upon the

unpaid actions of millions of people who kept organisations such as the Red Cross, Surf Lifesaving and Legacy going. Although competition was pushed as the noblest of human values, a majority of people showed that they preferred co-operation through their support of sporting, school and community organisations. Without endless efforts freely given to street stalls, fetes and raffles, Australia could never have recovered. The tragedy was that this willingness to help was used by governments as an excuse for not raising taxes from the rich to do the job properly. Ambulance services were perhaps the worst example of neglect.

ABORIGINES

A book about the position of Aborigines in Australia during the 1930s could be written simply by summarising the royal commissions and conferences that studied them. It would even be possible to show that these reports became more progressive in outlook. Such scholarship would be a complete waste of time, because the investigations made no improvement in the daily lives or long-term hopes of Indigenous people. A single incident came closer to the truth about what life meant to the original inhabitants.

Towards the middle of 1933, there began an affair which showed the change that had come over the Northern Territory as a result of the Coniston massacre. No longer was it safe to boast about murdering Aborigines legally.

The incident began when some Aboriginal men speared three Japanese pearl fishermen to death. Reports in the southern press said that a white hunting party had gone out to retaliate but had found no Aborigines to shoot. Over a year later, four constables and four trackers landed on Woodah Island off Arnhem Land. They walked for thirty kilometres and found a newly abandoned camp site. Nearby, they captured four Aboriginal women whom they handcuffed and questioned about the spearing of the Japanese. A report that Aboriginal men were nearby led three of the constables and two of the trackers to search for them. When they returned there was no sign of the women, the trackers or the fourth constable, McColl. McColl's speared body was not found until the morning. Reports of this latest white shooting party again aroused those southern whites who felt sorry for the Aborigines.

Protest meetings in Melbourne and Sydney raised a collection to send a missionary party to the area to negotiate. When the missionaries arrived on Woodah Island they talked an Aboriginal man named Tuckiar into going to Darwin with them. There he was arrested and brought to trial. Only two witnesses spoke at the trial. Neither of them had seen the killing. Both offered statements that Tuckiar had confessed to them that he had killed Constable McColl. Their statements wildly disagreed with each other's. Neither could speak any English and their evidence was given to the court in Pidgin, through another Aboriginal man who had been one of the trackers on Woodah Island at the time of the killing of McColl.

The first of the witnesses to give evidence was named Parriner. He claimed that Tuckiar had told him that he had killed McColl because he was afraid of him. Tuckiar is alleged to have hidden behind a tree and thrown a spear which McColl removed with one hand while getting his pistol out with the other and then firing three shots.

The second witness was Harry, who was employed on the boat that had brought Tuckiar to Darwin. He had talked to Tuckiar during the trip at the suggestion of the boat's captain. According to Harry, Tuckiar told him that he had come across McColl sexually assaulting one of Tuckiar's three wives. When Tuckiar asked McColl for some tobacco, McColl drew his pistol and fired at him. Tuckiar had then thrown his spear and killed McColl.

After the first lot of evidence, the judge asked the defence lawyer if Tuckiar had been questioned about the truth of Parriner's evidence of a confession. The lawyer said 'No'. The Court then adjourned. After Harry gave his evidence, the defence lawyer said that he had been placed in 'the worst predicament in all his legal career'. The judge, the lawyer and the Chief Protector of Aborigines then talked in private.

When the trial resumed, no further evidence was given. The jury asked the judge what they should do if they felt that not enough evidence had been presented. The judge took this as a criticism of the prosecution for not presenting more evidence to convict Tuckiar. He informed the jury that their duty was clear: they had to convict Tuckiar. If they acquitted him two things would follow: first, he could not be tried again for this offence; secondly, it would be a slur on the character of the murdered McColl.

The prosecution then called a character witness for McColl, before the judge gave his summing up. No full record was kept, but he did say:

> You have before you two different stories, one of which sounds highly probable, and fits in with all the known facts, and the other is so utterly ridiculous as to be an obvious fabrication. What counsel for the defence asks you to do is to take up the position that you will not believe either of these stories. Tuckiar has told two different stories to two different boys, and both of these stories have been told to you in Court. Which one is true? For some reason Tuckiar has not gone into the box and told you which one is true, and that is a fact which you are entitled to take into consideration. You can draw from it any inference you like.

The jury found Tuckiar guilty. Tuckiar's lawyer got up and said that during the first adjournment Tuckiar had admitted his guilt. During the second adjournment, the judge had told him to carry on with the case 'because if you had retired from the case it would have left it open to ignorant, malicious and irresponsible persons to say that this Aboriginal had been abandoned and left without any proper defence'. The judge then condemned Tuckiar to death.

When news of the trial reached southern Australia, more protest meetings were held and a fund set up to appeal to the High Court to have the verdict set aside. In November 1934 the appeal was heard by the full bench of the High Court and unanimously upheld. The High Court said that the judge should not have said anything about Tuckiar's not giving evidence. Nor should the jury have heard evidence about McColl's character. The bench attacked the defence lawyer's failure to call for an acquittal on self-defence or manslaughter, and for breaking Tuckiar's confidence after the verdict had been given. Under these circumstances, the Court felt that a fair trial would not be possible in the Northern Territory and ordered that Tuckiar be set free.

A legal lynching of an Aborigine had been prevented by southern appeals to the High Court. There was still no way of stopping the daily doings of Territorians. Tuckiar left Darwin but never got back to Woodah Island. His body was never found. In 2003 the Tuckiar and McColl families conducted a ceremony of reconciliation in the presence of the Chief Justice of Australia.

VIEW OF THE WORLD

By the 1930s, almost no non-Europeans tried to enter Australia. The Immigration Restriction Act was used against anyone for any reason. Late in 1934, an anti-Nazi writer from Czechoslovakia, Egon Kisch, tried to visit Australia to speak to a conference against war and fascism. This meeting had been planned for the same time as Melbourne's Centenary Celebrations, which were being used to drum up support for military spending. On 11 November the Duke of Gloucester attended the opening of the Shrine of Remembrance in St Kilda Road, built by the unemployed for the dole. Travelling with the

Duke were three British military experts. The London-to-Melbourne Air Race was another part of the celebrations related to preparing for war.

Egon Kisch had been in one of Hitler's concentration camps. He had a great reputation as a writer in Europe and spoke a wide range of languages. No sooner had Kisch asked for a visa to visit Australia than the British secret police told the Australian authorities that he was an undesirable person. When he arrived at Fremantle, his bags were searched for communist books but nothing was found. Nonetheless, he was told that he would not be allowed to land in Melbourne. An appeal to a magistrate failed.

On 13 November, just as his ship was pulling out from its Melbourne wharf, Kisch leapt over the side. Police rushed forward. The boat reversed. Kisch had injured his leg. Still, he was put on board for Sydney. Supporters claimed that he had broken his leg in two places. Opponents said he had merely sprained his ankle. Everyone agreed 'he was game'.

Shortly afterwards, the High Court in Sydney said that the government had no right to hold Kisch. When he came ashore, officials of the Department of Immigration used another part of the Immigration Act to exclude him, namely the dictation test. They asked him to speak fifty words in Scottish Gaelic. Although he failed the test he was free until his case came before a magistrate. Two days later he spoke to a rally in Sydney's Domain.

After Kisch was declared to be a forbidden immigrant because he had failed the dictation test, another appeal was organised. This time, the full bench of the High Court ruled that Scottish Gaelic was not a European language. Once more, the government would not let matters rest. It hoped to put Kisch onto a Nazi ship. The government compromised and agreed to drop its charges and to pay a good part of Kisch's court costs if he agreed to leave Australia, which he did on 11 March 1935.

Kisch brought home to Australians what Hitler's Germany was about. He exposed the lengths to which the Australian government would go to stop the expression of opposing ideas. Although Kisch had come to speak against war, the long-term result of his visit was to awaken Australians to the need to fight fascism, both at home and abroad. After fifteen years of uneasy peace, Europe was once more disturbing Australia.

Australians were not well informed by their papers which took most of their news from conservative sources in London. Keeping people ignorant about foreign affairs fitted in with the Australian government's idea of how the country should be run. The Minister for Defence put this clearly late in February 1938:

> We, the Government, have vital information which we cannot disclose. It is upon this knowledge that we make our decisions. You, who are merely private citizens, have not access to this information. Any criticism you make of our policy, any controversy about it in which you may indulge will therefore be uninformed and valueless. If, in spite of your ignorance, you persist in questioning our policy, we can only conclude that you are disloyal.

Supporters of the Movement Against War and Fascism could not equate ignorance with patriotism.

Few if any Australians knew that the Nazis were exterminating Jewish people until late in 1944. The fact that the Jews were being persecuted had been known throughout the 1930s. Several important Australians criticised the Commonwealth government when it tried to help by letting a trickle of Jews take refuge here.

In the 1921 census almost 22 000 Australians described themselves as Jewish. This total was less than one half of one per cent of the population. During the 1920s, only another 2000 Jews came to Australia. Because of the depression, it was almost impossible for anyone to enter Australia. To get in, a person needed £550 and a close relative here already. When

this rule was eased, the Australian government admitted 500
refugees from Nazism a year. In 1938, this quota was increased
to 15 000 over the next three years. Before the outbreak of war,
some 7100 Jewish refugees had arrived.

Radicals thought that larger numbers of Jews should be
allowed in to save them from Nazism. Most Labor politicians
said they were sorry for the Jews but did not want them here
because there were not enough jobs for Australian workers. A
few Labor people attacked the Jews in much the same terms as
the Nazis used. Conservatives supported the government's
policy of admitting limited numbers but were unhappy about
any immigrant who was not British. A very noisy group
thought Hitler was doing the right thing and that the Jews
deserved whatever they got. Because Catholics saw Hitler as a
defence against communism, they were reluctant to show fascism in a bad light. Their spokespeople in Victoria opposed
Jewish immigrants and tried to play down the Nazi persecu-
tion. The most powerful opponents of Jewish immigrants
were the doctors, who tried to stop some of Europe's leading
medical men from practising here on the grounds that they
had not been properly trained.

Keeping refugees at bay was easier than preparing for an
armed onslaught. The virulence of Australia's opposition to
Japan immediately after the Great European War had died
away once German New Guinea and White Australia were
secure. Japan signed a Naval Agreement (1921) with Britain
and the United States to keep the tonnage of its warships down
to about one-third of the other two powers combined. The
fear that Japan would one day attack Australia remained. But
the feeling was abroad that 'we had merely to drink to the
Sydney and damnation to the *Emden*, to feel at once secure'.

Japan began armed action in Manchuria on 19 September
1931. Australia, concerned with economic worries, had cut
spending on defence by more than half. Although the government opposed Japan's actions, it was pleased that Japan had

moved west and not south. The more Japan got bogged down in China, the better for Australia.

Japan was not bogged down. Early in 1933, Tokyo left the League of Nations. This departure did not upset Australians, who had never been very keen on the League. In fact, Australia supported Japan's refusal to hand back the ex-German Pacific Islands. Canberra did not want the League to take New Guinea away. Japan's withdrawal from the 1921 Naval Agreement was more upsetting and Australia started to re-arm. Canberra also sent a goodwill mission to Japan in 1934. The change in outlook was summed up by a November 1933 Sydney newspaper headline: 'War with Japan is inevitable'.

Australia was back where it had been before the Great European War, chasing British and United States support against Japan. In this pursuit, Australian governments tried all manner of maneouvres. Sometimes they offered friendship to Japan, as in their 1937 call for a Pacific Pact. Sometimes they angered both Japan and the United States, as in the 1936 Trade Diversion Policy, which turned to Britain for imports. Always there was the demand for Britain to finish its Singapore naval base. As war in the Pacific came closer, Canberra sent its own ambassadors to Japan, China and the United States. No longer could Australia rely on Britain. Yet, without a firm promise of direct US support against Japan, Australia could not do without Britain. Although Australian policies from 1931 to 1942 look confused and contradictory, they had the continuing aim of finding a powerful ally against Japan.

1938: BINDING THE WOUNDS

On 26 January 1938, three months of celebration started for the 150th anniversary of the landing of Captain Arthur Phillip. Although supposedly a national occasion, the celebrations were largely confined to New South Wales. Even there, they were biased against the working class.

Australia-wide support was lacking not merely because Western Australia (1929), Victoria (1934) and South Australia (1936) had just celebrated their own foundation days. There was more to this inter-State rivalry than reluctance to praise the arrival of convicts. Under the shock of the depression, Federation suffered a number of blows. The most obvious was Western Australia's two-to-one vote early in 1934 to break away from the Commonwealth.

If Australian nationalism had been born at Gallipoli in 1915, it did not continue to keep Australians together. Other loyalties — to class, to region, to religion — broke up Australian sentiment until only the threat of external attack kept it alive. Inside Australia, national pride appeared as little more than the anger of writers and painters. They showed their discontent by giving first prize in the official competition for a great Australian novel to an attack on pioneering life, *Capricornia* by Xavier Herbert.

Even within New South Wales, voices were raised against the festivities. Aborigines objected to the re-play of Phillip's landing and several hundred met to protest against 'This festival of so-called "progress" ' which in fact 'commemorates

150 years of misery and degradation imposed upon the original native inhabitants by the white invaders of this country'. Disagreement was also clear in a call by the Sydney Trades and Labour Council for separate working-class celebrations. The small but vigilant Communist Party organised that alternative between Lenin's birthday and May Day.

So what was being celebrated? Not even the officials appeared certain. Why start on 26 January and conclude on 25 April? Did they still believe that the convict stain could be washed away only by the blood of Anzacs? Convict origins were publicly taboo. In reaction, Miles Franklin and Dymphna Cusack wrote *Pioneers on Parade* as a sharp attack on the desire of Australia's ruling classes to deny the convict origins of their families or their wealth.

Anzac traditions found an outlet in the stress on sport. The official film of the celebrations, *March to Nationhood*, described lifesavers at a surf carnival as 'knights of civilisation' and 'modern Vikings'. The youth parade carried this identification further when thousands of children performed pagan dances for wheat and the sun. This interest in Australia's vitality was supposed to warn off external enemies and to reverse our falling birth-rate. Political and social issues were never far away from even the most light-hearted activities. Examples from the poetry competition include:

> *Ye girls of British race*
> *Famous for your beauty*
> *Breed fast in all your grace*
> *For this is your duty.*
> *As Anzac gave in war*
> *So daughters at your call*
> *Will quick respond the more*
> *To replace those that fall.*

As an orgy and as a show, the celebrations were rather a success. At the official dinner in the Sydney Town Hall, thousands of distinguished guests were filled with oysters, turkey and Diplomat Pudding. For the rest, attendance figures at the Royal Easter Show went over a million for the first time. An outbreak of polio no more spoilt the general fun than the break-down of the air force float upset the Australia Day procession.

Still, there were few signs that Australia's divisions had been ended, either by the pleasure or by the propaganda. When the celebrations closed on Anzac Day, the acting Governor-General was still asking Australians 'to make a legal unity with heart and mind and to renounce State and class prejudices'. As Governor of Victoria, his words were of special importance because two leading soldiers, Sir Harry Chauvel and Sir Brudenell White, had just refused to take part in the Anzac service at the Melbourne Shrine because, out of politeness to Roman Catholics and Jews, Protestant prayers had been replaced by two minutes' silence. Memories of Irish disloyalty to the Empire continued to divide Australia.

The attempt at a national revival had extra importance in New South Wales. From the rail strike of 1917, through the rebellious conditions on the northern coalfields in 1930, to the near civil war between Langites and the New Guard in 1932, New South Wales had been bursting apart. Anger against British bankers had found voice during the 1932 bodyline cricket tour. In addition, 'Langism' still meant opposition to Canberra and to the Empire.

To be entirely successful the 150th anniversary needed to achieve three results: restore the bonds of Empire; bind up the wounds of class conflict; and show a united, active people to possible invaders. For these very reasons, convicts were played down for fear that they might recall some less pleasant bonds of Empire and thereby spotlight more recent social problems. That the organising committee failed in these aims is hardly surprising. Three years later not even the spectre of a Japanese invasion could establish them.

1939–1945
THE FIRST
PACIFIC WAR

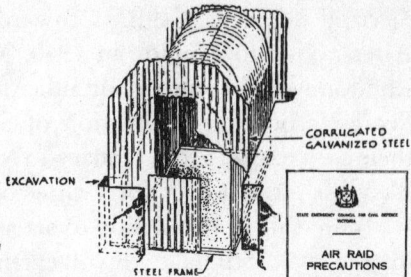

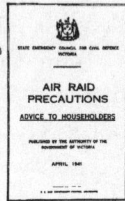

CORRUGATED
GALVANIZED STEEL

EXCAVATION

STEEL FRAME

STATE EMERGENCY COUNCIL FOR CIVIL DEFENCE
VICTORIA

AIR RAID
PRECAUTIONS

ADVICE TO HOUSEHOLDERS

PUBLISHED BY THE AUTHORITY OF THE
GOVERNMENT OF VICTORIA

APRIL 1941

Although the British Empire declared war on Nazi Germany on 3 September 1939, very little fighting took place until the following April. The shadow boxing, occasional dog fights and lightweight sparring of the first seven months led people to nickname this period 'the Phoney War'. France surrendered almost without a struggle on 22 June 1940. Not until Germany invaded the Soviet Union in June 1941 did massive land battles begin. Australia experienced its own 'phoney war'.

The making of the film *Dad Rudd, M.P.* was nearly over when the Second European War started in September 1939. The ending was rewritten so that 'Dad' could give a few patriotic words during his first parliamentary speech. Australia's leading comedian, 'Mo' (Roy Rene), did not have his contract renewed because the theatre owner thought that people would not go out as much. In fact, they went out more than ever. Prime Minister R. G. Menzies called for 'business as usual' to head off the economic slump that his government feared would follow the start of the war. Three weeks later, *Rydge's Business Journal* called capitalists on to patriotic effort by reminding them of the profits that had been made during the Great War. Business went on as usual. Fewer than 15 000 joined the three fighting services before the end of September. The phoney war was off to a flying start.

During the first year of the war, the Menzies government

directed its military efforts towards the defence of Britain. After a visit to London in 1940, Menzies doubted whether London would come to our aid. After the Japanese attack on Pearl Harbor, the population of Sydney took matters into their own hands. From January to March 1942, they built up a 'People's Army', with forty-three branches. Its aims were to: '1. Train civilian population to act as Auxiliaries in the case of invasion; 2. Stimulate involvement in Volunteer Defence Corps, etc.'

The president of this Army was the popular author Ion Idriess, who had been a soldier in the 1914–18 war. Years later, Idriess recalled:

> A crowd of us formed that nucleus of a defence force because at the time the enemy were expected to 'fall on Sydney from the skies!'. Parachute army; and we were informed that there was absolutely no defence for citizens, even soldiers on guard duty were mostly armed with dummy rifles, the armed forces would be away, barely armed at Lithgow, even our 1914–18 rifles had been hurried away to England. Our idea was that at least the government should arm us with rifles and sporting guns from all commercial stores so that at least we could give enemy parachutists in particular and beach landings as hot a time as possible before they could set our coastal towns afire. The idea developed swiftly.

The People's Army stopped growing because it had no weapons, because the government expanded the Volunteer Defence Corps, and because of the arrival of US forces.

Within a week of the Japanese attack on Pearl Harbor on 8 December 1941, the United States decided to use Australia as a base for supplying operations in the Philippines. In a New Year's message, Prime Minister John Curtin told Australians that they would have to smarten up if their white society were to survive. Looking overseas, he appealed to the Soviet Union for aid, hoping for a renewal of armed conflict between the Japanese militarists and the communists in Siberia. When US forces arrived in Australia their wealth contrasted sharply with local shortages. Beneath the upheavals, heartbreaks and excitements of the First Pacific War, some threads continued. Total war demanded total support from the civilian population, especially from workers who would not be tricked as easily a second time with promises of a 'land fit for heroes to live in' when the fighting finished. War brought forward social welfare reforms that had been promised for thirty years.

LIFE IN THE CITIES

When nearly 200 Sydney people were asked in 1941 if they thought that news reports on the war were true, about 40 per cent said 'No', while an equal percentage had doubts. Some of this disbelief carried over from the exposure of the lies that the Australian and British governments had pushed during the Great War. Doubts arose also because the newspapers printed reports that readers knew from their own lives to be false. In January 1941, a Melbourne journalist, Cecil Edwards, wrote an example in his diary:

> Minister for Supply Senator McBride said a union steward had been dismissed for preventing men speeding-up on war production. The union claimed the steward had drawn attention to the fact that a new man had been speeding-up with the result that much work had to be done again. Steward reinstated, and we hear no more about the wasted material. The editor suggests we should always place strike news alongside the casualty lists.

Public skepticism survived the Japanese thrust. The Department of Information put out propaganda under the slogan 'We've always despised them — NOW WE *MUST* SMASH THEM!' So great was the outcry at this racist attitude that the advertisements were withdrawn two weeks later.

Rationing of goods did not start until the middle of 1942. The delay was due partly to the time needed to print and give out ration cards and partly to the changed situation brought about by the entry of Japan and the United States into the war. Japan's conquest of Java meant that tea had to be rationed to

225 grams per person every five weeks, or about enough for two cups a day. Other items were in short supply because U-boats had sunk international shipping and thus cut imports to Australia. Some items were no longer being made in Australia because workers were put onto more important jobs. Other goods were made in greater volume but were needed by the fighting forces of Australia and by the half-million Americans who came in 1942. Yet other foodstuffs were being sent to Great Britain.

To make sure that everyone got a share and that no one was overcharged for scarce goods, the Commonwealth government brought in rationing and controlled prices. The need for price control can be seen from examples such as one included in a letter from a senior public servant to a relative in October 1939:

> I experienced a queer little instance of profiteering the other day. I paid 3/4 for a lb. of tea — then came the war and, immediately, it went up to 3/8. Nothing had happened in the meantime, and the tea had been in stock long before the war was even thought of.

Price control did not become effective until April 1943, by which time a great deal more profiteering had taken place. Towards the end of the war, a young poet, John Goss, voiced the anger which most people felt towards those who had done well out of the depression and were now growing rich from the war:

> *He made his millions from the people's bread.*
> *They paid him tribute; every hungry slice*
> *Was cut a little thinner by his price ...*
> *Sir William's wheat in William's ships was borne*
> *To mills that nothing ground but William's corn,*
> *And William's bakers kneaded every hour*
> *The loaves of Midas from Sir William's flour.*
> *He made his millions. Now Sir William's dead.*
> *But though beneath this stone his body lies*
> *His prosperous soul is busy in the skies.*
> *The Bread of Life exclusively he vends.*
> *And grinds the Mills of God for his own ends.*

By mid-1944, severe drought further restricted each person to 60 grams of tea, 450 grams of sugar, 170 grams of butter and 1 kilogram of meat each week. Sausages, fish, poultry and bacon were not rationed. Special arrangements were made for young children, pregnant women and the sick. The purchase of each piece of clothing needed a given number of 'coupons': thirteen for a dress, six for a hat, and twelve for a shirt. Detachable collars became popular again. Increased industrial production strained the power supply. Hence, daylight saving was introduced from 1 January 1942 for the summer months of 1942, 1943 and the first half of 1944. Paddle steamers, manned by Italian prisoners of war, carried timber down the Murray to help overcome Melbourne's fuel shortages.

The use of Australia as a refitting station for US troops transformed the economy. Construction of Beaufort bombers and Mustang fighters, the mass production of small arms, notably the Owen submachine gun, and the fashioning of precision instruments and machine tools required more skilled trades. Education would be changed to meet their requirements.

Disruptions to the daily life of Australian children did not start until the 1942 school year. Bombs, fear of invasion and tens of thousands of American troops caused the upheaval. The army took over several inner-city state high schools, along with some private boarding schools. Queensland held up the re-opening of all schools in the northern coastal districts until trenches could be dug in the grounds. When these schools re-opened, children under six were not admitted; compulsory attendance was not enforced again until October 1944. Only 4500 children were touched by these requirements. Very many more were upset when mothers and children were sent away from coastal areas likely to be bombed, to the greater safety of inland towns. The arrival of these extra students strained the already overloaded bush schools. The demand for correspondence lessons increased, although mothers had less time to watch over them, either because they had to do their own housework or because they were doing war work.

Despite wartime upheavals, major education reforms came in New South Wales and Tasmania. Homework was cut for very young children, the role of inspectors restricted and the leaving age raised.

HEALTH

One scheme for improving children's diet was the 'Oslo lunch', so called because it had been developed in Norway by Dr Carl Schiotz in 1932. A six-month trial in Australia started in September 1940. Fifty primary school pupils in Collingwood (Vic.) were chosen at random. For lunch each day they were given three slices of wholemeal bread, well spread with butter and cheese; half a pint of milk; half an ounce of wheat hearts, and an orange. The improvement was remarkable. The children in the trial gained more than twice as much weight as other children, they had more energy, fewer colds and minor ailments, and their cuts and scratches healed quickly and no longer became scabby sores. The main lack in the Australian diet had been Vitamin B1, which the wheat hearts and wholemeal bread supplied. After this experiment, 'Oslo lunches' were adopted by mothers' committees throughout Australia, almost as a compulsory part of school life. This reform was no more than a first step towards overcoming the neglect that the depression of the 1930s had merely made worse.

Alongside improved nutrition, powerful drugs came into general use. A small, separate radium clinic opened at Sydney's Prince Alfred Hospital, which had been using radiotherapy for skin conditions since 1900. The same hospital had started electrocardiography for heart diseases six years later. Although insulin had been discovered in 1921, it was not widely given to diabetic patients until the early 1930s. People's ignorance had to be overcome before diabetes was seen as a disease. An education campaign, for sufferers and the public alike, was launched around a 1936 film called *So I'm a Diabetic*. Deaths from tetanus fell by nearly 50 per cent once injections were given for most serious cuts and abrasions.

The greatest breakthrough was the development of 'sulpha' drugs against pneumonia and all manner of infections. The drugs revolutionised medicine. For instance, they halved the death-rate of women from childbirth. Doctors acquired those magical powers that 'quacks' had always claimed and that the profession had long desired. As an example of what became possible, take the case of a 76-year-old South Australian, Samuel Worst, who fell off the roof of his son's house in 1954 and broke his neck, his collar bone and some ribs. After being moved 260 miles (420 kilometres) to the Nuriootpa Hospital he got pneumonia and it was found that a rib had pierced his lung. Such extensive injuries in so old a person would have been fatal before the 'wonder drugs'. Worst lived on to ninety years of age.

ABORIGINES

The main impact of the Pacific War on the Aboriginal population was through jobs on construction projects in northern and central Australia. Full award wages were paid, the work was constant, adequate housing was provided and health standards were enforced. The government showed that the pastoralists' claim that Aborigines were poor workers who deserved low wages was untrue. According to Charles Rowley, the war in the Pacific 'may be taken as indicating the end of the process of destruction of Aboriginal society'.

This turnaround could not mean that every difficulty was improved at once. For example, in 1941 Western Australia tightened its Native Administration Act to stop Aborigines moving south of the 20th parallel, known as the 'leper line'. Constant employment and high wages made the Aborigines attractive customers for the shopkeepers of small country towns. In addition, social service payments were made to most detribalised Aborigines from 1941 to 1944. This spending power, however, did not make the Indigenous people welcome as citizens. At Katanning (WA), one day a week was set aside for them to shop.

Joining the army did not bring Aborigines all the rights enjoyed by white troops. They were often denied drinks in hotels. There were several reports of Aborigines expressing delight at the idea of a Japanese victory. The army believed that, after 150 years of European ill-treatment, Aborigines might be less than enthusiastic about the war effort. So in June 1942 a Special Mobile Force rounded up all unemployed Aborigines from the Midlands (WA) and gaoled them as 'possible potential enemies'. Meanwhile, Aboriginal men such as fighter pilot Len Walters were joining the battle for Australia.

VIEW OF THE WORLD

The troop of cowboys and Indians that starred at Sydney's 1939 Royal Easter Show gave notice of the American occupation of Australia three years later. By the time the battle of the Coral Sea had been fought in May 1942, the initial feelings of thanks towards the US soldiers were being mixed with other emotions:

> They saved us from the Japs,
> Perhaps;
> But the place is at present too Yankful
> For us to be decently thankful.

The concern was not so much that they were 'over here' as that they were 'over-paid' and apparently 'over-sexed'. While the Australian basic wage was £4 13s 0d a week and Australian troops earned 6s 6d a day, GIs were paid £15 a week. Taxi drivers could not see anyone not in American uniform: in Brisbane, one woman finally got home from the hospital with her new-born baby only because a passing GI hailed a cab, put her in it and paid the driver treble in advance. Yet a soldier's kindness could not do much about problems such as those in Townsville where people were unable to buy ice for their kitchens because it was all going to cool water for US officers' baths.

Presents for girlfriends included stockings (the first nylons), orchids and frangipani posies with their stems in silver paper. Australian men complained and fought back, but Australian women appreciated this polite lovemaking, at least before marriage. Despite some outward increases in sexual freedom, the law and the newspapers showed few signs of change. The press had a full range of phrases which they used instead of referring directly to sexual activities: 'capital offence' for rape, 'certain condition' for pregnancy, 'women of a certain class' for prostitutes, and 'night attire' for pyjamas. Even the divorce reports in the cheap weeklies such as *Truth* used the Latin words *flagrante dilecto*, which gave ordinary sexual actions a largely undeserved excitement.

Early in 1942, the Australian government protested to the United States about Negro GIs being sent to Australia. The reply was to the point: 'If you ask for help you'll take what you're given'. MacArthur promised to keep the Negroes out of the big cities. By the end of the year, half of the 7000 Negro troops in Australia were in or around Mt Isa. To reduce sexual contact between the races, the American army set up Negro-only brothels in North Queensland, but staffed by Australians. One prostitute's bank balance rose by £3800 in less than a year. For a short while in 1944, a leave centre for Negroes operated in Sydney but caused such an outcry that it was transferred to New Guinea. Australians were fussy about whom we would let save us from the Yellow Peril.

Diplomatic contact was not easily established from the US side. Late in 1942 President Roosevelt wanted to send a political friend, Ed Flynn, as ambassador to Australia. This appointment was unpopular in both countries, where he was confused with the ex-Tasmanian film star Errol Flynn, who was facing a carnal knowledge charge at the time. Ed Flynn was the victim of growing American opposition to Roosevelt and was accused of stealing public funds. In the first such move in more than fifty years, the US Senate refused to approve Flynn's appointment.

From the beginning of this phase of US involvement with Australia, some Australians, such as the anti-conscriptionist member of parliament Maurice Blackburn, knew that 'Friendship did not bring Americans to Australia'; 'they are here because it is a convenient base for operations against Japan'. By early 1945, official Australian newsreels of the war complained that the rest of the world did not know of the feats of Australian troops in the Pacific because some unnamed ally was taking all the credit.

Japanese thrusts

Japan's attack on Pearl Harbor came as no surprise to Australians who had expected something like it for nearly fifty years. Most felt safe until two days later when the Imperial Japanese Navy sank the *Prince of Wales* and the *Repulse*. Panic set in. The attack on the Americans could be good for Australia. Defeat of the Royal Navy presaged disaster. Singapore was in danger. In the middle of February, that impregnable fortress surrendered to the Japanese. By this time, bombs had already fallen on Port Moresby. On 19 February 1942, four days after the fall of Singapore, bombs fell for the first time on Australian soil when Darwin was attacked for the first of sixty-four times. The last raid took place on 12 November 1943. During those twenty-one months, the Japanese bombed nine other towns: Broome (WA) was hit four times and Townsville (Qld) three times. The raid on Darwin startled Australians and sparked arguments about courage and cowardice, which a Royal Commission did nothing to stop.

What happened on the morning of 19 February 1942 is clear enough in outline. Two air raids took place. The first came at 10 am and the second at 11.55 am. The first raid was wide-ranging. The town area of Darwin, its docks and airport were all attacked. The second raid was confined to the airfields. Damage was extensive. At least 250 people were killed, including 53 civilians. Between 300 and 400 were injured. Six ships were totally destroyed and three others severely damaged. Half of those killed were on two of the ships. Nearly twenty planes were totally demolished, half of them on the ground. Government offices in the town were also completely wiped out except for a few rooms in the civilian hospital and at Government House. The Japanese lost a handful of aircraft. For the Japanese it was a complete victory.

The reasons for the attack are equally clear. The Japanese wanted to knock out the only possible base from which their enemies could launch a counter-offensive into the Netherlands East Indies. The raids were pre-emptive attacks, not the start of an invasion, an interdiction, not the prelude to an onslaught.

The response of the Australian defenders was much more confused. For a start, many of the locals had been dissatisfied with the way the Northern Territory was being run. In 1919 these grievances had led to the overthrow of the Administrator and to the appointment of a Royal Commission. In 1941 the Administrator was a former anti-Labor cabinet minister, C. L. A. Abbott, who was unpopular with the workers.

As soon as news of Pearl Harbor reached Darwin, the authorities became active, holding their first air-raid alert three days later. This exercise provoked a confrontation between the citizens and the Administrator. A deputation forced Abbott to wire Canberra to arrange for the women and children to leave Darwin. Approval came the same day and by the end of January 1000 women and 900 children had gone south. Another 300 left before the raid, by which time only sixty-five white women remained in town. Before this evacuation, Abbott had annoyed the locals by placing controls on petrol, beer and food. On Australia Day, all the civil defence wardens resigned in protest. They complained that the civil defence plans involved using Boy Scouts as runners, even though there were no longer any Scouts in town.

As the Japanese planes passed over Melville Island at 9.30 am, the missionaries there sent a message which, if acted upon, would have given Darwin twenty minutes warning. The Air Force did not react because false alarms had lowered morale. The siren was sounded by the Naval Station staff after they saw bombs falling on them. Some men stuck to their posts. Others moved to positions of extreme defence, one soldier reaching Melbourne in time to read of the appointment of a Royal Commission twelve days after the raid.

The Commissioner, Mr Justice Lowe, heard seventy witnesses in Darwin and another thirty in Melbourne before reporting on 27 March 1942. He did not take evidence from Abbott, who had moved his administration, along with his china plates and silverware, to Alice Springs. Lowe was very critical of the officers in charge of the RAAF station, who were replaced. He was also less than happy with Abbott's performance, but this criticism did not prevent Abbott's staying on as Administrator until 1946.

Meanwhile, the Japanese had failed to secure Port Moresby by sea. Early in May 1942 United States and Australian aircraft clashed with Japanese planes over the Coral Sea. Their warships never sighted each other. In terms of tonnage sunk, victory went to the Japanese. In terms of pilots lost, the battle ran in favour of the Allies. However the outcome is calculated, the Japanese did not see the Battle of the Coral Sea as a check. That perception would not strike until June at Midway. Certainly, the outcome in May did not cause the Japanese to abandon plans to invade Australia. Invasion had never been part of their strategy.

Papua New Guinea

Although Australia had argued in 1919 for annexing German New Guinea as a first line of defence against a possible Japanese attack, very little had been done to arm either New Guinea or Papua. So, in July 1939, the Lieutenant-Governor of Papua, Sir Hubert Murray, wrote to his daughter:

> We are up to our neck in preparations for a Japanese invasion. They have worked out an elaborate Defence Scheme which we have to put into force. It is a fine piece of work, but has little relation to reality. For instance, one of the Government Secretary's duties is to look after the carrier pigeons, and an anticipated advance on Kokoda from Buna is to be opposed by a Company of Infantry with Machine guns. And so forth. We have pointed out to the Defence Department that we cannot carry out all these things — but they reply by telling us to carry out as many as we can.

When war came to New Guinea in 1942, the Japanese almost reached Port Moresby after a heroic drive across the island.

Australians liked to think of the Papuan carriers on the Kokoda Trail and elsewhere as 'fuzzy-wuzzy angels' who willingly accepted heavy loads to help their white friends. Papuans had other memories. Patrol officers told the Papuans that the Japanese were evil. Albert Maori Kiki pointed out that his people had quite different ideas about the Japanese:

> They thought that 'Japanese', 'German' and 'kiavari' (helpful spirit of a dead person) all sounded much the same. The Japanese, then, were the Germans of the First World War, and were our dead relatives making another attempt to come to us and bring us cargo. They had returned once more in a new disguise. Little or no attempt was made to tell Papuans what the war was about. The official newspaper for Papuans came up with the comparison that bombs 'were like cassowary eggs, only bigger'.

Recruiting of Papuans was supposed to be voluntary, but the Australians used violence to stop carriers leaving and to keep them working. A song, which was still being sung in the 1970s, ended:

> The white man has brought his war to be fought on this land;
> His King and Queen have said so.
> We are forced against our wishes to help him.

Throughout the war, carriers for the Australians were given poor clothes and food. One village group remembered getting two or three navy biscuits and a tin full of rice each day. After the war, they were paid between £7 and £13 for two years carrying. The money they received from Americans for carvings was confiscated on the grounds that it must be stolen, as were any gifts from Australians whom they had helped.

In the late 1960s, a teacher from the University of Papua New Guinea, Ulli Beier, spoke to surviving carriers from one village:

> About two-thirds of the men spoken to made at least one attempt to escape. The carriers often held meetings to discuss plans for escape, but only some plucked up the courage. Reasons for wanting to escape were given as follows: poor food, sore shoulders from carrying, beatings, cold, bombs.

If a man did escape, his sons would be threatened with recruitment in his place and so the father had to return, usually to a beating as well:

> The most terrifying punishments remembered were the so-called drum beatings in Kerema. These were carried out by the district office clerk, and were allegedly ordered by the District Officer. A fire was lit in a 44-gallon drum and when it was hot the unlucky carriers were put across the drum and beaten.

Considering the way that settlers had treated Papuans before the war and how they were treated during it, it is no wonder that they had little enthusiasm for the white man's war. The impact of the war did not cease with the end of fighting in August 1945. The Australians had to manage 150 000 prisoners. Papuans were conscripted to help. The vegetable gardens were besieged by snails that the Japanese had introduced to help their forces live off the land. These invaders evolved into giants with armour-like shells. Their combined weight was enough to topple pawpaw trees as they searched for food. To get rid of them, they had to be collected by hand, put into huge drums and drowned in salt water for twenty-four hours.

8 1946–1953 RECONSTRUCTION

Between the 1880s and the 1950s, the hopes of a majority of the Australian people had been met for only two brief periods. One of these interludes had been just before the Great European War. The other was a moment early in the 1920s. Most of the fifty-five years from 1890 to 1945 were marred by depression, drought or war. The years following the First Pacific War brought progress and enthusiasm, yet they were not easy going. The threat of a new war loomed, this time with atomic bombs.

Winning the First Pacific War required promises to rebuild Australia. A Department of Post-War Reconstruction was set up in 1942, although almost nothing had been destroyed by the war. Rather, factories had expanded. Australia moved into a new stage of development. Yet, because so much had been left undone since the 1880s, there was more than enough to keep everyone busy. The key projects were the Snowy Mountains scheme to supply electricity for nuclear weapons and for the industrialisation that would guarantee full employment despite immigration. So important were these developments that, although the Liberal and Country parties had opposed them at first, they kept them going after they defeated the Chifley Labor government late in 1949.

The new Menzies government lifted most of the controls on the economy. Then it failed to manage the boom from the

Korean War. During 1950, the cost of living went up by 16 per cent. A year later, employers complained of a 'Starvation Christmas'. In March 1952, the *Chartered Accountant* noted that Australians 'have almost imperceptibly moved into a position where the idea of a depression has begun to be a topic of conversation'. By May, half the people felt worse off than twelve months before. The Menzies era of 'free enterprise' had got off to a terrible start. The ALP opposition was the clear winner at the half Senate election in 1953.

WORK

All through the Pacific War, Australia's Labor government thought about the kind of Australia it wanted once the fighting was over. Its leaders knew that people would not fight the new war wholeheartedly if they could not look forward to a future brighter than the 1920s and 1930s. From 1945, workers again fought for a better deal. Long and bitter strikes erupted, especially in the railways, on the waterfronts and at the coal-mines.

The government said that its aim was 'full employment'. In practice, it hoped that unemployment would be less than 5 per cent of the workforce. If this level were to be achieved, the economy would have to be transformed. Australia could no longer rely on selling primary products to pay for its industrial imports. Instead, industrialisation would need electrical power and more workers from assisted immigration.

New Australians

British immigrants had been helped to come to Australia in the past but never on as large a scale as was planned in the 1940s. Each year would add one new arrival for every hundred Australians. These 70 000 people a year would be more than twice as many as had come at any time since the 1850s. In 1950, 170 000 immigrants arrived, 100 000 more than had been expected. The government cut the intake back to below 80 000 a year until it could cope with the larger numbers.

One result of this influx was that newcomers were not well looked after. Most Australians thought that immigrants should be happy to be here at all. No matter how rough conditions were for them, they were much better off here than they had been in Britain or Europe. Hostility showed in the names that Australians called the immigrants: 'reffos' for refugees, and 'Balts' for East Europeans. In an effort to ease the tension, the government decided that the official name for immigrants would be 'New Australians'.

Although people were coming to Australia from many countries and for diverse reasons, individual stories offer some idea of common experiences. An English woman, married to a carpenter, with a five-year-old child and a one-year-old baby, left England in April 1949. Her husband was tied to the Victorian State Electricity Commission, which promised him a house and a job. They decided to emigrate when her husband borrowed a copy of the Melbourne *Age* from a workmate who had already decided to go:

> We were fascinated by some of the advertisements, particularly those regarding foodstuffs and the 'positions vacant' columns, and from this arose our feeling that it might be to our children's advantage to emigrate. The first thing we both remember of Australia was standing outside a butcher's shop in Fremantle, and gazing open-mouthed at the quantity of meat in the window: we had been accustomed to a very small meat ration, and it hardly seemed possible there was so much meat in the world as we saw in that window. The next thing, of course, was the fact that clothes could be bought without coupons, and we had a good spending spree.

The couple had been shown photographs of Yallourn by officials at Australia House in London. She later found out that these snaps were of the older parts of the town and not the new areas where her house was: 'We were more than horrified to find ourselves in East Newborough, knee deep in mud, with no roads, footpaths, street lights, sewerage, shops, schools, doctors, or halls in our area'. With the help of her new neighbours, she formed a Tenants' Association, and battled to improve conditions and to organise social activities: 'The interest we have in Australia stems largely from the fact that we feel we have helped to make one small portion of it grow'.

A Polish woman described in detail the conditions on many of the early immigrant ships. The crew were helpful but could do nothing about the overcrowding:

> There were 60 women and children to a room. Men were much better off because they were alone while we had to look after the children. Besides, the women had to clean the cabins, shower-rooms, toilets and corridors and to wash and iron, so they had very little time left. The food was very bad and there was not enough fresh water, so that on the Red Sea it was turned on only three times a day, one hour at a time. The heat and the shortage of water were driving us mad. At night, one could not breathe in the cabins. Mothers were fanning their children who, although completely undressed were crying, gasping for air. The bed-sheets were saturated, the ventilators did not work and we were in despair. We were not allowed to remain on deck after 11 pm.

These ships were scraped together from what was left afloat after the war. During the 1950s, most immigrants came on a better class of ship. In the 1960s, many were flown out by Qantas.

The reason for bringing immigrants here was so that they could work. Until 1951, many were told what they had to do and where they had to go. An engineer from Latvia told how he signed a contract agreeing to work for two years in any job in any place chosen by the Australian Employment Office:

> After three weeks the Employment Office put me to work at SEC in Yallourn. For the two years under contract, that is, the first two years in Australia, I worked as a labourer. When my contract expired I first worked as a surveyor's assistant and then as head of the Building Section's laboratory.

Highly trained people were forced into unskilled jobs. University professors and leading musicians from Europe worked in forestry camps. At the other extreme, Jurek, a Polish migrant, spent his first two years in Australia in an iron foundry. Then he became a jam salesman. On a trip to Cooma, he took a job with the Snowy Mountains Authority as a hydrologist. He told the Authority that he knew nothing about the work, but they needed men and said they would train him.

The Snowy

On 17 October 1949, the Governor-General set off the first explosion in the Snowy Mountains scheme. The plan was for fifteen power stations, 220 kilometres of tunnels, 400 kilometres of water diversions, seven major and twelve smaller dams. The first stage was completed in 1955 when the Guthega power station started feeding electricity into New South Wales. The next stage was the Adaminaby dam which began to fill two years later; it eventually held eight times as much water as Sydney Harbour. This project was the largest single undertaking in Australian history. It supplied water to farms and power to factories. The authorities recognised its potential in creating plutonium for nuclear weapons. Explaining the scheme to parliament, the Minister for Works had said that Australia would need four million tons of coal, or 547 million gallons of oil, to produce the same amount of electric power each year as would be available from the Snowy. All the major aspects were finished by the early 1970s.

Great as the engineering works became, they needed men and women. Five thousand men, most of them emigrants from more than thirty countries, worked there. Some had their wives and families with them, living in townships such as Island Bend and Cabramurra, which had been built for them. Others lived alone or in the work camps. Major Clews, a surveyor, had come from England thirty-seven years before he started work with the Snowy Mountains Authority (SMA) in 1950. Clews had left the army to build a shack in the Blue

Mountains, miles away from anywhere. He agreed to give five years to the Snowy. Island Bend was too big for his comfort and he preferred a tent with timber sides for the winter.

Specialists came with firms that had contracts to build parts of the system. For instance, 400 Norwegians arrived in 1951 to help build Guthega. Others were picked by a team sent to Britain and Europe which were still suffering from the war. Thousands were anxious to come, but they had to be checked to make sure they were not war criminals or communists. A German couple who heard of the scheme asked to join:

> *Dear Sir,*
> *I and my wife have tried to emigrate to Australia previously. There is living in our village a man whose daughter resides in Canberra. She rang her father last Christmas-time, all the way from Canberra, and of course, such a long-distance call made great local news, and was reported in our district press. We read about it, and wrote to [the man's daughter] to sponsor our coming to Australia. So far she has been unsuccessful. It is a matter of housing. Perhaps you would help us.*
> > *Werner Rauch.*

At first the men had to leave their wives and children in Europe. If they stayed on when their two-year contracts were over, the Authority would lend them the money to bring their families to join them. The men refused to wait two years and they forced their employer to lend them half the fare if they put up the other £60. Families started arriving during 1952.

Because of opposition to the scheme, the SMA rushed to finish one sector as a showpiece to convince the public and the politicians of its worth. This rush meant that almost no attention was given to the men's living and working conditions, which were rough and hard. In 1951, there was no doctor in Island Bend. A vet treated the men for their recurrent laryngitis. The SMA did not employ social workers to help the immigrants, who were not taught English, or anything about Australia on the ships coming over.

Mona Ravenscroft, a sociologist who lived on the Snowy for six months in the mid-1950s, wrote up her researches in a book *Men of the Snowy Mountains*. In a letter to a friend she explained that when she started her survey she had false notions about the Snowy, which she quickly shed:

> I had believed that a project as great as the Snowy Mountains Scheme, expending in the long run more than four hundred million pounds, would throw up at least two worthwhile communities of permanent use after the actual building of the scheme was finished. I also believed that it would be the Australian Government's policy to co-operate with the workers on the scheme in encouraging the human values associated with it. Living in the Snowy made me aware of the glamorous facade that surrounds the scheme, and I realised that I had entertained a misguided idealism.

Churches and communities were not part of the SMA's building program. No money had been set aside for social activities. The workers and their wives had to provide those services for themselves.

Working conditions were no better. Because so much of the work was new, there were no set wages for many jobs. A new group of workers appeared — PNECs, persons not elsewhere classified. When the Arbitration Court came to the Snowy, a union leader said: 'I saw Judge Foster walk across the mud. He was perfectly dressed; I hadn't had time to brush up. I felt he could never understand the way we felt and work'. By working overtime, a man could earn £40 a week after tax, which was almost three times as much as workers elsewhere. Whether it was the high wages or the people's own community spirit that kept them working, very few strikes occurred on the Snowy during its twenty-five years.

Eight hours' rest

One of the proudest boasts of Australian working men in the nineteenth century had been their achievement of the eight-hour day. Not everyone had won it, and those who did benefit still worked a 48-hour week. In the 1920s a 44-hour week came, and went, in some industries. The working week was cut to forty hours in 1948. This reduction provided most workers with a two-day weekend. Those still obliged to work on Saturdays were in businesses servicing the public, such as banks, shops and post offices.

Although weekly hours of work had fallen from forty-eight to forty in twenty years, most workers did not have more time at home or for leisure. Because of the higher cost of living, more people sought overtime, or had two jobs. In addition, people needed longer to get to work. In the 1920s, most Australians had lived within a couple of kilometres of their jobs, or could get there with one public transport trip. From the 1950s, it became more common for people to travel for up to an hour each way. As poorer people moved further out of the big cities in search of cheaper land, they also moved further away from their workplaces, and further from public transport. Daily train trips of twenty or thirty kilometres were possible. To work in Sydney, some people came each day from Gosford, Katoomba or Wollongong. Driving a car through peak-hour traffic became another source of stress.

Paid holidays did not become widespread until after the 1930s when metal unions won a fortnight's leave. By 1949, eight out of ten workers had some paid holidays. The proportion among unskilled and farm labourers, however, was only six out of ten. At that time, only one-half of the population could afford to go away for a holiday. They stayed at guesthouses, visited their relations, or camped at the beach. During 1953 half the population went away for two weeks, and another quarter for three.

Motoring was the usual means of travel. As car ownership spread, more people travelled, perhaps with a caravan instead of the tent. Queensland soon became the most popular destination. In 1952, Queensland had thirty-six caravan parks, with two hundred more in preparation. Outside the cities, garages and petrol stations remained few and far between. Australians on the road needed maps, took colour slides and bought blocks of ice from automatic dispensers. Most of all, the drivers needed roads. Long stretches were hardly even bush tracks. Even the main highways were single-lane, with more potholes than signposts. Hotel construction expanded from the mid-1950s after almost twenty years of none being built. The Chevron opened at Surfers Paradise just in time for the prison gates to close on its promoter, Stanley Korman.

Women's work

Women, like men, are brought into the workforce when their labour power is needed and expelled from it when their labour is no longer required. Their preferences remain secondary. The failure of women to enter the workforce in large numbers before 1940 had been another part of the inability of capitalism to find work for even the male breadwinners. When women were needed, propaganda poured out calling them to get away from dull housework. Once they were no longer required, the propaganda was full of the joys of home life.

The *Australian Women's Weekly* played its part in forming attitudes to women and work. The magazine had started in 1933, selling hundreds of thousands of copies each issue. In its early days, the *Weekly* supported a more liberated woman. This approach flipped over to endorsing the woman as wife and mother. This view changed again with the First Pacific War. Even then, women were told to get behind their men, not to compete with them.

Large numbers of women were called into factory work during this war. In 1939, only 574 of the 5055 employees in government munitions factories were women; by 1943, there were 22 548 out of 54 758. This total had fallen to 2166 out of 12 413 three years later.

As soon as the war ended, the *Women's Weekly* found a new job for women as homemakers. Returning soldiers would once more enjoy 'children's laughter and the sight of a small sleepy head upon a pillow — an armchair by the fire and clean sheets — tea in the kitchen and a woman's tenderness no longer edged by unspoken fears'. Not all women wanted to return to their old situation. One short story in another magazine ended with the wife telling her husband: 'Well Jim, I've got a union meeting tonight, so I'll leave you to wash the dishes. And then see the babies are in bed by eight'. To combat this independence, the *Weekly* published stories such as 'Albert — Le Petit Lapin'. 'Albert' was a rabbit in a story written by Wendy who gave up her job as an advertising copywriter to marry her work-mate, Peter. Peter knew that Wendy was better at her job than he was at his: 'Not that I'd tell her that, mind you'. Wendy's serial became popular and she argued with Peter to let her go on writing:

> A little extra money would come in handy. You never know when there'll be three or four of us to provide for, and I don't see why I shouldn't do my share. After all, the house is so modern that there's hardly a thing to do, and, besides, I have really wonderful ideas. Just because you married me and put me up in a home, does not say I have stopped thinking up ideas.

Peter was jealous and wanted to be fussed over full-time. Yet he felt that his attitude was not quite right and did not tell Wendy to stop until his boss ordered him to have 'Albert' killed off because its popularity was hurting the business of one of the advertising firm's customers, Freeman Rabbit Traps Ltd. This excuse was the escape Wendy had been waiting for. She sighed: 'Yes Peter. I didn't know you could be so masterful'. She then told him that she was going to have a baby. Peter's life was complete.

Not everyone could afford to stay home. A mother of four told the *Women's Weekly* in 1951 that, when 'things started getting dearer and dearer, I started to get nervy, and giddy turns and blackouts'. Her doctor advised her 'to get part-time work and get my mind off not having enough money'.

LIFE IN THE CITIES

Not many new houses had been built in Australia from the beginning of the depression in 1930 to the end of the Pacific War in 1945. The arrival of tens of thousands of New Australians added to the shortage. Many people had to live in slums, in ex-army camps, in tents or in temporary dwellings, which were usually made from fibro. Amateur builders found fibro-cement walls cheap, available and easy to put up. The percentage of Australia's houses with fibro-cement walls rose from 2 per cent in 1933 to 6 per cent in 1946 and 12 per cent in 1954; by 1961 they were one-sixth (17%) of all dwellings.

Tiles, bricks and clay pipes were in short supply and were often second-rate because they were being produced on machinery installed in the 1920s. Under the Labor government, prices of building materials were controlled. After 1949, the Menzies government removed the last of these restrictions and the cost of a private house doubled. In December 1949, a man in Brisbane paid £1100 for a 70 square metre weatherboard and fibro dwelling. A year later, his best friend paid £1900 for a slightly smaller but otherwise similar place. They were the lucky ones who could afford a new house and could find a builder to put it up for them.

Others built their own at weekends. This do-it-yourself approach brought changes to the shape of suburban homes. Flat roofs and box-like floor plans were easier for the amateur. When extra rooms were added later, these homes started to look like the letters of the alphabet: L-shapes, T-shapes and U-shapes were common. There were even S-, O-, Z-, and W-shaped ones.

New Australians had special problems getting a house because they had to start completely from scratch. A Polish couple found it very difficult to save money after the husband was sent to work in the bush where there was no room for his wife and children:

My husband came home only for weekends. He was not earning much and it was very expensive to keep two houses. For a whole year I had to live in camps. Only after a year did my husband find a room in a private house for which we had to pay £2/2/6 per week. On top of that I had to work without pay: laundering, ironing, cleaning and looking after children. The landlady treated me almost as her property merely because she let us the room for which we were paying.

To get away from this house, the family bought a block of land. With the help of friends, they put up a two-roomed bungalow in six weeks. After another six years, they got a loan from the bank and started to build their own four-roomed house:

> The building took my husband a year and a half. He worked in his spare time and I was his only help, for there was no money to hire anybody else. It was hard work. We had no rest and no pleasures. I moved into the house when it was not quite finished. Inside, we have not much furniture because we are still paying off the bank. Besides, there are improvements to the property to be made and prices are very high today. After paying the bills nothing remains from my husband's earnings.

In the big cities, it was just as hard to find a house. Young couples with families crowded into single rooms in the inner-city slums.

Conditions in these areas were brought to public notice early in 1947 when Ruth Park won the *Sydney Morning Herald*'s fiction competition with her novel *The Harp in the South*. The newspaper serialised her story, which told of everyday life in Surry Hills but did not please everybody. Protests poured in from people who lived in comfortable homes on Sydney's North Shore. They claimed that it was wicked to write novels saying that Australia was not perfect. One letter-writer alleged that *The Harp in the South* was 'a wallow in depravity, filth, and crime, playing down to the lowest-minded readers'. To find out the views of people who lived in Surry Hills, a *Sydney Morning Herald* reporter spoke

to forty locals. Sixteen had never heard of the novel. The fourteen who were following it day-by-day were almost all enthusiastic in their praise. Asked what she thought about living in
Surry Hills, an elderly widow replied:

> I've got a pension of 32/6 a week. The rent's 12/6 (two rooms and
> a kitchen). Grocer's bill is seven bob [shillings]. No bugs since the
> house was repapered and had new floorings two years ago after a
> rat plague. There's gaslight down here — penny in the slot, I take a
> lamp upstairs. I've got no bath but I manage to wash all right.
> Quite a lot of places in the district have got both, but there's not a
> bathroom in this street except for what some have made for them-
> selves in their backyard.

Baths and bugs were common topics of conversation. A
working man pointed to his baby's arm: 'See those marks.
Bugs. I spray the beds every week with kero, but they come
back'. A returned soldier, with two children, liked the novel
but thought it would do good only 'if it's followed up by
someone with influence about slum clearing'. A young mother
also enjoyed the story; she pointed out 'there's bits in it that
made me think. Our kids ought to have a playground, for one
thing'.

Living a long way away from the inner-city slums was the
1948 winner of the *Australian Women's Weekly* competition
for the most economical yet nutritious menu on which to feed
a couple with two children. The successful entrant, Mrs Keith
Morris, of East Malvern, Victoria, identified herself by her
husband's given name. Her weekly menu included two meals
of rabbit, two of nut loaf, and one of liver. Evening meals finished with a homemade cake or pudding. Breakfasts always
included fruit, porridge, meat or egg, with milk for the children and coffee for the adults. The Morrises graced their home
with an old piano, his oil paintings, and shelves of Everyman
classics, poetry and travel books. They used some of her £1000
prize to buy a new piano and a refrigerator. Although they
rented, they would not use any of their windfall to purchase a

place of their own because he was a bank clerk who would be moved between branches anywhere in the State. They were the 'Forgotten People' at whom R. G. Menzies had directed the Liberal Party that he had launched in 1944–45. Menzies appealed to the middle class who, he believed, 'provides more than perhaps any other the intellectual life which marks us off from the beast: the life which finds room for literature, for the arts'. While Mrs Morris devised her menu, Mr Morris would have been knocking on doors to explain to his neighbours the evil of the bank nationalisation proposed by the Chifley Labor government. Nor did the Morrises plan to buy a motor car.

Cars

Before the Pacific war, Australia had imported almost all its cars, assembling some here and making quite a few of the bodies. Australia's ten most popular automobiles in 1937 had been Chevrolet, Ford Canadian, Vauxhall, Morris, Chrysler/ Plymouth, Dodge, Austin, Oldsmobile, Pontiac and Buick. Together, they accounted for three-quarters of the new registrations. In the late 1940s, the major change was a swing from US to British designs, because Australia could not afford the necessary dollars for imports. For a time there was a total ban on importing cars from the United States. Three British firms (Rootes, Rover and Austin) set up factories in Australia.

The 1950s saw the mass production of 'Australia's own car', the US-owned 'Holden'. Late in 1944, the Australian government had asked motor firms to send in their post-war plans. General Motors worked out a scheme for an Australian car. Head office in Detroit killed this proposal. Finally, production of the Holden was paid for by unrepatriated profits and loans from the Commonwealth Bank and the Bank of Adelaide. Not one cent of US money went into it. On 29 November 1948, the first Holden came off the production line at Fishermen's Bend in Victoria. It sold for £675 plus tax. By the end of the year, another 162 were ready. The demand was so great that in 1951 salesmen refused to accept orders. Within three more years, production reached 100 cars a day. The millionth Holden was sold in 1962, when Japanese imports were starting to appear.

During the 1950s, car ownership grew from one vehicle for every nine people to two for every seven people. Australia was the world's fourth leading car-owning nation on a population basis. The increase in car numbers brought parking meters to Melbourne in 1954 and Sydney's first parking station by 1956. With the spread of suburbs, the motor car became the family's shopping basket.

Despite the new models that appeared each year from most of the companies, the car itself changed very little. The industry was attacked as 'technologically stagnant'. Even worse, local designs were two years behind US models. In 1960, the Holden still had no automatic transmission. The main reasons for new sales were marketing and the fact that cars were no longer being built to last. Between 1955 and 1958, the VW 'beetle', with its rear engine, revealed the power of small cars by winning all but one of the round-Australia rallies.

In 1946, the preferred colour for family cars was black, followed by cream or navy. Ten years later, only one new buyer in ten wanted black. A quarter then favoured a pastel two-tone. An equal number wanted a pale colour, or one of the greens. This change did not represent a shift in taste, but a change of paint chemistry. Before the war, only black or olive had not faded rapidly. By 1958, Ford V-8s came in twelve body colours with sixteen more shades for the flash along the sides. To supply the tones that buyers wanted, dealers installed repaint shops. The desired colour combination 'can influence a customer to buy, on the spot, probably more quickly than any other feature offered in a car', the *Australian Motor Manual* reported in 1958.

Car interiors also changed from mostly green to tartans,

maroon, blue or pale grey. Men fretted that women were taking over, with pink paint and with accessories such as make-up mirrors. No repainting disturbed gender stereotypes more than Farley-and-Lewers concrete trucks which, early in 1967, went from red or green to pink. The colour for baby girls sold concrete to blokes more accustomed to seeing pink elephants after a weekend on the shick.

Drinking

During the ten years after the war, annual beer drinking doubled to 110 litres per head. The years immediately after the war had found plenty of pubs with no beer. In the 1914–19 war hotels suffered from would-be prohibitionists. During the 1941–45 Pacific war, regular drinkers suffered from publicans who saw beer rationing as a chance to make up for the hard years of the depression. Some sold black-market cigarettes and butter. Others found that beer supplies went no further than the Yankee dollar. Most pubs opened for only two half-hour 'sessions' when the swill was worse than ever. As a result, no drinker had a good word to say for publicans.

In the mid-1950s, a series of changes began to shake the hotel industry: the country's first motel opened in Canberra (1955); the first drive-in bottle department started up in Adelaide; and the first international-class tourist hotel opened for business at Broadbeach on the Gold Coast. In 1956, poker machines became legal in New South Wales, where the number of licensed clubs had grown tenfold from a mere eighty-five in 1945. Ten o'clock closing came back to NSW in 1954. Victorians had to wait a further twelve years.

LIFE IN THE COUNTRY

From the late 1920s to the late 1940s, Australia's rural industries were hit by one disaster after another. The depression ruined exports. This collapse meant less money to improve farms throughout most of the 1930s. During the Pacific War years, there was money for labour and machines but neither could be had. Against this background, the 1944–45 drought was 'particularly serious because of the dilapidated state of the farms, and of the efforts to increase production with limited manpower, which had led to higher livestock numbers with very limited fodder conservation, limited fertiliser and little or no increase in water storage for stock watering'. Wartime shortages of men and materials continued till the early 1950s. Rabbits made everything worse. Some experts worried that Australia would not be able to grow enough food even for her own people.

New problems came in the early 1950s with the economic boom during the Korean War. Wool prices rocketed and pastoralists bought Holdens with their wool cheques. They also bought tractors. Mechanisation came in full force. In 1939, farmers had 42 000 tractors. By 1951, they had 70 000 more. Then they added another 20 000 in one year. The wool boom came just as myxomatosis killed off most of the rabbits, allowing a great increase in the number of sheep that could feed on the grass. Tractors and myxomatosis were only two of many improvements. The absence of copper and cobalt in West and South Australian pastures, which had been identified in the late 1930s, was now redressed. Although every farmer was likely to suffer flood, fire or drought, the farmers who were always badly off were those whose properties were too small ever to make money.

That lesson had been gained the hard way on the road to Gundagai, five miles past Wagga Wagga. In 1934, the original settlers at Gumly Gumly had won ballots among the unemployed for blocks of 2 to 7 hectares. Bringing little beyond dole tickets and a few pots, they pitched their tents on Gumly Common. They began to clear the land by hand, and to help build each other's houses. They formed a Progress Association which brought them a local school, erected a community hall and maintained two football teams.

Mrs Argus, JP, with ten surviving children, marked the moments of her life in verse. After the first year in a tin-and-timber hut, she had tempered pride in their efforts with this recognition:

Money is our great drawback
But with hard work and care
We hope that in the future
Real comfort we will share.

It was 1951 before the water came to the forty-two farming families of Gumly Gumly. The state government funded a spray irrigation system from what a reporter called 'the swiftly flowing Murrumbidgee'. Hopes ran high in the year after myxomatosis had wiped out the rabbits. One small-holder looked forward to sowing vegetables all year round, putting lucerne in the paddock, maintaining a flower patch and having a corner for onions. At last their farms would become paying propositions. The fight to get the water connected was the latest battle for survival. Some of their wells had already run dry; water had to be carried from neighbouring properties in a 'Furphy' tank on a horse and cart. When the reticulated water came, the farmers overcame the post-war shortage of pipes by pooling whatever lay about their blocks. No accolade was more valued than to be known as 'a wonderful worker' for the community.

Not only in hamlets such as Gumly Gumly did bush families wait for government services. Outside the larger towns almost half of the houses had no electricity, more than three-quarters had no gas, half had no running water, and a quarter had no bathroom. In five out of six rural homes, the most usual means of cooking was on a wood stove. These conditions were hardest on wives doing the housework and on children trying to study. Without electricity, farms had fewer of the appliances that were making domestic labour easier in the cities: no vacuum cleaners, no washing machines, no

lightweight irons, no electric mixers. Water had to be heated
on the stove and lifted to the sink. An English woman who
married an Australian grazier remembered 1946:

> We were living in a corrugated iron shed, which also served as a
> garage and a hay shed. The rainwater tank was empty, and every
> morning my husband carried two kerosene-tin buckets of water
> up from the creek. There was a dead calf in the hole, so the water
> was foul as well as muddy. I allowed it to settle, then I boiled it,
> skimmed it, and left it to boil a second time, before boiling again.

Children studied by the light of a kerosene lamp, which did
not help them win scholarships. Though life outside the capital
cities was becoming less of a pioneering challenge, it was often
harder and materially less rewarding than suburbia. The
steady drift off the land continued despite any number of
government-backed schemes to open up new farming country.

HEALTH

During the depression, many more Australians than ever had
not been able to take care of their health. If they did have a job,
they dared not stay home when they were sick. Although
'wonder drugs' proved effective, they were also costly. Governments would not levy the taxes to pay for major health programs.

Good health was vital to the war effort. The Commonwealth government took the opportunity to lay the basis for a
wide-ranging system of public health care, to continue after
the war. Its six components were sick pay, general practice,
hospitals, chemists, tuberculosis and research. The scheme
would cost more because its elements were to be available to
those who needed them, whether or not they could pay. Most
importantly, doctors would have to agree to help.

Pensions had been paid to permanent invalids from 1910.
From 1944, the Commonwealth government made payments
to sick people who were unable to work for short periods.

Recipients had to be out of work for a week before they could apply. A married man got only one-third of the basic wage. People were still expected to support themselves from their savings. If they had none, or after they had used them up, a little money would come in each week.

The Labor government wanted a health scheme which would be completely free to the patient. The community would pay through taxation. Doctors would get a wage from the government, hospitals would be financed from government funds, and prescribed medicines would be issued free by chemists who would send the bill to the Department of Health. Only the free hospital part of this programme ever operated. Doctors refused to use the official forms. When Labor was defeated in 1949, the Liberal–Country Party government took up the doctors' plans.

Under the doctors' scheme, some medicines would be free. In order to receive a government subsidy for medical bills, however, people had to pay into a private health fund. In addition, patients had to pay part of the bill. This arrangements helped a majority of Australians but it was of little use to the people most in need. Large families on small incomes could not afford the weekly fees to the health fund. In South Australia, unpaid medical bills were the main reason for jailing people who had not paid their debts. Immigrants who had been accustomed to their governments' paying for all health care did not find out that they were supposed to join a health fund until they became ill, when it was too late. Not until the late 1960s would the government pay the contributions of very low income groups, or give immigrants six months free membership. Even then, about a million Australians still had no health insurance.

Tuberculosis

In the nineteenth century, people suffering from consumption (tuberculosis, or TB) came to Australia to be cured. Dry heat and mutton three times a day often made them well. With the growth of cities and the development of deep-shaft mining, tuberculosis became a major killer in Australia. In 1915, almost 4000 people died from consumption. Although deaths from TB fell both in total and as a percentage, it remained a major killer into the 1940s.

TB had been looked upon as something to be ashamed of, along with VD, leprosy or madness. The Commonwealth government called a section of its Health Department the Division of Tuberculosis and Venereal Disease. A popular name for TB was the 'White Plague'. The feeling of shame arose because TB was viewed as a slum disease, the result of dirt and drink. Or worse still, the fable was that the condition was passed from parents to children, not by contact but through the blood. People would not marry into a tubercular family. The worst feature of TB was that most people thought nothing could be done about it. Once people had it, they often kept working till they collapsed and died. Or, as a medical conference had put it in 1911: 'Generally speaking, it is not treated at all'.

Although TB was known to be catching, governments did not make people report that they had it. The authorities feared that the shame of being a known TB sufferer would stop people seeking medical help. In particular, the patients would lose their jobs. Small pensions were paid, but only when sufferers were complete invalids and too sick to work at all. By then, it would be too late to do much to help them. Moreover, their families would also be infected. Sixty per cent of children living with TB sufferers caught the disease.

To make matters worse, the pension almost cut out when the patient went to hospital. Hence, fathers would stay at home for as long as they could so that they could get the pension for their families. This delay further increased the chances of wives and children becoming infected.

Treatment had to begin in the early stages. But in the early stages the sufferer looked healthy and could do a day's work.

The public and the politicians were not willing to spend money on people who could keep themselves. So sufferers went on working until they dropped; only then would the state and private charities give them some aid. A medical congress in Adelaide in 1937 pointed out: 'The economic factor is definitely the most important aspect of the campaign against tuberculosis'.

Before that financial problem was solved, three scientific improvements helped. In 1938, a simple form of X-ray was developed in Brazil, which made it possible to examine people for a shilling a chest. When this method was used on soldiers in the First Pacific War, one in every two hundred who had been passed A1 was found to have TB. This X-ray method later made possible the compulsory examination of entire populations. New 'wonder drugs' and lung operations cut the time in hospital from twelve or eighteen months to three or five months.

These breakthroughs could not help those most in need unless they could afford to go to hospital. That opportunity became possible after 1948 when the Commonwealth government took three steps. First, it offered money to State governments to pay for new hospitals, equipment and upkeep. Secondly, in return the States were to pass laws making X-rays compulsory for every Australian over fourteen years of age. TB sufferers were also to be forced into hospital if they would not go of their own accord. Thirdly, a special, generous, pension would be paid to all sufferers during their treatment so that they would not have to worry about their families and thus could afford to spend as long a time in hospital as was necessary. The payment of this pension brought 4000 new cases to light in the first year. So successful was this public health scheme that by the 1970s deaths from TB were down to about twenty-five a year.

Nutrition

Dairy cows were a prime source of TB infections. Although laws controlling dairies and milk had been introduced early in the twentieth century, they were not very effective. The task was still to bring fresh, pure milk from the country to the cities. The solution called for clean dairies, quick transport and good door-to-door delivery. Dairies were far from clean. In 1937, officials estimated that 8 per cent of all cows had TB, which could be passed on to humans who drank their milk. Refrigeration and pasteurisation were two answers to these problems. Victoria passed a law in 1949 which brought about the pasteurisation of milk supplies in most of Melbourne within five years. Farms were also changing so that by 1948 more than two-thirds of the dairies supplying Sydney had installed milking machines. Taking the milk to the cities was made safer by refrigerated road tankers. Bottles took the place of billycans for home deliveries. By 1943, half of Melbourne's supply came in bottles. In New South Wales, the percentage of milk sold in bottles leapt from 35 to 95 per cent between 1952 and 1955. Until then, milk was not a safe, pure food.

Nor was there always as much milk as was needed. From 1939 to 1951, New South Wales rationed supplies during the winter months. To make sure that children got their share, free milk was distributed at school. During the 1940s the amount of milk drunk daily increased from 280 millilitres to 380 millilitres for each Australian. Milk was no longer looked on as a food for the young, the old and the sick, but as a desirable part of everyone's diet.

Poor diet was one reason why dentists worried that the teeth of Australian children were so bad that fillings and extractions would never keep up with the rate of decay. Experts called for fluoride to be added to drinking water to prevent caries. The experiment seemed to work, because the rate of tooth decay fell and successive generations had stronger teeth. When fluoride was proposed, its loudest opponents were political cranks who saw fluoridation of the public water supply as the first step towards a communist dictatorship. Some scientists would note how flouride had become a profitable sideline; the costs of disposing of a pollutant had been abolished by pouring it into the water supply. The success of fluoride was debated. By the time Sydney's water had been fluoridated in 1968, the level of tooth decay had already fallen to a half that of the early 1950s. Brisbane has never flouridated its water supply. Yet between 1954 and 1977 the rates of decay among its 6–14-year-olds had halved. Changing diets and improved oral hygiene were contributing to better teeth.

ABORIGINES

Australian governments endorsed assimilation as their policy for Aborigines. On paper, 'assimilation' meant that Aborigines would become white people with black skins. In practice, it meant that Aborigines would remain under the control of government officers, missionaries, pastoralists and mining companies. The destruction of Aborigines as a distinct group of people with their own culture was to be stepped up. Aborigines were supposed to be helped to work for wages. For as long as they let whites control their future, they got some encouragement to become self-supporting. They felt the truth about assimilation as soon as they tried to take charge of their own lives in any collective way.

Nowhere was the nature of assimilation made clearer than in the Port Hedland district of Western Australia. The West Australian and Commonwealth governments smashed several attempts by Aborigines to set up mining and pastoral ventures. Yet nowhere did Aboriginal resistance burn more strongly. Each defeat gave rise to new activity, starting with armed resistance in the 1860s, passing through a planned uprising in 1900, and on to the establishment of their own organisation thirty years later. The Pilbara mobs had a rich past of struggle behind them when, in 1946, they struck for a wage of thirty shillings a week.

Their demand for more pay was immediately and almost completely successful. Yet they did not return to work on the pastoral stations, despite arrests and gaolings. Instead, they set up their own settlement at Twelve Mile Creek outside Port Hedland, where they built and ran their own school. Strikes spread across the north-west. In 1949 Aboriginal workers wanted three pounds a week, plus two pounds a week in keep. These rates had already been agreed to by station managers who had arranged them through a white man, Don McLeod.

McLeod had worked with the Pilbara Aborigines since 1943. In 1949 he joined a small group of Aborigines mining for tin near Marble Bar. Within two years the community had grown to 600. Its total income for 1951 was nearly £50 000, most of which was spent on new machines and land. Among the stations the group bought was Yandyerra which became the site of a large settlement and included a school, a hospital and homes for the aged.

Before these plans could be carried through, the West Australian government forced the two companies that the Aboriginal group had set up to go broke. It also took back Yandyerra station. A high-ranking official was forced to admit that 'self-reliance has been engendered in these people. It is tangible, and probably unique in the history of this State. It may rest with this Department whether this spirit is nurtured or crushed'. The state and federal governments spent a lot of time trying to crush the independence of the Pilbara people, who went on to form two other mining companies. The authorities were determined to assimilate the Pilbara people. Two of the leading Aborigines were tricked into splitting up the group. Those under state control were driven towards hopelessness.

In 1960, pastoralists were allowed to poison waterholes, thus killing the kangaroos that were vital to the group's survival. For two years after 1959, the State Government threatened that Aborigines would not get Commonwealth social services unless they put themselves under the control of the Department. This ruling was used in 1965 against those Aborigines who had left the government reserve in order to form another cooperative, Nomads, further south at Roebourne.

The experiences of the Pilbara Aborigines revealed how fierce governments would be to prevent Indigenous people taking charge of their own affairs. Similar intimidation would be shown against the Gurindji at Wattie Creek. One Australian characteristic that Aborigines were not supposed to assimilate was independence.

To contain the drive for self-determination, governments limited the education of Aboriginal children. Its purpose was shown on the Cape Barren Islands in Tasmania, where the only government officer combined the professions of policeman and teacher. More than in most schools, training for Aboriginal children was a form of labour discipline. In their case, they had to learn how to serve as domestics or bush-workers.

Education for Aborigines was often racially separated, and almost always of a poor standard. In New South Wales until 1940, schools on reserves expected pupils to reach only third grade by the age of fourteen. Until 1945, no Aboriginal child could attend an ordinary State school. Teachers in Aboriginal schools were rarely trained. None had special skills to reach Aboriginal children. A study in 1941 had shown that teachers of Aboriginal classes were likely to be retired or broken-down men whose previous jobs ranged from third-mate of a tramp steamer and an army sergeant-major to a maker of breakfast foods. The same study found one school with an untrained teacher in charge of 100 pupils. Almost none of the schools had a clock. Shortly afterwards, another expert reported:

> Native schools lack even the most essential equipment, in particular they lack facilities for healthy recreation and for education in

practical hygiene and manual training. The black child's education is jeopardised by a colour consciousness that is unworthy of any democracy.

Bad as most education was, a few brighter spots existed. Roman Catholic priests at Beagle Bay (WA) and Lutheran missionaries at Hermannsburg (SA) had taught Aboriginal children in their own languages of Nyul-Nyul and Arrernte since about 1900. In the 1940s the outstanding innovation was the Presbyterian mission at Ernabella (SA), where children were taught in Pitjantjat-jara, could come to school naked, and could live with their parents. Within six years, fifty of them could read and write in their own language. Church-going was not enforced. All the Aborigines were free to come and go. The school teacher at the mission, Mr Trudinger, could boast:

> No family tie has been broken, no superior complexes set up. The child still finds his most satisfying impression and expression in the nightly corroboree; he still seeks most the family circle and the society of his kind.

The significance of Ernabella was in showing that Aborigines could be educated formally if appropriate methods were used. Furthermore, Ernabella demonstrated that those methods could succeed if governments wanted them. Ernabella was important not only for what it did but also for its exposure of the otherwise almost total failure of the public instruction of Aborigines.

WHITE AUSTRALIA

During the Pacific War, several thousand Asians had come to Australia to escape from the Japanese. The refugees were told that they could not stay forever. Nonetheless, some of them married Australians, or had other reasons for not going home. The man in charge of sending these Asians back, Arthur Calwell, was also in charge of bringing tens of thousands of people from Britain and Europe. Trade unions were not happy with the Labor government's plan for large-scale immigration; they feared that the new arrivals would add to unemployment and be used to undermine working conditions. Calwell worked hard to convince them otherwise. In the process of selling European immigration to his trade-union supporters, he took up an increasingly tough stand on the White Australia policy. He seemed to be saying: trust me with European immigration and I will not let even one Asian stay. Calwell's ready wit landed him in trouble in December 1947 when he answered a question about the deportation of a Chinese called Wong from an opposition member named White: 'Two Wongs', quipped Calwell, 'do not make a White'.

The tenacity with which Calwell deported Asians boiled over with the case of Mrs O'Keefe. Annie Maas O'Keefe had been born in the Celebes in 1908. She escaped from the Japanese with her Dutch husband and seven children in September 1942. Her husband was killed two years later. In June 1947, she married a British citizen, which was how she had become Mrs O'Keefe. When the government tried to deport her in 1949, she appealed to the High Court, claiming that her marriage to an Australian entitled her to stay. The judges were not impressed by this argument but agreed that she could stay because she had not broken any law to enter Australia. The law as it then stood did not apply to her. Calwell had a new law passed by which he could deport Mrs O'Keefe. Although public opinion was strongly in favour of a White Australia, many Australians objected to this hounding of a woman with a large family. Newspapers asked if it was right to break up a marriage? Calwell replied that her marriage was only a trick for getting around the law. Before Mrs O'Keefe could be sent back to the Celebes, the Labor government was defeated. The new Minister for Immigration said he would enforce the White Australia policy but with charity.

The O'Keefe case made it possible for a few hundred war refugees to remain here. But the controversy also made the

Labor and the Liberal–Country parties more determined in their support for White Australia as a policy. Labor became firmer when it closed ranks behind Calwell, feeling that it had lost votes in the 1949 election in defence of a principle. The Liberal–Country parties became inflexible because, in order to let a few hundred Asians stay, they had to be seen to be as committed to the principle of White Australia as the Labor Party was. Otherwise, they too might lose votes.

The mentality behind White Australia went further than skin colour. 'White' implied pure in body and mind. The government imposed strict medical and political tests on non-British immigrants. In 1951, the Italian authorities proposed 8191 single men as suitable. Fewer than 2000 passed the health checks. Removal of those who had voted Communist cut the number down to sixty-two.

Opposition to White Australia continued, but was largely confined to academics and to parsons. In 1945 one of Sydney's leading Methodists, Rev. Alan Walker, published a pamphlet which went further than almost any earlier opponent of White Australia. Walker wanted Asians to come to Australia so that Australians could gain from contact with foreign cultures. He opposed assimilation and wanted cultural differences to grow so that Australia would be a more exciting country. Most other opponents wanted to ease the White Australia policy so that it would not offend our Asian neighbours.

VIEW OF THE WORLD

Japan's defeat brought only a passing sense of safety to Australians. They worried that Japan might re-arm as Germany had done in the 1930s. More importantly, Asia did not settle back into the pre–Pacific War system of control by Britain, France, the Netherlands and the United States. Everywhere in Asia, revolutions and civil wars flared. The old empires that had been driven out by the Japanese could not take up where they had left off. By 1947, the Communists were winning in China; India was about to become independent; and the Dutch would be driven out of Indonesia. Wars also raged in Vietnam, Malaya and the Philippines. Could Britain afford to fight another Asian war? Would the United States move in again? These questions worried Australians so much that a world-wide opinion poll showed that Australians were more convinced than any other people that there would be another world war.

In the 1930s, leading Australian newspapers had called the Indian independence leader, Gandhi, a 'fraud' and a 'humbug'. India had been important to Australian defence planning. Under enemy control, the sub-continent could have become a dagger aimed at the shipping lines that were supposed to bring the British navy to Singapore. Once Singapore had surrendered to the Japanese early in 1942, keeping India on the British side became more important than ever. Tokyo was promising India its independence. An Indian National Army fought with the Japanese in Burma, adding firepower to Gandhi's pacifism. Prominent Indians started a 'Quit India' movement to get rid of the British. In order to keep Indian support, more Australians came to favour granting her full Dominion Status within the Empire. This reform would have made India as self-governing as Australia. Early in 1947, the British Labour government said that India would become independent during the year. Australia's Labor government agreed that this concession was the wisest and safest course, providing India stayed within the British Empire and Commonwealth of Nations. The Liberal Party Leader, R. G. Menzies, however, told the federal parliament that, on reading the news in his morning paper, 'my first feeling was one almost of shock'. Matters were moving too far and too fast, Menzies went on; he thought 'that to abandon control of a people who have not yet shown a real and broad capacity for popular self-government is to do a disservice to them'. Later, he was horrified when

India was allowed to remain in the Commonwealth after becoming a republic. As Prime Minister, Menzies looked down on Indian Prime Minister Nehru as a 'savage'.

During 1942, Australia had welcomed Dutch officials from what was then called the Dutch East Indies, now known as Indonesia. At the end of the war, Australia expected that the Dutch would take control once more, although they might have to grant a little more self-government. In 1947, Canberra stopped supporting the Dutch against the Indonesians. Not all Australians were happy to have an independent Asian country so close. Crucial support for the Indonesians came from trade unionists, especially waterside workers who had worked with Indonesian refugees in Sydney during the Pacific War. Sydney wharf labourers refused to load ships carrying arms to put down the Indonesians' struggle for independence. The Labor government showed its new-found sympathy for Indonesia by not forcing the waterside workers to change their stand. The waterside workers' action won Australia a deal of goodwill in Indonesia.

When Mao Tse-tung proclaimed the People's Republic of China on 1 October 1949, most Australians were too concerned about local matters to take much notice. Some leading newspapers did not report the declaration at all; only two or three gave the Communist victory in China any close attention. The usual noises followed about the Red and Yellow perils. The reaction was a general wait-and-see. The Labor government declined to recognise the new Chinese government because an Australian election was to be held in two months and the Liberal–Country parties were already winning votes by claiming that Labor was pro-communist.

Fears of Communist China intensified after the civil war in Korea became an open conflict late in June 1950. Australians joined a United Nations force which, under US control, defeated the North Koreans and kept moving towards the Chinese border. Beijing saw this advance as the start of a war of intervention, just like the one waged by the Allies against Bolshevik Russia after the Great European War. To defend its border, China sent volunteers into North Korea. Heavy fighting continued around the 38th parallel, which later became a truce line between North and South Korea. China's defence of her border was portrayed as proof of her aggressive plans and warlike nature. Within a year of its establishment, the People's Republic of China was one of the two Asian countries most feared by Australians. The other was Japan.

Communist victory in China led the United States to change its policy towards Tokyo. Instead of being a defeated enemy to be punished and stopped from ever making war in the future, Japan was needed as an ally in the fight against Communism in Asia. On 8 September 1951, the United States signed a Peace Treaty and a Security Treaty with Japan. To lessen Australian and New Zealand fears of a revived Japan, the United States had signed the ANZUS Treaty a week earlier. As the Australian Minister for External Affairs, Percy Spender, put it: 'the risk of Japan again being dominated by a militaristic and hostile clique at some future time was too real to be disregarded because of any short- or long-term advantages of a soft peace treaty without any safeguards'. Washington looked on ANZUS as a device for committing Australia to the defence of the demilitarised Japan. Its wording did not commit Washington to doing anything. According to the US special negotiator for ANZUS, John Foster Dulles, 'treaty words in themselves have little power to compel action. Treaties mean little except as they spell out what the people concerned would do anyway'.

Australia must prepare for war within three years, Prime Minister Menzies announced in 1951. The alarm was clear in Melbourne's *News Weekly*, the voice of Catholic Action:

> If we refuse to fill this country with people to the full limit of its resources, we must always be on the defensive against 12 hundred million pairs of hungry eyes — and not only against 86 million

pairs of Japanese eyes. If it is not Japan, it will be China, and if it is not China, it will be somebody else.

By the middle of 1954, the Menzies government faced an Asia as tumultuous as it had been in early 1942. India and Indonesia were independent, neutral and drifting towards socialism. Japan was regaining strength with the support of Australia's only effective ally, the United States. Britain was still active in South-East Asia but was no longer the major power in the region. China was communist. Communists were fighting in Malaya and the Philippines, and were winning against the French in Indo-China. The Australian government jumped at the chance to join the South-East Asia Collective Defence Treaty, signed on 8 September 1954. This new grouping, known as SEATO, brought the old Imperial powers of Britain and France together with the new strong man in the Pacific, the United States. In a world where nothing stood still, SEATO offered Menzies a chance to turn back the clock to Alfred Deakin's 1908 plan for a grand Pacific alliance. SEATO did not satisfy *News Weekly*, which described it as 'weak' and 'toothless'.

Holden goes further ahead
with new styling, new features and substantially reduced prices

HOLDEN SPECIAL

1954: 'NOT SO MUCH A VISIT, MORE A WAY OF LIFE'

When King George VI died on 6 February 1952, his elder daughter, the Princess Elizabeth, was in Africa on her way to Australia. She flew back to England at once, but her Coronation was not until June 1953. Five months later she left for a tour of the West Indies, Fiji, Tonga, New Zealand and Australia. She became the first reigning British monarch to visit this continent.

The Commonwealth government printed a booklet telling Australians what to wear and how to behave in the presence of their Queen. Women were advised that 'Her Majesty has expressed the wish that no one should be put to unnecessary expense in buying clothes'. Their husbands were informed that 'Her Majesty does not wish anyone to stay away from a function to which he has been invited because he feels he has not the correct clothes to wear. The basic principle to be observed for Garden Parties is that men should wear the best they have, whatever it may be'. The general public was notified that Her Majesty did 'not accept gifts from firms engaged in trade or commerce', nor would she 'give autographs or sign photographs'. Those who were to be presented to Her Majesty were reminded that 'the correct procedure is to address Her Majesty in the first instance as "Your Majesty", and thereafter as "Ma'am" '. The caterers had to be reminded that neither the Queen nor the Duke enjoyed oysters.

Arriving in Sydney on 3 February 1954, the Royal party

was not due to leave until 1 April, fifty-seven days later. Reports from the New Zealand tour that Her Majesty was tired were repeated here after she did not dance at a ball given in her honour. Tired though she might have been, Australians did not tire of going to see her. A poet claimed that:

> To cheer you, Ma'am, along our foreshores men
> Who fought in France and Egypt march again,
> And sailors, once in Crete,
> Or your Korean Fleet.
> 'A Queen', they say, 'whose courage shames our own.'
> ('Great heart in little bodie'!) It is known.
> Oh, nothing daunts your strength!
> — No day's unending length

A fortnight after the Queen's arrival, an editorial in the *Women's Weekly* found the reason for 'the enthusiastic scenes which greet the Queen everywhere she goes' in the need that human beings have to look up to and admire someone. The attribute that people admired about the Queen was her goodness:

> Goodness was a virtue that seemed to be going out of fashion. To say that a man or a woman was good was often to imply that he or she lacked other more attractive attributes. The Queen has brought goodness back into fashion.

Others saw more direct political gains from the visit. The retired professor of Political Science and History at the University of Adelaide, G. V. Portus, saw the Queen as 'the bond of the Commonwealth of Nations'. To those who claimed that the Crown was only a symbol, Portus replied:

> That may be so, but its uniqueness lies in the fact that it is a symbol embodied in a living person. Can anyone suppose that a flag, a national anthem, or an emblem like a monogram, a swastika, or a hammer-and-sickle could serve these purposes as well?

For those who wanted a reminder of the royal couple, their coronation robes, some of the furniture from Westminster

Abbey and a few imitation crown jewels were exhibited throughout Australia.

The day before the Queen left Australia another editorial in the *Women's Weekly* was pleased that 'she gave every appearance of enjoying the tour'. Australians had done so, but to understand why, it is important to recall some other events. At the simplest level, the 1954 Royal Tour fulfilled promises made in the 1940s. Yet the outbursts of popular loyalty and pleasure were more than the usual feelings of a British people towards their monarch. Australians seized a moment of relief from the tensions of world affairs. The presence of the Queen recalled the days when Britain was all-powerful and God was in his Heaven. The excitement of holidays and the splendour of parades made it possible to forget, if only for a while, the re-armament of Japan, the wars in Korea and Indo-China, and the explosion of the world's first hydrogen bomb.

The comfort of the British presence was hollow. During the planned 1952 visit to Canberra, the Queen was supposed to have lain the foundation stone at Australia's memorial to the US troops. Two years later, she was in time to unveil the 70-metre column topped by an eagle, which soared above the British lion on which the sun was setting. At the same time, the Elizabethan Theatre Trust was established to bring to the Australian theatre the vigour that the English stage had exhibited in the reign of Elizabeth I. Instead, the Angry Young Men took the limelight.

Twelve days after Her Majesty left Australia, Prime Minister Menzies told the federal parliament that a member of the Russian Embassy staff in Canberra, Vladimir Petrov, had given evidence of a Soviet spy ring to the Australian Security Intelligence Organisation. A Royal Commission would follow up these charges. A federal election was due seven weeks later. The Labor Party won 51 per cent of the votes but lost by four seats. Its leader, Dr Evatt, alleged that Menzies had pulled the Petrovs out of a hat to steal victory. Labor supporters repeated this conspiracy view. If Menzies did stage an election stunt, it was the Royal Tour. In 1954, nothing could have done more to remind Australians how conservative they should be than the presence of their monarch.

9

1955–1962
FOREVER
AMBER

The 1950s came to be pictured either as a golden age of economic prosperity or an ice age for culture and politics. Neither summary fits the facts. A reporter for European magazines believed that the 'most important generalisation is that life in Australia since the late forties has always been several paces ahead of the utterances of her public figures'. The 1950s were not stagnant. Experiences broadened and expectations expanded. Both were held in check by the Cold War, and even more by financial shackles.

The crux of the economic problem was how to balance overseas payments and receipts. An economy riding on the sheep's back would always be hostage to the weather and to world demand. In 1956, the reserves of gold and money were so low that additional import controls were imposed, even on materials vital for production. Export earnings surged in 1956–57. Wool prices then collapsed for the first half of 1958. An upswing in the second quarter of 1959 resulted in a tiny trade surplus. The *Chartered Accountant* observed that this pattern looked more like a gaming table than a set of national accounts. Critics complained that the economy was lurching between Stop and Go. A politician said the national traffic signals were 'forever amber'.

The discovery of bauxite in 1957 promised an escape hatch. Very large crude carriers would take several kinds of dirt (bauxite, iron ore and coal) to Japan. The Japanese would send back lots of money. Henceforth, any trade imbalance would be positive. Before that exchange had got started, Prime Minister Menzies placed his biggest bet early in 1960 by removing import controls. The volume of imports skyrocketed. Exports remained the same. His government reacted by increasing the sales tax on vehicles and cutting the funds available for home loans. General Motors-Holden laid off 8400 workers for two weeks without pay. Late in 1961, Menzies clung to office by a handful of donkey votes in one Brisbane electorate. The golden fifties would not arrive until 1963. Nonetheless, mass marketing had entered everyday life.

WORK

From 1942 to 1974, less than 3 per cent of the Australian workforce was unemployed. These numbers led working people to hope that unemployment would never again be a lasting problem. Some employers, however, were calling for an unemployment rate of 4.5 per cent. Maintaining full employment, they said, had strained the economy by pushing up wages. In 1953, the Industrial Court abolished the automatic increases in the basic wage to match price rises. By 1958, the purchasing power of the basic wage had fallen by 5 per cent while average earnings had not moved.

Australian workers were still drifting away from the bush towards the cities. During the half-century to 1961, the percentage of the total workforce in the rural and mining sector had declined from a quarter to one-tenth. The secondary sector had grown to nearly 40 per cent and the tertiary sector to almost 50 per cent. The age structure also changed, with fewer young and old people. In 1911, 44 per cent of males over the age of seventy were still working; by 1961, this portion had dropped to 18 per cent. Earlier retirements resulted from more and better pensions. An inability to keep up with the pace of operations also encouraged those who lived past the age of sixty to take it easy.

Forklifts made work lighter after the US military brought some during the First Pacific War. In 1951, a local firm sold 600. By 1958, some 5000 were in use. Before then, motors had powered the forklifts and later allowed some models to raise pallets several metres. In October 1956, G. J. Coles opened a distribution centre in Port Melbourne to supply its 130 stores in five States, replacing three older warehouses. The delivery trucks had been designed to match the pallets, forklifts and hydraulic lifting trucks. Their full benefit required computer-ised stock control throughout the Coles network. In 1960 Woolworths installed the first IBM Ramac 305 in Australia to manage its supply chain. Operating a forklift eliminated much of the laboriousness from the movement of goods, and with it the risk of back injury. However, the drivers sat alone in a cage-like structure with their lines of vision blocked by the crates. As a result of this isolation, they suffered high levels of stress.

Technical progress did not mean safer work. Industrial inju-ries cost Australia five times more than strikes in 1958. That year, 400 workers were killed, 3500 were maimed and 350 000 hurt.

New South Wales railways introduced the '60' class Beyer Garratt steam engines early in the 1950s. The tonnage increased. The productivity figures did not calculate the human misery. More than any other twentieth-century train engine, the '60' class earned the title 'widow maker'. Tempera-tures reached 55°C in their cabins on a hot day. Not only the cabin crews suffered. Electricians had to replace the wiring blown out of place in tunnels by the engine's exhaust. Those wires were sulphurous, but no 'dirt' money was paid. One ex-driver wrote to the Sydney *Sun* shortly after the last steam engine in New South Wales went out of service on 4 March 1973: 'We retired men all regret (with arthritis and bronchitis) ever having been loco men. Only a train-lover could have any affection for these filthy "60" class monstrous railway anachronisms. Stick to the diesel, grandsons'.

LIFE IN THE CITIES
Television

A few days before the start of the Olympic Games on 22 November 1956, two Melbourne television stations began transmitting programs to the 10 000 Victorian families rich enough to afford £300 for a set. Two years earlier, the federal government had agreed to the introduction of television. From July 1955, stations had screened a few programs to gain experience and to let the retailers of electrical goods show the public what television would look like. By the middle of 1957, Melbourne and Sydney each had three channels, and each one screened forty hours of programs a week. Adelaide, Brisbane and Perth followed in 1959.

After 1 January 1957, each household with a television set had to pay a £5 licence fee. By the middle of 1959, almost 600 000 homes held licences. More than half of Sydney's families had a set. Groups still stood outside shop windows at night watching programs. A visit to TV-owning friends could still be a nice night's entertainment.

In a June 1959 interview, the editor of *TV Times* named the most popular shows:

> Oh I suppose 'Mickey Mouse', 'Clint Walker' ['Cheyenne'], 'Wells Fargo', 'Gunsmoke' and, of course, 'Perry Mason' and 'Sunset Strip'. Sport particularly seems to be almost the program for which television was invented, and you've got to hand it to all three channels in that respect.

Favourite teenage shows were 'Bandstand' and 'Six O'Clock Rock'. Two years later, a Sydney survey showed that the four most popular programs were 'The Untouchables', 'Pick-a-Box', 'Perry Mason' and 'The Perry Como Show'.

The commercial channels met the government's program standards of ordinary good taste, respect for individual opinions, proper regard for the needs of children, and 'respect for the law and social institutions' with cops and quizzes.

The ABC answered a public desire for something more than goodies and baddies when in 1961 it commenced its weekly current affairs report, 'Four Corners'. The need for lifelike drama was filled by British programs such as 'Z Cars', 'Coronation Street', and later by 'Callan' and 'Family at War'. Yet these offerings remained only a very small part of most television programs. Hollywood comedies and cop shows and repeated movies still took up most of the time. The imported shows met the need of the commercial networks for cheap programs between the advertisements. Actors and writers complained about the absence of Australian content, especially dramas. The ABC presented more local entertainment than the commercial channels. Yet, when the latter screened 509 episodes of 'Homicide', or Graeme Kennedy's naughty 'In Melbourne Tonight', they drew ever larger audiences. The managing-director of Channel 9 explained that his business was to make money by supplying a 'diversion' for the majority of workers who were 'wrecked from a hard day'. Australian winner of the Arthur C. Clarke Award for Science Fiction, George Turner, mocked television as 'the Triv'.

Before television started, experts had worried about its effect on families, social life and school work. People certainly stayed home more. The queues outside local picture theatres on Saturday nights shrank. Hundreds of theatres closed. A 1959 survey showed that, in Sydney, fifteen-year-olds watched television for between nine and twelve hours a week, which was more time than they spent on any other single pastime. Children slept less, read less and listened to the radio less. These changes affected their formal learning.

Education, however, faced larger problems than students' watching the screen rather than doing homework. In 1953, the

Australian Council for Education Research noted: 'The central problem in Australia since 1940 has been a shortage of teachers'. The lack of graduate teachers prevented three States from raising the school leaving age. No State had been able to reduce class sizes. The effort to secure more teachers distracted the attention of parliaments, administrators and professions from the purposes of education. That harsh judgment would remain true. Indeed, some of the methods used to overcome the teacher shortage produced new problems. The lack of effective secondary teachers in the 1950s diminished the quality of education once their poorly prepared pupils became the next generation of teachers.

Teenagers

As well as places for instruction in reading, writing and arithmetic, schools remained centres for instilling social attitudes. This aspect grew with concerns about the behaviour of juveniles. For example, a high school in the Sydney suburb of Fairfield was broken into thirty-nine times in less than three years. From convict days, Australian cities had had young men and women whose clothes, language and outlook offended their elders. They bore various names: 'cabbage tree mob', 'larrikins', 'hoods'. They were described as 'flash', 'swaggering', 'drop-outs'. Violence had often been seen as the answer. Sydney's larrikin pushes were hit in 1887 when six young men, some of them allegedly innocent, were hanged for rape. In the 1920s, the razor gangs ended after the whipping of a larrikin. Belief in a 'strong right arm' reappeared in the 1950s. Melbourne's Lord Mayor wanted 'vandals, litterbugs and young hoodlums put in stocks before town and shire halls'. The *Sydney Morning Herald* said they should be put 'into the army under a hard-driving drill sergeant'.

Others tried to find out why there were juvenile delinquents, which was the official name for young people who caused trouble, or who merely dressed differently. Broken homes were said to be a major cause. Victoria's divorce rate had risen from 650 a year in the 1930s to 1600 a year in the 1950s. The Catholic Church launched a campaign around the slogan 'The family that prays together, stays together'.

In 1957, a Sydney newspaper printed the life story of a six-teen-year-old boy who was in a reformatory because he had stolen £15 after running away from home:

> My father went away when I was five, and he and Mother were di-vorced. I was put in a home. I went back to live with her when I was 10, and she was married again. They never took any interest in what you did at school and I didn't get on too good. When I left school I got my apprenticeship with a plumber. If I stayed home at night I used to go to bed to get out of the way. I got £5 a week and gave her £3 to keep me. I didn't think £2 was too much to spend on clothes.
>
> When she told me I'd have to give her my whole pay-packet I decided she was making a bit of a good thing out of me. I shot through one night with my whole pay in my pocket and a bit I'd saved — about £8. I didn't have any proper meals — only pies and things. I mucked about and didn't get a job until the fourth day. By that time I only had 3/4d in my pocket so I took £15 out of the till. They caught me a quarter of an hour later. Now I'm appren-ticed again at a different trade.

The determination of this young thief to become a skilled worker indicated how conventional a delinquent could remain.

Juvenile crime, drinking and promiscuity were not spread-ing. Many adults mistook the outward appearance for the real thing. This overreaction arose because most Australians in the 1950s had grown up in hard times when they would have been lucky to own a new pair of shoes. The depression and the war accustomed them to simple, plain-coloured clothes. Also, Australian men refused to dress for the climate. Felt hats and three-piece serge suits were common sights around sub-tropical Brisbane in summer. Shirts were white in the office, or

blue for factory workers. Trouser bottoms were at least eighteen inches (forty-five centimetres) wide and turned up. It was
not very hard to stand out in that crowd. The wearing of a
bright pullover was enough to label a boy a 'bodgie'. Men did
not wear jewellery or any toilet preparation apart from hair
oil. Anglo-Celtic Australian men were reluctant to use toilet-
ries in case they were suspected of being 'poofs'. Deodorants
were marketed through chemists to appear medicinal. One
brand was labelled '12 Gauge' and packaged like a shot-gun
cartridge to make cologne seem masculine.

So-called 'bodgie' gear included tight-fitting black slacks
which showed inches of lime green or watermelon socks above
black pointed-toe shoes. Ties were only three centimetres
wide and shirts were the same colour as the socks, although
black was acceptable. Long hair was cut straight at the neck
and trained to a curl in front. Long hair meant longer than one
centimetre at the sides. The thing that shocked some citizens
the most was that men were interested in clothes at all. Fashions were for women. It was enough for a man to be neat and
clean.

The 'criminal' bodgie with his motor bike and black leather
jacket was much harder to find. Most teenagers could afford a
bright shirt and socks, but a motor bike cost over £150, which
was a year's wages for an apprentice. The closest most Australians ever came to seeing 'bodgies' were Marlon Brando in *The
Wild One* or Jimmy Dean in *Rebel Without a Cause*. 'Bodgies' were the first in a line of youthful fashions pushed by marketing.

Marketing

As an extension of that sales effort, businesses had invented
Mother's Day in the 1920s. In the 1950s they adopted Father's
Day. Marketers formed a Father's Day Council in 1957.
Fifty-nine firms signed up in Perth. Throughout Australia, the
organisers attached their selling to good causes. They named a

'Father of the Year' to combat juvenile delinquency, idealising 'Dad' as both pal and disciplinarian. In 1960, the Victorian branch of the Father's Day Council got £125 000 of free publicity by linking their marketing to War Orphans Day, which collected an extra £650 in donations. The first Sunday in September became an occasion for expanding the range of goods that men would use. For instance, during the 1950s the percentage of Australian men using electric shavers rose from 10 per cent to 40 per cent. Because their average price was around the basic wage, trade-ins were accepted and hire purchase available.

The image of 'Dad' in Father's Day advertisements shifted. In 1950, he was a rigid and remote pipe-smoker in an armchair reading a classic. In 1960, he was 'colourful', 'playful' and 'Dandy dad' for his kids to 'pamper' or 'butter up'. By then, advertisements in the *Women's Weekly* portrayed husbands as prone to stray. They therefore had to be wooed homewards with red lipstick. In 1962, Father's Day cards that 'took a quiet shot at Dad' were popular. 'Perhaps the Mums took delight in reducing Dad's ego a bit', noted the trade journal for newsagents.

Housing

So great was the demand for housing in 1956 that 3000 families applied for the 841 units built at the Olympic 'village'. A two-bedroom, brick veneer home there cost £2460, excluding the land. According to Melbourne's Board of Works in 1954, 105 000 families lived in third-class homes. Six years later, Victoria's Housing Commission suggested that eight suburbs, covering almost 400 hectares, be rebuilt. That would have taken fifty years. A quick answer was found in high-rise blocks of flats. A typical Melbourne block went twenty storeys up, with ten flats on each floor. Each tower held 700 people, a quarter of whom were children under five years of age. Notwithstanding this pattern of residents, the blocks offered no social services such as child-minding. Because families had to be poor to get a Housing Commission flat, both parents often had to work. Couples without friends or relatives nearby left their children at home alone, which gave rise to the term 'latch-key kids'.

Although each block had its own playground, these areas did not appeal to children, many of whom liked something less organised and more secret. A ten-year-old boy described life in his high-rise:

> I live in a flat. Most people who live in houses say that people who live in flats are better off. No, I believe this is not true. First of all, people living in houses have much more privacy than people living in flats. In the flats you can't open your front door to find a crisp fresh lawn. Instead you open your door to concrete. In a house you find your bread, milk and newspaper all safely perched on your doorstep. In a flat your bread and milk are nearly always stolen, your clothes are stolen. It is different in a house because you can hang out clothes confident that they won't get stolen. And to the flat people's inconvenience the teenagers rip doors off hinges, smash lights, knock down fences, break glass, rip up public seats and form gangs and attack people.

High-rise blocks did not have to be as bad as this description. The wealthy did just fine in apartments on Macquarie Street, Sydney; atop Brisbane's Highgate Hill; or along Domain Road, South Yarra. The Housing Commission ones needed to be planned as homes in which people could thrive. They had been stuck up to be rid of an eyesore.

Yet many families were pleased to get out of broken-down houses at high rents and to have a dry, rat-free home. Others found that the break-up of their community was too big a price to pay. Talking over the fence was a great way to spend an hour. Having neighbours watching out for you made it less likely that a pensioner was indoors, too sick to ask for help.

LIFE IN THE COUNTRY

Australian city-dwellers had long been attracted to literature about life on the land. The yarns of Henry Lawson and the verse of 'Banjo' Paterson became national treasures. The 'Dad and Dave' stories of 'Steele Rudd' gained a new audience as a radio serial and as feature films in the 1930s. In keeping with this tradition, two scripts about life in the country shared the first prize for a new Australian play in 1955. The winners were *The Torrents* by Oriel Gray and *Summer of the Seventeenth Doll* by Ray Lawler.

Gray set her drama in a mining settlement in the 1890s. Her message was to irrigate the interior, a project then seen as progress. She based her enthusiasm on the dams being built in the Snowy Mountains, Tennessee Valley, and Dnepr in the Soviet Union. Gray had been a member of the Communist Party, which supported engineering solutions to social and natural problems. Her approach is now recognised as a source of environmental degradation through salination. Gray got into her stride as a writer in the 1970s for the television serial *Bellbird*, set in a Victorian township.

Lawler's drama focused on a pair of canecutters who came down to inner Melbourne each year after the cutting season. The action is set in the early 1950s, on their seventeenth stay-over. Each year, one of the men had presented his female partner with a kewpie doll, hence the title. Lawler had pictured a disappearing world. Machines would soon replace men in the canefields, just as Europeans had displaced Pacific Islanders fifty years before. Opportunities for seasonal labouring were shrinking. The leading male character found work in a paint factory, that emblem of urban prosperity. *The Doll* won approval from local audiences because of its Aussie accents and idiom. (Gray's dialogue sounded like the Irish playwright George Bernard Shaw.) Censorship meant that the men said nothing stronger than 'bloody'. *The Doll* also succeeded in London, despite the five-shilling bet by Prime Minister Menzies that it would flop. A Hollywood producer turned *The Doll* into a film with imported stars. Lawler made a career as an expatriate writer in London. Although the old Australia was retreating, as Lawler recognised, another decade would elapse before the new Australia began to support its authors and performers.

The drift of canecutters into factory work was one strand in the tug-of-war between the city and the bush. Bill Bauer had been born on his father's farm in the early 1920s. The property was thirty kilometres north of Pinnaroo, a township of around 1000 people, 200 kilometres east of Adelaide, almost on the Victorian border. Sand dunes twenty metres high cut across the arable land. Bill's father had rolled down the Mallee scrub; he survived the collapse of wheat prices in the 1930s depression by selling Mallee roots as firewood. The clearing and ploughing left the thin earth vulnerable to drought and winds. In 1944, dust from their fields had soiled snowfields in New Zealand. Average rainfall was around 340 millimetres. The Brauers could survive two years of drought. A third dry year would tip them towards bankruptcy. One solution was to buy up the properties of neighbours as they abandoned the struggle. That expansion let Brauer leave more of his land lie fallow for longer. Another solution had been to replace labour with machines. Both moves reduced the population of Pinnaroo. Its shops began to close.

HEALTH

Very little medical research had been carried out in Australia before the Great War. The Institute of Tropical Medicine was set up in 1910 to look into problems of the white man, and the white mother, in the tropics. A nimble-footed share deal in 1913 funded Melbourne's Walter and Eliza Hall Institute. It had to wait till 1919 to obtain a director, because the man who had been offered the job died of wounds at Gallipoli. Individual doctors published their own findings in the *Medical Journal* . Small agencies, such as the Commonwealth's Quarantine Service under Dr Cumpston, were active. Large-scale medical research did not begin until the John Curtin Medical School opened in Canberra in the late 1940s.

Medical science delivered wonder drugs and surgical procedures with the promise of ever better ways to cure people once they became ill. In 1957, the Walter and Eliza Hall Institute developed a vaccine against 'Asian flu'. A 1960 Nobel Prize for Physiology and Medicine went to the Institute's director, Macfarlane Burnet, for his work on immunology. The Heart Foundation was set up in 1961 to fund research. Two years later, a pacemaker was developed; in 1968, the first heart transplant was made in Australia. Researchers emphasised fixing up parts of the body that had broken down under abuse. Most attention went to new drugs and machines. Improvements to ways of living came a poor second.

The vanquishing of TB overlapped with the conquest of another scourge. Australia's most serious outbreak of poliomyelitis began in 1951 when 4735 people were affected. Some died, many were crippled for life and a few lingered on in iron lungs. Young healthy people were commonly the victims. Panic spread through Australia until 1954 when the epidemic ended. In April 1955, a means of prevention, the Salk vaccine, was discovered in the United States. The first injections here were in June 1956; within a year a million had been given. By 1961, the new cases of polio were down to about 125. In the late 1960s, the vaccine could be taken orally. This development made prevention easier, as people needed more than one treatment in their lifetimes to be completely safe.

WHITE AUSTRALIA

In 1955, non-Europeans could enter Australia only as students or as tourists. Changes in the White Australia policy started in 1956 when more non-Europeans were allowed to become Australian citizens. Some Chinese were allowed to stay rather than be deported to the People's Republic of China; 'distinguished and highly qualified non-Europeans' were also given permission to remain. During the next three years, the rules about bringing in non-European husbands, wives and children were relaxed. Before 1962, only a thousand non-Europeans had been admitted under the new rules. Although these changes pointed towards a new interpretation of White Australia, they in no way undermined its basic principle. Australians became indignant in 1957 when the fraction of immigrants from the United Kingdom slipped below 50 per cent. Just how strict the White Australia policy remained showed up in the case of a sixteen-year-old Scottish boy, Kenneth McBride, who tried to come to Australia in 1961. He told a newspaper reporter:

> It is generally thought that none of my grandparents was coloured. But nobody is certain because I'm a war orphan and have no living relatives who can say whether this is true. All I know is that both my grandparents were dead before I was born and that my parents were born in Scotland. I have no family yet the authorities seem to think that family is more important than anything else. I think it's the person who counts.

Calls increased from inside Australia to relax the policy. Public opinion polls showed a slow, unsteady edging away from opposition to all Asian immigrants. The fraction opposed came down from 61 per cent in 1954 to 45 per cent in June 1958. In 1957, 55 per cent were against letting in even fifty people from every country. By 1965, only 16 per cent opposed admitting a total of 1000 skilled Asians each year. That intake would have been about 1 per cent of total immigration. The drift did not indicate that all Australians had changed their mind about keeping Australia white. A defence expert hinted at what was happening: 'We need to let enough

coloured immigrants in to show that we are not racially prejudiced, yet not so many as to reveal that we are'.

VIEW OF THE WORLD

In November 1956, the Olympic Games brought the world to
Australia. The Soviet-led invasion of Hungary late in October
drew blood during the game between the Hungarian and
Soviet water-polo teams. With competitors from sixty-seven
countries came the foods to suit their tastes. The North Americans imported Soccotash (a version of tinned sweet corn),
pancake mix and maple syrup. Asians brought bamboo shoots
and ginger. Europeans asked for smoked sprats and eel. The
South Americans drank *mate* and used ground maize for torti-
llas, described as 'akin to the damper'. Australian efforts to
please were heartfelt but limited by resources and experience.
That restricted outlook appeared in the Olympic Dinner menu
proposed by the European-born chef from Melbourne's Food
Trades School. His meal opened with turtle soup, to be followed by a choice of baked schnapper or barramundi, or roast
lamb with mint sauce, accompanied by baked potatoes and
green peas. The meal would end with Australian-Olympic
pudding in a passionfruit sauce.

While Melbourne was preparing for its sporting visitors, the
British government was conspiring with France and Israel to
invade Egypt to regain control of the Suez Canal. A
drug-dependent British prime minister, Anthony Eden, had
sent Menzies to Cairo to mediate. External Affairs minister
Richard Casey supported Washington's criticism of their
aggression. Commentators remarked that Canberra faced a
situation which was like mummy and daddy fighting. Five
years later, the United Kingdom tried to join the Europe Economic Community, provoking fears in Australia about a loss
of trade outlets.

The years from 1955 to 1962 brought a relative calm to

Australia's near north. The flash points were all in the northern hemisphere — over Suez in 1956, Berlin in 1960, and Cuba in 1962. Australia got through the transfer of West Papua to Indonesia without firing a shot. Nagging concern remained about fighting along the unmarked border between China and India.

Fear of communist China went hand in hand with ignorance. A hundred Melbourne adults were questioned in 1969 about why they thought China was a threat to Australia. They gave answers such as 'I wish they still threw their babies in the Yangtze like they used to, then they wouldn't be so over-crowded'. But when asked how many Chinese there were, the same people guessed between 80 million and 6000 million, nowhere near the true figure of 600 million. When asked whether there were two Chinas, they came up with answers such as:

A second China: that would be Korea; the government has split that off now; they have broken away.

There is another but I don't know its name; it's ruled by Madam Gandhi; she has a husband, General someone or other; he is deceased.

Yes in some provinces there is Chiang Kai Shek. I think he is in the north, but I think Mao's got the numbers now.

Well there is Chiang Kai Shek — he is a communist. [Chiang was the anti-communist who had fled to Formosa/Taiwan in 1949.]

There was some doubt about where China was, although it was widely believed that it was 'up on top of us there some-where'. Some people said they got their information from *Reader's Digest* and TV. Others mentioned that they had gone to school with Chinese, or had known Chinese market-gardeners.

The Queensland poet Bruce Dawe reflected on one of the

ways in which Australians had closed their Venetian blinds
against the world:

For a while there we had 25-inch Chinese peasant families
famishing in comfort on the 25-inch screen
(if I remember rightly Grandmother dies
with naturally a suspenseful break in the action
for full symphony orchestra plug for Craven A
neat as a whistle probably damn glad
to be quit of the whole gang with their marvellous patience).
We never did find out how it finished up ... Dad
at this stage tripped over the main lead in the dark
hauling the whole set down smack on its inscrutable face,
wiping out in a blue flash and curlicue of smoke
600 million Chinese without a trace ...

The rest of the world neither knew nor cared much about
what Australians were doing. Egon Varro was 'Australian
Correspondent' for European publications. Even during the
height of the Soviet spy scandal in 1954, his editors told him
not to put them to the expense of cabling his reports: 'continue
using air-mail unless half of your continent gets blown away'.
Varro learned that stories about the impact of immigration
were his best sellers. His editors wanted to hear

of how the Old Australia — decent, stolid, coarse, and prudish,
narrow-minded and generous like a *Bulletin* cartoon — is meeting
the impact of minestrone and espresso, of higher building and
hire-purchase, of Yankee slickness in ads, of finicky German fit-
ters and exasperatingly serious Finns. My stars have been
Namatjira, Sister Kenny, the Flying Doctor, and Clem Walton (remember the cabbie who made Rio Tinto what it is today?) and
King Booze. I have written more about the six o'clock swill than
about section 92 of the constitution.

By the late 1950s, Varro observed what he called 'the
Southern Hemisphere complex'. This was the conviction that
developments in Australia were the biggest ever in the
Southern Hemisphere. Its promoters neither knew nor cared
about the size of Rio de Janeiro.

10 1963-1970 STRIKING IT LUCKY

By selling coals, iron and bauxite, as well as its old standbys of wheat and wool, Australians, at last, could import whatever we needed or felt like: mainframe computers or magnums of champagne, diesel engines or designer clothes. The 1950s had arrived. When Donald Horne in 1964 dubbed Australia 'the lucky country', he was being critical. Australia under Liberal Prime Minister Menzies, Horne wrote, was being 'run by second-rate people who share its luck'. He accused some executives of glorying in 'a look-no-brains attitude'. The mining bonanza meant that Australia's leaders did not have to become clever managers. Looking back from 1971, the chairman of the Commonwealth Banking Corporation, Warren D. McDonald, reckoned:

> We missed a generation in management. Our industrial growth was so rapid that many firms moved from being backyard operations to complex national organisations in a few years. Father, who often started in shirtsleeves and with perhaps a limited education, had to compete with immense problems and back-breaking work. Instead of his better-educated, better-trained sons taking over in the natural course and being able to handle the new problems, as in older industrial societies, he had to do everything himself in a few years or he failed to survive. He often did not possess the time to be concerned with marketing research and scientific management techniques.

Instead, a cargo cult mentality prevailed. The rest of the world would make us rich. The two biggest saviours were the old enemy of Japan and the current threat of Red China.

WORK

Industrialisation impacted on every aspect of life. Industrial estates were constructed at Altona in Melbourne and at Botany Bay in Sydney. Mining towns dotted remote areas of the north-west Pilbara. Abattoirs adapted assembly lines. The building trades were re-skilled. Computers entered machine-shops. The poor quality of management gave workers an extra reason for taking charge of the production process. The following survey illustrates these elements.

On the western side of the continent rose the industrial site of Kwinana, twenty-five kilometres south of Perth. In the 1940s, the area had been a holiday resort. In 1955, British Petroleum started processing crude oil, which it piped to Fremantle Harbour. Petroleum by-products attracted other industries. The State's Electricity Commission built an oil-fired power station. Western Australia's mineral boom brought still more firms to Kwinana's 2800 hectares. Broken Hill Proprietary agreed to build an iron-and-steel industry in return for leases on iron deposits at Koolyanobbing. The government constructed a railway to carry that ore for the blast furnace that started in 1968. Bauxite, from the nearby Darling Ranges, fed Alcoa's alumina refinery. Nickel from Western Mining Corporation's Kambalda site, south of Kalgoorlie, was refined using ammonia provided by a large fertiliser company, which in turn used by-products from the oil refinery. Oil acted as the spark. Even before the energy crises of the 1970s, concerns arose about the environmental impact of such giant developments. David Ireland's novel *The Unknown Industrial Prisoner* (1971) portrayed the dangers and how workers responded.

During the 1960s, the Liberal–Country Party government had made strikes in effect illegal. The law bottled up workers' complaints, all of which burst open in 1969 when half-a-million unionists stopped work in support of the secretary of the Victorian Tramways Union, Clarrie O'Shea. O'Shea had gone to gaol for refusing to pay a fine imposed on his union for an earlier strike. Victory in the O'Shea struggle made workers more confident. It also frightened the government so much that it did not dare use its laws against strikes. The combination of almost continuous over-full employment until late 1974 and rapidly increasing prices gave workers both the opportunity and the reason to strike for higher wages.

Further north, the mining boom brought new chances for young men willing to trade a few years' very hard work for a bigger bank balance. Mining companies paid high wages for long hours, providing air-conditioned cheap houses for families. Herman and Helen Driesan decided to try their luck at Mt Newman (WA). Herman had just finished his apprenticeship as a toolmaker in Perth. The Driesans reckoned that they would never be able to afford a deposit on a house. After two years at Mt Newman, they had a home in Perth with rent-paying tenants, a car, money in the bank and no debts other than the mortgage. But, as Helen explained: 'Herman has paid for everything we have achieved — up on that hill. He works a six-day week, ten-hour day for his money, in that appalling dust and heat'. Back in Perth, Herman wanted a clean job.

During 1962, the big three meat-handling firms introduced production-lines. Before then, the carcasses had been cut up and boned on tables. Now, the beast passed down a mechanised line of thirty boners, each with a different task. Each man had a little over a metre in which to work. Their moves were timed to the second. If one boner fell behind, he had to invade the space of the next one along. The men saw from the start that the system would not work. They advocated operating in teams of two or five. After five years of disputes, the company agreed that the workers had known better than the experts.

Automated production came in 1963 with the first numerically controlled lathe. Within ten years, Australia had another 278. Most were in the government sector. The simplest were run by a tape prepared on a separate computer. These machines saved labour-time and wasted less material. The more advanced models had computers built-in which could modify the tape. Small firms could afford versions that allowed an unskilled operator to produce at the speed and quality of fully trained tradesman. One sign of this development was that the Amalgamated Engineering Union in 1969 changed its name to the Amalgamated Metal Workers Union.

Professional engineers took over from architects in the management of building projects. In Sydney, the Dutch-born engineer G. J. Dusseldorp led the way in reorganising the construction industry through his firms Lend Lease and Civil & Civic. Prefabrication reallocated tasks between professions and within trades. Instead of a tradesman hand-crafting a cupboard, a labourer trained on the job would assemble, or perhaps only install, kitchen units made in a factory. Modular standardisation was extended to office blocks. The volumes of ready-mix concrete used in Australia went from 1442 cubic yards in 1956–57 to 6603 cubic yards in 1965–66, almost five-fold in ten years. High-rises required taller cranes. The higher the buildings went, the deeper went the foundations, bringing massive machinery onto city blocks. Unionists took advantage of the new techniques to enforce safety and to preserve historic sites.

LIFE IN THE CITIES

More Australians were living in flats. In 1953–54, only 3 per cent of the money spent on new housing units went on flats.

Twelve years later, that figure was 21 per cent. Or, put another way: in 1952 in Sydney, only one new dwelling in forty had been a flat; by 1967, more than one in five was a flat. Higher-density housing did not end the sprawl of Australian cities. In fact, the areas being filled with apartment blocks often had falling populations. Bringing 2000 people together on a block of land where only 200 had lived before required additional parking space, access roads and areas for garages and shops. One measure of the suburban sprawl around Melbourne was that after *Melway* first appeared in 1966, each new edition added 2000 streets.

Suburbia

Early in the 1950s, a Melbourne architect, Robin Boyd, had attacked the way in which Australians built their cities. In *Australia's Home* he claimed that the millions of private dwellings were 'Collectively an achievement. Individually they are prey to thoughtless habits, snobberies and fickle sentiment. This is the story of a material triumph and an aesthetic calamity'. Boyd concluded: 'Out at the end of the Australian suburb, where raw new houses stood in shadeless yellow grass beside the rutted tracks, one seemed to suffer all the disadvantages of city life and enjoy none of the advantages'. Boyd was concerned about more than the material and artistic sides of suburban living. It seemed to him that life in the suburbs had changed the Australian character for the worse. 'What', he asked, 'has happened to the spirit, the gusto, the faith? The Wild Colonial Boy is selling used cars.' Boyd was nonetheless hopeful: 'The vision will return. Australia will advance again'. Before he died in 1971, he felt little reason to justify his earlier hope. His last book was a satire on the country he loved, and hated to see spoilt.

Barry Humphries personified Australia's uncertain attitudes towards suburbia when he created Mrs Edna Everage in 1955. Within three years, she and hubby Norm were leaving

Moonee Ponds to try it in Highett. In that new suburb she could peek through her Venetian blinds and worry whether to say 'pat-tio' or 'payshio'. Edna would not have found anything unkind in the 1966 description that Sydney broadcaster Alan Ashbolt gave of life in the suburbs:

Behold the man — the Australian man of today — on Sunday mornings in the suburbs, when the high-decibel drone of the motor-mower is calling the faithful to worship. A block of land, a brick veneer, and a motor-mower beside him in the wilderness — what more does he want to sustain him, except a Holden to polish, a beer with the boys, marital sex on Saturday nights, a few furtive adulteries, an occasional gamble on the horses or the lottery, the tribal rituals of football, the flickering shadows in his lounge room of cops and robbers, goodies and baddies, guys and dolls.

That was rather how Mrs Everage liked it.

Critics of suburbia were attacked, in turn, for being anti-democratic, anti-working class and ignorant of the human relationships that supported community bodies. Just as Robin Boyd was the keenest critic of suburban living, Hugh Stretton became its noblest defender. Stretton had been a professor of history in Adelaide and later advisor to the Australian government on housing. In his 1971 book *Ideas for Australian Cities*, he claimed:

you don't have to be a mindless conformist to choose suburban life. Most of the best poets and painters and inventors and protestors choose it too. It reconciles access to work and city with private, adaptable, self-expressive living space at home. Plenty of adults love that living space, and subdivide it ingeniously. For children it really has no rivals.

Supporters of women's liberation suspected that Stretton's views were arguments for keeping women at home looking after hubby and the kids.

Although the debate over suburbia had gone on for a long time, and had been sharp on both sides, there was something unreal about it. Suburbia did not exist as a single way of life.

Life in working-class suburbs such as Green Valley, Inala, Sunshine, Elizabeth and Victoria Park was different from life in the posh suburbs of Woollahra, St Lucia, Camberwell, North Adelaide and Peppermint Grove. Frank Hardy's 1971 novel, *The Outcasts of Foolgarah*, highlighted the class divisions that made suburbia possible: the garbos at the bottom of the hill lived in an extended family; the toffs on top of the hill entertained the prime minister.

The fact that so many Australians lived in the suburbs was not proof of their preferences. When people did not have much money, and there was a housing shortage, they lived wherever they could afford. In Melbourne, the government had parked thousands of families in high-rise apartment blocks. Other government rules had also driven people to live on suburban blocks. Later, different laws, and the chance of a quick profit for developers, shepherded people into flats. If Australians did not want to live in the suburbs, the assumptions about the Australian character based upon a life-long passion for a sliver of land, 8000 bricks and a hunk of tin from Detroit, collapsed. If most Australians ever live in high- or medium-density housing, we still will not know anything about the 'national character'. We will know only that apartments and town-houses had become profitable for developers who will be living somewhere else.

Going up?

Inner cities shot up as the suburbs continued to move outwards. Tall buildings were a recent addition to the Australian skyline. They had become possible because of iron frames. That form of architecture was not understood in Australia until the 1920s when the new BHP iron-and-steel works at Newcastle supplied the materials. Before then, some local authorities had ruled that iron-framed buildings had to have the same base wall-width (a little over a metre) as stone ones. Taller buildings required fast and easy lifts. Australia's first

electric elevator was installed in Melbourne in 1923. Cantile-
vered awnings had appeared in 1908, but they too had to wait
for the development of a local steel industry before becoming
common.

Until 1956, Melbourne had a building limit of about
forty-five metres. The twenty-storey ICI building was the
first office block to go above this height. That record was
broken in 1961 when the CRA building reached twenty-three
storeys. For a long time, Sydney's pride was the AMP's
twenty-six storeys at Circular Quay. In 1975 Australia's tallest
building became the 259-metre Centrepoint in Sydney. By
then, twenty-storey blocks were being knocked down to make
way for buildings twice as high. Central Business Districts
flaunted signs reading 'WHELAN THE WRECKER WAS HERE'.
The cities suffered from filling their inner areas with endless
rows of office blocks. After six o'clock, and at the weekends,
the streets were dying. During the day it was hard to find a
sunny spot. Most of the new buildings were dull imitations of
each other. One Australian designer observed on his return
after several years working in Britain: 'Australia is busy
pulling down a lot of ugly old buildings to put a lot of ugly
new ones up in their place'.

These developments threatened older structures. Because
Australia had had so brief a European settlement, it had been
assumed that few buildings had historical significance. When
the National Trust in New South Wales started in 1947, its task
was to identify buildings worthy of preservation and to save
them. In the beginning, the Trust spent most of its time and
money on a couple of showpieces, the mansions of the rich. In
later years, resident action groups and builders' labourers
struggled to save whole blocks of houses such as those in the
Rocks area of Sydney. Protestors forced private developers to
save Melbourne's Regent and to replace Sydney's Theatre
Royal. Local councils set aside buildings and land for historical displays. Fremantle's maritime museum opened in 1970 in

a convict-built structure which would otherwise have been knocked down.

Corruption

Urban redevelopment made local government into a corruption zone. Most councillors were paid little more than their expenses for council duties, which often involved a lot of social spending. That demand provided one motive. The opportunity arose because councils had the power to decide whether developments should go ahead. For a bribe, councillors were known to change their votes. Between 1940 and 1975, seven councillors and a mayor from four Sydney suburbs were gaoled and three councillors fined for corruption. These figures did not point to large-scale corruption in Australian local government. Yet they were only the ones who had been convicted.

The way in which corruption worked was exposed in 1966 when two members from the Warringah Shire Council were gaoled for taking bribes. The details of the case came out in court much later. This account will use initials instead of the councillors' surnames because in New South Wales the libel laws protect the guilty.

In December 1965, Councillor X was elected to the Warringah Shire Council. Shortly afterwards he was asked to a Liberal Party social by Councillor Z. Over a drink, Z allegedly told X that his friends had the council fixed up and they would do very well out of it. Later X got $400 to vote for a hotel application and was promised money on five other matters before council. On 1 September 1966, a land developer applied to subdivide fifteen hectares at Killarney Heights. An executive from the developer, Mr Stewart, was asked to meet the council's works committee, which decided to inspect the site the next day. The following morning, Councillor X arranged to meet Mr Stewart privately and told him that unless his firm 'came to the party' there would be no approval for the land development. Councillor X demanded $8000, to be split eight ways, to buy council support. Stewart went to the police who told him to go ahead with the payment, while they took steps to catch Councillor X red-handed.

At 5 pm the same day, Stewart, with a wire recorder, went to Killarney Heights. He promised that, if the council gave its approval on 19 September, the money would be paid the next day. Councillor X threatened that the council could reverse its vote.

On the morning of the 20th, Stewart took $8000 in twenty-dollar notes from his bank and drove past Councillor X's garage: X followed in his truck, with the police watching. In Stewart's car, the money changed hands. Councillor X was arrested. Later, he confessed everything and, with another councillor, went to prison. Despite claims by a councillor that several more councillors were involved, no one else was arrested. The State government removed the entire Warringah Shire Council in April 1967.

Corruption in local government is significant because municipalities control the issues that touch the everyday lives of most Australians. If a council were bribed to let a petrol station be built where there should have been a playground, the lives of ordinary people would be disadvantaged for years to come. Bribery also added to the advantages that the rich had over the poor, who could not afford to bribe anybody. Big companies did not always need to bribe councillors to get what they wanted. Business executives used the mantra that 'growth is good' to convince authorities to approve development projects. The process was summed up in the title of Leonie Sandercock's book, *Cities for Sale*.

Lifestyle

Urban redevelopment was one aspect of the dilemmas investigated by US economist J. K. Galbraith in his 1958 book, *The Affluent Society*. Marketing penetrated every aspect of life, from the holidays Australians took, to the clothes we wore and to what we drank and ate.

More Australians, particularly the young and retirees, were venturing overseas. Short trips abroad became feasible with the introduction of jet aircraft in the early 1960s. Flights to Bali and Hong Kong began. Ships remained popular with retired couples; hundreds booked a *Women's Weekly* 'Cherry Blossom Cruise' to Japan. Sea passages to the United Kingdom and Europe were cramped but cheap. After four weeks' annual leave became the norm in the 1970s, middle-aged Australians could draw on their long-service leave to spend three months driving around their continent. Attracted by Namatjira tablemats, and shocked by the scenery in Chauvel's film *Jedda*, more wished to experience the Red Centre than had been willing to rough it. Caravan parks were packed with campervans.

Adults were less shocked by youthful fashions than earlier generations had been, because they were promoted by advertisers, the arbiters of taste. The merchandisers provided the young with their own sub-cultures. Teenagers no longer competed with their parents at the pictures on Saturday night. By 1969, men's hair was longer and fathers wore coloured shirts to work. Paisley neckties for men were becoming as common as the mini-skirt was for young women after Jean Shrimpton wore one to the 1965 Spring Racing Carnival at Flemington.

Tea or coffee?

Before the First Pacific War, Australians used 3 kilograms of tea per head per year against 250 grams of coffee. By 1971, tea was down to 2 kilograms per head while coffee had increased fivefold. The trend continued until the 1980s when tea fell to 1 kilogram and coffee reached more than 2 kilograms. One explanation offered for this turnaround is that it was one of the changes that European immigrants introduced to Australian eating and drinking habits. Coffee, wine and pizza replaced tea, beer and meat pies. Certainly, salami went on sale in super-markets as well as in delicatessens; many shops had gourmet sections selling seeded mustard, olive oil, brie and Twinings teabags. Yet branded pet foods also became widespread at this time, and no one suggests that they were a European delicacy. Nor did Italians smuggle jars of Maxwell House instant coffee into the country in their suitcases. The influence of Continentals and Asians on Australian diets has been exaggerated. The adoption of coffee was not a sign of multiculturalism but of '*mall*-ticulturalism', a shopping arcade of synthetic ethnic flavours. The Chicko Roll was invented by the 'Chinaman' Frank McEnroe, Dial-a-Dinos was founded by the 'Italian' Richard Wescombe, and Papa Giuseppe pizzas were cooked up by that other 'Italian', the Hungarian Joe Piazs.

Missing from the conventional wisdom is any recognition that coffee, like pet food, was promoted by multinational corporations. Only a few thousand Anglo-Celtic Australians frequented *expresso* bars when they opened in 1956, compared with the millions opening a jar of Nescafé in 1969. The immigration of capital was more significant than the movement of people. For instance, a Swiss firm, Nestlé, influenced the choice of beverages even though Australia had almost no Swiss settlers. Of course, pre-war levels of tea-drinking had been no more natural than the subsequent swing to coffee. From the 1930s, the Tea Market Expansion Bureau and its successor, the Tea Council, had advertised that product.

Similarly, more cheesecake was eaten because of the sales efforts of Sara Lee than because of an influx of Austrian chefs. Sara Lee products fitted into freezer compartments like an up-market ice-cream. The popularity of French cuisine far exceeded the number of new arrivals from France. Magazines promoted the branded foods that advertised in their pages. Early in 1972, the *Women's Weekly* explained that 'quiche' should be pronounced 'keesh', and was an open-faced savoury tart. A few years later, most quiches were bought branded and frozen.

The switch from tea to coffee was only one of a number of changes to beverage consumption. Coffee did not replace all the tea that people used to consume. For the young, colas and fruit juices took over. Between 1964 and 1985, the sale of soft drinks went up from 182 litres a year per person to 332 litres per person.

Mass marketing, however, was not the whole explanation. Tea declined because it needed so long to brew. Instant coffee took only seconds. By 1971, 70 per cent of coffee was instant. The speed-up of working lives also brought the tea-bag. Its sales quadrupled to 1350 million a year between 1972 and 1975 once Lipton's television commercials made jiggling a national pastime.

LIFE IN THE COUNTRY

In 1955, one Australian in five lived outside towns with a population of more than 1000. By 1971, only one in seven lived in such small communities. The drift from the country-side slowed down because there were fewer people who could leave. In bad times the exodus quickened. For example, during the wool slump of 1968–71 the population of western Victoria and western New South Wales fell by as much as 10 per cent.

One reason for this shift was an unwillingness by men and women to put up with the grind and the boredom. A grazier's wife who had spent nearly thirty years on a property in southern Queensland described her loneliness:

My husband and son leave home early in the morning and may return for lunch, but often do not. Even when I see them in the middle of the day, they are only home a short while before going out again until dark. When they return they are physi-cally tired, and answer my questions in monosyllables. No one asks me what sort of a day I have had, whether or not I have been lonely. It is even farther from their thoughts to ask me how I should like to spend the evening. The nearest neighbour is eight miles away by road. If we go to town more than once a fortnight, we are being very gay. This has gone on for years and years.

Our mail is left in a petrol drum, six and a half miles from the house. We put up our own telephone line. I waited twenty-six years for a septic and the same year — glory be! — we got electricity. The roads about here can best be described as car-wreckers; but TV is our greatest disappointment. Although there is a transmission service from Roma, and in spite of boosters and a sky-high antenna, we receive a good picture only when conditions are ideal. All these things have lessened hardships caused by isolation in country areas but it is still there.

A young mother in the outback recalled being without a radio transceiver for a month: 'It was really horrible, like being on a desert island and quite frightening'. Educating children added to the stress for women in remote areas. One of them pointed out that 'the tremendous, overriding factor in our lives is that children have to be marshalled into school each day and taught. And unless we do it, no one else will worry'. The next obstacle was finding jobs for young people in the country: 'on the farm, they get paid half as much as in the cities' and 'get about two weeks holiday every two years'. This difference explained why so many country areas had few people aged between fifteen and twenty-five.

In the 1930s, the journalist-poet Kenneth Slessor had pictured country towns:

And farmers bouncing on barrel mares
To public houses of yellow wood
With '1860' over their doors,
And that mysterious race of Hogans
Which always keeps General Stores ...

By the 1970s, some of these towns no longer existed. Their pubs and shops were closed. The towns that remained had usually grown in order to survive. Instead of horses there were

Holden utes; instead of public houses there might be a motel or at least a service station with a restaurant; and the Hogans would be working for Woolies or Coles.

One suggestion for stemming the loss of population was to accept that the smallest settlements were dying. Larger towns would be helped to grow to around 5000 people. Communities of that size could provide services and entertainments. Farmers could drive out to their properties, as many of the wealthier ones already did. This reallocation paralleled plans to build up one or two regional growth centres, such as Albury–Wodonga and Bathurst–Orange.

A few districts were revived by the arrival of Pitt Street or Collins Street farmers. These city businessmen and doctors bought farms, did them up, and perhaps sold them, as a way of not paying taxes. Between 1967 and 1972, the number of Hereford studs in Victoria grew by 40 per cent because of this kind of investment. The city-slickers made their money by buying a debt-ridden, cleared property and holding on to it for five years. High-income earners could make 60 per cent more this way than if they had put their money into suburban flats. The *Real Estate Journal* recognised that 'Pitt Street farming still rewards the rich'.

The quality of living in the country depended on where you lived and what you did for a crust. Country towns differed as greatly as suburbs, as can be seen by comparing Heyfield (Victoria) with Bowral (NSW). Heyfield had about 1500 people, about one-third of whom depended on the timber industry. It had a greater proportion of children and middle-aged people than did the rest of the State. Its proportion of unskilled and semi-skilled workers was almost twice as high as the Victorian average. About one-fifth of its 500 houses were rented. There was no sewerage. Although Heyfield had a milk factory, many people bought their milk raw; two of the three butchers did their own killing; there was no longer a local baker. Heyfield was small, quiet and declining.

Bowral could hardly have been more different. Its population was slowly increasing towards 6000. Nearly half of its workforce had white-collar jobs. It also had a high proportion of wealthy retired people. In 1968, the town enjoyed performances from the Australian Ballet, the Bath Festival Ensemble and the University of California Chamber Singers. One of Bowral's most noticeable features was its social divide. That barrier existed throughout Australia but it was easier to see in the country. A widow from the rich part of town told how Bowral's class system worked:

> If you have money and a lovely home you are accepted socially. But older families are accepted more on family than on money. There are a lot of beautiful homes, and this makes for more plums in the mouth and that sort of thing. Money, homes, and family are the main things. People are not friendly.

The social divisions decided which golf club Bowralians could join. The old families, the professional people, the graziers and the retired rich kept the rest of the town out of their club. As one of them explained:

> We just have a rule that no one who is in trade in the town can be a member. We like to have a quiet drink in a pleasant atmosphere. Can you imagine what it would be like if we let the local shopkeepers in? They would be getting drunk, making a noise, and playing the poker machines all night.

The cliché that Australia was a classless society meant only that it was free of most of the feudal trappings in Europe. The class divide of capitalism between the owners and the workers ran as deeply.

Slessor observed advertising posters 'Sprayed with the sarcasm of flies'. When city-dwellers went on a picnic, a bush-walk or an outback trip, nothing spoilt their fun more than flies. Although the bush fly is native to Australia, its numbers had multiplied because Australia's ecological balance had been upset by the introduction of European cattle. In 1788, the largest animal here had been the kangaroo, which drops small dry dung, quickly broken up by a variety of insects. By contrast, cattle drop an average of twelve large pads a day. If not gotten rid of, the pads from twenty beasts would cover a hectare in a year. That expanse does not include the largely inedible grasses that grow around the edge of each pad. Ten cows might degrade a hectare of grassland each year. Thirty million cattle in Australia threatened as much as three million hectares a year. Native insects were too small and too fussy to carry the cattle pads away, and flies bred in them. CSIRO scientists experimented with imported dung beetles, setting the first ones free in northern Australia in 1967. A variety of beetles was needed to cope with all our climatic conditions. Success offered three benefits. Outdoor social life in Australia would be much more pleasant; more grass would be available; and the grass would be of better quality since dung beetles break up the dung and carry it underground, providing fertiliser. The only complaint came from a pastoralist who had used dried-out dung pads to even up his irrigation pipes. He had to carry blocks of wood around with him instead. In the time it has taken to read this section on dung beetles, as many as half-a-million cattle pads have been dropped in Australia. The attack on flies was an example of public health.

HEALTH
Hatch, Match and Patch

Demographic and social factors contributed to the percentage of married women engaged in paid work: more women were getting married, they were marrying younger, and they were living longer after their last child went to school. Compare a woman born in 1945 with her grandmother born fifty years earlier. On average, the grandmother married when she was aged twenty-five, had her last baby when she was forty, and died aged not quite sixty. By contrast, her granddaughter married when she was twenty-two, had her last child when she was thirty and could expect to live to seventy. In other words, the granddaughter would have at least twice as many years to work after her last child went to school as her grandmother had had. These changes in turn helped the proportion of married women in the workforce to grow from about 8 per cent in 1947 to around 40 per cent in 1974.

Contraception became one of the silent forces shaping twentieth-century Australian society. Its impact occurred despite efforts to keep people ignorant. For a time, advertisements for birth-control devices were illegal. Nonetheless, couples learned how to limit pregnancies, and to make them more predictable. Children could arrive at times that suited a mother's social and economic situation. Around 1935, slightly less than half of all married fecund women practised some kind of contraception. Or, it might be truer to say that their husbands did, since the most widely used method was withdrawal. The total number of couples who were practising contraception rose to two-thirds in 1945–49. By 1970–71, it reached over 90 per cent. The fraction of those practising withdrawal remained at around 20 per cent. Another change came after 1960 with 'the Pill', taken by about 40 per cent of all fecund married women in Australia. The increased use of contraceptives did not greatly reduce the birth-rate.

Dying is as much a part of life as getting sick or becoming well. During 1967, 102 703 Australians died, which was 8.69 per 1000 in the population. This death-rate had been fairly stable since the 1930s. Life expectancy had also stayed about the same for men, at 67 years; for women, it rose from 63 years in the 1920s to 74 by the late 1960s. Sulphur drugs had reduced the number of women dying during childbirth. Between the 1930s and the 1960s, the death-rate of infants under one year of age fell from 7.4 to 3.9 in every hundred live births. Causes of death also altered. In 1931, more than 3000 Australians died from tuberculosis, as against only 320 in 1966. In 1948, only one-sixth of traffic deaths were of women, a percentage which grew as more women drove cars.

People not only died later and from different causes but their remains were treated in new ways. Instead of being buried, more bodies were cremated. The first crematorium had opened in 1903 in South Australia. Sydney did not get one until 1926, when 122 bodies were burnt. In 1967, almost 40 per cent of corpses were incinerated. By 1978, the figure for the capital cities was closer to 70 per cent. One difference between Melbourne and Sydney is that Melburnians preferred to be buried than burnt. Funeral directors performed some of the tasks that had been done at home in the days when more people died in their own beds rather than in hospital. Even those who died at home in the 1960s were taken away as quickly as possible. In the past, they would have been laid out in the family house for grieving relatives to gather round while friends paid their respects.

The price of dying went up along with the cost of living. In 1950, the average Melbourne funeral had cost about £50. By the late 1960s, the bill had risen to around $350, and then to more than $1000 by 1980. A memorial over the grave site had gone up from $40 in 1958 to $500 in 1980. Some families spent many times these amounts as their way of expressing sorrow. Others thought that most funerals were impersonal when conducted by a clergyman who had never met the deceased. Families began to devise their own services. 'I did it my way' displaced 'Abide with me'. A few preferred 'no fuss' or even 'do-it-yourself' arrangements whereby relatives made the coffin and shifted it in their panel van.

ABORIGINES

Aborigines in the second half of the twentieth century took back control of their own lives. In 1955, the typical organisation interested in the Indigenous population had been a welfare society whose members were white Australians concerned to help people who were not allowed to help themselves. In the 1960s, Aborigines turned those bodies into activist groups aimed at rebuilding Aboriginal society outside settler control. All over Australia, Aborigines strove to take charge of their own affairs. At cattle stations they walked away, leaving the whites to fend for themselves. In the cities they set up their own legal, health and social services. As Aborigines regrouped, they brought changes to the way the rest of society thought about them. In 1960 the Indigenous population had not been a political issue. By 1970 it had placed itself centre stage.

Small improvements were made to the law and to government welfare policies; more white experts peered into the Aboriginal question; some money was spent on houses, schools and hospitals. Yet the more fiddling there was, the more Aborigines complained that little was improving. And nothing much would change, they said, until land rights were won.

In June 1966, members of the Gurindji tribe working on Wave Hill station in the Northern Territory 'walked off'. They set up a camp in the dry bed of the Victoria River and refused to work for wages anymore. Early in the next year, they asked that 1300 square kilometres be cut out of the 16 000 square kilometres of Wave Hill station, which was leased by the British firm of Vesteys Ltd. Although the company agreed to give up some land, the Liberal–Country Party government blocked the transfer. The Minister for the Interior, Peter Nixon, told parliament in 1970: 'The government believes that it is wholly wrong to encourage Aboriginals to think that because their ancestors have had a long association with a particular piece of land, Aboriginals of the present day have the right to demand ownership of it'. Aborigines, he said, could own land, but only if they got it in the same way as other Australians. Presumably he did not mean that Aborigines should steal it. Ted Egan, a Northern Territory white folk-singer, answered Nixon's demand:

Poor bugger me, Gurindji
Peter Nixon talk long we:
'Buy you own land, Gurindji
Buyim back from the Lord Vestey'
Poor bugger blackfeller Gurindji
Suppose we buyim back country
What you reckon proper fee?
Might be flour, sugar and tea
From the Gurindji to Lord Vestey?
Oh poor bugger me.

Donald Horne joined those Australians who saw the Aborigines as the unluckiest people in their own country.

On 27 May 1967, almost 90 per cent of Australian voters agreed to amend the Constitution to allow the Commonwealth government to make laws relating to Aboriginal people and to include them in the census. The referenda did not give Aborigines the vote or bestow citizenship — both those conditions had been available for a long time, though unevenly applied. Nine months later, the Commonwealth appointed a Minister for Aboriginal Affairs. Aborigines hoped that the constitutional amendments would mark a new deal for them. They looked forward to the end of repressive State laws, to better living conditions, and even to some granting of land rights.

Meanwhile, Aboriginal people struggled to say alive. In that regard, there was nothing unusual in the death of Evelyn Young. She was, after all, an Aboriginal baby. The death-rate of Aboriginal children was six to eight times higher than that of white Australian children. What was unusual was that her mother, Nancy Young, was tried, convicted and gaoled for Evelyn's manslaughter. After Evelyn's father deserted the family, Nancy had $6 a week to keep herself and her two children. When Evelyn was about five weeks old, she got gastroenteritis and was in hospital for eight days. She was sent home because she 'looked better'. No tests were carried out on her and her mother was given no instructions about feeding or check-ups; nor was she given any vitamins or medicines. Nancy kept Evelyn alive on Sunshine powdered milk, with some Farex, custard and vegetables if she could afford them.

When Evelyn was four-and-a-half months old, she again became very sick. Late on Saturday, 6 July 1968, her mother carried her three kilometres to the Cunnamulla Hospital. An untrained nurse abused Nancy, gave Evelyn glucose and water, but did not call the duty doctor. On Sunday the doctor began what a specialist later called entirely incorrect treatment. Two days later, Evelyn died.

Apart from the inquest and a couple of interviews by the police, nothing more happened until the following November when Nancy Young took Evelyn's older sister to the hospital with gastroenteritis. The next day, more than three months after Evelyn's death, the police charged Nancy Young with Evelyn's manslaughter. The grounds were that she had failed to provide adequate food and did not seek medical treatment soon enough. The magistrate set bail at $1000, three times Nancy's annual income, and Nancy spent three months in gaol awaiting trial. Several aspects of the hearing were strange, including the judge's advice to the jury. Found guilty, Nancy was sent to prison for three years of hard labour.

The ABC television program 'This Day Tonight' ran a ten-minute item on the case. As a result, protest meetings in Sydney initiated an unsuccessful appeal to the Supreme Court. An appeal was then made to the Governor of Queensland who sent the case back to the Court. This time, the judges knew they had to find that 'fresh evidence was available'. They set aside Nancy Young's conviction. She was released one month before she would have been freed anyway.

Between the hearings of the two appeals, another ABC television program, 'Four Corners', had screened an in-depth study of Cunnamulla and its Aboriginal population. The broadcast stirred up the State government enough to send a welfare officer. When rumours spread that the officer had bought a house in the town for Nancy Young, three petrol bombs were thrown at it. The local shire installed another tap at the reserve so that its water supply was equal to that of the cemetery next door. Indeed, the shire spent more on the cemetery each year than it did on the Aboriginal reserve, which was bounded on the other side by the town's sewerage outlet. There was no sewerage on the reserve.

At the time of Evelyn's death, Cunnamulla's bowling club, two of its three hotels and the best seats in the cinema were off limits to Aborigines. In such a town it was not surprising that no one much cared if an Aboriginal child died. Nancy Young's offence was not that she did not look after her children. Her crime was that she had upset Cunnamulla's whites by bringing her sick children to their hospital. A documentary film by Dennis O'Rourke in 2000 illustrated the persistence of the prejudices faced by young people, black and white, in places such as Cunnamulla.

WHITE AUSTRALIA

From time to time, the government still deported non-Europeans. The case of a Filipino led to a debate in the United Nations and to demands that Australia be expelled from SEATO. The White Australia policy was also getting in the way of Australia's trade with Asian countries. Nonetheless, the white supremacist Prime Minister Menzies threw out proposals by members of his own cabinet to make non-European immigration less restrictive. In March 1966, two months after he retired, sweeping changes were introduced.

The new regime meant faster naturalisation. More families could come here sooner and more easily. The rule about coloured people being 'distinguished and highly qualified' was eased to 'well qualified', which included nurses and teachers. The result of these amendments benefited non-Europeans already here. There was a small increase in non-European newcomers. By 1968, about 40 000 non-Europeans (not counting the Indigenous population) lived in Australia.

Whether or not a non-European could stay depended on the Minister for Immigration. The 'Nancy Prasad case' revealed the extent of the minister's powers, just as Nancy's story revived one element of the origins of White Australia. That policy had aimed to repatriate the Pacific Islanders who had been brought here to work in the sugar industry. To serve sugar giants such as Australia's CSR, the Prasads had been sent to Fiji as indentured labourers, that 'new system of slavery'.

In September 1961, Mr Shiri Prasad came to Sydney from Fiji on a holiday to visit his two sons who were married to Australians. He got a job, but was told by the Immigration Department that he had no right to work here and that he would have to return home. Mr Prasad claimed later that he had been told also that he could return to Australia once he had turned fifty; then, he could claim to be dependent on his two sons. Mr Prasad went back to Fiji, resigned from its public service, and got £2000 in superannuation. When he asked to enter Australia permanently, the officials told him, 'Not a chance in the world, mate, for you blacks', but gave him another visitor's permit. In April 1962, he brought his wife, four children and mother-in-law to Sydney. On his fiftieth birthday, Mr Prasad went back to the Immigration Department, to be told that he could not settle here under any circumstances. Yet he was allowed to stay on holiday for a whole year. He bought two houses. His wife had a baby daughter. In April 1963, he was given permission to stay until September but only to fix up his business affairs. On 5 November, he left for Fiji, leaving two of his daughters in Australia. The 21-year-old daughter had married an Australian. Five-year-old Nancy was in hospital.

In March 1964, the government ruled that Nancy had to go back to her parents in Fiji. Shortly afterwards, one of her brothers said that Nancy was in hiding from the police and that his sister wanted to adopt her so she could stay in Australia. Several court cases agreed that Nancy should return to Fiji and that she could not be adopted.

Early in August 1964, her brothers and sisters gave in and took Nancy to Sydney airport where students protested against the White Australia policy. Just as Nancy was about to board the plane, she was nabbed by a student leader and driven away. This last-minute move had been worked out with her brothers, to whom she was returned later the same night. Three days later she finally left for Fiji.

Even then, the case was not over. Newspapers and leading Australians attacked the deportation. The *Daily Mirror* (Sydney) called it 'lumbering, insensitive, boorish, overbearing, pig-headed, undiplomatic and pompous'. When the government changed the entry rules eighteen months later, people claimed that it was because of the trouble caused by the Prasad case. This was not true, though the case was one of a number of instances which the government felt were spoiling friendly relations with our Asian neighbours. Early in 1973, the Whitlam Labor government let Nancy return permanently to Australia.

VIEW OF THE WORLD

White Australians had depended for defence first on Britain and then on the United States. Behind one of these great powers, Australian governments felt almost safe. This sense of security faded in the late 1960s as Britain retreated from east of Suez and the United States got bogged down in Indo-China.

Indonesia looked dangerous, especially from 1961 until 1965. Jakarta got the Dutch out of West Irian in 1962. Next year came Jakarta's opposition to Britain's formation of a

Malaysian Federation to contain the radical leader of Singapore, Lee Kuan Yew. In response to Indonesia's policy of
'confrontation', Canberra introduced two years of compulsory military training for some twenty-year-olds; it also
ordered F-III fighter-bombers. Indonesia seemed frightening
because of its close links with Red China and because of its
own very strong Communist Party. Then, late in 1965,
anti-Communist generals seized power, slaughtering
half-a-million opponents. The Australian government was
anxious to help the new dictatorship of General Suharto.

Australia had only one treaty of any possible use, namely
ANZUS (SEATO no long existed.) Yet the United States had
proven over Indonesia that the ANZUS alliance did not auto-
matically ensure US support. To secure Washington's commitment, the Australian government jumped at the chance to send
an infantry battalion to Vietnam in 1965. On the evening of 29
April, Prime Minister Menzies lied to the parliament when he
claimed to be reading a request from the prime minister of
South Vietnam. The letter arrived hours later. Moreover, it
made it clear that the initiative had come from Canberra.
These deceits typified how the government handled the war
for the next seven years.

Because young Australians were conscripted to die and kill
in Vietnam, opposition to the war spread through schools and
universities. As the Vietnamese victory became obvious, Australians rethought their attitudes towards Asia in general. The
ignorance was rampant. For example, when a Liberal member
of the Australian Parliament visited Indonesia, travel
narrowed his mind:

> We Australians never look down on Asians you know, we never
> treat them as inferiors. But it's amazing to see these people. Their
> Asian heads only came up to my ponderous stomach and their
> tiny wrists are no bigger than my finger. Australia must help these
> people. We all know an Australian can work for a week without
> feeling tired, but an Indonesian becomes tired after three hours

driving. We are the people who have been chosen to lead Asia, and we can help them. You know, Asians live on only a small handful of rice a day so it's not hard for us to supply them with food.

From June 1965, Teach-Ins on Vietnam challenged this mess of prejudice.

The growth of understanding can be traced in how one person reacted. From 1956 to 1965, Gregory Clark served as a diplomat with the Department of External Affairs. His work showed him that Canberra's approach towards Asia was wrong. Like a large number of younger Australians, Clark moved from being a very conservative supporter of the government to become its radical critic. When Clark had joined the Department of External Affairs, one of his first jobs had been to find facts to support Australia's anti-Arab policy. He had 'to add up the guerilla attacks on Israel'. Even then, he could see that there was something wrong with 'condemning the other side's violence *after* the much greater violence of one's own side'.

His early training as a diplomat was all to do with Europe. The wisdom around the Department was that 'Asia was messy and mysterious'. Then, in order to escape from Canberra, Clark took a course in Chinese at Point Cook, outside Melbourne. 'To learn Chinese, you are forced to realise that a large slice of the human race manages and has managed its affairs perfectly well without the help of Western genius.'

Late in 1962, Clark's view of world politics started to shift with the Indian invasion of China. The media presented this war to Australians as if the Chinese had attacked India. At the time of the fighting, Clark used 'some CIA material to confirm Indian misbehaviour' in a background paper he wrote for the Department of External Affairs. The head of the South-Asia branch blocked Clark's paper. His superior thought that it was 'in the Western interest to see the Chinese and the Indians at each others' throats'. In 1968 some of the most vehement anti-China spokesmen of 1962 had to admit that they had been wrong. Their change of mind came with the publication of *India's China War* by an Australian, Neville Maxwell, who had been Indian correspondent for *The Times* (London) from 1959 to 1967. The Australian High Commissioner to India in 1962, Walter Crocker, wrote a review of Maxwell's book for the *Age* (Melbourne), headed 'When Nehru took India to war with China'. Rohan Rivett's review in the *Herald* (Melbourne) had the heading 'How India led the world up the garden path'. The truth came too late to stop the Australian government using the big lie that China had attacked India as one argument for sending troops to Vietnam. They were supposed to be holding back a Chinese thrust between the Indian Ocean and the Pacific Ocean.

Fear of China became irrational. When the Minister for External Affairs, Paul Hasluck, went to Moscow (where Clark was working), Hasluck tried

> to recruit the Russians as allies against the Chinese by warning them of Chinese territorial ambitions to take over Sinkiang. The Soviet Foreign Minister Gromyko took it calmly. Then he reminded Hasluck that Sinkiang had long been Chinese territory.

On Clark's return to Australia in 1965, he resigned from the Department of External Affairs because 'the intense US killing was opposing a genuine nationalist movement, to protect a corrupt regime' in South Vietnam. His protest made little difference to the External Affairs Department, which continued to get reports from Australian ambassadors in South-East Asia 'on the popularity of the local strongman just before his overthrow. On one famous occasion the report was delayed in the mails and arrived in Canberra after the *coup*. (The ambassador involved went on to better things and ended up as head of the department.)'

Because of Clark's job and his special information, he could see the realities of Vietnam before many other Australians.

Papua New Guinea

Throughout the 1960s Australians became interested in what Papua New Guineans thought of them. A favourite way of finding out was to ask a class to write an essay on how the peoples saw each other. In a group of 216 students from all parts of the Territory, one-third were critical of Australians, one-third were happy with them, and the other third balanced criticisms with praise. The critics were angry at the way the Australians talked to them:

> When a New Guinean does a little bit of a mistake the European swear at them. 'Bush kanaka' is the main swearing word. Bush kanaka really means primitive which isn't fair at all. The other foul word is Black Bastard, which is really worse than bush kanaka. This is another fact, whenever a European speaks there must be a swearing word.

Even the students who were friendliest towards the Australians had complaints. A nineteen-year-old trainee teacher reported:

> The Europeans were a race I naturally respected and looked up to. In the Territory some of the Europeans still make me feel uneasy because they tend to act superior. I do think it's necessary for Europeans to be aloof at times, but it is not necessary to obviously stick out as a superior race. In Australia, I accept all Australians as my own people because they make me feel the same towards them. It's only when I'm in the Territory that I have a dislike for some Europeans, but most are helpful and understanding.

The commonest act of superiority on the part of Australians was their expectation that they would be served first. Until 1972, Papua New Guineans knew that they had to wait at the airport until all the whites had gone through customs. This rule even applied to members of the House of Assembly.

1970: GREAT EXPECTATIONS

Aborigines who, in 1770, had seen Captain James Cook's *Endeavour* sail past what became known as Sydney Harbour made up stories about the ship. Their children perhaps expected the strange object to come again. When Europeans did return in 1788, the local peoples started to get sick and within four years most were dead. A new legend spread among them: the pillars that held up the sky had fallen down. In 1970, Aborigines from all over Australia protested against Cook's claim to possess eastern Australia. They threw wreaths into Botany Bay to mourn their people who had died from European diseases, dispossession or massacres. Images of Aborigines appeared on the panel of stamps issued to commemorate Cook's 'discovery'. Armed with spears and shields, they appeared to be threatening Cook and his men. This image was one of the few official acknowledgments that Indigenous people fought in defence of their country.

Twenty-eight different images appeared on Australian postage stamps during 1970. Their subjects displayed Australian attitudes. Hence, two stamps were issued for the third visit by Queen Elizabeth II. Although ties with Britain remained strong, economic links with Japan were becoming more important, and so two stamps came out for Expo '70 held at Osaka. One displayed the Southern Cross beside some Japanese characters which read 'from the country of the south with warm feeling'. The feelings of many Australians towards Japan remained 'hot' rather than 'warm' because of memories

262
262 Social Sketches of Australia

of the First Pacific War. Mineral sales to Japan had given Australia the chance to shop around the world, yet fear and hatred had not totally surrendered to profit-taking and pleasure.

One in three of the stamps issued during 1970 celebrated aspects of 'national development'. That phrase had been plastered on every money-making scheme for more than a century. Transport was vital in what every commentator called 'a big country' which suffered from 'the tyranny of distance'. The first new stamp dealt with the completion of a standard-gauge rail link between Perth and Brisbane. Two others celebrated the fiftieth birthday of Qantas, the initials which stood for Queensland And Northern Territory Air Service. From such beginnings in 1920, Qantas began testing its first 'Jumbo jets' by 1970. A set of four stamps came out under the heading 'National Development'. One dealt with the Snowy Mountains Scheme, which was at the end of its construction period. Another showed the Ord River Scheme, in the Northern Territory, which even then was proving to be a waste of money and a blight on nature. The third stamp was labelled 'Bauxite to Aluminium', even though almost no processing took place inside Australia. The final image was of 'Oil and Natural Gas', which helped to cut down the costs of importing petrol from the Middle East. Two other stamps pictured cows. One referred to grasslands, so much of which had been spoiled by soil erosion. The other was about dairying, which was getting large amounts of government help to keep inefficient farmers on the land in order to protect National (Country) Party politicians against extinction.

Australia did not issue a stamp to mark the first visit by a Pope, Paul VI, who arrived on 30 November. Disputes between Roman Catholics and other Christian churches were still sharp. Hence, it would not have been smart politics to honour the Pope in the same way as the Queen, who was head of the Church of England. The Vatican, however, produced its own stamps for the Papal tour. One showed the Virgin and

Child Jesus as Aborigines. No Australian stamp has ever been so daring. Indeed, the local Christmas stamp for 1970 highlighted how unsure some Australians still were about their country's place in the world. The design had nothing Australian about it but was a blurred image of the Virgin and Child, trying to look like a European 'Old Master' painting. Art and religion were seen as remote. Pipelines and dams were proper objects for Australians to worship.

While the government encouraged Australians to place their faith in great national projects, stock exchanges were placing their bets on companies with names such as 'Harrietville Hot Rock'. The name that took the punters' fancy was Poseidon, an exploration get-up named after the god of earthquakes and the sea, lord of the earth, a violent character with savage giants for children. Fifty-cent shares in Poseidon nickel were going for $1.90 at 10 am on 29 September 1969; by 3 pm they were selling at $6.70. On New Year's Eve they hit $210 each, and by February 1970 stood at $280. Poseidon's founder tried to explain: 'People just don't understand that the millions referred to in the Press are just stage money'.

Most people knew only that fortunes were being made and they wanted a slice. Stockbrokers could not handle the volume of business. One dealer reported this conversation with a customer who phoned at a very busy time:

> Broker: 'We're all in turmoil'.
> Client: 'Buy me some too'.

If the boom needed the greed of investors, the frauds flowed from boosting by people in authority. After the bubble burst early in 1971, a Senate Committee looked into the share market and found crooked dealing to be so widespread that only a few cases could be written up. Brokers had used insider information to make their killings. Journalists had praised companies in which they owned shares. The public had been at the mercy of sharks in suits.

Hard as it was for families to lose their money in the crash, Australia as a whole suffered more in the longer term because people would not invest in working mines. Corporations borrowed more from overseas, leaving Australia in debt to the future. The head of CRA, Sir Roderick Carnegie, warned:

> People don't realise the cost. If you get four dollars in 1979 from overseas invested in equities, those owners want a dollar a year from 1990 onwards forever. That's a very high price, and in political terms it doesn't seem a high price because they see four dollars coming in today, but in 10, 11 years' time, a dollar a year out is an enormous price to pay.

Despite the record of rip-offs around the Sydney Stock Exchange, its hundredth birthday in May 1971 would be honoured with a postage stamp. According to the Senate Inquiry, several of that Exchange's leading members should have been in prison, along with company directors and financial writers. When a few charges came to Court, judges were unwilling to convict or to impose severe sentences. A businessman was no ordinary criminal. The two-hundredth anniversary of Cook's first voyage into the Pacific called for fireworks. The flickering of the Poseidon boom sparked a bonfire of 'stage money'.

11 1971–1980 BOOM, BUST — BOOM?

For thirty years after the end of the First Pacific War in 1945, Australia's economy moved upwards, despite repeated recessions. Unemployment would rise from next-to-nothing towards 3 per cent of the labour force, before falling back towards zero. One of these downturns helped Gough Whitlam lead the Labor Party to a narrow victory late in 1972. For the next eighteen months, the economy boomed as never before. Governments had a treasure chest of taxation to spend and could borrow more. Exports of minerals removed all worries about the cost of imports. By April 1974, three US dollars were needed to buy two Australian ones. Cheaper imports and more expensive exports laid waste to the local manufacturing industry.

World economic forces were heading downwards, and Australia felt their impact during the second half of 1974. The 'trough in unemployment' was coming to an end. Unemployment had risen to 4.5 per cent by the end of 1975 when Whitlam lost the elections because his party had bungled the economy. Most people believed that a change of government would put Australia back on the road to prosperity. Nothing much improved until the late 1970s when the Fraser government claimed that Australia was about to benefit from a resources boom through the production of shale oil, coking and steaming coals, and the smelting of alumina. In short,

Australia would return to prosperity through the luck of its natural endowments. The promise was not met. The shale oil project never got started; the expansion of open-cut coal-mines helped to force down the price per tonne; and only half of the aluminum plants came on stream. Unemployment stayed at around 6 per cent. Between 1974 and 1979, the value of the Australian dollar fell from 422 yen to 243 yen. More people suspected that whatever had gone wrong with Australia's economy in 1975 could not be cured by changing prime ministers. 'Luck' would no longer be enough. Donald Horne wrote about 'the death of the lucky country'.

While the economy began to decline, Australia's cultural life flourished. The opening of the Sydney Opera House, on 20 October 1973, coincided with the award of the Nobel Prize for Literature to Patrick White. These headline events were surrounded by a revival in Australian theatre and film-making, and by widespread activity in the crafts. Peter Weir's *The Cars That Ate Paris* (1974) broke away from the Ocker sex comedies such as *Alvin Purple* to present Australia as a society addicted to motor cars and living off their wreckage, human and mechanical. That grim mood and the refashioned vehicles prepared the way for the cinematic ballet of *Mad Max II* (1982). Australian rock bands had been accepted by Australian audiences since Johnny O'Keefe and Col Joye in the 1950s. Generations grew up expecting some of their stars to be locals. 'Sharpies' established a style which owed nothing to overseas fashions. Young men clipped their hair at the back and sides but kept a tail; they wore cardigans known as 'Connies' and chisel-toed boots called Venus. The Australian television serial *Number 96* became a scandalous success in 1972, sending up the rival soaps and introducing the first positive homosexual character to our screens. *Prisoner* rated highly from 1978 with a cast of tough women who were far from being merely victims of men or the system. An amateur finish to Australian-made shows disappeared. The ABC combined social and historical issues with audience appeal in *Power Without Glory* and *Rush*, the theme music from the latter topping the hit parades. As well as Film Commissions in most States, Canberra set up the Australia Council to fund these cultural activities, with its Boards for Literature, Craft, Visual Arts, Theatre and Music. Governments also added 'Arts' ministries to their cabinets. The expectation was that everyone would have so much leisure that they would need to become active in the crafts and the arts.

WORK

The percentage of the labour force out of work rose from 2.3 per cent in 1974 to 5.8 per cent early in 1979. Three aspects of this increase presented complications. First, the jobless were not evenly spread across the continent; cities such as Wollongong (NSW) and Whyalla (SA), which had depended on the big employer BHP, were the worst hit. Families who owned houses in those places could not sell them at a price which would allow them to move away to find work. Secondly, the average number of weeks that an unemployed person spent without a job had gone from seven in 1971 up to twenty-eight by 1979. Thirdly, young people had the greatest difficulty getting jobs. Of those who had left school, 20 per cent of females and 15 per cent of males aged between 15 and 19 were out of work in 1979. In Whyalla or Woollongong, these percentages were twice as high and the average length of time without work stretched to twenty-eight months, not twenty-eight weeks.

Immigrants were more likely to be unemployed than were the Australian-born. The more recently people had arrived, the more likely they were to be out of work. This situation meant that they were less likely to have savings or friends to tide them over. Also, it could mean that their English was not good enough to fill out the forms at the unemployment office.

If a wife were working, the husband did not get any unemployment benefits. This was the case with M. who was out of a job for five weeks in 1972. He had come to Australia a year earlier and worked for a car-maker where he earned $57.00 a week. After tax, his wife brought home another $31.00 from a chocolate factory. Their cost of living each week was:

Rent of flat	$17.00
Hire purchase for fridge and TV	8.50
Creche for baby	8.00
Hospital benefits	2.10
Gas and electricity	4.50
Food	15.00
Clothing	5.00
Fares	5.00
TOTAL	$65.10

When they were both working they saved $23.00 a week. With M. out of work, they were $34.00 a week short. In order to cope, they spent seven weeks' savings.

M.'s story was not one of great hardship. However, if his wife had not been working, they would have had no savings and they would have had to live on unemployment benefits of $29.50. That income would not have paid for their food and rent. Moreover, M. would not have got any money for the first week that he was out of work; his first unemployment cheque would not have arrived until seventeen days after his last pay day.

Daring to win

During the 1960s, the Liberal–Country Party government had made strikes virtually illegal. The law bottled up workers' complaints, which burst open in 1969 when half-a-million unionists stopped work in support of the secretary of the

Victorian Tramways Union, Clarrie O'Shea. O'Shea had gone to gaol for refusing to pay a fine imposed on his union for an earlier strike. Victory in the O'Shea struggle made the workers more confident. They also frightened the government so much that it did not dare use its laws against strikes. The combination of almost continuous over-full employment until late 1974, and rapidly increasing prices, gave workers both the opportunity and the reason to strike for higher wages.

A dispute at Ford's Melbourne plant in the middle of 1973 added to local grievances. The pace of work on the assembly line brought a rapid turnover of labour in the motor industry. The strike began on 18 May after the union called a meeting of 4000 workers and told them to stay at work. The men voted against the union and struck for higher wages and more holiday pay. On 12 June, the union told the men to go back to work. One section agreed, but most of the workers in the car assembly plant refused. The next day, anger turned into a six-hour riot when 500 strikers broke windows and knocked down a two-metre-high brick wall. Over a hundred police were needed to control the strikers. The men returned to work shortly afterwards. They got almost nothing out of the Arbitration Court decision a month later. Two aspects stand out about this strike: one was the gulf between the workers and the unions; the second was the hatred of the workers for their bosses. These attitudes grew out of the way that Ford ran its plant.

In some ways, Ford's assembly line was worse than others. It had been built to produce forty cars an hour with two models. In 1973, it was making fifty-four cars an hour with at least a dozen models. Eighty per cent of the workers were immigrants and, of these, one in five could speak no English. Union leaders did not explain their policies to these workers, and did not understand what the immigrant workers felt. Any listening was left to activists on the job, to men such as Lokman Kaleshi, a Vehicle Builders Union shop steward. He had worked at Ford for three years before the strike. Kaleshi, aged thirty, had come to Australia from Yugoslavia, via Turkey, in 1969. In a newspaper interview during the strike, he gave this account of working on an assembly line:

> [the line] often goes too fast and we can't keep up. It doesn't go at the same speed all the time — sometimes it stops for a few minutes because of a breakdown, so they increase the speed to try to make up. When this happens, the workers are in trouble trying to keep up. Sometimes they leave a job incomplete. When the inspector sees it at the end of the line, he has to send the car back. But the foreman knows who had to do that job, so he shouts and yells at the worker.
>
> The worker doesn't understand English usually, so he is taken to the personnel office, where the foreman tells them that the man can't do the job. Some of the tools are no good. For example, an air-gun is not operating, and the worker complains to the leading hand. He is often too busy to do anything about it, so the worker is obliged to work with the poor gun. Then the foreman comes and shouts because the work is not done.

Another worker told reporters:

> [I] always pictured the car coming down the line as being like a great queen bee cruising down the line as the workers swarm over it servicing it and then jumping off as they move onto the next, only to be replaced by other workers repeating their jobs fifty-four times an hour, 400 times a day, two and a half thousand times a week.

A third worker said that he had often had to wait for more than an hour before he could leave the line to go to the lavatory. He had to explain why he had been away sick, just like 'fronting the teacher'. Two of the men's demands during the strike were for a six-minute afternoon tea break, and to have the holes in the roof fixed.

Frustration with management in general led to movements for worker control of industry. The incompetence of experts had led to the collapse of Melbourne's Westgate Bridge in October 1970, killing thirty-five workers. Unionists took over the running of factories and power plants. During a sit-in at the Union Carbide plant in 1979–80, a senior tradesman could no longer contain his contempt for the engineers and executives:

> When you say safety what you really mean, what is ultimately meant, is safety for the plant. Your main worry is the plant. A bloke gets hurt — yeah, that's bad news all right. But the worst news for you bastards is the fucking inconvenience of a bloke getting hurt, that's the thing, the bloody inconvenience of that being a spanner in your stinking, fucking works.

Nearby, at the Goodrich tyre plant, another unionist measured exposure to a proven carcinogen at twelve times more than the level that the Victorian government allowed. In addition, the company had issued defective masks. When workers complained, they could be sacked.

LIFE IN THE CITIES

In 1980, only one in five households cooked breakfast. One in ten had no breakfast at all. Most Australians ate a cereal, a few of which were half sugar. Several brands of toasted muesli contained 25 per cent sugar. Half a cup of milk contained more protein than a normal serve of these sweetened breakfast foods. The most popular cereal remained the high-fibre Weet-Bix. Many people could not recall what they had eaten the day before and most were uncertain of the value of what they ate. In 1980, first-year university students in Adelaide did not understand how fats, proteins and fibres worked in their bodies. Primary school students knew that 'sweet, fatty' foods were bad for them but did not know which foods were loaded with sugar and fats. With more Australians overweight, dieting became a national pasttime. A few diets related to particular illnesses or allergies. A much larger group aimed at losing kilos of fat, often on 'crash' programs.

Australian eating and drinking habits altered between the

1960s and the 1980s. In 1970, only one baby in five was being breastfed at three months; ten years later, half of them were. The increase at six months was even greater, going from one in ten to more than one in three. Coffee became as popular as tea; margarine overtook butter; beer drinking fell while the intake of wine rose. Consumption of cheeses increased from three to five kilograms per head in the ten years to 1974. Three times as much poultry was eaten, most of it bred in batteries. The ideal of a good dinner being a large T-bone steak, covered in gravy with two fried eggs, mashed potatoes and peas, did not disappear. Vegemite also retained its place. Few Australians could resist a meat pie, which one company marketed in the United States. Fish and chips remained popular but pizzas attracted the under-35-year-olds. No longer could a single menu describe Australian food preferences.

Women's liberation

Despite women's liberation movements, so-called women's work was still rarely done by men. The choices were driven by the demands of work, especially on employed mothers. During the 1950s, Australian families had paid off their first refrigerator, saying goodbye to the ice-man. The early models included a small freezer section for home-made ice-cream and ice-blocks. By the 1970s, the freezer had become a separate compartment with its own door. Many households were also paying off a freezer unit in which they kept supplies of TV dinners and stacks of frozen vegetables, meats and juices. Meals were bought in rather than being prepared at home. The larger freezers became popular because they let families shop only once a week, or perhaps only once a fortnight, depending on how often wages came in.

The need to reduce the time spent on shopping grew as both parents took jobs outside the house. The extra money that mum earned gave her enough to pay off the freezer that she needed because her job meant that she no longer had time to go to the shops every other day. Paid employment also meant that she had less time to prepare meals and so the family got more frozen meals, or takeaways. Electrical appliances are often described as 'labour-saving'. Working women found them 'time-saving' in the sense that they reduced the amount of time needed to perform each household task. The appliances are better described as 'labouriousness-saving' because they did away with many of the heavy and boring aspects of cooking and cleaning. The time and energy thus saved could then be sold to corporations for wages.

One drawback with frozen food was that it took longer to heat. By 1980, the family meal was beginning to move out of the freezer and through the microwave oven, another time-saving device that mum could work to pay off. The increased pace of work and living meant that the ritual of heating a teapot, adding one teaspoon of tea for each person and one for the pot, pouring on boiling water and then waiting for the tea to draw had become a luxury. The tea-bag followed sliced bread as a time-saver.

The women's liberation movement appeared in Australia late in the 1960s. It made headlines shortly afterwards when an Australian woman living in London, Germaine Greer, published her book *The Female Eunuch*, and returned to Australia for a lecture tour. In 1971, another Australian, Dennis Altman, published *Homosexual* in the United States. Australians were setting the pace in a cultural upheaval.

Women's liberation had not appeared out of nowhere. Australia had a history of women's struggling for their rights. Usually, those campaigns were over single issues, whether equal pay or the vote. Some women had always argued that the attainment of equality would need more than a shopping list of separate reforms. In the 1930s, Australia's women writers, such as Eleanor Dark and Christina Stead, had illustrated how women were treated as inferior to men because they were physically different.

At the end of the 1960s, three factors combined to revive the international women's movement. First, the increase in the number of women working made more of them aware of the problems of competing with men on unequal terms. Unionists campaigned for equal pay for equal work. A growing number of women had university degrees or other specialist skills, which were not being rewarded. Secondly, the development of a reliable contraceptive pill gave more women a chance to enjoy sex without the fear of a baby ending their careers. Thirdly, the world-wide protest movements for racial equality sparked an understanding that oppression was not a law of nature. From a demand for racial equality, it was a short step to a demand for sexual equality. Liberationists saw that Blacks were treated as second-class citizens because of their skin colour, and women were treated as second-class citizens because of their physiology. Moreover, these demands for equality arose during protests against the war in Vietnam, when younger people questioned all manner of views.

A part of the 1970s wave of feminism was the demand that women be allowed to control their own bodies and their own sexuality. This desire brought opposition to advertisements that depended on sex appeal. Liberationists also changed the law regarding rape so that women would be protected rather than persecuted after they were attacked. That reform was not enough to encourage all victims to report sexual crimes.

Just before the 1972 elections, the Women's Electoral Lobby (WEL) started as a means of finding out what candidates believed. WEL continued as an activist organisation supporting women's rights to equal pay, child-care centres and the right to an abortion. Some members thought that women were emotionally different from men, but argued that these differences should not count in social, political or economic issues.

LIFE IN THE COUNTRY

Throughout the nineteenth century, industrial processes such as canning and freezing had extended the sales life of farm produce. In the twentieth century, the application of machines and chemicals to the land improved crop yields. Industrialists developed new products, or substitutes, such as margarine and instant coffee. Livestock, fruits and vegetables were redesigned to match the needs of the supermarket. Chickens spent all their lives in cages and were treated like egg-laying machines; pigs were bred so that their bodies gave better-looking slices of bacon; lambs were looked on as 'woolly pigs' which might also be kept indoors. Experiments were made with chemical shearing. In the late 1970s, the McDonald's hamburger chain told Tasmanian potato farmers to change their crop to Russets because that type was five inches long, slender, and had a low water content which was ideal for chips. Tomatoes were bred so that their skins would not burst. Many types of apple disappeared because they were too small or did not look glossy enough. As one grower commented: 'The apples definitely look better, but I won't say they taste any better. All the old varieties we used to like have gone'. Cox's Orange Pippins, Cleos or Croftons had to be sought at roadside stalls.

Despite ways of industrialising the flavour, colour and appearance of agricultural products, these foods were still the offspring of plants and animals. The mass marketing of food could not wait for nature to adapt its gifts to sit on supermarket shelves. New varieties had to be invented if products were to be standardised. That need for profitable packaging led to 'bio-engineering'. Plants were manufactured in laboratories and their genetic codes patented like any other invention. These plants belonged to private companies who could stop farmers growing them or other firms copying them. Control of farming passed to corporations known as 'agri-businesses'. Farmers got their funds, fuel, machinery and breed stock from Elders–IXL or Adsteam. Families owned the mortgages, paid the interest and took the risks of drought. Their produce was contracted to corporations which set the prices and took more of the profit. Family farms were becoming another kind of 'franchise', like a McDonald's hamburger outlet.

Mining towns

Mining sites tended to become boom towns, rising and falling within a few years. Several larger towns owed their existence to mining. Queenstown in Tasmania and Broken Hill in New South Wales survived for almost 100 years. Their futures were uncertain by the 1970s because they had used up their profitable ore bodies. Ghost towns such as Coolgardie in Western Australia became tourist attractions, while nearby Kalgoorlie balanced tourism with gold mining.

Mining towns varied in their ways of living. The older ones retained a sense of themselves with firm, even oppressive, local traditions. Many of the newer mining settlements in the north of Western Australia had little if any community feeling. Young couples moved there for a few years to save enough to set themselves up in the suburbs of Perth. The husband worked hard and long while the wife stayed at home with pre-school children. He drank with his mates while she found it hard to make close friends:

> I'm careful about my emotional involvements. I tend to keep to myself, because if you talk to some people, everyone knows your business. There's the feeling that friendship with the people in the street isn't going to last.

These younger women were a long way from their parents who could give advice or baby-sit. Few Europeans in the Pilbara wanted to be buried there. Most who died were flown south or east to a resting place which was not in danger of becoming another ghost town.

To attract workers to these remote settlements, the mining companies offered high wages, low-cost housing and air-conditioning. The same support was not always available for the families of school teachers who had been sent there:

> Temperatures of 52 degrees Celsius have been reached in my kitchen when I'm trying to prepare my dinner. The electrician who installed my air-conditioner estimated $35 a week for 24-hour use. However, the enormous cost of running one of the units makes it impossible for me to afford 24-hour service. The cost of living generally (tomatoes $1.75 to $2 a kilo all year round is one small example) makes the district allowance absolutely inadequate. In the two years we have been in Karratha our savings have diminished rather than increased.

Some visitors fell in love with the north-west. After a round-Australia holiday a tour-bus driver and his family agreed that Port Hedland was the best place for them.

The weathering that exposed mineral outcrops also had rendered Australian soils shallow, often no more than 15 centimetres. After a dry spell, storms could wash away as much as 100 tonnes of soil per hectare. But when the land was planted with a summer crop, the loss of soil went down to two tonnes per hectare. Farmers cannot prevent droughts and floods, but they can reduce soil erosion. Wheat growers in the Namoi Valley (NSW) suffered in the 1978–79 season when erosion filled a creek with silt. Water then covered their fields, leaving the soils so soggy that 320 hectares could not be planted. One farmer lost $60 000 of income. Nearby, another 265 hectares of farmland could not be sown because of erosion.

On the coast

Coastal towns throve when they became holiday resorts where amateurs went fishing, for fun or a feed, with a hook and line. Surfers Paradise was famed for its sun, surf and sands from the early 1950s. Then the sand stopped coming. A tussle began to keep any kind of beach at the Gold Coast. In Queensland, tropical storms and cyclones whip up breakers which wear away beaches but do little to create new sand. Most sand was formed from shells and rocks, broken up by the sea. Certain soft sandstones were worn away at the rate of a metre every twenty-five years. Holiday-makers went back to a favourite beach only to find that it had disappeared. Victoria's narrow beaches were pounded by seas from the Southern Ocean, moving sands along the coast. Portland (Victoria) built a harbour in the early 1960s and lost its beaches through erosion. Instead of holidaying there, tourists moved to nearby Port Fairy. Local economies rose and fell with these changes to the shoreline.

By the 1970s, the whaling that had begun just after European occupation was running down because of the numbers that had been taken. Despite the use of spotter aircraft, the kill fell from 1172 to 624 during the two years to 1977. Only the Albany (WA) station continued, and it would close after 1980. Meanwhile, commercial fishing moved towards exports and became an industry. Cheap meat had meant that Australians did not need the cod that kept the poor alive in Europe. Those who fancied cheap fish here ate mullet or deep-fried shark, known as flake. By 1970, Australians still consumed only 6 kilograms of seafood per head a year. Factory ships with nets appeared around the coast. Japanese fleets based themselves in Hobart. Rock lobsters, prawns, crabs and abalone became delicacies to be frozen and flown around the Asia-Pacific. At home, squid became popular as deep-fried calamari. Fish landings grew three times as rapidly as the population. Greek and Italian immigrants took up the ocean trawling that they had practised in the Mediterranean. Most of the professional fishing was by families, some of whom formed cooperatives, such as SAFCOL. A quarter of the catch went into cans as tuna and salmon; nonetheless, Australia needed to import twice those volumes. The extension of sovereignty in 1979 to 200 nautical miles offshore gave Australia a vast fishing zone. However, the increase did not meet the local demand, which exceeded 11 kilograms per head in the late 1990s. By then, more than half of the Australian breeding grounds had been over-fished, leaving both common and exotic species in danger.

HEALTH
Nurses

For a hundred years, doctors had put down nurses as little more than 'expert bum washers'. From the 1970s, Australian nurses stuck up for their rights. so that wages and training improved. New South Wales nurses demonstrated in 1966 and nurses went on strike in the Australian Capital Territory in 1970. A campaign in Victoria that year resulted in an increase in wages of 75 per cent for sisters and over 100 per cent for matrons.

Qualifications for nursing advanced. As one matron put it: 'it is no use any more having a nice, kind, gentle little girl who will muddle through'. A director of nursing added: 'university graduates who decide to nurse under our two-year training program are always amazed at the academic content of the course'. By the 1970s, entrance standards were closer to those for a university. These qualifications added weight to the nurses' demands to be seen as professionals alongside doctors. A Melbourne nurse, Suzanne, pointed out that when Christian Barnard did his heart transplants:

> He had a team of thirty-two who did the bulk of the work, and they were nursing staff. Those patients were in hospitals for months afterwards, being taken care of by nurses. And *he* got all the glory.

For those still trained only in hospitals, the situation did not improve much, if at all. Lorraine, a Sydney nurse, gave this account of her training:

> Most of the lectures and clinics were in your time, and when you're already working a 40-hour shift all your spare time is valuable. I was unable to shut off. It was compulsory to attend a certain number of lectures. Sometimes you'd be on night shift and have to get up in the middle of the day to attend lectures.

Lessons often remained genteel. One nurse recalled that when she was at Royal Melbourne Hospital, a friend had asked the tutor sister for a lecture on contraception and abortion: 'The sister got up and said "This disgusting, filthy girl!" and refused to give the lecture'.

Some doctors, especially surgeons, treated a nurse as someone on whom to work their tensions out. One Easter, a group of trainees was sent into theatre to watch a plastic surgeon working on a burns patient:

> He was cleaning the wound. It's called debriding [pronounced as in *breed*]. He looked at us and snapped, 'OK you three stooges. What am I doing?' We were too terrified to answer. Then the shyest one whispered, 'I suppose you're debriding the wound.' She said it like in *bride*.
>   He absolutely bellowed at her, 'De-bride-ing, de-breed-ing — depends on what school you went to!'

The worst aspect was that even fully trained nurses, who spent all day with their patients, were rarely asked for their opinions. The longer nurses worked in hospitals, the less patient care they were likely to do because they were promoted to fill out forms.

Doctors

Nurses with tertiary qualifications and a range of paramedical staff challenged the status of doctors, who were no longer the single source of medical knowledge and experience. In addition, most doctors were untrained for the work they spent much of their time doing.

One-half to two-thirds of the people who went to their local doctor did not have a physical illness. Bodily symptoms were often the result of some emotional problem. Hence, the most commonly prescribed drug in the 1970s was Valium to relieve anxiety. Patients became addicted while the drugs did nothing to remove the causes of their tension. Concern about other side-effects led to a reduction in the use of Valium by the one-in-four women who reported suffering from depression. Two other drugs took over as what became known as 'Mother's Little Helper'. In 1984–85, 2.5 million prescriptions were filled for Serapax, 1.65 million for Mogadon and 1.5 million for Valium, or one for every three Australians. One woman commented:

> It's the Australian tradition of women taking pills whereas men drink. It was the bromides at the turn of the century, then the barbiturates, the compound analgesics and now it's Valium and Serepax. Definitely the role of women is tied up with women getting into tablets.

Many patients sought advice and comfort from a person whom they could trust to be intelligent, informed and bound to secrecy. In particular, doctors were seen as a safe source of advice on sexual and marital difficulties. Social work and psychiatry were very low on the list of subjects for a medical degree. Recognising the failure of its training, the University of Sydney started a new course which included a full year of social medicine.

A study carried out at Monash University in Melbourne documented just how poor the education of doctors was on these matters. Some 820 medical students, from first to sixth year, were asked 135 questions about their sexual knowledge, activities and attitudes. Queried about contraception, a third did not know what the rhythm method was; 70 per cent were wrong about its safety; and 40 per cent were wrong about the length of the 'safe period'. Questioned about masturbation, one in ten thought that it 'will often lead to severe psychological illness'. Tested further on this most common of all youthful sex concerns, 2 per cent thought it would lead to blindness or insanity; 20 per cent suggested sport as an alternative; and 29 per cent wanted to refer patients to psychiatrists. Only 29 per cent knew that 'there is no such thing as "excessive" masturbation'. Asked how they had got their knowledge of sex, 70 per cent said they had learnt more from growing up than from their university courses. Answers of this low grade did not improve the public's confidence in their GPs. Hence, books such as Alex Comfort's *The Joy of Sex* and Derek Llewelyn Jones's *Everywoman* sold readily.

Sex education has always taken place at school. Children heard jokes in the playground or passed around snippets of information about why changes were happening in their bodies. Sex education in the classroom countered the half-truths and prejudices that children whispered to each other. Some people believed that only parents were entitled to provide such information. One problem was that some parents knew little more than their children, and so handed on fears and falsehoods about how the human body works. Many teenagers at Brisbane private schools were far from sure how women became pregnant, or how best to limit the chances of pregnancy. More than one student in four wrongly believed that condoms were more effective than the pill. Almost half believed that 'spermatozoa' was a contraceptive. The ones who knew the most were those who had attended sex education classes.

The taking of so many pills for depression and anxiety was only one part of a spreading sense of being unwell. A 1977–78 survey showed that 45 per cent of Australians had suffered a chronic illness lasting more than six months. One person in five had been to the doctor during the fortnight before the survey, and one in fifteen had spent a day in bed. More than half had taken some form of medication during the preceding forty-eight hours. Australians liked to see themselves as sun-bronzed, sport-loving and active. Yet, in the words of the professor of social and preventive medicine at Monash University, Basil Hetzel, Australians were 'by generally accepted health standards one of the unhealthiest peoples among those to which we belong by tradition and standard of living'. The death-rate was higher at all ages than Sweden's; it was higher than that of England and Wales for those aged between one and sixty-five years.

Hetzel saw four major epidemics in present-day Australia: violence, from motor cars or suicide; heart disease, the most common killer; cancer, especially of the lung; and strokes. All four had social causes to be prevented rather than cured. Prevention needed changes in the Australian way of life. Australians were driving, drugging, drinking, smoking and eating themselves to death. Most of the money spent on health care in Australia went to doctors and hospitals. Both were largely helpless in the fight against the major killers. General medical practice looked after people who were sick but could do almost nothing to stop their becoming ill in the first place. Hospitals were the net into which fell those who became seriously ill. Only a redirection of services towards public, social and preventive medicine would improve Australian health, Hetzel argued.

A combination of laws and education was needed to reduce drunken driving, cigarette smoking and poor diet. Only lung cancer was on the rise. Tobacco consumption increased from about half a kilogram per head a year in 1947 to two kilograms per head a year. Compared with the advertising budgets of the cigarette companies, anti-smoking campaigns by governments were nearly worthless. They had little impact on total sales of tobacco. Similarly, motor-car makers encouraged fast driving, while breweries promoted 'expert drinking'. Merchandisers spread the term 'lifestyle' and were responsible for promoting the most prevalent death styles. In each of these diseases, corporations had too much at stake to give up their profitable activities without a battle.

Another Melbourne Professor, Louis Opit, named a fifth epidemic. He accused the typical suburban medical practice of spawning 'an epidemic of procedures'. A group practice of five doctors with 8000 possible patients would see 6000 of those people each year. Those consultations gave rise to 500 visits to specialists, 1800 X-rays, 6000 blood tests and 800 general anaesthetics:

> No varicose vein seems entirely safe from surgery, no drooping breast with an unhappy owner will escape an implant, no uterus free of foetal longing will remain. Only 58 out of every 100 women will be allowed to give birth without drugs or surgery.

This epidemic of tests and operations was one by-product of the increasing number of doctors. In 1971, there was one doctor to every 792 Australians; by 1985, there was one for every 478. Most were anxious to maintain the quality of their own lives by non-essential medical procedures and tax avoidance schemes.

For health workers to be useful, they needed to become more like community welfare workers and less like drug-dispensing machines. In the 1972 words of Monash University's professor of surgery, Hugh Dudley, Australia had to put a stop to a medical profession which was 'far more interested in the quality of its life than in the quality of its service'. The fee-for-service concept made doctors 'quite unable to move from sickness care to health care, quite unable to educate for a profession as distinct from a group of medical shopkeepers.

Doctors wanting to practise preventive and social medicine were often unable to do so. Their patients needed attention for illnesses that had arisen from years of neglect. Money was available for 'fee-for-service' but harder to come by for community programs on diet and fitness. One attempt to improve health by altering lifestyle began on the north coast of New

South Wales in 1978. A 'Quit for Life' anti-smoking campaign included newspaper, radio and television advertising. It contained the message:

> The human lung is like a sponge; a sponge designed to soak up air. But it also soaks up smoke. If the average smoker were to wring out his lungs once a year he would find a cup-and-a-half of cancer-producing tar. It's enough to make you sick. Very sick.

After tobacco companies complained, the advertisements were stopped for fifteen weeks. During that time, advertising for cigarettes in one local paper, the Lismore *Northern Star* , increased by 260 per cent. Organisers of the 'Quit for Life' campaign pointed out that all the complaints about 'unsupported generalities' being 'applied to individuals' could be levelled against cigarette advertising that featured airline pilots and cowboys.

ABORIGINES

Land rights became more urgent during the late 1960s with the mining boom across northern Australia. Mining companies got access to areas that had been set aside as Aboriginal reserves. Bulldozers did more than flatten sacred sites; they wiped out the tracks of ancestors. In 1970, the Yirrkala people went to court to stop the Nabalco company mining their land around the Gove Peninsula in the Northern Territory. The Commonwealth government entered the case on the side of the company. Almost a year later, the court decided that the Aborigines had no legal claim to their land. The judge sympathised with the Aborigines but said the law was clear. If land rights were to be won, parliament would have to change the law. This road meant pressure on politicians. On Australia Day 1972, the Aboriginal tent embassy was set up outside Parliament House in Canberra.

The Labor Party had promised 'land rights' for Indigenous people. Within a fortnight of becoming prime minister, Mr

Whitlam gave Mr Justice Woodward the job of working out ways of securing 'land rights'. His instructions upset the Aboriginal activists because the guidelines dealt only with the Northern Territory; in the following May they were extended to the States.

Labor continued the Liberal–Country Party's policy of buying land for Aborigines. Unlike the Liberal–Country Party, Labor passed legal ownership over to the original inhabitants. The first grant Labor made was to Nomads Ltd for a final payment on land near Port Hedland where the group had been going it alone since 1946. Then the government announced that it would take 4000 square kilometres from the Vestey lease at Wave Hill for the Gurindji.

Because of the 1967 change in the Constitution, the Commonwealth could make State governments remove laws that discriminated against Aborigines. All the States except Queensland agreed to the reforms. Finally, the Queensland government brought its laws into line, but it broke the spirit of its promise by failing to consult with Aborigines, reserving wide powers to public servants, and continuing to deny basic human rights. The Queensland Parliament discussed the legislation for less than four-and-a-half hours. It had been circulated less than a week before the debate. Not even Queensland's Aboriginal senator, the non-Labor Neville Bonner, saw the final draft. Under the law, powers to manage property, to control entry to reserves, and to set working conditions were given to officials. There would be only a slight chance of appealing to a court against their decisions. A professor of law at the University of New South Wales pointed to eleven articles of the United Nations' Universal Declaration of Human Rights broken by the new Queensland law. Those sections dealt with arbitrary arrest, free movement, rights to property, democratic government and working conditions.

Even in the Northern Territory, which the Commonwealth controlled directly, medical and health services remained second-rate. In 1972, an official inquiry criticised the situation there:

> [Health services to Aborigines] consist of predominantly pater-nalistic programs of preventive medicine and European-type cu-rative services rather than an integrated service based upon the cultural and traditional needs of the recipients.
>
> The term ... 'hospital' is an inaccurate descriptive term which can convey the wrong impression ... health centres are ineffec-tive ... [and] are in need of urgent revision.

The Aboriginal mortality rate was still twice as high as that for the Australian population generally.

Under Labor, Commonwealth spending on Aboriginal ser-vices more than doubled. Poverty was not the only problem facing the Indigenous population. They believed that they would not be healthy or prosperous unless they controlled their own lives, free from kindly officials who only wanted to help by taking away their children.

If white women and black men had uphill struggles, it was very much harder to be both female and black. Aboriginal women were often bashed by black males or raped by white men. Gracelyn Smallwood was a double-certificate nursing sister whose work in Townsville had alarmed her:

> Black women are at the bottom of the social ladder, we all know that. There are a lot of black women that I know who have to go and lie down with a white man to get money to feed their children. Now, what constitutes rape? To me, that's rape, not just physical rape, but mentally and emotionally.

Black women were often too frightened to report even the most violent assault cases. They believed that the police would not do anything to help. Among those willing to complain was a 24-year-old Townsville woman who took her case to a Queensland senator:

> I had gone to a friend's place to watch television, when I was told that some white men were outside and wanted me. I came out and the man, who I knew, said 'You ran away from me last night. I

want you to come with me'. I got into the vehicle and he drove me to the airport. I said to him 'Aren't you taking me to the city?' He said 'Just shut your bloody black mouth up'. We got out of the car and with force he made me take all my clothes off. He told me to lie down and then he had intercourse with me without my consent. After he had finished with me he said 'I don't want you to tell anyone or my wife will hear about this'. He threatened he would lock me up all the time for no reason at all and flog me to death. He also made me wash the car, before he left me at the airport.

The senator complained that the police commissioner had taken no action about this information.

WHITE AUSTRALIA

European immigrants had been glad to come to Australia after the Second World War had devastated their homelands. From 1947, the policy towards these immigrants had been to treat them as 'New Australians'. They were supposed to turn themselves into carbon copies of British settlers. Northern Europeans did a fair job of pretending to be British. Italians, Greeks and Spaniards could not be assimilated so readily. They were abused for not becoming one of the 'weird mob'. By the late 1960s, almost as many Mediterraneans returned home as arrived. This rush of departures made a mockery of a population program based on immigration.

During the 1970s, governments moved away from fitting everyone into a single Anglo-Celtic mould. Ethnic organisations were encouraged to make more of their customs than costumes and folk dances for Australia Day parades. The new policy later became known as multiculturalism.

Ethnic groups, however, were divided by gender and class. Lebanese women complained that they were more often abused in their traditional cultures than in contemporary Australia. Workers said they had as much in common with Australian-born unionists as with Lebanese bosses. Greeks were split between the Orthodox who backed the fascist junta in Athens and those who supported the communists or socialists. British-born labourers reckoned that they also suffered disadvantages as both immigrants and workers through their regional and class accents. Because they were Anglo-Celts, they got no attention.

The chances of assimilating new arrivals were reduced further once thousands of Turks and Asians began arriving. Asian immigration had gone from a few hundred in 1965 to a yearly intake of almost 10 000 by 1967. Most were professional people. These newest Australians were not exactly white and often not from Christian backgrounds. White Australia as a national ideal had been put on the back shelf.

By the early 1970s, non-Europeans entered as permanent residents. The government did not pay their fares. Their numbers were still very small compared with total immigration. On paper, those who qualified for entry were treated the same as Europeans. Although there was no longer any hint of skin-colour in Australia's immigration rules, they retained a clause about the newcomer's ability to integrate into the community. In practice, an illiterate European could get in as readily as a university professor from China.

The victories of the Indo-Chinese by May 1975 gave rise to an exodus of those who had sided with the US military. When the war ended, about 1300 Vietnamese lived here, half of them war orphans, as well as some students. Between 1966 and 1981, their total number went from 2427 to 41 000. Only 2000 of these arrived as 'boat people'.

After 1975, the orderly retreat from strict controls on non-European immigration was capsized by the volume of Asians who came. After a brief war between China and Vietnam in 1978, many Chinese fled Vietnam. The total number of Chinese immigrants grew towards 20 000 a year. Some lacked the skills necessary for an urban, industrial economy; others were unable to speak English. Because total immigration declined, its Asian component rose to 31 per cent in 1979.

VIEW OF THE WORLD

Until the end of 1972, Canberra refused to recognise that the Communists had taken control of China in 1949. Instead, Australia kept up relations with the Nationalists who had fled to the island of Formosa. From being a closed book to most Australians, the People's Republic of China became a favoured country to visit, usually on a packaged tour. Australians had learned recently to enjoy Chinese food; they now became fascinated by acupuncture and other traditional skills. The fraction of Australians who saw China as a threat fell from 21 per cent in 1969 to 9 per cent in 1980.

The Liberal Party's asset at elections had been to stoke the fear of Asiatic communism. The Coalition always argued that to stay safe, Australians needed a close alliance with the United States. From the 1968 Tet offensive onwards, it became clear that the US strategy was not winning. Opposition to the war grew with moratorium marches in 1970. The Australian government wound back its commitment until all the troops had been withdrawn before Labor won the 1972 elections. By then, most Australians had accepted that our military involvement in Vietnam had been immoral, futile or counter-productive. The mainstay of Liberal Party electoral strategy was in tatters. The Labor Party's open attitude towards Asia became more acceptable.

Defeat in Vietnam brought home other lessons. The United States could no longer dominate the world. The cost of the Vietnam War had undermined its dollar. Other countries took note of what the Indo-Chinese had done and they too defied the United States more openly. Middle-Eastern countries no longer feared a US invasion, as had happened to Lebanon in 1958. The Organisation of Petroleum Exporting Countries

(OPEC) demanded higher prices to offset the falling value of the US dollar.

With the election of Whitlam's government, relations between the ANZUS partners soured. The United States appointed a career diplomat, Marshall Green, as its ambassador to Canberra. His dispatch indicated the depth of Washington's disquiet at Labor's approach. Shortly after Green's arrival, conflict broke out in the Middle East. The United States used its base at North-West Cape (WA) to alert its forces in the Indian Ocean without consulting Canberra. Green later regretted that incident as 'one of the greatest embarrassments to me during my time in Canberra'.

> It was an oversight but one that certainly would not have occurred if it had been Nigeria or some other country. Somehow there was an assumption in Washington that no matter what the hell happened the Aussies would go along with it. It was this over-identification that caused the problem and of course the fact that ... successive conservative governments had been so close to Washington, running on slogans like 'All the way with LBJ' and so on.

Under Green's professional leadership, working relations were back in place before his departure early in 1975.

A second crisis over the US bases broke out in October 1975 when Prime Minister Whitlam pointed to links between the leader of the National Party and a CIA man from the Pine Gap base, near Alice Springs. In those days, the CIA still denied that it had any connection with Pine Gap. Whitlam pushed on with his attack until three more CIA agents in Australia had been named. On 8 November, CIA headquarters in the United States contacted the Australian Security and Intelligence Organisation's representative in Washington who cabled his superiors in Canberra:

> Does this signify some change in our bilateral intelligence security related fields? CIA can not see how this dialogue with continued reference to CIA can do other than blow the lid off those installations in Australia where the persons concerned have been working

and which are vital to both our services and countries, particularly the installation at Alice Springs.

CIA can understand a statement made in political debate but constant further unraveling worries them. Is there a change in the Prime Minister's attitude in Australian policy in this field?

CIA feel that everything possible has been done on a diplomatic basis and now on an intelligence liaison link they feel that if this problem can not be solved they do not see how our mutually beneficial relationships are going to continue.

Three days later the Governor-General, Sir John Kerr, sacked Whitlam as prime minister. Some Labor supporters suspected that the CIA had played a part in the dismissal, as it had in other countries that were its allies, such as Greece.

Papua New Guinea

In September 1972 the House of Assembly voted for full internal self-government as soon as possible. Three months later, the Whitlam Labor government was anxious for Papua New Guinea to become self-governing and then independent. Self-government was achieved on 1 December 1973. Independence followed in 1975. Although political independence had been achieved within three years, Australian governments had not been working for this outcome. Apart from a slight hurry in the early 1960s, there had been no expectation of self-government until early in 1972. This failure to prepare kept Papua New Guinea's economy dependent on Australia.

Bougainville's copper mining became an example of the difference between the Australian government's view of good economic development and that of Papua New Guineans. In 1967, the Australian government had signed an agreement with Bougainville Copper Ltd, which meant that the company would not pay tax until 1980 on its profit of hundreds of millions of dollars. After that time, its tax rate would be between 22.5 per cent and 50 per cent. As soon as Papua New Guinea became self-governing, its leaders tried to rewrite the agreement. In October 1974, the company agreed to pay tax from 1

January 1974 at 33.3 per cent on the first $87.5 million profit each year, and 70 per cent on any profits over $87.5 million. This offer promised Papua New Guinea an extra $500 million in ten years, depending on the world price for copper.

Money was not the only aspect that distinguished the Australian from the Papua New Guinean view of development. In March 1974, Prime Minister Michael Somare flew to Sydney to speak to a conference of company directors:

> There are various Papua New Guinean concepts which make our investment rules different. Firstly, there is the concept of property rights. In Western society, the individual's absolute right to the use of his own property is a very important value. But in our society, there may be other values that are more important. For example, a clan or a village group often holds land rights exclusively. Similarly, much of Western business practice is based on the objective of receiving a return on capital investment. But in Papua New Guinea, return on capital is not as important. A pig freezer might be preferred to highly profitable popcorn machines.

The world economic crisis from 1974 hit the income for the new government, but most Papua New Guineans did not suffer because they remained self-sufficient.

Soviet threats

After 1975, Liberal Prime Minister Malcolm Fraser positioned the USSR as the primary threat. When 100 000 Soviet troops moved into Afghanistan late in 1979, Fraser led a campaign to boycott the 1980 Moscow Olympic Games. That year, 28 per cent of Australians thought that the USSR was a threat to Australia, compared with only 16 per cent two years before. The percentage who felt threatened by some other country reached 65 per cent, far above the usual figure of 52 per cent.

Fraser's opposition to the Soviet Union led him to conclude that the longer fighting continued in Zimbabwe, the greater would become Soviet influence over the independence movement that would eventually form the government. Fraser convinced the British government to accept a Marxist regime in order to limit Soviet power in all of southern Africa. Many of Fraser's fellow-Liberals could not follow his logic; they abused him for betraying 'the white tribes of Africa'. He extended his strategy for containing Soviet power in South Africa by working to end apartheid. In support of the United States, Fraser also recognised Pol Pot's Khmer Rouge regime in Kampuchea (Cambodia) against the Vietnamese invaders. He was consistently anti-Soviet, but flexible in which communists he would back.

The 1975 change of government in Canberra brought no change in policy towards Indonesia. The developing friendship continued until late in 1975 when Indonesian troops invaded Portuguese East Timor. A revolution in Portugal early in 1974 had promised independence for its colonies. From being ruled by a very reactionary government in Lisbon, East Timor seemed likely to pass to the control of local left-wingers. Indonesia claimed that conflicts within East Timor compelled it to take charge of the other half of the island, which lay within the Indonesian archipelago. People fight and die across the world every day without the Australian media paying much attention. The 1965–66 massacres in Java and Bali had not stayed in the headlines. Timor was different because the invading Indonesian troops murdered five Australian journalists. While Australian governments of both parties supported Indonesia's take-over, sections of the media remained critical of Indonesia's suppression of the Timorese. In 1969, only 4–5 per cent of Australians had feared Indonesia; after 1976, the figure more than doubled.

12 1981–1988 IN DEBT TO THE FUTURE

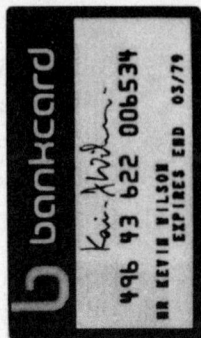

During the 1980s, the Hawke ALP government threw out most of the policies through which the Australian economy had been managed. The restructuring began by floating the currency. The value of the Australian dollar fell against the currencies of its major trading partners. It declined against the Japanese yen from over 200 in 1981 to under 100 by early 1988. Prices for minerals and farm produce also fell. In May 1986, the Treasurer, Paul Keating, warned that Australia was in danger of becoming a 'banana republic'. Two months later, the Wall Street brokers Salomon Brothers warned Keating that, if he went ahead with a tax on foreign investments, loans would be difficult to raise and the Australian dollar would plunge further. Keating abandoned the tax.

'Banana republics' are known for their submission to foreign financiers, unstable economies, authoritarian governments and sharp divisions between the rich and the other 90 per cent of the population. In 1976, Sir Roderick Carnegie, then head of the mining company CRA, had warned that Australia's dependence on foreign funds ran the risk of turning the country into the 'Uruguay of the South Pacific'. 'A society raised on champagne tastes', Carnegie reflected, 'may not be a polite or a pleasant one if it is reduced to a beer income.'

WORK

Unemployment remained high throughout the 1980s, never falling below 7 per cent. Few expected that it would return to the 1–3 per cent that had prevailed between 1942 and 1974. Governments established training schemes for young people and to retrain those older workers whose skills were no longer needed. With the closure of the ship-building yards, for instance, shipwrights had to take on other tasks if they were to have any kind of job in the metal trades. That sector suffered a massive decline in the early 1980s. More jobs became available in the service industries which required fewer skills and involved lower pay and fractured hours. These places suited students looking for part-time work but they were not much use for breadwinners. McDonald's denied its teenage staff trade union protection over hours and conditions. By promising fast service, the corporation used customers as spies to make sure that the youngsters were flat out, always giving the 'Welcoming Smile' and trying the 'Suggestive Sell', before ending with the 'Friendly Farewell'.

Older men found it impossible to believe that their capacities were no longer saleable. A teenage son who accompanied his father to the Employment Service observed:

> My father had worked for the whole of his life, ever since he was fourteen and suddenly he had to get unemployment benefits to support his family. And I went in with him and I saw him sit there and it took him a good half an hour just to get in the line and then he just walked out. You know. And he was just so put down with himself that he couldn't get a job and he had to go on the unemployment benefits. He found it hard to adjust but after a while he accepted it. You know, because there was no other way he could have supported his family and that was his priority.

His sense of shame was reduced when he got a sickness benefit rather than 'the dole'.

The chances of finding work were unevenly distributed. Queanbeyan had become one of the largest country towns in

Australia because it was so close to Canberra where most of the jobs were created in the building and service industries. By 1981, the town's rate of unemployment had reached 8.5 per cent. Then, construction of the new parliament house revived the local economy.

As the newest arrivals, Vietnamese suffered most when the semi-skilled manufacturing industries contracted. In 1981, 60 per cent of Vietnamese with jobs were in car plants, clothing factories or building suppliers. By 1991 that rate had fallen to 40 per cent. The men who lost jobs in the recessions of 1981 and 1991 could not get back into the workforce. Some moved into self-employment until every second shopping strip supported a Vietnamese bakery and restaurant, where family members laboured for long hours for small profits.

In textiles, clothing and footwear, women and children were driven to 'outwork' for rates of pay reminiscent of the 1880s. As the leading authority on Indo-Chinese immigration, Nancy Viviani, commented: 'the ugly face of ethnic business could not flourish unless supported by Australian and international firms'. Even when Vietnamese had perfect English, their accents counted against them. Graduates employed by banks to deal with other Vietnamese had no career path; they suffered from a 'sticky floor'.

The rising numbers of mothers in the workforce created job opportunities in child care. Between 1981 and 1990, the places available trebled to 120 000. In 1991 they shot up by a further 50 000 with the introduction of subsidies for commercial providers.

Bosses and workers both welcomed flexible patterns of work, but for contrary reasons. The firms wanted to cut costs, whereas employees hoped to balance their hours with life-long education, family needs and leisure activities.

Both paid employment and housework can be dull or rewarding. Some days, a Sydney mother was pleased that she had a job 'because it gets me out of the house and it is an escape from loneliness. But when I'm working it's boring'. Another woman preferred staying at home because she was her own boss and had 'time to see my friends and do the things I like'. Skilled or self-employed men were happier at work than most other employees: 'It's very responsible, diverse. It gives me opportunities to travel. I have been there for 31 years. I feel I belong'. An electrician expressed satisfaction because he found the trade itself interesting: 'As I drive around at night I see all the houses lit up, and I think "I did that" '. A butcher enjoyed 'talking to people'. For these workers, any problems on the job came from outside their workplaces, such as red tape from head office.

As much as many people enjoyed being at work, they still looked forward to a vacation. During the 1960s and 1970s, more Australians could afford to take a holiday away from home. Many took packaged trips organised through the airlines. By 1988, only 4 per cent of the population had never been away for a week's holiday. Half of the population had travelled during the previous twelve months. Half had gone to the seaside. A third still stayed with friends or relatives. These figures had not changed much since 1980, except that more people were going overseas or interstate. In 1988, one in five people had taken their most recent holiday outside Australia; of those, one in four was a retiree. Many sold their homes and travelled north to warmer climates by the ocean. Queensland's Gold Coast filled with high-rise apartment blocks peopled by widows, a long way from their grandchildren.

Any prospect of retiring had become widespread only during the twentieth century. Until then, there were no pensions or superannuation schemes. Most people had worked until they were sent to an institution, were kept by their families, or died. From 1980, people were encouraged to take early retirement at fifty-five. Some had not been able to adjust to automated offices or computer-aided manufacture. Unemployment was hidden under the label of 'early retirement'.

LIFE IN THE CITIES
Shopping

Broken and longer working hours led to longer shopping hours. First came late-night shopping one night a week, then shops were open on Saturday afternoons, and eventually Sunday trading came in. Suburban family outlets did business until 8 pm, seven days a week. Control of the grocery trade had been transformed since the late 1950s when the first super-markets had opened and chain stores expanded. The inde-pendent corner grocer almost disappeared. The few who remained could survive only by obtaining their supplies through a chain of suppliers to get lower prices. Even then they could not compete with the massive orders placed by Woolworths, Coles or Franklins.

The buying power of the big three retailers squeezed both small manufacturers and smaller outlets. Unless suppliers could pay to advertise their products, the giant retailers were not interested in stocking them. The result was further con-centration of ownership at each stage of the food chain: manu-facture, wholesale and retail.

During the 1950s, oil companies had paid wild prices for corner blocks on which to build service stations. Twenty years later, those outlets began to close. The survivors became all-purpose shops. In the 1980s, the local garage rented videos and stayed open twenty-four hours a day. The pumps became self-service to cut labour costs. At the same time, oil compa-nies bought up chains of food stores, such as Seven Eleven, installing petrol bowsers at the front.

Small shopping centres survived if they were not in direct competition with the drive-in ones. Handiness could prove more of an attraction than price. In order to prosper, the neighbourhood shops had to sustain a butcher, a supermarket, a fruit-and-vegetable shop, a chemist, a newsagent and a women's hairdresser. If any one of those goods or services was absent, customers would drive to a larger outlet to do all their shopping.

'Just me and the kids'

Since 1961, Australia had had a uniform divorce law, with fourteen grounds for divorce. New rules about divorce began from January 1976 under the Family Law Act. Henceforth, the only reason would be that the marriage had broken down and could not be put together again. The new system promised to make divorce easier and cheaper. The average number of divorces granted between 1971 and 1975 had been 17 000. In the first year of the Family Law Act, the total shot up to over 60 000. People took advantage of the simpler laws to turn longstanding separations into divorces. Many of those divorcees intended to marry the person with whom they had been living. In the next year, the number of divorces fell by 30 per cent to settle at around 43 000 a year, or more than twice as many as before the Family Law Act.

The new divorce laws came at around the same time as reforms to the status of children born outside marriage. Single mothers had formed a support organisation in 1970. The Commonwealth introduced a Supporting Mother's Benefit in 1973. Most of the legal disadvantages of being illegitimate were removed by 1974. The number of unwanted pregnancies was being reduced by contraception and quasi-legalised abortion. Moral attitudes also softened, removing much of the stigma of bearing a child out of wedlock. One result was that fewer children were available for adoption. IVF programs assisted couples unable to have their own children.

Sixty per cent of divorcing couples had one or more children. In 1983, 52 000 children experienced parents divorcing. Although the Family Law Act took some of the pain out of divorce proceedings, no legislation could remove the fears, heartache and anger of a family break-up. Some divorcing parents still fought over the right to look after or spend time with their children. The homes of Family Court judges were attacked, presumably by fathers who had not got what they wanted.

Children had rights under the 1975 Act but they could not will their parents into loving each other. One mother reported difficulties with her preschool child:

> He went against me — blamed me. Started to bed-wet, dirty his pants, have nightmares. I had to take him to a psychiatrist. He thought he was responsible for the separation even though he was only three.

Teenagers were better able to cope than younger children, though all were upset. One fifteen-year-old girl lamented: 'I felt really sad, really upset. I felt like I was a rag doll being pulled by both arms because they both wanted me. Didn't know which way to turn'. Some older children said they were pleased because their fathers had been drunken or violent. Most children came to accept their parents' separation, or even to see its good side. Nonetheless, more than one child in ten remained upset or sad six years later.

With nearly 40 per cent of marriages ending in divorce, the number of children in single-parent households increased. By the mid-1980s, more than half-a-million children were living with only one parent because of divorce, death or unmarried motherhood. Mothers usually had the care of these children, although a growing number of fathers acted as single parents. The fathers often had fewer financial problems than the mothers but were less used to the emotional and domestic sides of parenting. One dad with two teenagers admitted: 'I hadn't ironed a shirt for 17 years. I wouldn't have been able to survive without my mother'. Another man started out working full-time and trying to be a sole parent:

> It was very difficult for the children. I'd pick them up after work, go home and start cooking, but four nights out of five they would be asleep before I had the tea ready. Well I solved that problem by buying a microwave.

One employed father organised his working time to have days off during the week. Yet another did the housework after his children had gone to sleep so they could spend their waking hours together.

Although it was unusual for fathers to be sole parents, their appearance signalled a transformation in the typical household. Only one in five Australian homes had 'Mum, Dad and two kids'. More adults lived either alone, as sole parents, or in group houses. Of course, most of these people had been part of a traditional family or intended to establish one.

Fast foods

The new pattern of households altered the preparation and consumption of meals. The fraction of a family's average weekly food expenses that went on eating out grew from 15 per cent in 1976 to 21 per cent in 1989. Fast food in the form of pies and 'fish 'n' chips' had long been part of the Australian diet. What was different was the arrival of American chains such as McDonald's, which opened in 1971. By 1988 the corporation had almost 200 outlets. KFC sold thirty-five million chicken dinners each year. The value of sales by fast-food chains grew from $183 million in 1978 to over a billion dollars in 1988. As work and living pressures increased, the fast-food industry took a further step by offering home deliveries and 'Dial-a-Pizza'.

Two billion fast-food meals were served during 1983. On average, every Australian had two or three fast-food meals each week. In 1981, 9 per cent of Brisbane's population went to McDonald's about once a week. Nonetheless, one person in four had never been. Because of McDonald's marketing, it became the firm most associated with branded fast foods, yet in 1983 the chains had only 11 per cent of fast-food sales. Locally owned 'Greasy Joes' (hamburger joints) were still far more popular.

Despite criticisms of McDonald's menu, the nutritional

value of its products was no worse than the potato cakes deep-fried in batter sold by the old takeaways. Nor would McDonald's customers accept whatever was served up to them. Haluburgers, Onion Nuggets and Chicken Pot Pie were dropped because the public could not stomach them. Australians liked their hamburgers plain, with lettuce, tomato and perhaps beetroot. The US version came with pickles, which most Australians chucked out: 'We had pickles all over the store — sticking to the ceiling and the walls'. Another sign that Ronald McDonald could not have it all his own way came when builders' labourers prevented the construction of an outlet on the site of the Eureka stockade in Ballarat.

Mass marketing also reshaped the other essential daily need, namely for fluids. The sale of mineral waters grew from the late 1970s, partly because people wanted to drink less alcohol. Only in Adelaide did the tap water taste so dreadful that it could not be served at the meal table. Marketing campaigns encouraged people to spend money on 'spa' waters, including brands imported from France and Italy. The promotion of mineral water was part of a larger policy to get Australians to drink branded fluids. The lower consumption of tap water reduced the amount of fluoride that children got into their teeth. Coca-Cola and its related drinks had over 45 per cent of the Australian soft-drink sales, worth $800 million. Instead of trying to win customers away from other brands, Coca-Cola urged people to take up soft drinks instead of tea, milk and water. As its US chairman put it: 'Sometimes the competition is Pepsi. Sometimes it is water, sometimes it is wine'. Diet lines played their part in this attempt to turn the body's need for fluids into a profit-making choice between different kinds of colas. A related health issue was that more than half of the daily intake of calories came from beverages, including milk. Women got 1220 calories in food but 1880 from beverages, and so were not always aware of how many they were consuming. At the same time as people imbibed more, they were expending less energy. Remote controls eliminated the effort to cross the living room.

Screens

Colour television had commenced in 1975. By 1980, only 10 per cent of households still watched black-and-white sets. A mere 2 per cent had no television set at all. Television was challenged by a device which it had introduced, the video. In 1987, 55 per cent of households had one. For a long time, the owners of TV networks had defended their programming by saying that they gave audiences what they wanted. The popularity of videos proved that audiences wanted some shows that they were not getting and that they were being shown material that they did not want. In particular, video watchers zapped through advertisements with the fast-forward button. In the past, audiences had switched over from one channel to the next. During the 1980s, they switched off. Some started going out to cinemas again to enjoy a big screen with wall-to-wall sound. Complexes with four or five theatres opened. Videos were another defeat for drive-ins. In 1975, Perth still had twenty-two; by 1987, only twelve remained.

Australia's film industry won international, critical and financial success with *Mad Max* and *Crocodile Dundee*. Equally important for workers in the industry, and for Australian audiences, were the television mini-series such as *Scales of Justice* (1983) and a regular output of feature films such as Paul Cox's *Kostas* (1979) and *Lonely Hearts* (1982). Documentaries by Dennis O'Rourke on the South Pacific and by David Bradbury on Latin America reversed the usual flow of information from the United States and the United Kingdom.

An even smaller screen had greater influence over life and work. Computers went from IBM mainframes to Apple desk-tops and lap-tops. The new owners did need to know about Pascal, FORTRAN or MS-DOS. High-technology became user-friendly. Software provided business applications, notably spreadsheets. The first personal computers could display only forty letters. The rate of innovation was matched by the fall in prices. At first, people used their Apple Macs as little more than clever typewriters. They were not yet toys.

Changes in families and entertainment put strains on schooling. Education was blamed for every failure in society and the economy. Teachers were told to stop teenagers drinking and to find them jobs. Because of new teaching methods and subject matter, some parents and employers believed that students were leaving school unable to read, write or add up. These fears were strongest when there were no external examinations. Demands for a return to the 'three Rs' of 'reading, writing and arithmetic' concealed the call for a fourth R, namely learning by rote.

Australianising the entire curriculum followed the principle that people learn best when they move from the known to the unknown. The Academy of Science developed textbooks in biology, chemistry and geology grounded in Australian experiences and examples. Schools had used a US text which explained molecular bonding in terms of gridiron football, a comparison which made the material harder for Australians to comprehend.

LIFE IN THE COUNTRY

The NSW Country Women's Association had been formed in April 1922 to help deal with the loneliness of women living and working outside cities and big towns. Henry Lawson had written into Australia's popular memory the hardships and courage of such women with his stories 'The Drover's Wife' (1892) and 'Water Them Geraniums' (1901). Almost a hundred years later, radios, aeroplanes and telephones had reduced the isolation, yet a woman in the bush could have less power over life than her sister in the city:

I live on a farm. My in-laws live in the old homestead and their three sons have houses on the 400-hectare property. Right now, our bedroom needs curtains, and before I can buy the material the men discuss it at a meeting. They decide which daughter-in-law can have the money for curtains or some other thing for the house. We don't even go to the meeting. We wait at home like children waiting for Father Christmas.

Not all women in the country were farmers' wives: some were unmarried or widowed, or were themselves farmers; many were Aboriginal; others were the wives of doctors or miners; a few lived underground, some in caravans. Each group had its own concerns and its own ways of coping. An Aboriginal teenager living in Cammoweal was less likely to have an abortion than the daughter of the doctor she visited about her pregnancy. Drought constricted choice more than usual. Mothers worked in the paddock all day alongside husbands and grandfathers, leaving children to do much of the housework. A drought in the big cities usually meant nothing worse than restrictions on hosing the lawn, or higher meat prices. On a farm, it made every drop of water precious:

Bath night tonight, but only a few centimetres of water are put into the bath for all the family. After bathing, the water is transferred to the washing machine, then to the toilet for flushing.

Every year, a patch of the countryside somewhere missed out on rains. One farmer defined a drought as 'when you haven't got any feed, or the soil won't produce a crop'. That was the case within a 65-kilometre radius in East Gippsland when animals had to be hand-fed, some shot, others sold before their prime. Good seasons elsewhere had doubled farm incomes from $2.2 billion in 1977–78 to $4.6 billion in 1979–80. Those years helped to make up for the ups-and-downs of the 1970s. The boost also cushioned the impact of what followed. In the early 1980s, entire States were afflicted. Most of New South Wales and southern Queensland had a dry year in 1980. That spell was mild compared with the disaster of

1982 which ended in the bushfires of February 1983. Despite occasional rainfalls, drought conditions had lasted for nearly four years across south-eastern Australia, finally breaking in March 1983. By then, a new phrase had entered Australian speech, *El Niño*. Vocabulary had caught up with reality.

As the stock died, abattoirs closed. A total of 30 000 jobs were lost in rural New South Wales alone. The 1982–83 drought was the most severe since the start of the twentieth century. The value of rural production fell by almost 50 per cent. Wheat crops in New South Wales and Victoria were only one-fifth of their average during the previous five years. The severity of the drought linked farmers to the environment movement. They concluded that crisis management had never worked, and agreed to organise to care for the land by recognising its cycles and fragility.

HEALTH
Food

Although a balanced diet is vital for good health, most doctors got very little training in this subject. Food was 'touched on' in many courses within a medical degree but rarely were the aspects brought together. In the early 1980s, the University of New South Wales introduced three 90-minute sessions outside the formal lecture hours. Students could choose to study the links between food and health for four-and-a-half-hours in their six years of training.

Food was treated as a sideline because medical science focused on curing a disease in one person rather than preventing illnesses throughout the community. Surgeons were brilliant at operations on arteries that had been ruined by fatty foods, tobacco, alcohol and too much salt. General practitioners were neither skilled nor experienced in advising people how to avoid the dietary causes of cancers and heart disease. Yet the three biggest killers in Australia were still more easily avoided than cured: dangerous driving, tobacco and excessive alcohol.

One result of this failure by the medical profession was a public demand for books on nutrition and for health foods. Like medicine, health foods were subject to fads and fashions. Australia had almost as many health food shops as chemists, and both stocked a range of vitamins and herbal products. Perhaps one Australian in five took a dietary supplement, such as vitamin C for colds, bran for constipation, or vitamin B to relieve stress. Vitamin addicts were the people who did not need to take them since their awareness of the links between food and health had already led them to eat properly. Others took vitamins only when off-colour, for instance vitamin B as a hangover cure. Like curative medicine, health food became big business. The food company H. J. Heinz, and the brewers Castlemaine and Tooheys, bought up small firms. The pharmaceutical giants again conspired to inflate the price of vitamins.

In 1981, one in three primary school children ate no fruit, either fresh or tinned. A quarter had eaten no vegetables in the week before they were questioned. A typical daily menu was cereal or toast for breakfast, tuckshop for lunch and a takeaway at night. One-third of these children suffered from constipation and one-third were overweight. Children who went to school without breakfast, and those who ate no fruit, were the most likely to buy sweets during their mid-morning break, to get a sugar buzz. The most popular chocolate snacks were Kit-Kat and Mars bar, with Cherry Ripe third. Such foods increased tooth decay and the risk of bowel cancers. They remained popular because they were widely advertised, especially on television. The screening of cigarette commercials had been banned during children's programs. Parents called for a ban on the promotion of sweets to children. Others complained about the success of the 'Big M' campaigns which got people of all ages drinking sweetened milk. No equivalent promotion followed for fruit and vegetables.

An indicator of Australian fitness had been the number of gold medals won at Olympic Games. On the home ground of Melbourne in 1956, Australia took twenty-three gold medals in swimming, athletics and cycling. Four years later in Rome, the total was down to ten; in 1964 in Tokyo, our team brought home only eight, falling further to five from Mexico City. Success shot back up to eleven at Munich in 1972 (six for swimming and five for yachting). A disaster occurred at Montreal in 1976 when Australians did not win gold. Under a partial boycott, two Australian swimmers took gold at Moscow in 1980; in 1984 four Australians won gold medals at Los Angeles, and three won gold at Seoul in 1988. Winning only one silver and four bronze medals at Montreal in 1976 had driven home the decline in Australia's international sporting prowess.

The sag in elite performance reproduced the reasons behind the failure of health care: the triumph of drugs and commercialisation. To say that Australia was a sporting nation no longer meant that many Australians played a game or took regular exercise. Sport became a branch of the mass media, a spectators' inactivity, packaged and sold on behalf of the cigarette and alcohol firms that promoted themselves on telecasts.

Sex

Women had started to take 'the Pill' in the 1960s in the hope that it would be a safe and sure method of allowing them to decide when to become pregnant. By the 1980s, 90 per cent of women had taken one of the brands. They no longer swallowed it as the sole or simple path to sexual pleasure or managing pregnancy. The biggest risk was with heart disease in women over 35 years, especially if they also smoked. Regular and prolonged use diminished the risk of some cancers without increasing the chances of developing others, though a danger existed for young girls. For women between 20 and 35, the threats to life from contraceptive pills were fewer than those from giving birth. Doctors became aware of the need to prescribe pills of varying strengths to suit the bodily needs of individual patients.

Teenagers were unable to get the Pill or take it without their parents' finding out. More of the unmarried girls who became pregnant had abortions. The number of females under twenty years of age who had children fell from fifty-five per 1000 births in 1971 to twenty-five in 1983. The rate of teenage abortions went up by even more, from twenty to fifty per 1000 births. An eighteen-year-old woman thought the situation had got worse rather than better:

> I watched the end of Clive James' interview with Kathy Lette, co-author of *Puberty Blues*. Old Clive was appalled by the things Kathy described in her recollections of suburban teenagers. But Kathy was appalled by what happens now. And so she should be. At least the boys in *Puberty Blues* still used condoms! No one uses condoms anymore. Boys pride themselves on never having used one. Even 'nice, sensitive modern boys' seldom consider using them. The wonderful liberating pill has liberated boys from any responsibility for pregnancy, and the girls don't know about the things the pill can do to them.

That opinion was voiced in 1985 before the 'Grim Reaper' campaign warned about the spread of HIV/AIDS (Acquired Immune Deficiency Syndrome). For a while, the fear of AIDS encouraged young males to use condoms again. This scare campaign spared some women an abortion, single parenthood or a too early marriage.

HIV/AIDS hit the headlines in 1983, the year that competing scientists associated a virus with the epidemic. Fear of AIDS became so strong because it was tied to two matters that frightened many people, namely male homosexuality and heroin use. Another factor which added to the panic was that AIDS was the first deadly contagion for more than twenty years, since polio. With the arrival of antibiotics in the mid-1940s, Australians had become used to taking a pill when-ever they caught something, or to getting shots to prevent their becoming sick. No magic bullet existed to prevent or cure AIDS. Instead, Australians led the world in a harm-reduction approach by the distribution of condoms and the exchange of needles. This example of a preventive social strategy became a model for other diseases.

ABORIGINES
Woman-slaughter

The gaoling of a 24-year-old Aboriginal man for the killing of his wife was not the kind of story to make headlines. Yet the trial of Alwyn Peter became front-page news. Journalists scru-tinised how Aborigines were treated by the law. Instead of presenting the facts about Alwyn Peter's actions, his defence introduced evidence about the conditions under which he and his wife had lived. The lawyers argued that the destruction of traditional society had contributed to violence on Aboriginal reserves. Alcohol was involved in most of the attacks. At Maningrida (NT), the women locked themselves up for safety after the boat arrived with the fortnightly beer supplies. They kept a two-way radio to call for police help if their men broke in.

For a time, almost no one wanted to talk about alcoholism among Aborigines. To do so seemed to reinforce the old views of drunken no-hopers. Even Aborigines who hoped to ban alcohol from their communities did not want whiteman's laws to intervene. The right to drink had been the first step towards equality in the early 1960s. To give that right up in the 1980s looked like a step backwards.

Uniting Church missionaries with contacts in the Pacific Islands noticed how people there drank kava without becoming violent. The church introduced that drink to Aborigines as a way around the destructiveness of alcohol. Far from making matters better, kava made everything worse. Whereas the islanders drank kava as part of their social order, the Aborigines consumed it all the time, like beer. Instead of being aggressive, people on kava became unable to do the simplest tasks. Hence, children were not fed, no work could be done, no political organisation was possible. Aborigines had been better off on beer and plonk.

Yet drunkenness was rife among a smaller percentage of Aborigines than other Australians. In the Northern Territory, for example, 60 per cent of Aborigines did not drink at all, compared with only 12 per cent of whites who were total abstainers. The problem was that two-thirds of the 40 per cent of Aborigines who drank did so to dangerous levels. Hence, Aborigines had proportionally more teetotallers and more alcoholics than European Australia.

Although alcohol and drugs were the immediate causes of crime for many Aboriginal offenders, social, cultural and economic disadvantages had to be redressed. Aborigines recognised this need and organised their own campaigns against drinking. In the towns, some turned to fundamentalist Christian sects for emotional support in giving up alcohol. Others mixed their experiences with Bible stories. A student from north Queensland asked:

Who was born into a poor world?
  Me and Jesus.
Who had loving parents gently guiding?
  Me and Jesus.
Who was a carpenter and worked with wood?
  My dad, Andy, and Jesus.
Who preached of God, our father?
  My grand-dad, Dan, and Jesus.
Who fed so many hungry people?
  My Mum, Rose, and Jesus.
Who died a cruel and senseless death?
  My ancestors and Jesus.

Others accepted a literal reading of the Bible that the world had existed for only 6000 years. That belief denied 40 000 years of human occupation of this continent.

Missionaries had been in contact with Aboriginal people since the beginnings of European settlement. Parsons were among the first to record Aboriginal languages, doing so in order to translate the Bible and thereby convert Aborigines to Christianity. The missionaries recorded some languages that have had no speakers for over a hundred years. Because Aborigines from different language groups lived together on reserves or in missions, they had to find ways of talking with each other. Children mixed English with words from a number of Aboriginal tongues. The result was a new mixed language, known as 'Kriol'. 'Kriol' spread across the north of Australia, separating its speakers from their own cultures and the standard English spoken by the dominant white population. Some US churches in Australia encouraged the adoption of Kriol to make their missionary work easier. Instead of having to make a number of translations of their bibles, a Kriol version would have a wide audience.

Daughter of the Sun

Patricia O'Shane wanted to be a doctor. Only later did she decide to become a barrister. She went on to head a government department and to serve as a magistrate.

> It's been a long tough road. I can still remember coming home from school one day in tears after being called names by my schoolmates. My mother told me I had to fight my own battles, so when I was young I settled quite a few with my fists.

The eldest of five children, Pat O'Shane was born in 1941 at Mossman, a sugar town in far north Queensland. Her mother had been the daughter of a part-Aboriginal father and an Aboriginal mother; her father 'Tiger' O'Shane was Irish–Australian, a Shakespeare-reading socialist, wrestler and wharf labourer. Her family moved into Cairns where Pat matriculated before training as a school teacher. While at school, she had become active in the Aborigines and Torres Strait Islanders Advancement League. A turning point came late in 1972 after O'Shane had been ticked off by her headmaster for selling Land Rights badges to her students. 'Legacy, sporting and service clubs all sold their badges', she said. At 3 am the next morning, she wrote to the newspapers and gained national attention for her opinions.

Always close to her mother, she had joined the Communist Party with her on the same night in 1959. At Christmas 1970, Pat's mother choked on a chicken bone, spent a year in a coma and died on the following New Year's Eve. The strain of that year, and Pat's frustrated desire to study medicine, led to the break-up of her marriage, followed by a nervous collapse and migraines. After countless drugs and doctors, O'Shane threw away her pills to study in Sydney for a law degree. She received a grant for her fees and books.

> I suppose what finally made me reach the decision to be a barrister was when the Advancement League took two police officers to court for brutality against some Aboriginal women on a settlement outside Cairns.

O'Shane studied, earned money to live and adjusted to the big city. For inspiration, she put three photographs above her desk: that of her mother; an American black activist, Angela Davis; and the Vietnamese leader, Ho Chi Minh. 'Every day at 5 am when I got up to study I'd grit my teeth and say, "If they did it, I can do it".' In 1976, Pat O'Shane became the first Aborigine to qualify as a barrister. She worked in Alice Springs before joining a NSW parliamentary inquiry into Aboriginal conditions. After that job, she became a policy adviser in Canberra on women's affairs. In 1981, the NSW government put her in charge of its Ministry of Aboriginal Affairs, the first woman to reach that rank in the public service.

Late in 1982, O'Shane was chosen 'Woman of the Year'. She returned to Queensland to speak on the topic 'Who Cares?' to a luncheon of establishment women, including Senator Florence Bjelke-Petersen. When O'Shane praised the Aborigines who had been arrested for protesting in favour of Land Rights during the Brisbane Commonwealth Games, half of the well-to-do ladies hissed and booed. The others gave her a standing ovation.

O'Shane helped to devise the 1983 NSW Land Rights legislation that gave Aborigines freehold titles over what had been reserves:

> Aborigines need land rights not only to give them an economic base, but also to boost their morale. When land rights are granted I think the problem of alcoholism could be overcome by the communities themselves. A lot of things will improve once their self-esteem is restored.

Because of the amendments and compromises that are part of every piece of legislation, some Aborigines accused her of losing touch with their concerns. At the time of her appointment as Departmental Head in 1981, O'Shane said she would stay for only five years. In 1986, she became Australia's first Aboriginal magistrate. The New South Wales government was glad to be rid of her. She had gone on television to attack the Hawke government after it dumped Labor's Land Rights policy in favour of the mining companies. A few lawyers opposed her appointment as a magistrate because of her attacks on injustices within the law: 'I have been described as a controversial figure and God forbid I should have been a milksop. I hope I shall always dare to struggle'.

WHITE AUSTRALIA

The achievements of immigrants in learning English, starting a new life, and contributing to Australian culture, politics and the economy became the stuff of speeches on

multiculturalism. A neglected success of the post-war population growth was the adjustment made by the Anglo-Celtic
majority to the size and diversity of the immigrant intake.
Despite a scatter of difficulties, the absorption of a million
non-Anglo-Celtic immigrants and their children was achieved
without prolonged conflict, and still less without violence.

This 'capacity to absorb' was noteworthy in the case of
Asian immigration. Between 1965 and 1991, the total Asian
intake was around 200 000. The annual intake of Asians
between 1977 and 1980 had more than doubled, from 11 000 to
24 500. Their arrival coincided with the worst business down-
turn since the 1930s. No one advocating the end of the White
Australia policy in the 1960s would have predicted that so
many Asians could have been admitted with so little disorder
at so difficult a time.

After provoking alarms over the 2000 'boat people', the
mass media paid little attention to the difficulties of resettle-
ment during a recession. When Professor Geoffrey Blainey
spoke in Warrnambool (Victoria) in April 1984, he asked
whether the level of Asian immigration was becoming so high
that it might provoke a backlash among those competing for
jobs or houses. He said nothing about the government and
corporations that had created the unemployment. The media
blew Blainey's reflection up into an attack on the
'Asianisation' of Australia. Resentment at non-Anglo-Celtic
immigrants flooded forth. People wrote to Blainey com-
plaining about the smells from Asian cooking. These prejudices faded from the headlines until stirred up in 1988 by the
Liberal Party leader, John Howard, in an effort to improve his
popularity.

Throughout the 1980s, the arguments over immigration
became livelier than they had been for twenty years. Yet there
was less effort to inform community opinion than there had
been during the campaign to admit some non-Whites before
1965. Multiculturalism confronted its major test: could it be

extended from Southern Europeans to non-Europeans? Out of these controversies came a questioning of what it meant to be an Australian. Did 'Australian' involve more than living on the continent? If multiculturalism was the new national ideal, who was a typical Australian? What kind of ethnic mix should Australians aim at having by the year 2040? This rethinking opened out to questions about the structure of Australia's population. A government report recommended more skilled Asian immigrants. Ecologists raised concerns about the total size: if we continued to populate, would the environment perish? Opponents of non-European immigrants hid their prejudices under a call for Zero Population Growth.

VIEW OF THE WORLD

'Anzac' had become an Australian legend in 1915, though few Australians paid much attention to the initials 'NZ'. They appeared in other shorthand words such as ANZAAS and the 1951 ANZUS Treaty which was supposed to keep the United States as Australia's great and powerful friend. During 1987, Australia announced a policy of greater self-reliance. A few critics of the US alliance wanted Australia to become 'armed and neutral'. The population remained unsure about Australia's ability to defend itself. In 1980, 73 per cent of Australians believed that the country could not defend itself; by 1988, only 53 per cent held this view.

Politicians knew that the alliance with the United States depended, in fact, on its bases at North-West Cape, Narrungar and Pine Gap. Although the United States would not risk its own interests for the sake of Australia, Washington, and particularly the CIA, had to protect those installations. The importance of the spy systems also meant that the Soviets would have to 'take them off the map' as a first step in any armed conflict with the United States. This threat to Australia led to calls to remove the US bases. A few even wanted to break off the ANZUS Alliance. At the 1984 elections, the People for Nuclear Disarmament, led by the lawyer and rock musician Peter Garrett, took almost 10 per cent of the Senate vote in New South Wales.

The end of ANZUS came from an unexpected source when New Zealand refused to allow nuclear-armed ships into its ports. By the 1970s, New Zealand seemed a pleasant place to go for a holiday after you retired. The United States broke off naval training programs with New Zealand. ANZUS became a two-party agreement between Australia and the United States. A broken-backed ANZUS survived because negotiating a new treaty would have split the labour movement, and perhaps brought down the Hawke government. Henceforth, the presumption that ANZUS guaranteed US support was supplemented by a pretence that ANZUS still existed.

The disappearance of the three-party ANZUS was only one of the several changes in the way Australians came to view the world during the 1980s. Islam, the South Pacific and the environment provided three new concerns.

The so-called Arab world had hardly existed for most Australians until the price of crude oil went up in 1973. Immigration to Australia from the Middle East had expanded during the 1970s, at first from Turkey and then from Lebanon. After the overthrow of the Shah of Iran in 1979, 'Islam' replaced 'Arab' as the mass-media image. Instead of wealthy oil sheiks in front of a petrol pump, the television news served up religious revolutionaries waving rifles. Political, religious and ethnic divisions within Islam were sidelined. Nonetheless, Canberra supported Iraq's Saddam Hussein against Ayatollah Khomeini in Iran and backed the Mudjahadin in Afghanistan. Extreme views were presented as the only ones in Islam, as if all Christians were followers of the Reverend Fred Nile. During this time, Israel lost some support because of its behaviour in Lebanon and its treatment of the Palestinians.

During the 1980s, Canberra rediscovered the Pacific and

had to deal with its island governments. Although these states came together in a forum, they were divided by religious, political and ethnic backgrounds: Vanuatu's leaders were Catholic, left-wing and Melanesian; Samoa's were Protestant, right-wing and Polynesian. Fiji was split between Indians, who had been brought in as labourers for the sugar plantations, and the native Melanesians who controlled the army, which threw out an Indian-led government in 1987. French refusal to give independence to New Caledonia turned some of the locals towards Libya which was at war with France in North Africa. These disputes tilted Australian attitudes about the Pacific away from a sprawling holiday resort into a zone with political and military puzzles.

The significance of the French in the Pacific came from its testing of nuclear weapons, not because of its remaining colonies. France said it did not have colonies: New Caledonia and Tahiti were parts of France which just happened to be a long way from Paris. Atomic testing had started at Mururoa in 1966, more than a decade after the British had set off their series of bombs inside Australia at Maralinga, and the United States had exploded theirs around the Bikini atoll. French nuclear testing continued in the atmosphere until 1974, giving rise to fall-out which blew away from Australia. Opposition to France's role in the Pacific escalated after two of its secret agents blew up the anti-nuclear Greenpeace vessel, *Rainbow Warrior*, in Auckland harbour in 1985, killing one of the crew.

One area of the Pacific held less interest than before. Once Papua New Guinea had become independent from Australia in 1975, the former colony almost disappeared from Australian headlines. None of the disasters that had been predicted happened. Free elections continued, so a parliamentary system seemed safe. Papua New Guinea became of interest to Australians only when it was involved in conflicts with Indonesia.

In 1987, the Department of Foreign Affairs merged with the Department of Trade. That move highlighted the importance of economics to political relationships. Environmental issues also demonstrated that countries needed to redefine international politics. The High Court, for example, reinterpreted the foreign affairs power of the Constitution in 1983. The Commonwealth had power over the States on international agreements about heritage areas, such as the south-west of Tasmania along the Franklin River. Linking foreign policy with trade and the environment showed that the safety of Australia involved more than treaties and weapons. Without export earnings, Canberra could not pay for fighter-bombers.

International treaties linked the health of the planet to the well-being of people. Security had to become comprehensive if it were to succeed.

Pieces of paper could not outlaw natural processes. At most, human beings could increase our understanding of how the climate behaved. Information about why droughts happen remained scarce, but Australia's 1981–83 experience was linked to currents of warm water off the coast of Peru which the locals there have long called *El Niño*. Since 1957, scientists had recognised *El Niño* as part of a world-wide chain of atmospheric events. Warm moist air rose over Indonesia and moved east until it sank onto the colder waters off Peru. The results were felt across Africa as well as Australia. Bob Geldof's 'Live Aid' concert to help African famine victims went around the globe like *El Niño*.

Talk about *El Niño* encouraged the idea that the earth was a single ecosystem. That view gained support from three other areas of concern: nuclear winter, the greenhouse effect, and holes in the ozone layer.

'Nuclear winter' was the term applied to the effect that would be produced by the dust formed after even a limited nuclear war. This dirt cloud would limit the amount of sunlight reaching the earth's surface and thus upset the growing season for food crops, leading to famine. The 'greenhouse effect' referred to a heating of the earth's atmosphere and the threatened melting of the polar ice caps. The result would be a rise in sea levels. According to this scenario, lower-lying parts of Australia would be under water by the year 2025.

The ozone layer in the upper atmosphere screens out 90 per cent of the sun's damaging radiation. Even a 1 per cent loss of ozone could lead to a 5 per cent increase in some skin cancers, of which Australia already had one of the highest rates in the world. A hole in the ozone layer over the Antarctic had been spreading each spring since 1979. Chemicals used in air-conditioners, refrigerators, some aerosol spray cans, and foam plastics broke down in ways that destroyed our planet's protective mantle.

Running through all these issues is the question of whether human activity can reset the cycles of nature. Fear of the Yellow Peril and panic at the Red Peril had encouraged simple-minded solutions. A great and powerful friend would protect European, Christian Australia. That kind of fix became irrelevant in an era of globalised trading in carbon futures.

1988: BEYOND CELEBRATION

Unlike 1888 and 1938, the bicentenary of European occupation did not pretend that convicts had never existed. By 1988, some Australians saw convict suffering, resistance and achievements as offering a more appropriate mythos than the Anzac legend. The convict stain no longer embarrassed direct descendants, or Australia as a nation. Yet the invitation to 'Celebrate 88' remained selective about which events Australians were encouraged to remember. For example, two popular victories were not paraded. In 1916, and again in 1917, the Australian people had voted against conscription for overseas military service; in 1951, they had voted against banning the Communist Party. These popular choices in favour of democracy were left out of the 1988 celebrations.

The brief history of European settlement has seen some remarkable coincidences in dates. November 11 — Remembrance Day — was the day Ned Kelly was hanged in 1880; the day in 1918 when fighting stopped in the Great European War; and, in 1975, the day on which the Governor-General sacked Prime Minister Gough Whitlam. Another trio of significant events attaches to 26 January: in 1788, Captain Arthur Phillip sailed into Sydney Harbour; in 1808, John MacArthur and his accomplices deposed the king's representative, Governor Bligh, in their Rum Rebellion; then, in 1838, a series of massacres of Aborigines began at Waterloo Creek in north-east New South Wales, continuing for four-and-a-half months.

The 'Celebrate 88' slogan required Australians to forget

how the rich had overthrown the government on Australia Day 1808, and how their agents had slaughtered Aborigines thirty years later. Nor did the organisers mention how Aborigines had fought to defend their territories against European invasion. Actions that had shaped our history were wiped out.

Other stories were retold by novelists, such as Kate Grenville in her *Joan Makes History*, a fiction about how women had always influenced the nation's destiny. The band Redgum adapted lines by the poet John Manifold about the rebel Ned Kelly:

> *And so they took Ned Kelly and hanged him in jail,*
> *For he fought single-handed although in iron mail.*
> *And no man single-handed can hope to break the bars;*
> *It's a thousand like Ned Kelly who'll hoist the Flag of Stars.*

Some self-awareness came from television series and films, such as *Bodyline* and *Melba*. These popular sources stimulated interest in grandad's schooling or mum's first job. No country forgets its past. Individuals may be mistaken in the details of what they recall, but some outline of previous experiences form our perceptions of whom we wish to be. Much of this memory is carried forward by the stories told within families. A more elaborate study of history is necessary to understand our past as more than a collection of anecdotes. Yet simple experiences can lead to profound questions — for example, where is home?

Home

Aborigines never doubted that their home, their 'country', was located on this continent. What they experienced, before and after 1788, was their version of patriotism, which is a love of one's physical environment and an attachment to preceding generations of human activity, whether physical or imaginative. Tasmanian Aborigines transported to Flinders Island during the 1830s gathered on the beach, lamenting, to look south towards their homelands.

For the European arrivals, the situation was different. In the most immediate sense, their homes were somewhere else, since their families, friends and hearths were in the British Isles. Those early convicts and settlers who used 'home' to describe a place thousands of miles away were making a statement of fact. This identification with the northern antipodes continued for 150 years. The painter Fred McCubbin (1855–1917) recalled that in his youth 'Everybody who was grown up spoke of Home, the Old Country'. The Melbourne weekly *Table Talk* editorialised against this habit in 1887:

> Here is where you were born, and where you make your living. And until the natives of Australia recognise this fact there will be no national sentiment — no pride of country — no patriotism — nothing but aping of old-world styles, from the fashion of a dress to the form of a thought.

Yet three years later *Table Talk* itself was writing about England as 'home'. The practice was not confined to the conservative side of politics. Henry Lawson wrote about going 'home' before he left for London in 1900. The Scottish-born leader of the Labor Party, Andrew Fisher, issued a final election appeal in 1910 in which he spoke of Britain as 'home'. When Robert Gordon Menzies visited Britain for the first time in 1935 he noted in his diary:

> At last we are in England. Our journey to Mecca has ended and our minds abandoned to reflections which can so strangely (unless you remember our traditions and upbringing) move the sense of those who go 'home' to a land they have never seen.

Menzies was a true Englishman in his heart which, as he said later, he kept somewhere near his bootstraps.

Menzies's discomfit with Australia as 'home' annoyed a group of writers calling themselves Jindyworobaks, derived from the Aboriginal word 'to join'. In the 1930s, they aimed to connect Australian culture with life as it was lived here. One of their members responded in verse to a 1940 headline announcing 'Prime Minister to Go Home':

> *'I'm going home' said the Minister.*
> *'He's going home' cheeped the Sparrow.*
> *'Home' squeaked the Starling,*
> *'Home' blinked the Capeweed,*
> *'Home' said the Prickly Pear,*
> *'Home' barked the Fox.*
> *'How nice' said they all,*
> *'Let's go with him.'*

In 1942, the writer Vance Palmer had asked whether white Australians deserved to hold this land against a possible Japanese invasion: 'We could vanish and leave singularly few signs that, for some generations, there had lived a people who had made a homeland of this Australian earth'. In other words, white Australians were still fairly much predatory interlopers, like the fox and the prickly pear.

The Jindyworobaks also exposed what they called the 'British Garrison'. This occupying force, imported from the British Isles, comprised not only generals and admirals but also bishops, headmasters, professors and newspaper editors. These ideology-makers reproduced what Menzies called 'our traditions and upbringing'. In 1988, the 'British Garrison' lingered on, but with much less influence than in the 1930s. Its place had been overtaken by agents of influence for the United States, especially in defence and security matters. Company directors gave their loyalty to global corporations such as IBM. Rupert Murdoch traded his Australian citizenship for television stations in the United States. Despite the power of such people, they were a minority of the Australian population. In the bicentennial year of 1988, most settler Australians were as convinced that this continent was their home as Aboriginal Australians had always been.

13 1989–2000 THE MONEY GOES ROUND

In 1985, the daily turnover of futures contracts in the Australian bond market was $100 million. By 1999, the total each day was seventy times bigger, at $7 billion. Similar growth overtook foreign exchange, the money market and the share market. The annual total across these four areas reached $50,000,000,000,000. That run of noughts became so long as to appear meaningless. The fifty-trillion mark moved beyond comprehension as the buying and selling of money became central to so-called 'globalisation' and the 'New Economy'. Speculation and fraud were the offspring of deregulating the financial sector.

An Australian could still calculate how many rental properties she could buy with a $14 million win in Lotto, on which adults spent an average of $2.00 every week in 1997–98. Casinos, clubs and pubs took another $10 per head. Total outlays on gambling expanded during the 1990s to exceed $11 billion, with $6.5 billion tumbling into poker machines. State governments became addicted to gaming revenues of almost $4 billion a year. The big losers were the 300 000 problem gamblers who accounted for one-third of the turnover. Australia's tradition of Melbourne Cup sweeps cannot explain this explosion. Rather, clubs and pubs had trebled their promotional spending in the three years to 1998.

Money also took on new forms as a means of exchange.

Bankbooks became the preserve of the elderly. Personal cheques all but disappeared, and cash was not far behind. In their place were wallets of credit cards, ATMs, Eftpos at super-market checkouts, and banking by phone or shopping on-line.

Before the withdrawal from circulation of one- and two-cent pieces in 1991, coins had replaced one- and two-dollar banknotes. The plastic coating of five-dollar notes in 1992 made them more durable but also hinted at an artificial connection between wealth and well-being. That suspicion grew after 1999 when the plunge in share prices warned investors that their retirement savings could evaporate. Even Telstra and AMP dropped in value. Meanwhile, debts continued to grow. In 1978, the average household could have paid off all its loans with the wages from twenty weeks' work. By 2000, the clearing of debt would have taken the earnings from the entire year.

WORK

Despite this avalanche of money, almost everyone still depended on wages or salaries. Survival meant finding a boss to buy one's capacities. The employee then had to earn enough per hour, and rack up enough hours each week, to make a living wage. As governments tightened their welfare spending, workers had to earn more to cover more of the costs of medical care, education and retirement. In addition, most workers had to juggle the rising pressure on time at work with family responsibilities and with continuing education.

Between 1990 and 1997, the real wage of the top 10 per cent of employees went up by 10 per cent. The bottom 10 per cent suffered a fall of 8.5 per cent. In the expanding service sector, the difference was even sharper. Managers got 40 per cent more, while the lowest-paid dropped 14 per cent. This spread of inequality grew out of a return to patterns of work that had prevailed before 1941. The number of permanent full-time jobs shrank. Casual, temporary and part-time work became the only option for many people.

Quitting the workforce is one of the toughest transitions in life. The 1993 closure of another NSW government enterprise led to the dismissal of 620 blue-collars workers. They were given six-months notice to help them to adjust. Instead, morale crashed. They began taking lots of 'sickies'. Only after absenteeism disrupted production did the managers bring in the social workers. Those outsiders soon recognised that the problem was the way the place had been run before the announcement of its closure. The response from the shopfloor was that 'everything management says is lies'. The foremen had extra difficulties in adjusting to unemployment because they were used to giving orders. They therefore treated the counselling sessions as 'crap', although they welcomed practical advice on how to look for another job. Men had more emotional problems adjusting to the sack than women, who maintained more social connections outside their workplaces.

Once out of a job, older workers found it harder than before to get back into the paid workforce. From 1990 to 1997, the rate of the long-term jobless went up from 1.5 to 2.6 per cent. To hide this problem, the ALP government moved the long-term unemployed onto disability pensions. The numbers in that category almost doubled during the 1990s. The Coalition government hoped to get costs down by imposing work tests on the disabled from 2000.

Governments also redefined 'employed' as having one hour of paid work during a week. This criterion made comparisons with previous times tricky. Yet even the official level of unemployment in the 1990s stayed between 6 and 11 per cent. Jobless rates had returned to the norms prior to 1941. Other statistics showed how desperate matters were becoming. The numbers of 'discouraged job-seekers' went up from 780 000 in 1989 to 1.3 million in 1998. That rise pointed to half-a-million people who would have sought work if they had believed they had any chance of securing a job.

Reports of one in four young people being unemployed were misleading. That percentage referred only to the minority who were not in full-time education. By leaving school early, those teenagers were more likely to remain job-less. The ones who did find work entered a cycle of low-paid, temporary, casual employment. The young long-term unem-ployed were likely to become parents at younger ages. They often accumulated other problems through petty crime, drugs or alcohol. They had no chance to save for a house.

One reaction to the recession of the early 1980s had been to encourage students to go on to Year 12. In 1983, only 41 per cent of Australian students completed twelve years of educa-tion. Governments hoped to lift the retention level to 70 per cent by 1995. That increase would require more qualified teachers, more classrooms and a new curriculum to match a greater spread of aptitudes and ambitions. Before these sup-ports could be put in place, another recession saw 85 per cent of Victorian students stay on to Year 12 in 1992. Class sizes increased just as teachers were struggling with new subjects and a welter of administrative controls. Under these circum-stances, the extra years of schooling could not supply the hoped-for improvement in employment prospects.

Starting a first job was as stressful as losing one. A group of school-leavers from around Wagga Wagga (NSW) reported some of these difficulties. The adjustments proved as taxing for those who had worked part-time while at school as they were for those who had never had a job. The work skills taught at school did not help them to adapt. The beginners felt that they would have benefited from more attention to the informal aspects of working. They agreed that the hardest aspect of adapting to a full-time job was getting to work early enough every morning, and then staying punctual throughout an eight-hour shift.

The first day was difficult because the young person was often the only new employee. How well they coped depended on their supervisors. Employers called on young workers to show 'enthusiasm, reliability, commonsense and motivation'. Those qualities were also necessary for the boss. Some managers were clueless and resorted to bullying. One girl recalled:

> Before I went I was nervous and excited. But when I got home I was in tears. The head office guy was there that day. He was an arsehole. I had only been there for fifteen minutes and I was watching the other girls and trying to pick things up, but he was abusing me for not doing everything right. The shift seemed so long, I thought I'd never get home. I said to Mum, 'I don't want to go back'.

This girl found another job where the supervisors helped her settle in: 'I felt dumb but now I feel smarter'. Friends provided as much training as the managers. The beginners valued 'trusting relationships with other workers from whom they could seek advice'.

This reliance on fellow employees confirmed what experienced employees said made for a good workplace. Only 15 per cent mentioned fair and reasonable pay. One in four spoke of getting along with each other. Forty per cent gave satisfying work itself as the most important factor making for a positive experience. Thus, two-thirds of employees identified social connections as the most significant aspects of a workplace.

The less respect that workers got from managers, and the less secure they felt about their employment, the more they used wage demands to hit back at executives who were on bloated packages. Workers complained about the new generation of managers who had been trained 'to manage anything'. They did not know how any one thing worked. Despite the desire for sociable labour, not many workers thought of their tasks as creative. They complained about repetitiveness and of being rushed. Australians unable to find fulfilment at work sought those rewards in crafts, hobbies, home improvements or gardening.

The degradation of labour is clear when contrasted with an Australian who lived outside the wage system. Emily Kame Kngawarreye was a Anmatyerre woman from north of Alice Springs. Before her death in 1996, she became one of Australia's most admired painters. She had not put a brush to canvas until the 1980s, when she was over seventy years of age. She had developed her talents in body decoration. Decades of digging for pencil-yams had given her the knowledge of their root systems. That contact let her complete the 3 x 8 metre 'Big Yam Dreaming' in two days. She had also learned her pattern-making from decades of fashioning bead necklaces and ceremonial string-ware. Her work and art had been inseparable.

Among settler Australians, older women were remaining longer in the workforce. During the 1990s, the rate of employment among women in their late fifties rose by one-third to 44 per cent. This increase continued the higher levels of participation that had begun in the 1950s. Some had returned to work, or hung in, because their husbands were being pushed out of the labour market. Others were divorced or widowed.

One side effect was that fewer grandmothers were available for child-minding when their daughters went to work. Nonetheless, grandparents provided most of the care for children up to twelve. Only one-third of all minding came from formal providers. In 1999, one-half of pre-teens received some kind of care outside school. The highest rates were for three- and four-year olds, at 80 per cent. The usual reason was that it was good for them to mix with other kids. After they turned five, the main reason for seeking child-care was so that their parents could work the longer or broken shifts that were called 'flexible'.

Round the clock

A crisis in working time erupted every second of every day for
some worker somewhere. An alarm clock did not go off. The
porridge burnt. A car would not start. The bus sailed past your
stop, or the train was running late. Trivial as each incident
appears, any one could have contributed to getting the sack.

Those with jobs worked longer. In 1974, only one male
employee out of eighteen had put in more than eleven hours a
day. By 1997, the proportion was one in eight. The mobile
phone and the home computer meant that clerical and professional workers were always on call. People were also working
unpaid overtime. They feared that if they did not give that
extra hour they would be at the top of the next list of redun-
dancies. A warehouse employee reported:

> You're being monitored all the time, y'know; even though you're
> doing your best it's not good enough for them [management]. If
> you're over in the drinks aisle and you're picking seven to eight
> hundred cartons of drinks every day it's not good enough, and
> you're even picking twelve hundred a day and it's still not good
> enough, y'know? What can you do? No matter what you do, it's
> not good enough. How much do I have to do to keep up with this
> thing?

'Work ate my life', said one woman. When asked 'What
have you been up to?', more people answered 'Only work'.

In 2001, the average weekly hours for full-time workers in
Australia was forty-one. In metalliferous mining, the average
was forty-two. In Tasmania, the norm in such mines was
between forty-two and sixty hours a week, but exceptions
reached seventy-two. Overtime was compulsory. Fatigue
became chronic, in effect a medical condition. Repetitive tasks
made the exhaustion worse. Half of those on night shifts
reported nodding off regularly on the job. One-third had
trouble staying awake on the drive home. The menace
increased when miners worked more days in a row than they
had off. That roster denied them the time they needed to

recover. About one in ten seemed never to be fully rested. Four out of five workers reported bad effects on their family life. The long hours and exhaustion also deprived communities of the involvement of husbands and fathers in school, sport or social organisations.

Few people in the mining industry had been aware that these patterns of work were putting people at risk at work and beyond. Then the deaths of several miners along the north-west coast of Tasmania led the State to commission a survey of 1000 miners, their families, managers and public servants. The people surveyed belonged to five mining communities, extracting copper, gold, lead and zinc. World-best practice by some of the biggest global corporations sent men to labour underground in a blackness that is unimaginable, up to their thighs in water, with electric wires fastened by string.

The workforce was splitting. On one side, those with permanent jobs worked more hours than was good for them. On the other, those with casual work scrambled to get enough hours to survive. The number of permanents shrank while the casuals increased. Between 1998 and 2001, the percentage of Australians with full-time permanent jobs fell from 74 to 61 per cent. In 1988 one Australian in five had been a casual employee. By 2001 the portion was more than one in four. These changes fell unevenly on age and gender. The figures for women hardly changed at all. For men over fifty-five years, the extent of casualisation doubled. The same was happening to everyone in their early twenties. A single-mother with two part-time jobs realised:

> I haven't got a career. Like there were jobs where I was getting paid $6.50, $7.50 an hour and I was so desperate that I just hung onto the job basically because I needed that money for my son. So I'm hoping that these new jobs will go well but it's always a bit scary that it's not going to last more than two weeks.

Workers on casual and broken shifts could not get enough hours, could not get them when they preferred, and could not plan for a holiday. The permanent casuals had no entitlement to four weeks paid leave. Many had traded their holiday time for a higher cash wage because they could not get by on the award rates. Some then found that the promised higher rates were cut, or never paid at all.

The hospitality industry chased every chance to impose inflexible hours on its workers. To beat the competition and pay the rent, eateries stayed open outside the hours of 8 am to 6 pm, Monday to Friday. Employment in hospitality grew at twice the national average, but with low weekly earnings. The protections were few, and they were rarely enforced outside the major hotels. The federal government in 1998 sought to remove even those protections. A key concern for workers was the threat to penalty rates for Sunday. That extra hourly pay was essential for a living wage. Workers protested for months. Outside the Sydney Novotel they held up banners, with slogans painted on bed sheets, referred to as the hotel's 'dirty linen'. The Industrial Relations Commission upheld their penalty rates. The hotel chains tried to get their way via the back entrance. In mid-1999, the Hyde Park Plaza put its housekeeping staff on individual contracts. These most vulnerable of workers at once went on strike, picketing the premises. Three hours later, the managers caved in.

LIFE IN THE CITIES
Faster foods

Between 1991 and 1994, the number of cafés and restaurants in New South Wales more than doubled. Those 7000 venues responded to a change in eating habits. By the late 1990s, half of all Australian meals were being prepared outside the home. In the rush to get to work, the muffin offered breakfast on the go. There was nothing new about workers and students grabbing a bread roll or a pie and sauce for lunch. Big Macs became day-time fare at 730 outlets across Australia. Backed by $80 million advertising, McDonald's served one million of the sixty million meals eaten each day in 2001. Their turnover of $7 billion a year represented half of all the sales at branded fast-food outlets.

The major change was to the evening meal. One in four was eaten out. Dinner at home was transformed. Butchers, for example, prepared meats ready for the oven or pan. The pressures on time heightened the popularity of stir- fries. The retail chains also repositioned themselves. At Sydney's inner-city train stations, a new kind of supermarket opened in 1995 with Coles Express, soon copied by Woolworths Metro. The latter promoted itself as offering 'fine food without the fuss'. These small-scale outlets catered for individuals rather than families. Their menu was a step up from takeaway fast foods, but several steps easier than fully preparing a three-course dinner. Commuters queued for just enough provisions for that night and perhaps tomorrow's breakfast.

The inner-city residential projects included cafes and often a convenience store. Australia's first convenience store had opened in 1977. By 1998, 800 outlets were operating. The average transaction was only $4.50. From a million customers a day, their takings in the five years to 1997 rose four-fold, to almost $2 billion a year. The biggest selling item was soft- drink (to 63% of customers), followed in descending order by bread, milk, sweets, newspapers and magazines, ice creams, and then snack foods (26%). Customers were prepared to pay more for access and speedy service. After dark, the convenience stores attached to petrol stations provided well-lit parking areas where people felt safer than on the street.

Street stories

Most assaults were by young adults against each other or on teenagers. The fears that adults had of teenagers were matched by the teenagers' fear of adults. Girls and young women felt the most vulnerable. Yet every group was the victim of crime panics by politicians chasing votes, or the media in pursuit of ratings. Asked to name the most dangerous place in Australia, Tasmanians nominated Kings Cross, though few had ever been there. That response was way out of date. Sydney-siders nominated Redfern or Cabramatta. All over the country, people interpreted graffiti as threats.

Graffiti had began with Aboriginal rock carvings and on the sheets of bark under which Aborigines sheltered during the wet season. Schoolkids had carved their initials in desks or scrawled on lavatories. Political slogans such as 'Vote NO' survived for decades after the 1951 referendum that failed to ban the Communist Party. Around that time, Arthur Stace had been chalking his copperplate 'Eternity' on Sydney footpaths. From the 1970s, a group calling itself 'Bugger-Up' corrected sexist or cigarette billboards. In the late 1990s, Aboriginal activists stencilled 'Sorry' on John Howard's running track around Kirribilli.

Graffiti as street art got under way here in the early 1980s, following New York hip-hop and the marketing of enamel in spray-cans. The artists had their own vocabulary of 'crews', 'writer' for the artist, 'piece' for a mural, and 'tag' for the signature. Graffitists refused the anonymity of city life and defied its encroaching surveillance. The 'writers' were daring the police to catch them. The 'pieces' that camouflaged factory walls and beautified railway carriages had short lives, removed by authorities or painted over by the envious and less-talented. In celebrating transience, these street artists denied the art market's devaluation of creativity into a commodity. Nonetheless, the pieces were rarely political, more a version of folk art. As with gallery art, most pieces were third-rate, but no more so than the architecture that defaced the visual environment.

Shopping plus

Even in daylight, girls felt safer inside a shopping complex than on the streets. Almost half the people in the biggest shopping centres and malls said they went there to be entertained. Businesses pandered to this expectation by providing displays and performances. In April 2000, Westfield Plaza at Marion drew 18 000 Adelaidians to an appearance by the pop group Bardot. The food courts, the multiplex cinemas and the video games attracted the young, especially on shopping nights and at weekends. The retail centres were places where ethnic groups could mix. Boys and girls mingled without parental supervision.

However, the owners needed only the kids who were born to shop. Hence, they controlled their amusements, which were policed by security guards and surveillance cameras. The malls excluded skateboarders and environmental campaigners. Leaflets had to encourage youngsters to spend.

The average pocket money for kids doubled during the 1990s. One teenager in four got $50 a week. Yet almost half were given no pocket money. Instead, they got cash rather than presents for birthdays and Christmas, as much as $160 dollars a year. Many started working part-time once they turned fourteen. Children did not aspire to be super-rich, only well-off. The media had taught them that the rich and famous were not happy.

Children influenced as much as $4 billion in spending a year. Hence, marketers targeted them in order to influence their parents' choice of brands for foods and drinks, but also for family cars and electronics. The sales effort reduced the influence that parents had over their children.

Professor Fiona Stanley of Perth's Institute for Child Health Research worried about those she called 'trophy children'. Their parents would not let them be kids. She stressed the need to teach parents how to play with their children and to read to them. She feared that the 'child has become an extension of the big car and house and it's all part of aiming at perfection, and yet we might be missing out on that spiritual side'.

The old-fashioned mix of goodwill and profits came under threat. Adelaide's Rundle Mall lost Johnny Martins, the department store that had inaugurated the Christmas street pageant in 1933.

Three grocery chains controlled 80 per cent of the dry/packaged groceries. They also sold 43 per cent of all food, whether packaged, fresh, takeaway or eat-in. These giants drew customers away from specialist businesses, as they had done from corner grocers in the 1950s. Supermarkets expanded by adding a liquor store, a butcher shop, a chicken shop, a fishmongers, a greengrocery, a newsagency and a bakery. 'Super' had begun by meaning a vast floor space. It came to mean the scope of products. Suburban centres boomed while the inner-city stores lagged behind. Efforts to revive Adelaide's East End as a café/entertainment belt competed against the re-creation of its West End as a cultural precinct. In Melbourne, the up-market Japanese Daimaru department store closed, even though it had occupied a prime location above a railway station on the city loop.

A home is not a house

The hollowing out of the commercial hub contrasted with a simultaneous swing of residents into those districts. Developers converted hotels, office blocks, factories and warehouses into apartments. They also threw up multi-storey blocks of units.

The outer areas remained the destination for many of those who had sampled inner-city living. When they shifted out, they expected some of the lifestyle that they had enjoyed around town. The new suburbanites aspired to more than tossing another prawn on the barbie. The latté belt extended to shopping centres with bookshops, cinemas, galleries, boutiques and resort-like gyms. 'Suburban' no longer meant lacking in sophistication. The newer leafy suburbs were not arty or bohemian in the style of Brisbane's West End or New Farm, but they were no longer sub-urban.

In the late 1990s, one of the fastest-selling project homes in those outer communities was a double-storey model called the 'Regent'. It had a floor area of 356 square metres. Thirty years before, the average house size had been only 140 square metres. Even the young with high incomes had trouble saving for these castles. Rather than putting aside every spare cent to become mortgage-serfs, they borrowed for cars and holidays. They married later, had children later, and bought houses later. In 1989, 42 per cent of Australians between twenty-five and thirty-four years were either home-owners or mortgagees. Ten years later, that fraction had dropped by a quarter, to 32 per cent.

In the early 1990s, home-buyers had been hit by the double whammy of skyrocketing house prices and soaring interest rates. Many mortgagees were then shelling out 30 per cent or more of their pre-tax income. By contrast, in 2000 low interest rates made repayments more affordable. However, house prices had grown so much that fewer people could afford a deposit. In Sydney, the first-time home-buyer faced extinction as the median house price passed $375 000. The working poor had few chances of getting a foot on the ladder of home ownership.

The gap between the better-off and the battlers remained extreme in regard to both the affordability and the quality of housing. In the long-established and richest areas, less than one household in ten carried a mortgage. In the outer zones, as many as 60 per cent were paying off their homes.

The worst-off groups were still the poor who rented privately. They forked out as much of their income on housing as did those with a mortgage. They had no prospect of escaping from the rental market. Four out of five of these rent-paying households were under stress. In inner Sydney, a social worker looked for accommodation on behalf of a man and his disabled child. She reported on 100 properties which were asking $180 a week: 'Not one of them was fit. There was rising mould, rotting carpets, cockroach-infested kitchens'. The poor were back to the conditions described in Ruth Park's 1946 *Harp in the South*.

The difficulties for the renting poor had been made worse by a retreat from public housing. In 1990, governments completed 112 500 units. By 1999, the total had slumped to 5200. During the same period, the number of people receiving government subsidies on their rents to private landlords went up from 674 000 to over one million, almost a 50 per cent jump. Few of the long-term unemployed could afford to live close to the cleaning jobs in the central business districts. For every unit that the government could afford close to the inner city, it could build three in the outer rim, where there were fewer job opportunities.

LIFE IN THE COUNTRY

Despite a rush to the inner-city, the urban sprawl continued to eat into the land that had supplied city dwellers with their milk, chicken, eggs, fruit or vegetables. In Victoria, 70 per cent of chicken meat came from 56 million broilers housed around Western Port, just to the south-east of Melbourne. New residents objected to the smells. Sydney's poultry farms had to move from the western suburbs out to Goulburn, 170 kilometres from the factory at Liverpool. The consumption of chicken went from 6 kilograms per person a year in 1965 to 31 kilograms by 1998.

In another intersection of city and country, the number of hobby farms expanded. Their owners planted olives, grapevines or chestnuts, or husbanded deer or alpaca. By 2001, many of these ventures had withered. For example, fewer than one in five of the newer vineyards remained productive. The Tax Office abolished the dodges that had been needed to turn a profit. The owners shifted their expectations to chasing a rural lifestyle. Some erected fantasy dwellings on large blocks, an hour or more from the inner city where they continued to work.

Angora goats and ostriches were two other exotics that attracted investors. Time was when Australia had as many sheep as kangaroos. In 1970, 180 million sheep safely grazed. By 2001, the count was down to 100 million. The Queensland tally fell to the lowest point since statistics had been collected in 1885. During the 1990s, the production of mutton fell from 400 000 to 300 000 tonnes. Health-conscious consumers wanted lean cuts of lamb, not the fatty forequarter chops that had sustained families in the 1950s. Butchers stopped sawing legs off sides of mutton and began slicing lamb into strips for curries. Lamb wraps proved as convenient a takeaway as a hamburger or a pie. KFC had marketed chicken. Popular preferences rearranged the sheep-meat industry.

Government policy transformed dairying. Between 1971 and 2000, the number of farms fell from 44 000 to 15 000. The national herd, however, grew after 1990, but to only three-quarters of the 1970 total. This decline was balanced by increases in production per cow from 2850 litres in 1990 to 5000 by 2001. To pay farmers to quit the industry, the government imposed a levy of 11c a litre on retail milk. That burden fell on households with the most children. During the seven years that the surcharge will run, to 2007, a family of six would have to fork out an extra $600 to fund this economic rationalism. While milk prices in supermarkets shot up, many producers got less at the farm gate.

The penetration of supermarkets into regional centres such as Inverell (NSW) quickened the drift from its outlying settlements. The corporations squeezed smaller stores that had earned most of their profit by trading after-hours or on Sundays. Because the supermarkets stayed open till midnight, or even around the clock, these opportunities were lost. Even the bigger country towns usually had only one supermarket. That monopoly position let a store charge up to 16 per cent more than where it faced a competitor.

The loss of small businesses coincided with fewer bank services. Between1996 and 1998, 125 of the 1000 bank branches across New South Wales closed. Remote customers ridiculed the offer to bank on-line. Telstra failed to provide broadband or a second land-line or even to maintain existing telephonic services. With an inventiveness born of necessity, people turned to 'community banks'.

Although regional populations declined slightly, more significant shifts took place within those areas. In 1996, 122 regional cities and towns recorded populations of more than 10 000. Not all these larger communities had secure futures. Their prospects were linked to the source of their livelihood. Hence, the mining centre of Port Hedland (WA) and the tourist town of Broome (WA) enjoyed the highest rates of construction and investment. By contrast, the Queensland coastal shire of Burnett Heads–Bargara experienced the lowest level. As the jump-off point for the Great Barrier Reef, Cairns challenged Townsville for the title of unofficial capital of the North.

Tourist trail

Central Queensland illustrated these variations. The district's population fell by almost 5 per cent between 1991 and 1996. Isisford lost one-third of its 440 residents, whereas Longreach remained steady at around 4400. Nearby, Barcaldine and Winton were also stable. In an effort to save their communities, locals latched onto tourism as a lure for retirees, known as 'grey nomads', steering campervans around their 'Big Country'.

Central Queensland had no site with enough attractions to hold visitors for more than a night or two. To overcome this lack planners during the 1980s had invented eco-tourism, which highlighted natural attractions such as the district's opal fields and the dinosaur footprints at Lark Quarry. Cultural tourism was another innovation that looked beyond the construction of a Big Banana, a Giant Merino or a King Prawn. Governments funded museums. In the bicentennial year of 1988, Barcaldine got the Heritage Workers Centre to commemorate the foundation of the Australian Labor Party beneath the 'Tree of Knowledge' in 1891. Further west, the boot and clothing king, R. M. Williams, helped Longreach to create the Stockman's Hall of Fame. That heritage centre began by marginalising the contributions of Aborigines, Afghans, women and unionists to the pastoral industry. Longreach also got the Qantas museum, although the airline had been founded at Winton in 1920. As if by way of compensation, Winton received $3.3 million for the Matilda Centre. A. B. 'Banjo' Patterson had finalised the words for Australia's national song, 'Waltzing Matilda', near there in 1895. The road through these towns was renamed the 'Matilda Highway'. Along the route, family businesses trebled the accommodation available in licensed hotels and motels.

The prospects of every district depended on a mix of government, community and business initiatives. Regional universities trained the professionals to maintain the services to sustain populations in remote areas. Commercial ventures kept even small towns afloat. Buderim, on Queensland's Sunshine Coast, was almost a brand-name for ginger. Wineries added tourist attractions across the southern corners of the continent. Walcha, in New England, laid claim to being the nation's Lamington Capital. In Western Australia, Narrogin capitalised on the publicity from Albert Facey's *A Fortunate Life* by naming its four-star motel after the lad who had slaved on farms around the district before the First World War.

Narrogin

Narrogin, 190 kilometres south-east of Perth, had grown as a rail junction on the Great Southern Line to Albany. In the late 1960s, the railways had provided over 300 jobs. By 2001, fewer than ten jobs remained. Despite the disappearance of that employer, the population edged up between 1986 and 1996, from 4266 to 4500. The number of dwellings had grown from 1257 to 1541. Its citizens experienced more changes than is suggested by such modest growth.

Narrogin became the focus of the district's shopping and services, drawing customers away from some of the six surrounding towns. Its pivotal place also helped to make its population mobile. More than half the residents changed their addresses during the 1990s. Public servants and business people would spend a few years in Narrogin as one step on a promotional ladder back to Perth. In exchange, Perth residents were attracted to Narrogin as a rural retreat. Complicating the picture even more, some of the people working in Narrogin shifted to adjacent settlements for cheaper and larger blocks, or to escape social tensions.

Narrogin had been divided on class lines. The Housing Commission (now Homeswest) supplied the blue-collar workers with 'fibro' dwellings, clustered together. Their occupants had all been dubbed 'Railways'. They had maintained their own sporting and social clubs. By the 1990s, most of these workers were retired and in need of accommodation more suitable for the aged.

Many of the difficulties associated with housing in the metropolises also appeared in this country town. A three-bedroom house built in the 1970s sold for $95 000 in 1993; seven years later, it went for $132 000. Two out of three households were owner-purchasers. One-fifth were renting privately, 10 per cent from Homeswest. The stock of public housing, meanwhile, had slipped from 212 units in 1971 to 157 in 1996. Homelessness meant camping with friends or relations, or living out of the vehicle.

In 1996, Narrogin was home to 271 Aborigines, about 6 per

cent of the population. Until the 1970s, the Nungars had been fringe dwellers. Then, the government offered them housing in the town. The planners did not know whether to keep them together as a community, or to disperse them through the town.

Race relations were an undercurrent to social life everywhere. They gained a sharper edge in rural areas in the backwash from the 1996 Wik judgment. That decision allowed for shared usage by lease-holders and native title claimants. Racists stirred up fears that Aborigines would be able to invade properties. The racists tied this falsehood to the gun laws introduced in reaction to the 1996 shootings at Port Arthur. Those controls required farmers to surrender most of their rifles. The racists said that mobs of drunken black militants could terrorise the now defenceless homesteads.

The gun laws made farmers feel that they were being criminalised. The buy-back was another blow to their self-esteem, propelling a rush to Pauline Hanson's One Nation Party. The countryside felt itself deserted. The National Party had become the voice of agribusiness and mining conglomerates, advocating global free trade and a market in water.

Water

From 1788, settlers had been determined to make their new home as pleasant as England, or as emerald as Ireland. The sprinkler playing across a suburban lawn in Perth and the spray irrigation of the cotton fields at Wee Waa expressed this dream. Schemes to turn the coastal rivers inland, plans to drain the artesian basins and efforts to seed clouds were all refusals to accept Australia as a dry continent, subject to swings between drought and deluge. Environmentalists perpetuated this error by calling themselves 'Greens'. Most of mainland Australia is grey, ochre, olive or fawn.

Since the 1880s, governments had encouraged farmers to

use more water. One hundred years later, along the Murray River, 3400 rice growers drew as much water as all of South Australia. Thus, when governments took some water back to keep the Murray flowing, irrigators became angry. Any loss of water shrank the area of land they could farm profitably.

During the 2001 drought, some farmers sold their water licences and then bought back enough water to see them through the year. Others sold an allocation that they had never used. The trade in water licences thus increased the effective demand. The price of a licence doubled in the three years to 2003. In the words of a water trader: 'It doesn't depreciate. It doesn't need servicing. It doesn't need maintenance. It doesn't need looking after every day'. That claim was true of water licences. The reverse applied to the water itself. The Conservation Foundation worried that the failure to recognise the difference between a licence and H_2O would expand consumption.

An alternative way of reducing the volumes going to irrigation has been to replace open channels with pipes. Some farmers had installed drip irrigation instead of the flooding where most of the moisture evaporated before it got near a root or a leaf.

Irrigation also contributed to the spread of diseases such as Murray Valley encephalitis. Lifting the groundwater table had extended the salt marshes where the carrier mosquitoes bred. Leeton in the Murrumbidgee Irrigation Area suffered one of the highest rates of infection. Good health could not be assured by an increase of GPs in the bush.

HEALTH

At the start of the third millennium, Australian men could expect to live for 78 years and women for 83 —ten years more than in 1961. Variations persisted. Class remained the best indicator of health. The better-off lived the longest.

As Australians lived longer, eyes, teeth and eardrums needed more supports. Cataracts developed because of exposure to the sun. The corrective surgery became as routine as getting a tooth pulled. Meanwhile, half-a-million Australians could not afford to see a dentist, who charged $200 an hour. Those who could just afford to attend had their teeth pulled out rather than repaired. Extractions cost less than fillings. One Australian in three over the age of forty-five had none of their own teeth. In 1996, the Coalition government withdrew the Dental Health Program. Tens of thousands of kids went back to waiting for up to a year for treatment in public facilities. Meanwhile, orthodontists made fortunes out of cosmetic procedures. The young suffered hearing loss from music at dance venues or from headsets, even before they were exposed to decibels at work.

Hence, the quality of life did not always keep pace with its length. People feared that they might linger in agony, demented, or with loss of dignity. These concerns led three-quarters of the population to approve of voluntary euthanasia. Juries proved reluctant to convict anyone accused of assisting a loved-one to die, often when suffering from cancer.

Cancer rates went up by 25 per cent after 1982. Billions of dollars in research brought very little improvement in survival for the most common kind, cancer of the lung. The second most frequent was cancer of the stomach. That pair of killers were linked to tobacco and diet respectively.

Smoking contributed to 15 per cent of all deaths. By 1995 the percentage of the population who smoked had gone down from 37 per cent in 1977 to 24 per cent. By contrast, between 1990 and 1993 the rate of smoking among seventeen-year-old girls rose from 22 per cent to 31 per cent. Yet only 8 per cent of the taxes gathered from the illegal sale of tobacco to teenagers went into No-Smoking campaigns aimed at them. Some girls had taken up smoking as a weight-control device.

'Be In It!'

By 2000, half of adult males, one-third of women and nearly one-quarter of children were overweight. One in ten adult Australians had become obese, a 250 per cent rise during the previous twenty years. These changes brought on an epidemic of diabetes. One in twelve Australians was afflicted, half of them undiagnosed.

Four out of ten Australian adults were dieting. Those who could afford Health Clubs bought the physical activity essential to control weight. A major cause of gaining kilos had been the loss of everyday activities. Children were no longer allowed to walk to school because their parents were worried about 'stranger danger'. Gardeners gathered leaves with motorised blowers instead of a rake or a broom. Remote-control devices opened garage doors and switched channels on the television.

Millions of couch potatoes watched Australian elites win seventeen gold medals at the Sydney 2000 Olympics. The television coverage was enlivened by Roy and HG's 'The Dream'. Its mascot, 'Fatso, the fat-arsed wombat', expressed how many Australians felt about the ego competitions and corruption among Games administrators. The politicians had argued that the Games would encourage Australians to get fit. Others thought the money should have been spent on community programs. Netball, for example, met the cry of 'Life — Be In It' but was not an Olympic sport.

Almost a million women between the ages of five and forty played netball, with Fun Ball for five-to-seven-year olds and Netta Netball for those aged eight to eleven. Teachers from England had introduced the game to Australian schools around 1900. Junior competitions still could be a bit schoolmarmish, with teams penalised for not wearing the correct socks. Netball became popular because the rules were simple, it could be played on a variety of surfaces, and needed little space and only a limited amount of cheap equipment. It appealed as a game run by women for women and girls. With no body contact, netball flourished as a friendly activity with social benefits.

Although Australia has won most of the international netball tournaments since 1963, there was almost no link between playing socially and following the National League. By 1999 few suburban players had heard of Anne Sargent, the winning captain from the 1980s. Corporate sponsorship was hard to come by, despite the large numbers of players. Television coverage of even the National League was rare. The television networks claimed that netball was dull to watch. Its promoters argued that with more cameras and action replays it would be more exciting than cricket. Amateurs questioned the value of sponsorship of any sport from corporations promoting sugar-laden soft-drinks, fatty foods or alcohol.

Drug of choice

In the late 1990s, the average age for starting to drink alcohol fell to below fourteen years. Rules requiring proof of age had little effect. Forty per cent of thirteen- to seventeen-year-olds bought alcohol each week, with an average outlay of $22. One-third had gone to work or school while affected by drink. One in four aged between eighteen and twenty-one had driven under the influence. The advertising code for alcohol promotions remained voluntary, and was often broken. Commercials were supposed not to show people under twenty-five, or even actors who looked younger. Advertisements were not to present alcohol as the source of happiness or success. Only messages from the Drug and Alcohol Foundation depicted young drunks vomiting, or smashed by the roadside.

At the same time, binge drinking became widespread. Ninety per cent of the alcohol consumed by men aged between eighteen and twenty-four was during sessions with the sole purpose of getting pissed. Bingeing also prevailed among teenagers. A survey of 4500 Victorians aged from sixteen to twenty-four showed that one in five were drinking to excess two or three times a week. One-third of males and one-fifth of girls had consumed between nine and twenty-two standard drinks in the course of a day.

A gender divide operated on the choice of drinks. Blokes went for full-strength beer. Chicks preferred wine or premixed spirits. The GST in 2000 replaced excise duties with a flat rate of 10 per cent so that spirits became much cheaper. Their makers sweetened them to mask the alcohol. Hence, they became known as 'alcopops', or a 'five-buck chuck'. In addition, they were packaged to confuse consumers about their alcohol content. The level was often more than one standard drink per bottle.

The other major drug addiction was that of doctors to pharmaceutical companies. Writing in the *British Medical Journal*, the Australian investigative journalist Ray Moynihan pictured their being 'twisted together like the snake and the staff', the symbol for medical care. Advertisements from the drug firms financed many professional journals. Waiting-room pressures were making it harder for GPs to keep up with published research. They were therefore tempted to rely on the pharmaceutical sales force. Gifts ranged from a wall clock to an all expenses-paid trip to the Olympics or to a $10 000 medical congress. The companies also paid GPs $500–1000 for adding their names to a reference group to evaluate a new drug. Medical students began wearing T-shirts with the slogan 'Just say no to drug reps'.

Going public

The poor were more likely to get a drug than a diagnosis. They had more health problems but fewer doctors. They waited for up to four weeks to see a GP. When they did get an appointment, their consultation times were briefer. The shortage of GPs in poorer areas, and a lack of nursing-home beds for the elderly, put pressure on hospital emergency departments. The public hospitals worked well enough at birth, or when lives were in danger. In those circumstances, rich and poor were treated almost equally. The wealthy with private health cover still went to public hospitals because they had the most sophisticated services and equipment.

There were long waits for non-life-threatening procedures. A young man in Brisbane needed a hernia operation before he could start work in an abattoir, his first job. His GP found that he would have to wait ten months for a bed in a public hospital. Medical treatment 'would make or break this man's chances of getting a job'. Another of his patients was a six-year-old who needed an operation on his ear drum. He had to wait almost three years for the surgery. 'The child has been getting ear infections every two months, missing school. Hearing difficulties may turn into learning difficulties.' The delay would also impair his job prospects.

To reduce waiting lists, cut costs and lessen the dangers of cross-infection, hospitals sent patients home after two or three days instead of ten. The more rapid turnover added to the paper work and hence to the pressures on nursing staff. As one nurse observed: 'You hardly ever go home and think "I've done everything" '. A young nurse recognised: 'Experienced nurses are really stressed and burnt out. You just don't even want to ask them a question or for help so you're on your own as soon as you get to a ward'. Another pointed out that, in the past, the managers would say: 'Look we're short, we need more staff'. That response had been replaced by: 'You'll cope. We know you can do it'.

In 1999, the amount of unpaid overtime and working through meal breaks equalled 750 full-time nurses a week. In specialist units, nurses did seventy to eighty hours a week, often over seven days. Some went for three months without a weekend off. The under-staffing became so chronic in Victoria that nurses won compulsory ratios for the number of patients per nurse.

Mental hospitals had discharged many of their inmates in the 1970s. Cutbacks to government spending left the emotionally distressed without the day care they had been promised. Many were unable to manage their medication. The closure of inner-city boarding houses put large numbers out on the street. Police have controversially been involved in incidents relating to such people.

Mental illness gained more attention with publicity campaigns around long-term depression. Pharmaceutical companies funded one-quarter of the costs of Sane Australia. Their donation came out of their sale of drugs to the mentally ill worth $650 million. Pills could not touch the triggers for depressive episodes: unemployment, stress at work, homelessness and denial of benefits. The Nursing Manager for the Far West Mental Health Service in Broken Hill recognised that his patients suffered from a combination of 'biological, psychological and social factors'. Having a job put a structure into their days, enlarged their social contacts and provided them with some of the money to engage in meaningful activities. Unemployment, he knew, was 'one of the strongest predictors of suicide'.

Suicide was the fourth leading cause of premature death in 1995. Its incidence had increased 50 per cent since 1983. Experts were not sure whether that statistic recorded a real increase. Perhaps coroners were more open about suicide being the cause. Either way, the rates were higher in rural areas than in urban areas. Single-vehicle accidents on country roads could be unidentified suicides. Most young men who took their own lives hanged themselves; this was followed by shooting or asphyxiation with motor-vehicle exhaust. The incidence of hanging went up from 10 per cent of cases in 1974 to 40 per cent by 1995. The victims selected whatever means was the most readily available. Before the 1996 gun buyback, rural dwellers had been twice as likely as city dwellers to use firearms.

Yet levels of physical and psychological distress were higher in the bush than in a metropolis. Rural sufferers also received less care. Rural Australians had pictured themselves as healthier than those in the stressful cities. Yet any decline was more likely to be due to perception rather than reality. In the 1890s Henry Lawson had called the 'grand Australian bush' 'the nurse and tutor of eccentric minds'. The other change was that city dwellers now favoured the regional coast as their ideal for a sea change in their lives.

Among Aboriginal people, two-thirds of suicides were by hanging. The rates for young Aborigines were the highest in the bush because there they were at the extreme end of deprivation. Aborigines lived twenty fewer years than most Australians. Their infant mortality rate remained several times greater.

ABORIGINES

In 1967, Australians had voted to amend the Constitution in the hope of improving the lives of Aborigines. Thirty years on, their condition seemed grave. A majority of voters in 1967 had assumed that 'throwing money at the problem' would make it go away. During the 1990s, opinion slipped towards a suspicion that the case might prove hopeless. Were not governments throwing money away on corrupt black leaders? The nation split. The Howard government refused to make even a token apology for past injustices. At the same time, a million Australians crossed bridges as a symbol of reconciliation. The hard line was that Aboriginal sufferings had been greatly exaggerated, not to say richly deserved. The Mabo case stiffened white resentments.

Mabo

Koiki (Eddie) Mabo was born on Mer (Murray Island) in Torres Strait in 1937. Expelled from his home in 1959, he settled in Townsville, where he developed as a leader of its Indigenous communities. His efforts on health, education and the arts led to his appointment to national bodies. In the 1970s, he campaigned to keep the Torres Strait Islands as part of Australia, and not be handed over to an independent Papua New Guinea. This political activity brought him into contact with historians at James Cook University in Townsville, notably Henry Reynolds. Reynolds had argued that the dispossession of Australia's Indigenes had been contrary to English Common Law. This interpretation excited Mabo who had been amazed, and then angered, to learn that his family on Mer did not own the gardens that they had been working when Europeans had sailed past in 1606.

In 1982, Mabo and four other Torres Strait men began a legal action to assert ownership over their island home. Ten years later, 'Mabo' became known because his name had headed that list of claimants. The *Australian* newspaper named him the most newsworthy Australian of 1992, four months after he had died of cancer without most people knowing he had existed. In 1994, a gang of white supremacists desecrated his grave.

In giving judgment in favour of Mabo, the High Court in June 1992 refined the legal doctrine of *terra nullius*. Nothing that judges or scholars said, however, could remove the popular misunderstanding of what that Latin phrase means. The most common mistake was that *terra nullius* assumed that there had been no people here when the English arrived. Not even the law is so asinine. The doctrine of *terra nullius* dealt with systems of government and land use. Indigenous societies did not have social classes, a state or private productive property. London, therefore, had no way of matching its tribal law with that of the Indigenes. British courts had declared the

Australian continent empty of the political and economic forms that secured prior ownership. That was the point that the High Court reinterpreted.

The 1992 decision brought limited and technical changes. Much of what the Court announced in theory, it denied in practice. On the one hand, the judgment acknowledged prior occupancy. Aborigines welcomed that as a moral victory. On the other hand, the judges said that much native title had been extinguished by government action. In brief, the Mabo decision accepted that British claims of sovereignty by themselves did not transfer ownership of Australian land from its inhabitants. The judges applied the feudal test that only the Crown could grant land tenure. This legal fact meant that native title could be extinguished only by a deliberate decision of the Crown, such as the granting or sale of land. Where that transfer had happened, native title no longer existed.

The reasoning used by the judges played almost no part in the public's reaction.

Mining conglomerates and agribusinesses abused the High Court for interfering in politics. The complex thinking behind Mabo made it easier for vested interests to lie about the extent to which that judgment affected most Australians. Without a shred of evidence, real estate agents claimed that Brisbane backyards were in danger. The tragedy of the Mabo–Wik years was that the judicial process delivered so little to Indigenous people while inflaming prejudices against them.

In south-west Queensland, one lease-holder, Camilla Cowley, had begun by being frightened that she would lose her 9000-hectare woolgrowing property, North Yancho. She went to a meeting to support the extinguishment of native title. The lone Aboriginal woman present, Ethel Munn, put her case for shared use with the Gunggari people. Cowley listened, made contact with Aunty Ethel and came to realise how little her family was being asked to accept. She toured

Australia asking other graziers to listen to what Aborigines were seeking.

For the lawyers, two areas remained in doubt. The first concerned the grants made since the Racial Discrimination Act of 1975. To calm fears, the federal parliament passed a Native Title Act in 1993. That law validated all the land grants made to mining corporations since 1975.

The second issue involved the Crown leases over 42 per cent of Australia. Had they extinguished native title? The graziers pretended that their leases had given them ownership. In the Wik judgment of December 1996, the Court rejected this attempt to repeat the land grab that squatters had made 150 years earlier. The judges also limited native title to areas where Aborigines and graziers could coexist. Again, the Commonwealth passed new laws to deprive the native-title holders of much of the little that the Court had offered them.

A few agreements were reached under the 1993 Native Title Act. Several legal cases ended up back before the High Court. For instance, the Miriuwung-Gajerrong people claimed 7900 square kilometres in the east Kimberleys. After years of disputation, a lead claimant, Ben Ward, declared: 'I don't want to go through another court battle. It's a waste of taxpayers' money'. The parties accepted a negotiated settlement late in 2003.

Throughout the 1980s, Aboriginal communities had got tied up in court cases. White lawyers replaced community activists. After the Mabo decision, Aborigines from across Australia met at Eva Valley Station in the Northern Territory in August 1993 to campaign for land rights. In this spirit, and after a lapse of seventeen years, Aborigines had re-established their tent embassy outside Old Parliament House in Canberra in 1992. Coalition ministers complained that the tourist site looked like a blacks' camp. Its residents replied that that was part of their reason for being there. Its makeshift appearance was a permanent reminder that living conditions could not be swept under the ochre- and eucalypt-toned carpets of the new parliament house.

The tent embassy was a dry camp. Throughout much of Aboriginal Australia, alcohol drove domestic violence, perpetuating cycles of self-destruction. Aborigines moved to deal with these consequences of their deprivation. They came to accept that until they controlled those symptoms, they might never be in a position to secure their larger claims for country. This approach suggested a strategic retreat from sovereignty to survival. In the 1960s, activists had argued that land rights were an essential precondition for overcoming health, social and education problems. By the 1990s, the reverse applied. Overcoming addiction, poor health and ill-education were accepted as the basis for winning wider recognition.

Indeed, the spectre of a dying race returned. This time, the death would not be physical. Some 400 000 Australians were of Aboriginal descent. Rather, the death would be social and cultural, despite the prominence gained by Aboriginal artists.

Art

The visual arts became central to how Europeans evaluated Aborigines and how Aborigines valued themselves. The popularity of Aboriginal paintings, however, was limited by aesthetic preferences as much as by racial prejudices. Many Australians had as much difficulty understanding one of Rover Thomas's funeral headpieces as they did Jackson Pollock's *Blue Poles*. From 1971, European advisors had encouraged Aborigines to paint for the whitefella art market. At that time, the fashion for New York Abstraction celebrated the dot-painting from Papunya. This bias towards the formalesque ignored the fact that Aboriginal patterns were another form of story-telling.

Governments were more comfortable promoting Aboriginal art overseas than in meeting land claims at home. Yet the seemingly abstract works selected for postage stamps could be maps of disputed country. In 1963, the Yolngu people from north-east Arnhem Land had pasted their land-rights petition to the Commonwealth Parliament onto bark paintings. After Mabo, Walmajarri elders from around Fitzroy Crossing in the north of Western Australia worked on huge canvases, known as 'Ngurrara I' and 'Ngurrara II'. These paintings included the tracks and stories that established their connections to the Great Sandy Desert. In 1997, they presented the 9 x 11 metre version as evidence to the Native Title Tribunal. The Walmajarri walked over 'Ngurrara I' in their stock boots. To them, the painting was not the precious object it would become to an art dealer. Rather, it was a map of sacred places.

This difference in attitudes extended to all aspects of Aboriginal experience. For example, tourists bought didjeridus as portable pieces of visual art to put themselves in touch with the Dreaming. The Yolngu used them for ceremony.

Around 1000 years ago, Aborigines along the northern coast of Australia had taken advantage of saplings hollowed out by termites to create the didjeridu, or *Yidaki* to the Yolngu. By the 1940s, settler Australians were incorporating its rhythmic drone into symphonic orchestras. Aborigines from across the continent followed the white's appropriation by adopting the 'didge' as an emblem of Pan-Aboriginalism.

A member of the pop-rock band Yothu Yindi, Mandawuy Yunupingu, himself a Yolngu man from Yirrkala, used the didjeridu to champion 'both ways'. Aboriginal musicians strummed electric guitars, he said, so Europeans could play the didjeridu. During the 1980s the didjeridu also became a part of World Music. Its popularity, however, was destroying forests and thus depriving wildlife of their habitats. Those creatures were lucky that didjeridus were also being mass produced in Asia out of polystyrene. By the late 1990s, Australian law forbade businesses from claiming that a tube fashioned in Indonesia was a 'genuine' didjeridu.

The ban on the false marketing of didjeridus was one more example of the difficulty in deciding what was 'authentic' in Aboriginal life. Was a 'didge' a fake if it had been made by a person of Aboriginal descent from Tasmania, rather than by one from the areas of its origin, 1500 kilometres to the north? Tom Djelkwarrngi Wood, from Maningrida on the Gulf, denied that Aboriginal singer Kev Carmody should use the didjeridu: 'It doesn't belong to those down south'.

The tussle over the didjeridu highlighted a core issue for public policy. Who was an Aboriginal person? Should land rights and welfare benefits be confined to those with no mixed heritage? Is Aboriginal culture genuine only if it has been frozen in time?

One assumption was that 'genuine' equalled 'timeless'. That approach helped to defeat claims by the Yorta Yorta people for lands straddling the Murray River. The courts accepted that European invasion meant that traditions and customs could not stay exactly the same. The decision turned on whether the disruption had been so thorough-going as to wash away those connections in the tide of history.

Aborigines contributed to this reverse by boasting about more than 40 000 years of continuous culture. That phrase had no room for the glaciation that transformed the land around which Aborigines had created their cultures. In the 1960s, archeologists had begun to push the date of human arrival back from 12 000 years ago, past 40 000. Yet before contact Aboriginal people had had no need to count to 40 000. Nor did they have a way of doing so. The Dreamtime was not a number.

OFF-WHITE AUSTRALIA

On the New South Wales south coast at Wollongong in 1995, a Taiwanese-based Buddhist sect opened the largest temple in the Southern Hemisphere. The local council welcomed the $50 million structure as a tourist attraction. The few complaints came from Protestant sects. At the same time, the town of Young in central New South Wales became the sister city of Lanzhou in north-west China. The Young Shire Council built a Tribute Garden at Lambing Flat to recognise the Chinese contribution to the Australian community. Young's mayor apologised for the violence against Chinese miners there in 1861.

One hundred years after that riot, the White Australia Policy had seen to it that almost no Chinese or Buddhists remained. By 1999, a million Australians had their origins somewhere in Asia. The portion of the population born outside Australia still hovered at around 23 per cent. The difference was where the foreign-born had come from. During the 1990s, the percentage of Asians rose from 3.5 to 5.5; those from the United Kingdom or Ireland slipped from 7.3 to 6.5.

Multiculturalism

Abandoning White Australia as the national ideal left space for multiculturalism. The term had been imported from bilingual Canada in the 1970s. From the first, the aim of multiculturalism had been to break down the 'Anglo' definition of what it meant to be Australian. The Celts escaped by pretending to be an oppressed minority instead of the enforcers of 'Anglo' prejudices.

The government did not oblige minorities to give up their prejudices. For example, anti-Islamic and anti-Asian attitudes were as fierce among Greeks as among the Anglo-Celts. Similarly, long-term Christian Lebanese residents proved as disdainful of Muslim Lebanese as was any non-Lebanese. Left-wing advocates of multiculturalism saw it as the nationalism you had when you weren't in favour of nationalism. Left-wing critics complained that multiculturalism accommodated everybody's chauvinism except the home-grown.

A 1997 Newspoll recorded that almost 80 per cent of

Australians thought that multiculturalism had been good for them. They enjoyed a diversity of flavours. Multi-nationalism, on the other hand, was feared. Providing you could speak Australian-English, it was okay to retain one's mother tongue. Nostalgia for one's homeland, however, must not extend to involvement in its politics, there or here. More Irish pubs serving Guinness were fine. Financing IRA bombers was not on.

Some ethnic spokespeople would not stay within these bounds. In the 1994 dispute over the status of Macedonia, a Greek leader declared: 'We have power. We can use it on behalf of Greece. That is what a Diaspora should do'. In 1990, plenty of Melbourne citizens of Greek extraction had hoped that Athens would get the 1996 Olympics rather than their Australian birthplace. Ethnic fans would not barrack for the Socceroos unless the team included members from their community.

What multiculturalism allowed and did not allow became obvious through the addiction to sport shared by all communities. Soccer provided a case study of how immigrants re-invented national traditions for themselves after they arrived. Although soccer is 'football' to the British, it became 'wogball' in Australia. As a result, the ethnic teams had to play mostly against each other. These clashes sharpened hatreds, for example, of Macedonians versus Greeks, Serbs versus Croatians, and everyone against the Jews. Around Sydney, young Croatians, known as the BBB (Bad Blue Boys), supported their teams with Nazi salutes and cries of 'Kill the Serbs'. To reduce these tensions, the Soccer Board forbade the use of ethnic team names. Sydney Croatia became Sydney United. Its supporters used the initial 'U' to stand in for Ustashi, their wartime fascist organisation. Challenged about their behaviour, they said they were just 'taking advantage' of multiculturalism.

Nonetheless, all residents were becoming 'New Australians'. From the 1960s, governments and people had been shuffling from restrictive immigration towards a selective integration. By 2001, integration required different adjustments from those that assimilation had demanded of newcomers in 1951. Fifty years on, 'becoming Australian' meant becoming part of a Pan-European Australia, not of a 98 per cent British one.

That remaking came at differing rates. A Latin American woman could talk about 'her Australian side'. She recognised that living in Australia had allowed her personal freedoms to escape from macho males. At the same time, she saw her family's food, language, music, dances and festivals as superior to Anglo ways of life. For her, multiculturalism was one means to ward off the prejudices she was encountering as a Latin American in Australia and as a woman among Latin Americans.

Asian-Australians were introducing even more complexities. The composition of the Asian component was quite different from that in any country of Asia. Most of those nations were more homogenous. Others enforced laws to maintain a fictitious mono-culturalism. In contrast, Asian-Australians had come from Afghanistan in the west through to Hong Kong in the east. Australia included some 100 000 Filipinos, 175 000 Indo-Chinese, 160 000 from mainland China, another 65 000 Chinese from Hong Kong and 44 000 Vietnamese-Chinese, 100 000 Indians, 50 000 Sri Lankans, 80 000 Malaysians and 30 000 Koreans. Only the Japanese were underrepresented. Many of these Asian-Australians were Christians, but others were Islamic, Hindu, Buddhist and Sikh. If Australia ever becomes 50 per cent Asian, Asian leaders could no longer attack 'White Australia'. Instead, they would have to look down on us for not being as pure as they pretend to be.

By the late 1990s, the barriers had been lowered to include some people from all creeds, colours and communities. Yet handicaps remained even for some of the whites born here.

Steve Bracks, for example, concealed his Lebanese background
when campaigning for the 1999 Victorian elections.

Lebanese-Australians

While the Australian population was trebling between 1901
and 1947, the number of Lebanese who lived here was stuck at
around 2000. The total reached 10 000 by 1966, before rising
to 50 000 in 1981. Another 20 000 had arrived by 1996.

In 2001, the governor of New South Wales, Marie Bashir
was of Lebanese extraction, as was the novelist David Malouf.
That pair did not fit the criminal profile stereotyped by ALP
Premier Bob Carr and talk-back radio jocks. Their abuse of
Lebanese relied on the confusions that other Australians felt
about 'people of middle-eastern appearance'.

The complexities of being Lebanese were almost as great as
those of becoming Australian. The only cultural aspect
common to Lebanese was their speaking Arabic. Almost all
the early Lebanese arrivals had been Christians. A majority of
Lebanese-Australians still were Christian in 2001. They were
split into three sects, two looking to Rome and the third
towards Orthodoxy. Little intermarriage took place between
them.

A second civil war from 1975 to 1990 saw many more Muslims emigrate. They were divided between Sunni and Sh'iah,
with smaller numbers of Druse and Alawi. The most recent
arrivals have been Shi'ites who came from the most disadvantaged groups. Media attacks brought the Islamic sects closer
together. Australian-born Lebanese Muslims came to identify
more strongly with Islam. They wanted to live like most Australians but sensed that they were not allowed to. In the words
of a Sydney teenager, Ali:

> I have come to realise I am an Australian but I am not treated like
> an Australian. I do not act like an Australian. I am more Lebanese.
> I am treated like a Lebanese so I will stick to what I am treated
> like.

They also developed new ways of being Arab, Islamic or Lebanese. For instance, the Sh'iah mosque in Arncliffe (NSW) supported an active women's association which informed its community on topics as sensitive as HIV-AIDS.

The post-1975 Lebanese arrivals became process workers, with high levels of participation by married women. Then the shrinkage of the manufacturing sector took away many less skilled manual jobs. The chances for these Lebanese to establish themselves disappeared in the recessions of 1982 and 1992.

To make matters worse, governments cut back the services provided to newcomers. Half-a-million people could not gain access to the 500 hours of English as a Second Language to which they had been entitled. The government had also closed its hostels. Hence, the arrivals went to stay with extended families already here. Two-thirds of the Lebanese, for example, were grouped in Sydney suburbs such as Canterbury or Rockdale.

Refugees

During the 1990s, the only assisted immigrants were refugees. Each year, Australia welcomed some 10 000 refugees from every part of the globe. Boat people had been always far less welcome. The first had landed from Vietnam in 1976. Only sixty came between 1981 and 1988. Then the massacres around Beijing's Tiananmen Square in June 1989 upended selection criteria. Prime Minister Hawke allowed 50 000 mainland Chinese students to stay in Australia permanently. They also got the right to bring in close family members. The Department of Immigration was in a mess. In an effort to restore order, ethnically prejudiced officials led the ALP government under Paul Keating to impose mandatory detention in 1992. Desert camps became a deterrent.

Some 700 more boat people arrived in the four years to 1993. In 1991, public opinion was divided evenly between those who wanted to send them all straight back and those who thought they should be kept in custody. Another 2420 refugees turned up on boats between 1994 and 1998. In total, only 5250 had landed in the twenty-three years up to 1998.

Twice that number came during the next three years. They were no longer from Southeast Asia but from the Middle East. The earlier boat people had been in danger from pirates. Now, the boat people were paying pirates to deliver them. These changes summoned policy initiatives from a government not quite as unpopular as a boatload of 'queue-jumping' asylum seekers. In August 2001, the Howard government used the Navy to turn away the *Tampa* after it had rescued refugees. In the run-up to the October elections, the government excised islands from the migration zone, bribed bankrupt micro-states to process the claimants, and lied about their throwing children overboard.

Public opinion on immigration was being driven by more than prejudice towards boat people. Middle Easterners remained the least popular immigrants. Indeed, they became less popular in the course of the 1990s. Meanwhile, the percentage of Australians who thought that immigration was too high fell from 73 per cent to 41 per cent. The reasons that people gave for being against more arrivals also turned around. Those who worried about longer unemployment queues went down from 76 per cent to 50 per cent. The numbers pointing to environmental damage or social tensions shot up from 22 per cent to 48 per cent.

In terms of numbers, the biggest gain was from overseas students. Their total doubled in the five years to 2001, reaching 146 000. The rules were altered to make it easier for them to get permanent visas on completion of their courses. A related amendment, however, reduced family reunions. Visas for parents tumbled from 9000 in 1995–96 to a mere 500 in 2001. By 2001 most of the people applying to settle here were already inside the country.

Another policy change had more potential significance for

both Australian culture and Australian citizenship. The Coalition government threw out the key principle of Australian immigration. In 1999, the Minister declared that the entry of temporary workers was now the 'touchstone'. Importing guest workers rather than permanent settlers broke more than 200 years of nation building. They were not even to be second-class citizens. This switch produced 40 000 long-term temporary visas for skilled employees. The latest way of supplying the labour market was in keeping with the casualisation of the entire workforce.

GLOBALISED WARNINGS

Early in 1993, the US food conglomerate Campbells secured a majority shareholding in Arnott's Biscuits. This takeover provoked more anguish than any previous sell-out. The Arnott's brand evoked memories of families and friends sharing Saos, Scotch Fingers, Tim-Tams and Iced Vo-Vos over a pot of tea or cup of coffee. The ALP government supported the sale on the grounds that the US managers would benefit Australia by expanding exports to Asia. Eight years later, Campbells closed its Victorian plant, putting 600 workers out of a job.

In 1963, the prize for the best radio jingle had gone to Masterfoods for its kangaroo-tail soup commercial. The advertising agency responsible reported that it had wanted the sound of a didjeridu but had been unable to get it. Instead, they hired a visiting US comedian, Leo de Lyon, to imitate one so as 'to gain an authentic, arresting note'. The advertisers said that they had 'got the very sound we wanted — plus the "boing" of a bouncing kangaroo'. Forty years later, free-trade agreements over intellectual property rights meant that neither the Yolngu people nor the Australian Parliament could prevent US corporations from cashing in on the 'authenticity' of any number of Leo de Lyons.

The fate of Arnott's and of the didjeridu fell under the

heading of a 'globalisation'. Reaction to this phenomenon took many forms. In 1997, the One Nation Party rose on the back of protests against the importation of Canadian pig-meats. From the opposite political direction, demonstrators supporting the Maritime Union thought it 'un-Australian' to use dogs and guards in balaclavas against workers defending their jobs. People of varied viewpoints wanted their leaders to stand up for traditional Australian values, defined around a fair-go.

Commentators fretted over how the world saw us. They worried that the treatment of Aborigines or refugees was spoiling our reputation at the United Nations. In particular, the scribes worried about how Asians perceived Australians and Australian policies. Before the 1980s, most face-to-face contacts between Australians and Asians had been military. Australians had come carrying guns on behalf of the British or US empires in the war against Japan (1941–51), through Korea (1950–53), Malaysia (1950–) and then Indo-China (1963–73). From the 1960s, Australians had begun to travel through Asia, either as young backpackers or as retirees on tour parties. Asian attitudes toward Australian tourists were much the same as ours towards them as tourists here. They stayed friendly enough to take the Australian dollars. They were less comfortable with Australian ways of dressing and behaving. Australians took up much more personal space.

At the political level, Asians did not worry about Australia's being a monarchy. Many Asians remained fond of their own kings. They found it harder to understand how Australia could have a head-of-state who was also the sovereign of another country. Their experience of having been colonised led them to assume that Australia was more tied to Britain than it was in fact. Worse still, despite twenty years of a non-discriminatory immigration, the belief persisted that the White Australia Policy remained in force. Memories of old affronts or outrages lingered on both sides. The RSL

demanded that Japan apologise for the First Pacific War before
Canberra could dedicate a Peace Park with its sister city, Nara,
the ancient capital of Japan.

By 1990, a boom in the Japanese economy had made Australians more fearful of economic conquest than a military
attack. The tabloids ran scare campaigns about the Japanese
buying up all the boutiques and resort hotels between
Coolangatta and Cairns. Alarms rang about a Japanese initiative to construct a Multi-Function Polis in Adelaide, but that
bureaucrats' fantasy never got off the Tokyo drawing board.
Mistakes about a Japanese financial juggernaut were in
keeping with ignorance about its military power. Japan had no
nuclear weapons, its armed services could not project force
more than 200 kilometres from the archipelago, and most of its
weapons were aimed at Russia. Japan was still occupied by
tens of thousands of US troops, which would not let the Japanese invade its southern dominion. Then the Tokyo land
bubble burst. Its economy slipped into recession and then
down a deflationary spiral. By the end of the 1990s, any economic threat from Japan was its weakness.

As Japan stagnated, China appeared to boom. Australians
had trouble keeping up with its transformation. The mainland
ceased to be Communist in anything but name. Its leaders
maintained an authoritarian state to engineer the transition to
capitalism. The bureaucrats drew on the Confucian traditions
of Imperial China to install what was jokingly called
'Market-Leninism'. Australian authorities once more hoped
that demand from China would drive the Australian economy.
These ambitions sat uneasily with popular criticism of
Beijing's repressions in Tibet and its suppression of the Falung
Dong. For example, respect for the Dalai Lama underpinned
Australians' opposition to Beijing's being awarded the 2008
Olympics. Meanwhile, the governments and businesses that
had run the Sydney 2000 Games were touting their expertise
to the Chinese.

Indonesia

The gulf between official policy and popular feelings was even greater in regard to Indonesia. In 1995, ALP Prime Minister Paul Keating signed a goodwill agreement with Indonesian President Suharto. In 1999, Australia's armed forces entered East Timor, which Suharto's troops had invaded in 1975. The Howard government had boycotted the award in Oslo of the 1996 Nobel Peace Prize to the East Timor resistance leaders. Canberra also repulsed the democratic opposition in the rest of Indonesia. Deputy Prime Minister Tim Fischer praised Suharto as 'perhaps the world's greatest figure in the latter half of the twentieth century'. A Liberal minister in Victoria called for the disciplining of a professor at the University of Melbourne who had exposed Suharto as a murdering thief. In the following year Suharto was driven from office. Australian officials supported him to the bitter end. They opposed a referendum on independence for East Timor, even after Jakarta had accepted it in the belief that its side would win. When 80 per cent of the Timorese called for independence, Canberra ignored its intelligence warnings that the Indonesian troops would go on the rampage.

Official policy towards Jakarta had been directed by a mix of politicians, academics, church leaders, bureaucrats and business executives known as the 'Indonesia Lobby'. From 1965 they had been practising the art of sucking up to Suharto. Despite the upheavals in Indonesia after 1997, the Lobby pushed the old policies of supporting the thugs. Thus, the commander of the Australian forces that went to East Timor's aid, Major-General Peter Cosgrove, in 2003 revived military links with the Kopassus Group IV, whose members had murdered the five Australian journalists in East Timor late in 1975. Kopassus were backing the militia raids from West Timor that required Australian forces to remain in East Timor, and had set up the network behind the Bali bombing in October 2002.

Reporting of the brutality in East Timor stimulated the

belief that Indonesia was a threat to Australia. In fact, the Indonesians had never had the capacity to invade Australia. Its commanders were not able to eradicate even ill-armed guerilla groups in East Timor, or the Free Papua Movement fighting with bows and arrow in West Irian.

Nonetheless, panic-merchants in Australia pointed out that there were twenty times more Indonesians than Australians, and that the Indonesian army had 235 000 members compared with Australia's 24 000. In an age of high-technology warfare, numbers of people are no guide to military power. What counts in battle is equipment. Weapons require money, which in the 1990s Australia possessed but the Indonesians did not. The economic collapse in 1997 weakened the Indonesian armed forces politically and financially. Until then, Australia had spent three times as much as Indonesia on its armed forces. After 1998, Australia spent eight times as much.

By 2001, Australia had as many attack aircraft, helicopters and tanks as the Indonesians. For instance, the Australian army had 129 helicopters against their 122. The decisive factor was quality, not quantity. Australia had thirty-seven Blackhawk helicopters; Indonesia had none. Similarly, most of their naval vessels had been bought second-hand, years ago. The 1997 collapse of the rupiah meant that the Indonesians were not able to buy the spares they needed to keep this out-of-date equipment running. For instance, its air force had to halve its training flights.

Papua New Guinea

A volcanic eruption on the northern tip of the island of New Britain buried the town of Rabaul in 1994. None of its 20 000 people was killed. Four years later, a tidal wave did kill 2000 people on the northern coast of New Guinea, near Aitape. A once-in-a-century drought in 1997–98 shut down mines and hydro-power. These catastrophes put Papua New Guinea back on Australian television screens. Yet the havocs worked by nature were limited in time. The devastation of both nature and human welfare by mining and timber developments could run for decades. The mines at Panguna, Ok Tedi and Porgera proved more destructive than the three natural disasters.

On Bougainville in 1969, Paul Lapun had smoothed the way for the company to mine at Panguna. Twenty years later, he bewailed what he had wrought:

> You didn't tell me what would happen to my environment. When I was young they fooled me and now I am old and still alive to see the result of my decision I weep. Who cares for a copper mine if it kills us?

The ravaging of Panguna was about to be repeated at Ok Tedi, at Porgera, and across the border at Freeport in Indonesia. A politician from Porgera warned in 2002 that 'the people's cry, the pain that the people of Bougainville felt, is currently being felt by our part of the province'.

The Panguna copper mine had been provoking resistance from the start of exploration in 1964. Riot police seized land there in 1969. Even before independence, the PNG government had renegotiated the agreement with the British-controlled CRA to prevent the island's breaking away. Resentments deepened as the open-cut spread. Despair turned to rebellion in 1988. CRA closed its mine a year later. The economic losses slashed government revenues, cut 10 per cent off the National Domestic Product and a third from the country's exports. Civil war continued among the locals, and between them and the central administration. Canberra contributed helicopter gunships.

The political consequences threatened disaster. In 1996, the PNG Defence Force was involved in murdering the Premier of the Bougainville Transitional Government, Theodore Miriung, as he was negotiating a settlement with Port Moresby. To get around its own troops, the central government then hired mercenaries. The Defence Force arrested them during a coup attempt in March 1997.

Port Moresby's reaction to the outbreak of turmoil on Bougainville paved the way for the ecological crisis at Ok Tedi. Ok Tedi is the eighth largest copper mine in the world. It is halfway across New Guinea and almost on the border with Indonesia. An Australian company, BHP, was the major investor. In 1984, a landslide undermined the dam that it had built to hold the tailings. The PNG government granted temporary permission to let the wastes flow into the Fly river. Then the 1988 rebellion on Bougainville slashed government income. Port Moresby became desperate for the revenues from Ok Tedi. The waiver therefore became permanent. Since then, 700 million tonnes of tailings have gone downstream, clogging rivers, bursting their banks and spreading pollutants. Fish died. Vegetation died back over 1350 square kilometres. Along the rivers, cassowaries, pigs, pigeons and bandicoots died. Muck ended up in the Torres Strait. Coral died. In 1996, BHP offered 40 million kina ($A40 million) in compensation.

Early in 2002, BHP passed its 52 per cent share of the project over to the Papua New Guinea government. By then, even the locals who had suffered the most did not want the mine shut down. Closure would have made their prospects worse. They needed the mine to keep earning in order to fund at least some rehabilitation. Without those earnings, no improvement would be possible. Yet there could be no guarantee that the monies would reach those in need.

Nor can there be any certainty that tailings are the worst that can befall the environment. Extreme weather and perilous terrain heighten the dangers from mining in Papua New Guinea. In 1984, a barge loaded with 260 000 kilograms of cyanide sank at the mouth of the Fly. Few of the steel canisters were retrieved. In March 2000, a container with a tonne of cyanide fell from a helicopter into a Highlands waterway.

Porgera saw a repeat of the problems at Ok Tedi. Porgera is

an open-cut gold-mine, 600 kilometres north-west of Port
Moresby, and more than 2000 metres up in the Central Range.
It was directed by a Canadian company, Placer Dome.

Porgera opened in 1990, yielding eleven million ounces of
gold in thirteen years. Tailings went down the Strickland River
into the largest lake in the country, Lake Murray. The
dumping of wastes into rivers would never be allowed in
Canada, or Australia. Australia's CSIRO reported on pollution in 1996. The PNG Minister for Mines awarded the locals
15 million kina in compensation. They rejected the offer as 'a
joke'. Six billion kina would be extracted during the life of the
mine. The company argued that any environmental changes
were part of the cycles of nature. In June 2001, the local who
chaired the Porgera Environmental Advisory Komiti (PEAK)
resigned in protest after Placer Dome distorted his views into
what he called its 'propaganda'.

Delaying tactics by the company provoked the locals into
attacking its power lines. Production stopped for months at a
stretch. The Porgera highway became impassable because of
landslides or bandits. Other locals got something out of the
project by panning for gold on their own behalf.

New Guinea had been one of the earliest sites for agriculture in the world, starting some 6000 years ago. Its gardens
remain productive. Villagers keep a million pigs and three million head of poultry. Twenty hours of work a week is enough
to feed a family. Village production of food remains a more
secure means of gaining a livelihood than entering the cash
economy of mining giants and the World Bank.

The imbalances can be traced back to the decision by the
Australian government in the mid-1960s to rely on foreign
corporations for the territory's progress. Canberra believed
that taxes and royalties would fund the administration. Neither mining nor its revenues have fed the population. Minerals
supplied 72 per cent of exports, while agriculture sustained 85
per cent of the people. By 1999, the mines were employing

only 7500 people out of five million. The problem was not how to clean up the mess from mining. The task was how to balance agriculture, employment and welfare.

Only one in ten Papua New Guineans lived in the seven major centres. Yet the Port Moresby administration neglected local government. By 2000, one-third of village aid posts had been closed and others were unsupervised. The rate of maternal mortality was the second highest in world, 55 for every 1000 live births. Over one-third of the population lived below the poverty line.

Climate change

A different danger came from the Australian coal that corporations sold to Japan and China. These exporters influenced Canberra to refuse to sign the Kyoto Agreement on global warming. Environmentalists argued that coal-fired power stations produced greenhouse gases, which were pushing up temperatures; this would cause the icecaps to melt and the sea levels to rise, drowning many islands and inundating low-lying lands; Australia might then have to cope with hundreds of thousands of homeless Pacific Islanders, perhaps as immigrants.

Deciding what to do about these claims was difficult because knowledge of climate and weather patterns was limited. Accurate readings of sea levels were sparse and recent. However, ice cores taken from Greenland recorded 250 000 years of snowfalls. That data suggested that global warming could provoke a sharp drop in temperatures. A related factor is that the Earth is coming towards the close of an inter-glacial period. Its onset about 15 000 years ago happened within a ten-year interval. That sudden reversal caused the sea levels to rise, separating New Guinea and Tasmania from the mainland of Australia. In the next ice age, the oceans will shrink, ice-sheets will advance and rainfall will diminish. Much arable land will become barren. In such circumstances, the planet may not be able to feed one billion people, let alone ten billion. Adding to the uncertainty about what is happening is that temperatures have been rising since the end of the little ice age from around 1850. That cycle has to be distinguished from any effect from burning fossil fuels.

Nineteenth-century optimists believed that they could control nature for the best. Today, environmentalists are no less convinced that humankind is in charge, but for the worst. The assumption of human dominance persists. Another nineteenth-century thinker accepted the limits to human power:

> Thus at every step we are reminded that we by no means rule over nature like a conqueror over a foreign people, like someone standing outside nature — but that we, with flesh, blood and brain, belong to nature, and exist in its midst, and that all our mastery of it consists in the fact that we have the advantage over all other creatures of being able to learn its laws and apply them correctly.

From this perspective, the onset of the next ice age is outside human control. At most, we will be able to manage a few of its social consequences.

2001: A LONG MARCH

Alec William Campbell outlasted the twentieth century. Born in Launceston on 26 February 1899, he died at Hobart on 16 May 2002. At 103, he was the last survivor from the Australians who served with the Anzacs on Gallipoli. Campbell had volunteered on 2 July 1915. Four months later, aged sixteen, he landed in Turkey, where he worked as a water carrier but never fired a shot. By Boxing Day 1915, he had been evacuated to Egypt. He was home in Australia before his eighteenth birthday.

Campbell's story is like that of Jim Martin on whose life Anthony Hill based his 2001 novel, *Soldier Boy*. The difference is that Jim was killed before his fifteenth birthday. Campbell later reflected: 'It's hard to believe — all those young men — gone'.

After Campbell died, Prime Minister John Howard spoke of 'the respect we feel and the debt we owe to the Grand Old Man and those he came to represent'. But which Australians did Campbell represent? Howard also declared that 'Within this one life are illustrated the living values that transformed Australia'. Again, which values had Campbell's life illustrated?

When the Howard government gave Campbell a state funeral, his family broke from military custom by having five women relatives walk on each side of the gun carriage. 'Dad was not a man of tradition', one of his granddaughters recalled. 'After all, he was a republican. We thought this was a way of showing that.' The Australian Council of Trade

Unions called on its members to remember Campbell as a battler for the rights of working people. In the late 1930s he had talked about volunteering to fight the fascists in Spain. In the 1960s, he became an anti-Vietnam activist. In his hundredth year, Alec Campbell had voted for a republic against the monarchist John Howard.

During Campbell's military service, he had gone absent without leave and got into trouble for being drunk. He was a young tearaway who became a prize-fighter. After he married in 1924, he worked for the railways and was active in his union, serving as its president. His boxing skills came in handy as an unofficial bodyguard for the union's left-wing secretary, Bill Morrow.

Morrow later received a Lenin Peace Medal. The National Museum in Canberra put that award on display when it opened in March 2001. After Howard supporters criticised the Museum for being 'politically correct', Morrow's Lenin Medal was no longer to be seen. Its removal was one moment in the history wars. That fracas raised questions about which of the values that had transformed Australia should be respected. Should Campbell be remembered for his brief military service or his life-long radicalism? Or can both strands be valued? In Campbell's lifetime, changes overtook the ways in which both soldiers and strikers are remembered.

Anzac Day ceased to be Australia's 'One Day of the Year' after it was commercialised during the 1950s. Instead of a day when everything was closed, hotels, picture theatres, racecourses and fee-charging sports began opening after the morning ceremonies. Anzac Day became just another holiday in the land of the long weekend. When the fiftieth anniversary in 1965 fell on a Sunday, the clergy wanted the march postponed until after morning church services. The RSL refused. The Anglican Archbishop of Sydney, and several other leading clerics, declined to attend. A Methodist leader, the Reverend Alan Walker, accused the RSL leadership of 'undermining

Christian standards every Sunday' with their poker machines and liquor clubs, thereby instilling 'a pagan atmosphere'.

After 1967, the arrival of 20 000 emigrants from Turkey gave another twist to the Gallipoli story. The Turks helped their fellow Australians to see that the Turkish nation also laid claim to have been born on the shores of *Canakkale*, their name for the peninsula. The founding president of the Turkish Republic, Kemal Ataturk, had commanded its Ottoman defenders. Immediately across from the Australian War Memorial in Canberra is a Turkish memorial inscribed with Ataturk's 1933 pledge:

> Those heroes that shed their blood and lost their lives. You are now living in the soil of a friendly country, therefore rest in peace. There is no difference between the Johnnies and the Mehmets to us where they lie side by side, here in this country of ours. You, the mothers, who sent their sons from faraway countries, wipe away your tears; your sons are now lying in our bosom and are in peace. After having lost their lives on this land, they have become our sons as well.

A Turkish association in Hobart sent a wreath to Alec Campbell's funeral. Yet nearly ninety years of commemorating Anzac Day had not convinced Australians that Gallipoli was part of another country. Turkey had done nothing to threaten Australians. We had joined an invasion aimed at propping up the Czar of all the Russias.

During the 1990s, Australian backpackers headed for the Dawn Service at Gallipoli. Some turned up expecting a cross between a Melbourne Grand Final and Sydney fireworks; they came more prepared to chant 'Oi, Oi, Oi' than to observe two minutes' silence. Once there, they were shocked to learn of the slaughter and defeat. 'To be perfectly honest', admitted Luke from Geelong, 'I didn't know very much about Anzac Day whatsoever, other than the fact that Essendon and Collingwood played every Anzac Day.' How was it that young Australians knew so little about the events that had supposedly given birth to their national consciousness? The little they did know came from feature films and television mini-series.

THE HISTORY KILLERS

In the lead-up to the centenary of Federation, politicians fretted that so few Australians could name their first prime minister, Edmund Barton. This concern about historical ignorance was selective. The authorities were not anxious to celebrate the Australians who had voted in 1916 and again in 1917 to defeat conscription for overseas service, or to prevent the banning of the Communist Party in 1951. Yet those three democratic triumphs had done more to keep Australia an open society than had either the Federation plebiscites or the Gallipoli campaign.

State governments reacted to evidence of ignorance and confusion by reinstating Australian history to junior high schools. Its place had been undermined by economic rationalists who had prescribed subjects that would make students more saleable to their first employer. A gloss for this business conception of life came from biological determinists. They alleged that wars and capitalism were the inevitable product of aggressive genes. Hence, the study of humans making ourselves — history — was bunk.

The most pervasive of the history-killers, however, has been the mass media. They reduced the dynamics and structures of social life to 'news on the hour every hour'. Television documentaries patched together a vision of the past from images torn out of context. This method carried no capacity to explain. Instead, when film clips rolled from Gallipoli into Kokoda, the Anzacs of 1915 seemed to be saving us from the Japanese in 1942.

While the politicians were decrying the want of historical knowledge in children, they were clear-felling our sense of even the most recent past in order to escape scrutiny. Television news demanded thirty-second grabs from politicians and corporate executives, who employed spin doctors to take advantage of those rushed responses in order to erase even short-term memory. A favourite trick became to refer to the mistake they committed yesterday as 'ancient history'. When caught out lying and cheating, the ministers and managers posed as forward-looking. We will 'put that behind us', they bleated before promising to 'move on'. Their victims, meanwhile, were told 'to get over it'.

The disagreements over how to value Alec Campbell were part of the usual range of opinions about the past. We prefer to recall events that make us feel good about ourselves. Scholars seek to limit such prejudices by introducing details of who, when, where and what. Either an event happened or it did not. To that degree, the writing of history aims at being objective. One problem is that we cannot always be certain about what happened. What remains are inadequate sources of information. More taxing still is to explain 'how' something happened. Answers to 'why?' are never likely to win widespread support.

The historian works with the surviving evidence both to explicate selective memories and to challenge ignorance. In so doing, he or she will face hostility. 'Revisionist' should be synonymous with 'investigator'. In Australia, the issue is rarely a matter of revising history. Rather, researchers must trace the story for the first time; they set documentation against prejudice, statistics above rumour.

Tracing one's family history became popular around the James Cook bicentenary in 1970. Genealogical societies have areas set aside in State libraries. Their work helps people to see whether their family was unusual. Everyday experiences also let us appreciate that changes are happening all the time, even when there are no big events such as wars or depressions. The contraceptive pill and hire purchase have done as much to alter the way Australians live now as did the Anzacs on Gallipoli or the striking shearers around Barcaldine in 1891.

Thinking about the past in this way helps us to recognise that the events in schoolbooks were made by people like our aunts and our neighbours. History-making is not confined to prime ministers and generals, gold medallists and *prima donnas*. The people who voted and marched for or against conscription around the time of Gallipoli were not a special kind of people. They were like the million Australians who crossed bridges for reconciliation in 2001. Making our history continues through the present. Written history, of course, can be about only the past. Yet the kinds of human action that both made the lived past and contribute to its written accounts are also happening now. To see the present as part of history is to recognise that our future is being shaped by our creativity.

If men and women did not refine bauxite, program computers, fly aircraft, tend vineyards, bake pizzas and keep on teaching, nursing or experimenting, there would have been no Olympics, no Midnight Oil, no Timor Task Force, no High Court: nothing at all. As Mary Gilmore wrote:

> Shame on the mouth
> That would deny
> The knotted hands
> That set us high.

REFERENCES

Abbreviations used in notes

AFR	*Australian Financial Review*
AGPS	Australian Government Publishing Service
AGS	*Australian Geographical Studies*
AJARE	*Australian Journal of Agricultural and Resource Economics*
AJPH	*Australian Journal of Politics and History*
AJSI	*Australian Journal of Social Issues*
A&R	Angus & Robertson
ANU	Australian National University
AWW	*Australian Women's Weekly*
B&TW	*Broadcasting and Television Weekly*
CPD	*Commonwealth Parliamentary Debates*
CPP	*Commonwealth Parliamentary Papers*
CUP	Cambridge University Press
IMJA	*Intercolonial Medical Journal of Australasia*
JIR	*Journal of Industrial Relations*
MJA	*Medical Journal of Australia*
MUP	*Melbourne University Press*
NLA	National Library of Australia
NSWPP	*New South Wales Parliamentary Papers*
OUP	Oxford University Press
SMH	*Sydney Morning Herald*
UQP	University of Queensland Press
UWA	University of Western Australia
VPD	*Victorian Parliamentary Papers*
WA V&P	Western Australia Votes and Proceedings
YSA	*Youth Studies Australia*

1888: One hundred years of after invasion

Details of the Melbourne Exhibition are from the various official reports, catalogues and programs; those of the Sydney Show are from G. Mant, *The Big Show* (Sydney, Horwitz, 1972), p. 50; K. Swan, *A History of Wagga Wagga* (Sydney, City of Wagga Wagga, 1970), p. 162, tells of the Brooking affray, and E. Ross, *A History of the Miners' Federation of Australia* (Sydney, A. C. & S. E. F., 1970), pp. 60–65, of the Newcastle struggle.

1889–1901: 'Never Glad Morning Again'

Work: Griffith published in the *Centennial Magazine*, 1 (12), July 1889, pp. 833–842; the navvies' camps are described in the *Argus*, 20 May 1890; the mortality of miners is from R. Rivett, *Australian Citizen* (Carlton, MUP, 1965), p. 32; many of the details of working hours, conditions and laws are from R. Lawson, *Brisbane in the 1890s* (St Lucia, UQP, 1973), pp. 64–77; the Royal Commission witness on barmaids is in *Lone Hand*, June 1908.

Life in the cities: The Whittlesea line quote is from D. S. Garden, *Heidelberg* (Carlton, MUP, 1972), p. 134; details of Brisbane are from Lawson, *Brisbane in the 1890s*; the English lady's views are in *Centennial Magazine*, 1 (8), March 1889, pp. 586–89; Byrne's experience was reported in the *Herald* (Melb.), 11 September 1924; the description of Townsville comes from *MJA*, 1938, II, p. 808; many of the details of housing and of building generally are from R. Boyd, *Australia's Home* (Ringwood, Penguin, 1968), J. Freeland, *Architecture in Australia* (Ringwood, Penguin, 1972), and M. Shaw, *Builders of Melbourne* (Melbourne, Cypress, 1972).

Life in the country: Stagg's diary has been edited by Nancy Robinson as *Stagg of Tarcowie* (Adelaide, Lynton, 1973); the railway job figures are from J. Docherty, *The Rise of Railway Unionism* (unpublished MA thesis, ANU, 1973), pp. 73, 87–8; the Western Australian farmer's hut is from M. Bignell, *First the Spring* (Perth, University of Western Australia Press, 1971), p. 166; Murray's cry is in M. R. Casson and WRC Hirst, *Loxton* (Melbourne, Hawthorn, 1972), p. 18; payment by whisky is from Eugenie McNeil, *A Bunyip Close Behind Me* (Melbourne, Hawthorn, 1972), p. 24; details of Mt Gambier are from a book of that name by L. R. Hill (Leabrook, Investigator, 1972), p. 314.

Health: Use of alcohol is discussed by K. S. Inglis, *Hospital and Community* (Melbourne, MUP, 1958), pp. 48–9, and phosphorus in *MJA*, 1951, I, p. 2; D. M. Whittaker has written of the *Hospital at Wangaratta* (Wangaratta, 1972); some other hospital practices are from J. Templeton, *Prince Henry's* (Melbourne, Melbourne University Press, 1969), pp. 59–63, 76–7; election of honoraries comes from Inglis, *Hospital and Community*, p. 133; the Launceston quotation was cited in *MJA*, 1967, II, p. 950; the old burn comment is from *IMJA*, 1908, p. 653; the nurse's experience comes from D. M. Armstrong, *The First Fifty Years* (Sydney, Australasian Medical Publishing, 1965), p. 72; early appendectomies are recorded in *MJA*, 1944, II, pp. 655–58; Sister Harris is from *Victorian Historical Magazine*, December 1942, p. 123, and the Sydney nurse from Armstrong is from *The First Fifty Years*, p. 37.

Aborigines: Almost all the West Australian material comes from P. Biskup, *Not Slaves, Not Citizens* (St Lucia, UQP, 1973); the South Australian group's story is from N. B. Tindale, *Royal Geographical Society of Australia (SA Branch) Proceedings*, 1940–41, p. 81; Rowley's view is on p. 221 of *The Destruction of Aboriginal Society* (Ringwood, Penguin, 1972); the West Australian politician's attitude is to be found in R. M. and D. H. Berndt, *The World of the First Australians* (Sydney, Ure Smith, 1964), p. 431.

White Australia: M. Williard, *History of the White Australia Policy to 1920* (Melbourne, MUP, 1966), and A. Yarwood, *Asian Migration to Australia* (Melbourne, MUP, 1964) provide materials for this section; the Chinese unionists are discussed by A. Markus in *Historian*, October 1973, and *Labour History*, 26, May 1974, pp. 1–10.

View of the world: B. R. Penny's articles in *Journal of British Studies*, 7 (1), November 1967, pp. 97–130, and *Historical Studies*, 14 (56), April 1971, pp. 526–45 are the main sources for Australian attitudes; French's comments on the Field Artillery occur in *NSW Leg. Co. Journal*, 1897, 56, Pt I, p. 638.

1901: A continent for a market

The radical doubters are collected by Hugh Anderson, *Tocsin: Contesting the Constitution* (Melbourne, Red Roster Press, 2000); the *Economist* is quoted by David Kynaston, *The City of London, Volume II, Golden Years, 1890–1914* (London, Chatto & Windus,

1995), p. 48; the doings of Chamberlain and Reid are traced in J. A. La Nauze, *The Making of the Australian Constitution* (Carlton, MUP, 1972), pp. 172–75 and 263–64; Deakin's reaction is from his *The Federal Story* (Melbourne, Robertson & Mullens, 1944), p. 156; the account of Queen Victoria's death is from *SMH*, 24 January 1901; the *Bulletin*'s obituary, 2 February 1901; *Truth* on Edward VII comes from C. Pearl, *Wild Men of Sydney* (Melbourne, Lansdowne, 1965), p. 118; J. A. La Nauze retells *The Hopetoun Blunder* (Melbourne, MUP, 1957).

1902–1913: Frugal Comforts

Work: The salt farmers are described in *Lone Hand*, June 1908; women workers were the subject of a series of articles in *Lone Hand* from March to October 1908, and again March, May and October 1911; Victoria's starch industry is investigated by *Lone Hand*, July 1907; Walker's return is taken from N. Brennan, *A History of Nunawading* (Melbourne, Hawthorn, 1972), p. 100; Melbourne's cab drivers were subject to an inquiry, *VPP*, 1907, II; the Royal Commission on factory laws is in *NSWPP*, 1911–12, II.

Life in the cities: Sydney sewerage workers appear in *Lone Hand*, 9 July 1909; the report of the cost-of-living investigation appeared in *Commonwealth Year Book*, No. 5; impure foods are tested in *Lone Hand*, January to November 1908; Melbourne's cabs in *VPP*, 1907, II, and its seaside slums in *VPP*, 1915, II.

Life in the country: The Luritja rain ceremony is from T. G. H. Strehlow, *Songs of Central Australia* (Sydney, A&R, 1971), p. 449; the turn-of-the-century *El Niño* is from Mike Davis, *Capitalism, Nature, Socialism*, 10 (2), June 1999, pp. 3–46; the Commonwealth tussles over water rights are in Don Wright, *Federalism in Canada and Australia* (Canberra, ANU Press, 1978); eating during the drought comes from Casson and Hirst, *Loxton*, p. 40; Aston's memoirs are in *Canberra and District Historical Journal*, September 1973; for impact of new amenities see F. A. Law, *History of Merredin* (Merredin, 1961), pp. 95–9, and Hill, *Mt Gambier*, pp. 160–61; the Victorian inquiry's report is in *VPP*, 1918, I; the *Argus* article appeared on 13 January 1902.

Health: The Queensland Director-General was quoted by R. Cilento, *Royal Queensland Historical Society, Proceedings*, 1961–62;

the mothers of Adelaide appear in Deborah Brennan, *The Politics of Australian Child Care* (Melbourne, CUP, 1994), p. 20; the beginnings of child care are detailed in *MJA*, 1938, II, pp. 808–9, and 1939, II, pp. 641 ff.; the story of Australian dentistry has been put together from K. J. G. Sutherland, *Oral Medicine* (Perth, University of Western Australia Press, 1955), *Lone Hand*, August 1909, A. Chapman (ed.), *History of Dentistry in South Australia, 1836–1936* (Adelaide, ADA, 1937), and articles in the *Dental Journal of Australia* throughout 1952; the Bendigo doctor is quoted in *Centenary of Nurse Training in Australia* (Melbourne, 1963), p. 12; the retired nurse in *VPD*, 5 March 1918, p. 613; the treatment of pneumonia patients is from Armstrong, *The First Fifty Years*, p. 158; the diphtheria story is in A. A. Calwell, *Be Just and Fear Not* (Melbourne, Lloyd O'Neil, 1972), p. 27; quack cures became the subject of a Royal Commission, *CPP*, 1907–08, IV; the Collingwood dairy is described by A. H. B. Barrett, *The Inner Suburbs* (Melbourne, MUP, 1971), pp. 137–38; and the standard text-book is R. S. Maynard, *Australian Dairyman's Handbook* (Sydney, A&R, 1931), pp. 533–34; Tambo's hospital features in *MJA*, 1932, I, pp. 71–2.

Aborigines: Biskup's view is in *Not Slaves, Not Citizens*, pp. 6–7; Kickett's letter is cited by Biskup, p. 154, while the bone-crusher quote is on p. 113 and the WA booklet on p. 56; Favenc's opinions are in *SMH*, 1 January 1901; the NSW educational policy is from *Course of Instruction for Aboriginal Schools* (Sydney, 1916) and the Aborigines' Board Report is in *NSWPP*, 1911, II.

White Australia: Sending 'kanakas' home is based on P. Corris, *Historical Studies*, 15 (58), April 1972, pp. 237–50; the quotation about pearl divers is in *CPP*, 1914–17, vol. V.

View of the world: The *Tocsin* quote is from the issue for 3 October 1901, and Dawson's view is from *Tocsin*, 24 May 1906; chapters 1–7 of H. McQueen, *A New Britannia* (St Lucia, UQP, 2004), give this material in more detail; Kitchener's report is in *CPP*, 1910, II.

1914–1919: The Great European War

Work: The miners' motion is from J. Docherty, *Newcastle and Conscription* (BA (Hons) thesis, University of Newcastle, 1971), p. 4; the radical Simpson is portrayed in Peter Cochrane, *Simpson and the Donkey* (Carlton, MUP, 1992), p. 18; the other opposition is from L.

C. Jauncey, *The Story of Conscription in Australia* (Melbourne, Macmillan, 1968); the exchange with the magistrate from J. Main, *Conscription* (Melbourne, Cassell, 1970), pp. 24–5; the 'obedience, respect ...' remark is from *Victorian Historical Magazine*, June 1943, pp. 29–30; the school papers mentioned are Class IV, Victoria, May 1915, p. 53; the exam questions are from S. G. Firth, *Melbourne Studies in Education 1970* (Melbourne, MUP, 1970); war work in schools is described in E. Sweetman et al., *State Education in Victoria* (Melbourne, 1922), pp. 302–05; the injunction about 'both sides of the paper' is cited by C. Turney in J. Cleverley and J. Lawry (eds), *Australian Education in the Twentieth Century* (Camberwell, Longman, 1972), p. 36; the experiences of soldiers are all from Bill Gammage, *The Broken Years* (Ringwood, Penguin, 1975); Mackellar's poem was published in *Southerly*, 5 (4), p. 13; Andrew Moore reported North Sydney's training in *The Mighty Bears!* (North Sydney, Macmillan, 1996), p. 106.

Life in city and country: Anti-German activities are taken from a number of local histories and articles; see, for example, M. Lake's article in *Tasmanian Historical Research Association, Papers and Proceedings*, September 1972, and Critchley Parker, *If the Germans Won*, Political Pamphlets Vol. 15, Mitchell Library; the *SMH* correspondent's letter was reprinted by Jauncey, *Story of Conscription*, p. 137; the poem is from *Sunday Times* (Perth), 9 February 1919; the advertisement for parlourmaids was reported in *Labor Call* (Melbourne), 14 December 1916; the influenza epidemic is detailed by me in Jill Roe (ed.), *Social Policy in Australia* (Sydney, Cassell, 1976); the Russian soldier's example is from *Messenger*, 14 February 1919.

Health: The story of VD control is told by J. H. L. Cumpston, *Venereal Disease in Australia* (Melbourne, Commonwealth of Australia, 1919); VD in the first AIF is discussed by Sir James Barrett, *Eighty Eventful Years* (Melbourne, Robertson and Mullens, 1945), pp. 102–05, and A. G. Butler, *Official History of the Australian Army Medical Service* (Sydney, A&R, 1943), vol. III, chapter 3; Frank Anstey retells the 'Aspro' story in his memoirs, NLA, MS 4636.

White Australia: Hughes's letter is from W. R. Louis, *Great Britain and Germany's Last Colonies* (Oxford, OUP, 1967), p. 45; for contemporary support of this interpretation see *Bulletin*, 24 April 1919, p. 7, and *Western Argus*, 12 May 1919, p. 6.

1919: Moods of violence

The *Courier* and the *Daily Standard* are quoted from their 25 March issues; the attack on McDougall is in the *Ararat Advertiser*, 12 February 1920, and his poem in *Labor Call*, 14 January 1915; the Darwin rebellion is retold in *Labour History*, November 1966; the *MJA* editorial appeared on 5 July 1919.

1920–1927: The Terrible Twenties

Work: Life on Sydney trams was written up in *Workers Weekly*, 6 May 1932, p. 3; for industrial health facilities see *MJA*, 1926, I, p. 75; the Broken Hill miner's story is from a tape deposited by Mike Lavers in NLA; the account of working in North Queensland comes from a typescript in the possession of Terry Cutler at Wollongong University; Cusack's teaching is from her *Window in the Dark* (Canberra, NLA, 1991), p. 45.

Life in the cities: Hotels are described in J. Freeland, *The Australian Pub* (Melbourne, MUP, 1966); Murdoch's hanging of Ross is from T. C. Brennan, *The Gun Alley Tragedy* (Melbourne, 1922); the comments about newspapers are from *Newspaper News*, October 1928, p. 7, and December 1928, p. 12; the automobile industry is sketched in J. Goode, *Smoke, Smell and Clatter* (Melbourne, Lansdowne, 1969), and P. Stubbs, *The Australian Motor Industry* (Melbourne, Cheshire, 1972); the Holden workers appear in Peter Poynton, *Arena*, 58, 1981; the explanation of suburban spread is from Freeland, *Architecture in Australia*; opinions of the Harbour Bridge are from *Bulletin*, 16 March 1932, and *Workers Weekly*, 25 March 1932.

Life in the country: Prell's success is retold in *Australian Quarterly*, 15, September 1932, pp. 73–80; the *SMH*'s editorial appeared on 16 February 1922, and the *Bulletin*'s on 23 April 1925; the report of the Royal Commission into Soldier Settlement is to be found in *CPP*, 1929, II; Rees's success and the other account are from L. Grondonia, *The Kangaroo Keeps on Talking* (London, Victoria, 1924), pp. 216 and 189, while the woman's experiences are from G. Bolton, *A Fine Country to Starve In* (Perth, UWA Press, 1972), p. 43; the koala trappers are captured by Norah Howlett, *Bowyang*, 1 (2), Sept–Oct 1979, pp. 9–24.

Health: The nurse is quoted in Armstrong, *The First Fifty Years*, p. 148; the school menu is in P. Blazey, *Bolte* (Brisbane, Jacaranda,

1972), p. 15; Dr Arthur's evidence is on p. 356 of the minutes of evidence; the Adelaide man's case is reported in *Medical and Scientific Archives of the Adelaide Hospital*, No. 2 (Adelaide, 1923), pp. 39–40; the lead paint puzzle is discussed in *MJA*, 1922, I, pp. 150–52, and 1938, II, p. 807; the *SMH* quote is from 10 May 1920 and the doctor's opinion given to the 1925 Royal Commission, p. 528; the Commissioners' views are from *MJA*, 16 January 1926, p. 69; the nurse's story is from *AWW*, 31 October 1973.

Aborigines: The union organiser is quoted by Biskup, *Not Slaves, Not Citizens*, p. 85; the Dala affair is based on *WA V&P*, 1927, and the Coniston Affair on M. Hartwig's BA (Hons) thesis (University of Adelaide, 1960); the Maynards are from Heather Goodall, *Invasion to Embassy* (Sydney, Allen & Unwin, 1996), pp. 149–68, and *Australian Historical Studies*, 34 (121), April 2003, pp. 91–105; the sales of *Coonardoo* are in *Newspaper News*, December 1928, p. 12, and the editor's private reaction in Palmer Family Papers, NLA MS 1174/1/3357.

White Australia: The details of the Japanese proposals at Versailles are from W. MacMahon Ball, *Australia and Japan* (Melbourne, Nelson, 1969), pp. 29–36; Hughes's copy of Lloyd George's book is in the NLA; the medical and political debates are condensed from my article in *Australian Quarterly*, 44 (1), March 1972, pp. 92–102.

View of the world: The *Bulletin*'s editorial is dated 19 February 1925; Bruce's attack is in *CPD*, 3 August 1926, pp. 4801 ff; the *Bulletin* catalogued its enemies on 30 September 1926; the spoof was in *Truth*, 26 January 1919; the outline of Burns Philp comes from *Australian Encyclopaedia*, vol. 2 (Sydney, Grolier, 1963), pp. 189–90, and vol. 7, pp. 100–101, and a company history by K. Buckley and K. Klugman, *The Australian Presence in the Pacific* (Sydney, George Allen & Unwin, 1983); Murray's opinion is taken from his *Selected Letters* (ed. Francis West), (Melbourne, OUP, 1970), p. 99; Hughes's 1919 opinions are from *Daily Chronicle* (London), 29 January 1919, and *Foreign Relations of the United States*, Paris Peace Conference, 1919, III, p. 746; the nature of the 'C' class mandate is discussed by E. H. Carr, *International Relations between the Two World Wars* (London, Macmillan, 1959), p. 18; the final Hughes–Wilson clash is retold by L. F. Fitzhardinge, *The Little Digger* (Sydney, A&R, 1979), pp. 400–13;

the Royal Commission Report is in *CPP*, 1920–21, III, while Murray's view of it is from his *Letters*, p. 108.

1928–1933: The Great Depression

Work: Relief payments are detailed by F. A. Bland, *International Labour Review*, July 1934; the sale of bank books is from Calwell, *Be Just and Fear Not*, p. 68; the *Advertiser* advertisement is retold in J. D. W. Babbage, *Between the Ranges* (Adelaide, 1972), p. 98; the wood-chopping story is in the Spring 1972 issue of *Overland*, p. 43; the unemployable office boy comes from *The Accountant in Australia*, March 1932; the plight of younger children appears in Foster, *Preston*, p. 99, *Argus*, 1 January 1931, and E. A. Beaver, *Launceston Bank for Savings* (Melbourne, MUP, 1972), p. 143.

Life in the cities: Happy Valley was described in *SMH*, 10 June 1932; Byfield's death is reported by *Workers Weekly*, 19 February 1932; an account of the hostel in Darling Harbour appeared in *SMH*, 10 June 1931; drinking habits are detailed in Freeland, *The Australian Pub*, p. 179; the Attorney-General is quoted from *Argus*, 3 June 1931, and the widow from 8 July 1931; CSR's position is in *Argus*, 7 May, the gas company on 21 July, and Coles on 16 July 1931; Drew Cottle reveals how the rich lived in *Bowyang*, 1 (1), 1979, pp. 2–24, and 1 (2), 1979, pp. 67–102.

Life in the country: The WA bank report and living conditions are in J. P. Gabbedy, *Yours Is the Earth* (Perth, UWA, 1972), pp. 171–76; the auction sale is in Bolton, *A Fine Country to Starve In*, p. 145; the soldier's remarks are in NSW Archives, Closer Settlement File no. 11304, item P5805; BHP's call is in *BHP Recreation Review* 'Supplement', September 1931, p. 6; for false-teeth anecdote see Beever, *Launceston Bank for Savings*, p. 146.

Health: Problems of public health are set out in *Shire and Municipal Record*, 28 July 1932; the editorial quoted appeared in *MJA*, 1932, I, p. 19.

Aborigines: the stories from around Hermannsburg are in Barbara Henson, *A Straight-out Man* (Carlton, MUP, 1992).

View of the world: Monash is quoted in Geoffrey Serle's biography (Carlton, MUP, 1982), pp. 517–22; Roslyn Pesman documents the fondness for Mussolini, *AJPH*, 39 (3), 1993, pp. 348–66; the Colored Idea is from Andrew Bisset, *Black Roots White Flowers*, (Sydney,

Golden Press, 1979), pp. 43–5; the reactions against war novels are from *Reveille*, between June 1929 and March 1931; Lindsay's farewell is from John Hetherington's biography, (Melbourne, OUP, 1973), p. 189.

1934–1938: Very Slow Recovery

Work: The Belanglo forest camp is described in *Workers Weekly*, 13 July 1934; the Wonthaggi strike is told by Peter Cochrane, *Labour History*, 27, November 1974, pp. 12–30.

Life in the cities: Radio is the subject of books by I. Mackay, *Broadcasting in Australia* (Carlton, MUP, 1957), R. R. Walker, *The Magic Spark* (Melbourne, Hawthorn, 1973), and Lesley Stern, *The Unseen Voice* (London, Routledge, 1988); the rise of Coles is from *Rydge's*, October 1936.

Life in the country: Jean and Alan McIntyre, *Country Towns of Victoria* (Carlton, MUP, 1944); the Broken Hill librarian is from Norman Freehill, *Dymphna* (Melbourne, Nelson, 1975), p. 31; Stretton's reports are in *VPP*, 1939, II, and 1944, I.

Health: Hospital expenses are from Inglis, *Hospital and Community*, p. 86, the poetry royalties in Templeton, *Prince Henry's Hospital*, p. 73; the *Herald* editor's opinion is in C. Edwards, *The Editor Regrets* (Melbourne, Hill of Content, 1972), pp. 83–4; car accidents are from Inglis, p. 88; the blood transfusion service is described in Whittaker, *Hospital at Wangaratta*, pp. 67–8, Armstrong, *First Fifty Years*, pp. 156–57, and in December 1941 issues of *Salt*.

Aborigines: The Caledon Bay Affair is based on 52 *Commonwealth Law Reports*, 1934–35; water, Hermansburg, Albrecht and Namatjira are all in Henson, *A Straight-out Man*, chapters 6 & 7.

View of the world: Kisch has told his own story in *Australian Landfall* (Melbourne, Macmillan, 1969); Minister quoted by W. MacMahon Ball, *Press, Radio and World Affairs* (Melbourne, 1938), p. 33; the Jewish refugee story is based on B. Hooper, *Australian Reactions to German Persecutions of the Jews* (unpublished MA thesis, ANU, 1972); the Sydney–Emden quote is from Philip Lindsay, *I'd Live the Same Life Over* (London, Hutchinson, 1941), p. 63; the newspaper headline was in *Daily Telegraph*, 1 November 1933.

1938: Binding the wounds

Aborigines put their views in *Australian Abo Call*, January–June 1938; the bad verse is from *Southerly*, I (3), July 1940, pp. 15–21; the acting G.-G.'s plea was reported in *The Times*, 26 April 1938.

1939–1945: The First Pacific War

Life in the cities: The details of the People's Army are from Janice Whiteside's BA (Hons) thesis, University of Melbourne, 1972; doubts about the war were recorded by A. P. Elkin, *Our Opinions and the National Effort* (Sydney, Australasian Medical Publishing Co., 1941); Edwards's diary is reproduced in his *The Editor Regrets*, p. 89; the public servant was Hubert Murray, quoted from his *Letters*, p. 235; Goss's poem appeared in *Meanjin Papers*, 4 (3), September 1945; rationing details are from *Commonwealth Year Book*, 36, 1949.

Health: On Oslo lunches see R. A. Gardner, *The Value of the Vitamin* (Kew, 1941); Worst's experiences are retold in Babbage, *Between the Ranges*, p. 96.

Aborigines: Rowley's opinion is in *The Destruction of Aboriginal Society* (Ringwood, Penguin, 1970), p. 337.

View of the world: The clerihew was published by *Meanjin Papers*, 2 (1), Autumn 1943, p. 54; the US reply about Negroes is taken from J. H. Moore's article in *Sunday Review*, 13 June 1971; Blackburn put his views in *Against Conscription* (Melbourne, 1943); the Flynn affair is based on M. Leach, *The Ambassador Who Never Was* (BA (Hons) thesis, ANU, 1973); the account of the Darwin raids is based on the R.C. Report, *CPP*, 1945–6, IV; the anti-Japanese propaganda is from John Hilvert, *Blue Pencil Warriors* (St Lucia, UQP, 1984), pp. 116–8; the aftermath is from Ian Downs, *The Australian Trusteeship, Papua New Guinea, 1945–75* (Canberra, AGPS, 1980), pp. 18 & 52; Murray's view of defence is in *Selected Letters* (Melbourne, OUP, 1970), p. 232; Kiki's recollections are in his *Ten Thousand Years in a Lifetime* (Melbourne, Cheshire, 1968), p. 60; the song is reprinted from V. Eri, *The Crocodile* (Ringwood, Penguin, 1973), p. 157; other war experiences are from Kalamend Sukor, *New Guinea*, December 1970–January 1971, and Ulli Beier, *New Guinea*, September–October 1969.

1946–1954: Reconstruction

Work: The complaint about Christmas is in the *Clay Products*

Journal, January 1952, p. 11; the March 1952 issue of the *Chartered Accountant* (p. 530) reported talk of a depression; the migrant experiences are taken from J. Zubrzycki, *Settlers of the Latrobe Valley* (Canberra, ANU Press, 1964); work on the Snowy is from Mona Ravenscroft, *The Men of the Snowy Mountains* (Adelaide, Rigby, 1962), while its unspeakable purposes are documented by Wayne Reynolds, *Australia's Bid for the Atomic Bomb* (Carlton, MUP, 2000); caravan parks and motels are introduced by *Australian Motor Manual*, October 1952, p. 478, and August 1959, p. 58; Surfers Paradise is praised in *Vogue*, Mid-Summer 1957, p. 46; the Chevron is in *Clay Products Journal*, February 1957, p. 17; details of women in the workforce are from by K. Richmond in D. Edgar (ed.), *Social Change in Australia* (Melbourne, Cheshire, 1974); the role of the *Women's Weekly* is discussed by A. Wright, *Refractory Girl*, 2, Winter 1973, pp. 9–13.

Life in the cities: The Polish woman's experience is from Zubrzycki, *Settlers*, pp. 230–31; *The Harp in the South* controversy was in *SMH*, 11–18 February 1947; the Morrises featured in the *AWW*, 13 November 1948, p. 17, & 20 November 1948, pp. 20–21; the class prejudices of R. G. Menzies are in *The Forgotten People* (Sydney, A&R, 1943), p. 6; the Holden story has been told by L. J. Hartnett. *Big Wheels and Little Wheels* (Melbourne, Lansdowne, 1964).

Life in the country: The summation of the 1944 drought is from L. J. Peel in G. Alexander and D.B. Williams (eds.), *Pastoral Industries of Australia* (Sydney, Sydney University Press, 1973), p. 65; figures for tractors and the lack of amenities were found in various year books, also the 1947 and 1954 census reports; Gumly Gumly is described in *AWW*, 20 June 1951, pp. 12–13; the English woman's story appeared in *AWW*, 2 October 1974.

Health: Post-war health schemes and TB are based on C. Thame, *Health and the State* (unpublished PhD thesis, ANU, 1974); the account of milk supplies is constructed from *MJA*, 1937, II, pp. 813–20, N. T. Drane and H. R. Edwards (eds), *The Australian Dairy Industry* (Melbourne, Cheshire, 1961), K. Sillcock, *Three Lifetimes of Dairying in Victoria* (Melbourne, Hawthorn, 1972), and *Rydge's*, July 1936, p. 500.

Aborigines: The Port Hedland group is detailed by Biskup, *Not Slaves, Not Citizens*, pp. 211–57 *passim*; the 1941 study of NSW schools is Tindale, *RGSA (SA Branch) Proceedings*, 1940–41, pp. 144–45; the other expert is P. W. Beckenham, *Education of the Australian Aborigine* (Melbourne, ACER, 1948), p. 46, who also describes Ernabella, pp. 16–19.

White Australia: Calwell's fatal jest is recorded *CPD*, 2 December 1947, p. 2948; his handling of the O'Keefe case is based on A. C. Palfreeman, *The Administration of the White Australia Policy* (Melbourne, MUP, 1967); the opponent is Alan Walker, *White Australia* (Sydney, Christian Distributors, 1946).

View of the world: The opinion of Gandhi comes from the *Sun* (Sydney), 5 January 1932; Menzies's response is in *CPD*, 19 March 1947, pp. 854–55; Percy Spender's view is in his *Exercises in Diplomacy* (Sydney, Sydney University Press, 1969), p. 55; Dulles set out his approach in *Foreign Affairs*, 1952, pp. 175–87; *Newsweekly*'s fear of Asia appeared on 3 February 1954 and its dismissal of SEATO on 15 September 1954.

1954: 'Not so much a visit, more a way of life'

The poem was in the March 1954 issue of *Australian Quarterly*, p. 7; the *AWW* editorial was on 17 February; Portus's views are from *Australian Quarterly*, March 1954, pp. 14–15; *Australian Quarterly* outlined the role of the Elizabethan Trust, March 1955; and the closing *AWW* editorial was on 31 March 1954.

1955–1962: Forever Amber

Work: The European's view is in *Observer*, 2 April 1960, p. 12; the trade position is from *Chartered Accountant*, October 1954, p. 202; the composition of the workforce is shown by M. Keating, *Australian Economic History Review*, 7 (2), September 1967, pp. 150–71; the spread of forklifts is in *Australian Factory*, October 1958, pp. 45–46, and at Coles in *Manufacturing and Management*, November 1956, pp. 163–64; the Woolworths computer is in *Chartered Accountant*, February 1961, p. 396, while the spread of computers is from *Personnel Practice Bulletin*, 22 (3), September 1966, pp. 90–94; the workplace injuries are listed in *Architecture and Arts*, October 1958, p. 11; the widow-makers are from the *Sun* (Sydney), 13 March 1973.

Life in the cities: For viewing habits see W. J. Campbell, *Television and the Australian Adolescent* (Sydney, A&R, 1962); opinions about

delinquents are from *SMH*, 12 October 1960, and 30 January 1957; the bodgie's own story was published in *SMH*, 2 June 1957; the acceptance of male cosmetics is reported in *B&TW*, 4 March 1965, pp. 12 & 33; the creation of the Father's Day Council comes from *Nation*, 20 May 1961, p. 13; the promotion of electric shavers is explained in *B&TW*, 23 March 1961, pp. 10–11, and *Man*, August 1960; the changing images of 'Dad' are from advertisements in *AWW*, 26 August 1960, pp. 16 & 36, 24 August 1960, pp. 48–49, and 31 August 1960, pp. 30, 48–49 & 59; the straying spouse is from 8 June 1960, p. 20; the changing messages on greeting cards are from *Ideas*, 28 September 1962, p. 45; Olympic Village housing is discussed in *Clay Products Journal*, December 1956, p. 3; the young flat-dweller's life is from B. Hetzel, *Health and Australian Society* (Ringwood, Penguin, 1974), p. 54.

Life in the country: *The Torrents* was printed in *Australian Women's Writing* (Ringwood, Penguin, 1988); Oriel Grey published her memories as *Exit Left* (Ringwood, Penguin, 1985); the story of the *Doll* is in John Sumner, *Recollections at Play* (Carlton, MUP, 1993), chapter 6; the Bauers of Pinaroo are from *Economic Geography*, 53 (4), October 1977, pp. 385–87.

Health: Scientific achievements are listed in Robin Brown, *Milestones in Australian History, 1788 to the Present* (Sydney, Collins, 1986); for nimble-footed share deal see Sir Macfarlane Burnet, *Walter and Eliza Hall Institute 1915–65* (Carlton, MUP, 1971), p. 5.

White Australia: H. I. London's *Non-White Immigration and the White Australia Policy* (Sydney, Sydney University Press, 1970) is a basic source; the McBride quote is from K. Rivett, *Immigration: Control or Colour Bar* (Carlton, MUP, 1962), pp. 37–8; the opinion polls are tabulated in *Australian Quarterly*, March 1972, p. 101; the defence expert quoted is R. O'Neill in *Australian Outlook*, 24 (2), August 1970, p. 123.

View of the world: the Olympic menus are from *Restaurant Journal*, August 1956, p. 19, and *Australasian Grocer*, December 1956, pp. 90–91; the Suez affair is the subject of W. J. Hudson's *Blind Loyalty* (Carlton, MUP, 1989); attitudes to China are reported by A. Huck and J. King in *Australian Outlook*, 24 (3), December 1970, pp. 309–27; Dawe's poem is taken from *Condolences of the Season*

(Melbourne, Cheshire, 1971), p. 55; the Southern Hemisphere standard is explained in *Observer*, 2 April 1960, p. 13.

1963–1969: Striking It Lucky

Work: Horne's criticism is from *The Lucky Country* (Ringwood, Penguin, 1964), p. 12; the loss of managers is lamented in *Australian Marketing Projects* (West Ryde, National Committee of the Hoover Awards for Marketing, 1962), p. vi; Kwinana's development follows J. K. Ewers, *Western Gateway* (Perth: UWA Press, 1971); the mining camp experience is from *National Times* 'Supplement', 2 April 1973; retired Brisbane meat-worker, Jim Sharp, described the struggles at Borthwicks in a personal communication, October 2003; the adoption of computerised lathes comes from *Personnel Practice Bulletin*, 28 (3), September 1972, pp. 266–72; Dusseldorp is examined by Lindie Clark, *Finding a Common Interest* (Melbourne, CUP, 2002); the use of concrete is explained in *Concrete Industries News*, August 1965, p. 2, and its adoption documented by John Hutton, *Building and Construction in Australia* (Melbourne, Cheshire, 1970), p. 184.

Life in the cities: Boyd's two quotations are in *Australia's Home*, pp. 8, 294–5, and Ashbolt's in *Meanjin Quarterly*, 25 (4), December 1966, p. 373; Humphries is introduced in *Nation*, 8 September 1962, pp. 12–13, and 30 October 1965, pp. 13–14; lifts are from Jason Goodwin, *Otis* (Chicago, Ivan R. Dee, 2001), pp. 70–71 & 157–58; the CRA building is from *Australian Building Technology*, January 1963, p. 14, and high-rises generally from Jennifer Taylor, *Tall Buildings* (Sydney, Craftsman, 2001); the Waringah scandal is from Krirk-Krai Jirapaet, *Corrupt Practices … in NSW* (unpublished MEcon thesis, University of Sydney, 1971); travel preferences to Europe or the UK are from the *Age*, 11 October 1960, p. 13, and 3 January 1972; the flights to Bali are from *POL*, December 1969, p. 16, and *Dolly*, May 1971, p. 74; tourism to the Red Centre is from *Australian Motor Manual*, April 1955, p. 30, May 1962, p. 59; tea drinking versus coffee is covered in *Nation*, 8 September 1962, p. 10, and Denys Forrest, *The World Tea Trade* (Dover NH, Woodhead-Faulkner, 1985), pp. 172–5; the jiggling of tea-bags in *B&TW*, 28 January 1971, p. 7, and *Australasian Grocer*, May 1975, p. 23; the promotion of instant coffee is in *Advertising*, June 1959, 1 (11), p. 24, and *B&TW*, 6 June 1963, p. 10.

Life in the country: The grazier's wife writes in *AWW*, 9 October 1974; the other women are quoted in *Woman's Day*, 14 August 1972; the lines are from the poem 'Country Towns' by Kenneth Slessor (Sydney, A&R, 1944), p. 81; the suggestion was made by F. E. Emery, *Journal of Agriculture*, June 1973; Pitt Street farming was explained in *Rydge's*, October 1972; J. Krupinski et al., *A Community Health Survey ... of Heyfield ...* (Melbourne, Mental Health Authority, 1970) and R. A. Wild, *Bradstow* (Sydney, A&R, 1974); D. F. Waterhouse discusses the dung beetle in *Scientific American*, April 1974.

Health: The varieties of family planning come from *Population Studies*, 27 (1), March 1973, pp. 7–31, and the pill from Donald R. Lavis, *Oral Contraception in Melbourne*, Canberra, Department of Demography, 1975); the death statistics are from *Commonwealth Year Book*, 41, 1951, pp. 370–91, & 54, 1968, pp. 195–216, and Graeme M. Griffin and Des Tobin, *In the Midst of Life ...* (Carlton, MUP, 1982).

Aborigines: The Minister for the Interior's opinion is in *CPD*, 3 September 1970, p. 968; the riposte is in Ted Egan, *The Aboriginals* (Melbourne, Greenhouse, 1987), pp. 78–79; Horne is from Frank Hardy, *The Unlucky Australians* (Melbourne, Nelson, 1968), pp. x–xi; the Young affair is based on G. R. Robinson and J. C. Carrick, *Australian Quarterly*, 42 (2), June 1970, pp. 36–46.

White Australia: London, *Non-White Immigration*, documents the Prasad case, chapter 9.

View of the world: The Menzies lies are chaptered and versed by Michael Sexton, *War for the Asking* (Ringwood, Penguin, 1981), pp. 170–72; the parliamentarian's views are quoted by Wild, *Bradstow*, p. 85; Clark's experiences are in *Meanjin Quarterly*, 33 (2), June 1974, pp. 117–27; Crocker's and Rivett's reviews both appeared on 9 January 1971.

1970: Great expectations
The Poseidon details come from *AWW*, 7 January 1970, and Trevor Sykes, *The Money Miners* (Sydney, Fontana, 1979); Carnegie's judgment was in *Faces of the Eighties* (Sydney, ABC, 1980), p. 16.

1971–1980: 'Boom, Bust – Boom?'
Work: Details taken from W. E. Norton and M. W. Brodie, *Australian*

Economic Statistics, 1949–50 to 1978–79, Reserve Bank, 1980; the case study is from *Unemployment* (Melbourne, Brotherhood of St Laurence, 1973), p. 47; *Penal Colony to Penal Powers* is the apt title for Jack Hutson's account of the class nature of the courts (Sydney, AEU, 1966); the Ford strike is reconstructed from material in *Tribune*, 3 and 17 July 1973, *Age*, 23 June and 12, 13, 24 July, and *Sydney Morning Herald*, 17 July 1973; the Altona dispute is chronicled by Barry Hill, *Sitting In* (Melbourne, Heinemann, 1991), p. 75.

Life in the city: Changes in eating habits are from *SMH*, Good Weekend, 6 February 1988, and *SMH*, 13 October 1979; value of breakfast foods is from the *Sunday Sun* (Sydney), 22 July 1979; students' understanding of nutrition appeared in the *Australian*, 6 December 1980; the equal pay struggle is in Edna Ryan and Anne Conlon, *Gentle Invaders* (Melbourne, Nelson, 1975), chapter 6.

Life in the country: The comment on apples is from Catherine Watson, *Full and Plenty* (Hobart, Twelvetrees, 1987), p. 98; for bio-engineering and agri-business see Geoff Lawrence, *Capitalism and the Countryside* (Sydney, Pluto, 1988); comments about loneliness are from *AJSI*, May 1974, 19 (2), p. 109; the situation of the teacher's family is from *West Australian*, 25 September 1980; erosion is detailed in *Ecos*, 25, August 1980, pp. 3–4, and 19, February 1979, pp. 26–31; fishing is from *International Journal of Maritime History*, V (1), June 1993, pp. 95–126, and whaling from the *Western Australia Year Book*, 1973, pp. 382–83.

Health: The nurses' stories are from *Digger*, April 1972, *Current Affairs Bulletin*, June 1972, and *SMH*, 13 February 1988; Hetzel's views are in his *Health and Australian Society*, and Opit was reported in the *Age*, 28 July 1979; the number of doctors was discussed in *Search*, 18(1), January/February 1987, pp. 4–5; the North Coast scheme described in *New Doctor*, 18, December 1980–January 1981, pp. 25–26; valium prescriptions discussed in Arlene Levinson, *An Addict in the Family* (Ringwood, Penguin, 1986), p. 42; figures about going to the doctor come from the *Age*, 21 April 1979.

Aborigines: The Gove case is in 17 *Commonwealth Law Reports* 1971; Woodward's instructions and subsequent matters are from issues of *Australian Government Digest* (Canberra, AGPS, 1972–75); the Queensland laws are discussed in G. Nettheim, *Out Lawed* (Sydney, ANZ Book Co., 1973); the 1972 quotations about health are from Colin Tatz, *The Politics of Aboriginal Health*, supplement to *Politics*, November 1972; the Townsville women's stories appear in the *National Times*, 14 July and 29 September 1979.

White Australia: James Jupp, *Arrivals and Departures* (Melbourne, Lansdowne, 1966); Gillian Bottomley, *After the Odyssey, A Study of Greek Australians* (St Lucia, UQP, 1979); Nancy Viviani, *The Long Journey: Vietnamese Migration and Settlement in Australia* (Carlton, MUP, 1984).

View of the world: Figures for fears and threats are from *Australian Outlook*, December 1987, 41(3), p. 163; Marshall Green is in the *Bulletin*, 8 March 1988; the CIA worries are reprinted in Richard Hall, *The Secret State* (Sydney, Cassell, 1978), pp. 189–90.

1981–1988: In Debt to the Future

Work: Carnegie quotations are from *National Times*, 26 September–1 October 1977, and R. H. Carnegie, *A Forward Look in a Changing World* (Adelaide, AIM, 1976), p. 23.

Life in the cities: The economics of shopping centres are outlined in *Search*, 14, February/March 1983, pp. 1–2; the divorce statistics are in *Year Book Australia*, 1985 (Canberra, AGPS), pp. 92–4, and the children's reactions reported in *AJSI*, November 1987, 22(4), pp. 614ff; single-parent families are the subject of Diana Kupke's *Just Me and the Kids* (Ringwood, Penguin, 1987), pp. 19, 171, 175; drive-ins are discussed by Michelle Bowley, *Media Information Australia*, 47, February 1988, pp. 12–16; sales of fast foods are given in *Journal of Food and Nutrition*, 1986, 43(1), pp. 24–5; the pickles case is in J. F. Love, *McDonalds: Behind the Arches* (New York, Bantam, 1986), p. 435; the working conditions are in Karen Throssell, *Rip-Off Ronald* (Melbourne, Labour Research, 1980); the sales of mineral water are in *Business Review Weekly*, 13 November 1987, p. 127, and the Coke executive is from *AFR*, 15 March 1988, p. 42.

Life in the country: The curtains are discussed in *Australian Social Work*, 37(1), March 1984, p. 20; drought statistics are in *Bank of NSW Review*, October 1980, pp. 10–14, and *Ecos*, 49, Spring 1986, pp. 12–13; a drought is defined in the *Bulletin*, 6 May 1980, and the bath is described in *AWW*, 17 December 1980.

Health: Medical training is outlined in *Journal of Food and Nutrition*, 40 (3), 1983, p. 169; primary school diets are given in the *Age*, 20

October 1981; lolly preferences come from *AFR*, 4 August 1987; the vitamin takers are documented by *Ecos*, Summer 1985–6, 46, pp. 9–11; the quotation about teenagers and condoms is in *New Doctor*, 38, Summer 1985, p. 9; the risks of oral contraceptives are debated in Basil Hetzel and Tony McMichael, *The LS Factor* (Ringwood, Penguin, 1987).

Aborigines: Figures on Aboriginal teetotalism are from the *Australian*, 26–27 March 1988; Carol Fisher's Jesus poem is from *Black Voices*, 3 (1), July 1987, p. 30; Pat O'Shane's story is pieced together from *SMH*, 6 February 1976; *Woman's Day*, 26 April 1976, *Australian*, 14 October 1982, *National Times*, 26 December 1982–1 January 1983, and *Age*, 16 August 1986.

White Australia: Blainey puts his views in *All for Australia* (North Ryde, Methuen Haynes, 1984); the minister's views on trade were reported in *SMH*, 25 January 1988; the figures are from J. A. C. Mackie, *Australian Outlook*, 41 (2), August 1987, pp. 104–09.

View of the world: Attitudes towards defence capability are from the *Australian*, 23–24 January 1988; the portrayal of Arabs is from *AJSI*, 19(3), August 1984, pp. 207–17; *El Niño* is in *Ecos*, Spring 1986, 49, pp. 12–13, and *New Scientist*, 4 February 1995, pp. 32–35; ozone from *Ecos*, Winter 1987, 52, pp. 7–9.

1988: Beyond celebration
McCubbin's recollection is in *La Trobe Library Journal*, October 1979, 6 (24), p. 73; the *Table Talk* extracts are dated 30 December 1887 and 3 January 1890; Lawson's usage is in the Mitchell Library, MS3012/82 & 83; Fisher's comment is reported in the *Daily Telegraph*, 9 April 1910, and Menzies' diary reprinted in *Canberra Times*, 15 July 1982; the Jindyworobak verse is in their 1941 *Anthology*, p. 57; Palmer's judgment is from *Meanjin Papers*, 1(8), March 1942, p. 5.

1989–2001: The Money Goes Round
Work: The turnover of money is in *Reserve Bank of Australia Bulletin*, March 2000, p. 17; gaming statistics are in *Commonwealth Year Book*, 2002, pp. 601–02; debts are in *Reserve Bank of Australia Bulletin*, February 2000, p. 13, March 2003, pp. 1–11, and April 2003, pp. 7–16; the dismissal of the NSW workers is taken from *Australian Social Work*, 48 (1), pp. 37–40; the Wagga Wagga students' comment

is in *YSA*, 22 (1), pp. 12–17; *Australian Social Trends*, ABS, 2000; the information about overwork is from *Labour and Industry*, 12 (3), pp. 5–25; the packer is quoted in *JIR*, 38 (2), June 1996, pp. 196–212; the Tasmanian mining industry is detailed by Kathryn Heiler, *The Struggle for Time* (Sydney, Sydney University Press, 2002); the hotel strikes are from *JIR*, 42 (4), December 2000, pp. 535–50.

Life in the cities: Convenience stores are from *SMH*, 5 September 1998, p. 95; the inner urban supermarkets are in *AGS*, 38 (2), July 2000, pp. 204–18; youthful fears are from *YSA*, June 1999, pp. 17–23; Graffiti art is surveyed in *Art Monthly Australia*, 133, September 2000, pp. 4–7, and *Australian & New Zealand Journal of Criminology*, 35 (2), August 2002, pp. 165–86; malls as entertainment are reported in *YSA*, 22 (2), June 2003, pp. 19–24; spending patterns are from *SMH*, 4 June 2002, p. 10; Professor Stanley's comments are from *Sun–Herald*, 1 September 2002, p. 7; age of home buyers is in *SMH*, 4 June 2003, p. 10; the new suburbia is sketched in *Bulletin*, 24 September 2002, pp. 28–31; housing statistics are from *Australian Social Trends 2000* (Canberra, AGPS), p. 166; public housing is traced in *Australia's Welfare 2001* (Canberra, Australian Institute of Health and Welfare, 2001), chapter 3; housing prices from *SMH*, 12 August 2002, p. 4.

Life in the country: The chicken farms are in *AGS*, 41 (2), July 2003, pp. 156–70; eating of chicken is from Dianne Schultz-Tesmar, *The Inghams* (Liverpool, Regional Museum, 2001), p. 2; hobby farms are from *Sunday Age*, 22 June 2003, Domain 3; mutton and lamb consumption is from *Bulletin*, 12 August 2003, pp. 30–31; the dairy restructuring is in *AJARE*, 47 (1), March 2003, pp. 75–98, and *Australian Geographer*, 33 (1), March 2002, pp. 29–42; bank closures are in *AGS*, 38 (2), July 2000, pp. 182–203; relative expectations of towns is from *AGS*, 41 (2), July 2003, pp. 131–47; Central Queensland tourism is in *Australian Geographer*, 34 (1), March 2003, pp. 73–90; Narrogin is from *Australian Geographer*, 34 (1), March 2003, pp. 47–60; water licences are from ABC *Four Corners* transcript, 14 July 2003.

Health: Pharmaceutical rackets are in *New Doctor*, 70, Spring 1999, and *British Medical Journal*, 31 May 2003; *Age*, 13 December 2003, pp. 8–9; the price-fixing by pharmaceuticals is from Fred Brenchley, *Alan Fels* (Brisbane, Wiley, 2003), p. 128; dentistry is in *New Doctor*,

Winter 1998, pp. 4–8; support for mercy killing is from Miriam Cosic, *Right to Die* (Sydney, New Holland Press, 2003), p. 75; outline of Medibank is in *New Doctor*, 79, Winter 2003, pp. 28–32; mortality and morbidity statistics are from *SMH*, 25 October 2003, p. 2; teenage drinking is from the *Bulletin*, 9 September 2003, pp. 20–3; the netball history relies on *The Oxford Companion to Australian Sport* (Melbourne, OUP, 1992), pp. 254–56; the Hunter Valley doctor is from *Bulletin*, 1 October 2002, p. 25; teenage smoking is from *ANZ Journal of Public Health*, 22 (3), Supplementary Issue 1998, pp. 321–23; smoking and alcohol consumption comes from media briefs in 2003 issues of *YSA*; the hospital delays are from *New Doctor*, Winter 1998, pp. 18; see Ian H. Lester, *Australia's Food and Nutrition* (Canberra, AGPS, 1994) for food intakes, chapter 4; the working conditions of nurses are from Ian Watson et al., *Fragmented Futures* (Sydney, Federation Press, 2003), pp. 74–5, 102–05 and 133.

Aborigines: Mabo is examined in *Oxford Companion to the High Court* (Melbourne, OUP, 2001); the Walmajarri story is from *New Yorker*, 28 July 2003, pp. 61–7; the didjeridu is from the *Currency Companion to Music and Dance in Australia* (Sydney, Currency Press, 2003), and *Bulletin*, 8 July 2003, pp. 26–27; suicides are from *AJSI*, 29 (4), November 1994, p. 407, and www.mentalhealth.gov.au/resources/nysps/problem.htm.

Off-white Australia: The Wollongong temple is described in *Australian Geographer*, 34 (2), July 2003, pp. 223–38; numbers, policies and attitudes follow Nancy Viviani, *The Indochinese in Australia, 1975–1995* (Melbourne, OUP, 1996); the Greek spokesman is from the *Australian*, 12–13 March 1994, p. 25: the Greek–Macedonian dispute is laid out by Loring M. Danford, *The Macedonian Conflict* (Princeton, Princeton University Press, 1995); the Latin women are in *Journal of Sociology*, 39 (1), March 2003, pp. 81–98; the Lebanese background is from James Jupp (ed.), *Encyclopedia of the Australian People* (Melbourne, CUP, 2001); the ethnic gangs are in *ANZ Journal of Sociology*, 34 (1), April 2001, pp. 67–90; Ali's remark is from Jock Collins et al., *Kebabs, Kids, Cops and Crime* (Sydney, Pluto Press, 2000), p. 165; the stats and the policy switches draw on *Australian Social Trends 2001* (Canberra, AGPS), pp. 12–15, and K. Betts, *AJSI*, 38 (2), May 2003, pp. 169–92; the soccer example is from *Studies in*

Sports History, 10, 1997, and John Hughson, *ANZ Journal of Sociology*, 33 (2), August 1997, pp. 167–86.

Globalised warnings: The jingle is from *B&T W*, 11 July 1963, p. 22; how Asians think of us is the subject of Alison Broinowski's *About Face* (Melbourne, Scribe, 2003); Fisher's praise is from Clinton Fernandes, *The National Interest* (PhD thesis, Deakin University, 2004); comparisons of weaponry come from *Asia–Pacific Defence Reporter Yearbook*, 2000, pp. 29 & 38–9; the dilapidation of Indonesian equipment is from *Jane's Defence* Weekly, 12 November 2003, p. 16, the precipitation of another ice age is in *Nature*, 388, 1997, pp. 862–5; the paean to nature is from F. Engels, *Dialectics of Nature* (Moscow, Progress Publishers, 1964) p. 183; Lapun's lament is in Donald Denoon, *Getting under the Skin* (Carlton, MUP, 2000), p. 200; the Sandline affair is covered by Sinclair Dinnen, et al., (eds), *Challenging the State* (Canberra, National Centre for Development Studies, 1997); *AJARE* detailed the effects of mining on crime in 44 (1), March 2000, pp. 129–46, and the state of rural life 45 (3), September 2001, pp. 437–58; the resignation from PEAK is from *Independent*, 21 June 2001.

2001: A long march

Campbell's life and funeral come from *Sabretache*, December 2002, pp. 39–41; Audrey Johnston told Morrow's life in *Fly a Rebel Flag* (Ringwood, Penguin, 1987); *Daily Telegraph* reported Walker's denunciation, 8 April 1965, p. 1; the Ataturk pledge is in Vecihi Basarin, Hatice Hurmuz Basarin and Kevin Fewster, *Gallipoli: The Turkish Story* (Sydney, Allen & Unwin, 2003), p. 22; Luke's comment is from *Australian Historical Studies*, 33 (119), April 2002, p. 8; Jenny Macleod compares Anzac Day in 1965 with 1990, *War & Society*, 20 (1), May 2002, pp. 149–68; the future of our past is explored in my *Suspect History* (Adelaide, Wakefield, 1997).

ACKNOWLEDGMENTS

Giving thanks has become complicated by three editions of this book over thirty years. The first *Social Sketches* in 1978 covered the years from 1888 to 1975; in 1992 I brought the story up to 1988. This edition is different. There are few images. Their loss demanded changes to the text. In the previous editions, the large-format double-page spread accommodated stand-alone paragraphs. Readers integrated them into a collage of images, large and small, text and bold sub-headings. Discontinuities were not blatant. Once the material was reset as a flow of type on a standard-size page, the eye could no longer seduce the mind into composing an integrated story. The number of sub-headings had to be slashed and snatches of information incorporated into the surrounding material.

The need to reshape the mass opened the way to refashioning each sentence. Karen Lennard at University of Queensland Press keyed the original text onto disks, allowing me to rework the whole. Reading all of the original text for the first time in almost thirty years, I was relieved to discover that most of the content was okay and the grammar better than I feared. The syntax, however, was appalling. The passive voice proliferated, sentences started in the middle, and many were too long. I have taken every opportunity to oblige 'the reader over my shoulder'.

Once embarked on the style, I could not forbear to touch up the content.

Thirty more years of research on Australia during the long

twentieth century had increased my store of plums, several of which enrich this edition. Incorporation of a keener analysis was not so simple. I have stiffened some of the introductory segments, pointing towards the kind of book I would prepare were I starting from scratch.

Moreover, my interests have shifted. For instance, in 1974, I would have woven the bare bones of the High Court's Mabo judgment into a biographical portrait of Eddie Mabo. In 2003, I had to remind myself to include any of his life story. My fascination had moved to jurisprudence, which has small relevance in a volume of social sketches. Despite my efforts to regain the canter of the original, the pace of the 1990s chapter differs from the earlier ones.

The layers of research and rewriting mean that these acknowledgments must be even less complete than those in 1978. They still source the quotations and indicate general indebtedness for bits of information, with the former usually pointing to the latter.

More than old time's sake requires that the original paragraph of appreciation stands untouched. There were a number of people to thank for specific assistance: the staff of the National Library of Australia without whom I would never have put pen to paper; John Hooker and Bob Sessions at Penguin Books for fighting back; Roger Markwick, Chris Cuneen and John Farrow for their researches; Norah Howlett, Judy Middlebook, Mike Lavers, Ken Fry, Robert Darby and Jim Docherty for quotations; all the members of the Australian History III classes at the ANU from 1972 to 1974 for enriching my understanding; the masters and boys at Canberra CEBGS for letting me try out some of the material; Pat Romans, Mary Olds and Carol Hibbertson for their typing; Peter Spearritt, Hank Nelson and John Playford for their very necessary criticisms; and Judy McQueen for rewriting every line.

George Dale slaved on both the illustrated editions.

Caroline Lurie was my literary agent for the second edition, and Jenny Darling arranged the contract for the third. Peter Applegarth, Ruth Blair, John Buchanan, Peter Curtis, Peter Elder, Clinton Fernandes, Peter Lyssiotis, Andrew Moore, Craig Munro, Heather Radi, Peter Robinson, Walter Struve, Bill Tully, and John Walker brought the cheer, comments, cash or corrections that make writing possible. Comrades in the Socialist Alliance confirmed one of the strands throughout these pages: the struggle availeth.

INDEX

INDEX